CHRISTIANITY IN INDIA

Christianity in India

Two Thousand Years of Faith

LEONARD FERNANDO
G. GISPERT-SAUCH

PENGUIN
VIKING

VIKING

Published by the Penguin Group

Penguin Books India Pvt. Ltd, 11 Community Centre, Panchsheel Park, New Delhi 110 017, India

Penguin Group (USA) Inc., 375 Hudson Street, New York, New York 10014, USA

Penguin Group (Canada), 10 Alcorn Avenue, Toronto, Ontario, Canada M4V 3B2 (a division of Pearson Penguin Canada Inc.)

Penguin Books Ltd, 80 Strand, London WC2R 0RL, England

Penguin Ireland, 25 St Stephen's Green, Dublin 2, Ireland (a division of Penguin Books Ltd)

Penguin Group (Australia), 250 Camberwell Road, Camberwell, Victoria 3124, Australia (a division of Pearson Australia Group Pty Ltd)

Penguin Group (NZ), cnr Airborne and Rosedale Roads, Albany, Auckland 1310, New Zealand (a division of Pearson New Zealand Ltd)

Penguin Group (South Africa) (Pty) Ltd, 24 Sturdee Avenue, Rosebank, Johannesburg 2196, South Africa

Penguin Books Ltd, Registered Offices: 80 Strand, London WC2R 0RL, England

First published in Viking by Penguin Books India 2004

10 9 8 7 6 5 4 3 2

While every effort has been made to trace c
photographs used, this has not been possible in
will be remedied in future editions.

Typeset by R. Ajith Kumar, New Delhi

Printed at Chaman Offset Printers, New Delhi

Contents

Preface

Dear Reader,

As you pick up this book at the bookseller's or off a library shelf, you may wonder whether anything new can be said about the Christians of India. They are sufficiently well known in most parts of the country, a rather peaceful though marginal community. They live their own form of worship, they have their particular structures of social interaction and they contribute to the well-being of the country, especially through their social and educational activities. You may also be asking yourself whether there is anything particularly Indian about the Christians in this country, or particularly Christian about them that would be different from Christians in other continents.

It is somewhat strange that, although we know there were followers of Jesus in India probably from about the beginning of the Saka era, and certainly during the Gupta empire, few Christians are known at the national level to have left a trace in our ancient history. The Sanskrit sources do not remember them, although there were Indians following the way of Jesus before Kalidasa wrote his kavyas and Sankara his bhashyas. They had built churches before the great temples of central and South India were erected by our Hindu ancestors. They lived a way of personal relation with God as Father, and with Jesus as God's manifestation to us, during the long period when other bhakti currents were spreading from South India to the far-flung regions of the North. Their relative absence from the collective memory of the country is a phenomenon that begs for an explanation.

Nor is the situation, one may say, much better today. Of course most people know some Christians in their part of the country. They are generally harmless, though they arouse some angry reactions because they are seen to be too keen on 'converting' others to their faith. They may also be disliked for upsetting the social balance of the country by an over-concern for the relief, uplift and education of marginalized groups in our society. Real knowledge of who they are, how they think and feel, what their patriotic sentiment is and what their deeper religious drives are is rare among the general public. Not out of bad will, but simply because they are different. And the 'other', the outsider, is generally kept at bay in most communities. It also often happens that the unknown causes anxiety, and anxiety breeds rumours. Rumours are seldom tested against facts, and there is a tendency to judge people on the basis of untested rumour. Moreover, many people have experience of only one community of Christians and are not directly aware of the great variety of forms of Christian life in the country. They extend to all Christians the traits they observe in the community they know.

There is in contemporary India not only little public debate but also little exchange of basic civilizational ideas. This is in contrast with the best of the ancient Indian tradition where the brahmodyas, or theological debates, were highly respected in Vedic times, where scholastic controversy was forthright not only between the various Hindu, Buddhist and Jain schools but also within each school, as is evident in the bhashyas of our acaryas. In the sixteenth century Akbar the Great was not afraid of inter-religious debate. Even in the mid and late nineteenth and early twentieth centuries there was a vigorous exchange of ideas between the Pandits of Varanasi and some Christian missionaries, some of it conducted in Sanskrit (Young 1981). Only when the goal of political independence became the sole focus of the nationalist movement during the twentieth century did the exchange of views in other than political affairs practically die out. After Independence the debate has been mostly political and economic.

The identity of India as a nation was articulated in the Constitution of India and adopted by members of the Constituent Assembly on 26 November 1949, after more than half a century of efforts and deliberations. The preamble to the Constitution promises to secure for Indian citizens not only justice, liberty and equality but also 'Fraternity assuring the dignity of the individual and the unity of the Nation'. (An amendment in 1977 added 'integrity' to the concept of unity.) This preamble came out of the fusion of two texts, an early jejune preamble drafted by Sir B.N. Rau in May 1947 (Rao 1968, 5: 127), and the 'Objectives Resolution' that had been proposed in the Constituent Assembly by Jawaharlal Nehru on 13 December 1946 (ibid. 79, 121–22). In a letter to the president of the Constituent Assembly, Dr Rajendra Prasad, the chairman of the Drafting Committee said, 'The Committee has added the clause about fraternity in the Preamble, although it does not occur in the Objectives Resolution. The Committee felt that the need for fraternal concord and goodwill in India was never greater than now, and that this particular aim of the new Constitution should be emphasized by special mention in the Preamble' (ibid. 3: 510). Dr B.R. Ambedkar wrote these words on 21 February 1948, six months after Independence and the Partition of India, three weeks after the assassination of Mahatma Gandhi.

This book seeks to foster the 'fraternity' promised in the Constitution. Fraternity (today we might prefer a more inclusive word like 'fellowship') supposes mutual knowledge, but there is no personal knowledge without self-revelation. The book wants to be a self-revelation and therefore an act of trust. We want to say as simply as we can who we are as Christians in India, what makes us tick, what unites us in spite of our many diverse traditions of social life, customs, forms of piety and Church denominations. And also what are our differences, and why. We want to be known as we are, warts and all. The book has no apologetic intention. It does not try to justify our existence in India; our long history in the country does not need justification. We are children of India, proud to be that. Nor is the book an effort to proselytize. We shall of course discuss the question of conversions and mission orientation in its place, but let us make it clear from the outset that the book is not an instrument for attracting converts. It is an expression of dialogue.

'Dialogue' has become a catchword even in today's political vocabulary, and it endeavours to establish its sphere of influence against the policies of conflict and war. All people of goodwill, all humanists whatever their religious affiliation, if they have any, know that dialogue is essential for peaceful coexistence and the sine qua non for building. Dialogue is a 'word' (*logos* in Greek) exchanged between two or more people. But the 'word' of true dialogue is not just a word of information or a word of command or a word of supplication. It is primarily a *personal* word, a word of self-revelation. Self-revelation is an act of courage, an act in which we decide to trust and dare to expose ourselves to the 'outsider' to some degree or other. Dialogue expects acceptance, not necessarily agreement—acceptance of one's self by the other, even where there is disagreement of ideas, views, ideals and ways of behaving. Obviously a book does not constitute a dialogue. A book is one of the ways in which a dialogue may be initiated and the spirit of dialogue fostered. A book requires a world of readers ready to react to it, continue and complete its mission. A book in a sense speaks for a community to another community.

In a sense, however; not necessarily in an official way. The two authors of this book have no mandate from any Christian community in the country to speak on their behalf. They speak in their personal capacity. But they have been in long contact not with one but with many Christian communities of the country and are confident that most Christians in the country will recognize themselves in this book. Dr Leonard Fernando was born in the lively Christian communities of the Fishery Coast of Tamil Nadu and has a specialized knowledge of Indian church history, a subject he has been teaching for many years in the faculty of theology, Vidyajyoti College of Theology, Delhi, where he is now the principal. (This institution is one of the oldest theological institutions of higher learning in Christian studies in the country, having been founded in 1879 in Asansol, Bengal, and after several avatars having come to Delhi in 1972.) Dr George Gispert-Sauch was born in Spain but has been a resident of India since 1949; his special area of interest is the mutual contact and the relations between classical Indian and Christian theological traditions. The two authors' perceptions of the Christian reality of India, arising from their different cultural backgrounds, complement one another.

Some might regret that both belong to the same Roman Catholic Church, even if this church is the largest and most representative of the Christian presence in India. Practical considerations precluded other possibilities, but we hope that our ecumenical experience helps us to avoid a denominational outlook. Dr Fernando is not only a member of the ecumenical Church History Association of India but is also the editor of its journal, the *Indian Church History Review.* Dr Gispert-Sauch is also known in ecumenical circles and has contributed to the *Guidelines on Ecumenism,* published in 2000 by the Commission on Ecumenism and Dialogue of the Catholic Bishops' Conference of India.

Our book is not meant to be scholarly, although we are committed to make our affirmations factual and defendable in the forum of history. But even if the history of the Christians in India is part of this project, its focus will not be history as such but rather the way of life, acting and thinking of the various Christian communities. Its history will therefore not concentrate on the 'missionary movement' of the last few centuries but on the life of the Indian communities, although obviously the contribution of the missionaries will be gratefully acknowledged. Ours will not be a technical sociological study of one or other of the Christian communities in the country or of all of them. We claim no particular competence in sociology, and books giving detailed case studies are available for those interested in that aspect.

Our intention is to present a simple narrative of the various Christian communities of the country, which formed as the result of many historical circumstances. For instance, one must distinguish the community of the so-called Thomas Christians, at present concentrated mostly in Kerala, from its neighbouring communities in Tamil Nadu. Both are also very different from the Christian communities of the western coast of India. And all these are equally different, in history, mentality and social organization, from the communities of Christian tribals in central India and those of the North-East. Separate attention will be given to each of these communities. Equally distinct are the communities of Dalit Christians, spread throughout the country, from Tamil Nadu, Kerala and Andhra Pradesh to the Gangetic plains of North India, or in Punjab, Gujarat and Maharashtra. Each of these communities represents a specific form of Christian life, and to know the Christians of India one needs to distinguish between these various sociological groups. It is around this perception that this book is constructed.

But more important than the historical and sociological structure of the various communities is their basic religious outlook. How they look at themselves, how they relate to the Transcendent God, what the role of Jesus is in their life and prayer, how they live and understand themselves in relation to other communities, what their knowledge and perception of other forms of religion is, how they identify with the history and culture of the country—these are important questions for anyone who wants to know them. This theological interest is one of the characteristics of this presentation. We want to be known not only by our history and sociological composition, and not only by what we have contributed as a community to the welfare of our country, but especially by our self-understanding and our relations with one another and with God.

There are a few books covering the history of Christianity in India. The most scholarly and satisfactory presentation is that published by the Church History Association of India. The project is still incomplete. It is planned in six parts and several volumes. The first three parts, already published, cover the Christian movement all over India from the first to the eighteenth centuries. Parts four and five, in several volumes, will cover the nineteenth and twentieth centuries according to regions of India. So far only two volumes have been published, one covering North-East India and the other Tamil Nadu.

Statistics, whether official or private, are notoriously unreliable and it is easy to pitch one set of statistics against another. At any rate they can give only a general picture of the facts. We shall refer to the statistics of the Census of India. Unfortunately the statistics on religion for the 2001 Census have not yet been published. We shall therefore use those given by the 1991 Census, in Series 1, Paper 1, which was published in 1995 by the Registrar General and Census Commissioner. There is no reason to suspect, as some have done, that the Census has an anti-minority or an anti-Christian bias. None is observable in respect to the Muslim community; therefore it would be arbitrary to suspect one in respect to the Christian community. According to Paper 1 of 1995, Religion, Census of India 1991, there were 1,88,95,917 Christians in India in 1991, out of a total population of 81,61,69,666, a minority therefore at only 2.32 per cent of the total population. According to the *Statistical Yearbook of the Church 2001*, published by the Vatican, ten years after the Census there were 1,67,70,000 Catholics in India.

What will come as a surprise to many is that the percentage of

Christians in respect to the total population of the country *diminished* between 1981 and 1991 by 0.13 per cent, a decrease that confirms what was noted in previous decades. Whether this decrease is due to conversion of Christians to other religions or to Christians hiding their religion because of unjust laws regarding reservations or to lower fertility among Christians in general remains an area to be explored. Probably the last reason is an important factor.

At any rate the growth of Christians between 1981 and 1991 is recorded as only 16.89 per cent, in contrast to the growth of the overall population which was 23.79 per cent (Hindus 22.78, Muslims 32.76, Sikhs 25.48, Buddhists 35.98, Jains 4.42, others 13.19). These sober statistics as a whole should lay to rest for the time being the bogus notion of massive conversion of India to Christianity. If anything, the process seems to go in the reverse direction.

Although Christians are found in all states and probably in all districts in India, and they belong to most sociological communities existing in the country, their spread is very uneven. Among the relatively major states only Kerala has a significant Christian population. But even here, according to the Census of India, it amounts to less than one-fifth of the population. Tamil Nadu has a modest 5.69 per cent. The new states of Jharkhand and Chhattisgarh may have a respectable proportion of Christians, but we have not seen any official statistics in this respect. Only very few states with rather small populations like Goa, Manipur, Meghalaya, Mizoram and Nagaland have a substantial proportion of Christians, in the last three cases amounting to the majority. In other states the presence is minimal: often below 1 per cent, all below 4 per cent.

So Indian Christians, unlike those in other continents, but like Christians in most countries in Asia, are accustomed to being a minority—and are comfortable with this status. Except for the last ten years or so, they have not felt threatened and have lived in peaceful relations with their neighbours, although marriages take place mostly within their respective communities. Economically they are not a wealthy community. A good proportion of them come from the poorer levels of the population, especially tribals and Dalits. Many do agricultural work, and on the coast of India a fair proportion are fisherfolk. A good number are of course employed in cities and towns, some of them in middle- and upper-middle-class professions like teaching, health care, secretarial and managerial work, and government employment. Relatively few are in formal politics. The large net of educational institutions which the various Christian communities run have provided a sizeable though limited group with the opportunity of upward mobility. But the general economic and social level is still low.

This is not a source of discouragement. On the contrary. Many find inspiration in the fact that their situation is similar to that of the earliest and most dynamic foundational Christian communities around Palestine in the first century CE. St Paul wrote to the Christians in the city of Corinth around 55 CE, 'Consider your own call, brothers and sisters. Not many of you were wise by human standards, not many were powerful, not many were of noble birth.' Paul then gives them a religious insight into a deeper reason for this and provides them with a sense of purpose for their life in their world of Greece: 'But God chose what is foolish in the world to shame the wise; God chose what is weak in the world to shame the strong; God chose what is low and despised in the world, things that are not, to reduce to nothing things that are, so that no one might boast in the presence of God' (1 Cor 1:26–29). This sense of God's inversion of values, of a divine preference for the poor, runs deep in the Christian psyche, nourished as it is by a contemplation of the crucified Jesus. This is true even when the community becomes powerful, much more so when it experiences weakness. No doubt the same theme is found in other spiritual traditions: did not the author of the *Narada Bhakti Sutra* (Sutra 27) write around the tenth century CE, *isvarasya abhimanadveshitvat, dinapriyatvat ca* ('because God hates pride and loves the lowly')?

Two metaphors in the New Testament are a source of encouragement against the fear of a minority complex. One is found in the words Jesus used to address his disciples calling them a 'little flock' and encouraging them not to be afraid (Lk 12:32). Indian Christians feel they live up to this title. The second metaphor is that of the leaven in the dough that remains hidden but helps it grow. There is a role for minorities in society and in the world at large.

It is therefore without pretensions and without any intention to blow anyone's trumpet that we present these pages to our fellow citizens. We hope that they will help foster a deeper knowledge and understanding between the Christian and other communities. They want to be an honest and serene answer to the accusations that recent propaganda has thrown at our community as a whole.

We want to thank Penguin India for offering us an opportunity to share our lives with our fellow citizens. In a special way we want to thank Christine Cipriani, who proposed the project to us, and Ravi Singh and Jaishree Ram Mohan, who brought it to completion. To all our readers we wish God's peace and thank them for their interest in our community.

11 April 2004, Easter Sunday   Leonard Fernando
Delhi   G. Gispert-Sauch

When Christians Gather

The Sunday service ~ Worship and memorial ~ Death and life of Jesus ~ The covenant community ~ The Meal ~ The Church ~ The Bible ~ Literary styles in it ~ Three 'baskets' of the OT ~ The NT books ~ The Bible as a sacred book ~ The Bible in India

Perhaps the best-known custom of Christians all over India, indeed all over the world, is their weekly gathering on the 'Day of the Lord', as they call Sunday. In many villages of any state of India one can observe them: come Sunday morning and families or individuals, well dressed, Bible in hand and often carrying a bag of rice or other offerings, shuffle along dusty roads to converge possibly in a thatched hut that serves as their place of gathering, their 'church'. Elsewhere they may meet in a pukka building, often the only one for miles around. They gather there, for one or two hours, and can be heard singing hymns and songs in their local language. They have moments of mysterious silence and some quiet activity inside the hut. At some point during the service they approach the altar and pour out rice from their little bags into a common basket: every day of the week they have saved a handful of rice, before cooking the meal, to offer it to the poor on Sunday. When the service is over they come out happy and exchange their bazaar news with one another. On special feast days they may bring with them their drums and tambourines and start their tribal dances that may last one or many hours. The feast may then turn into a community celebration.

If we happen to be in Thiruvananthapuram or Chennai, Bangalore or Mumbai, Delhi or Chandigarh, Patna or Ranchi, Nagpur or Goa, Kolkata or Shillong, we may find the gathering more sober, generally shorter, though we will surely note a special excitement on big celebrations like Christmas, Easter or Pentecost days. The meeting place there is more impressive, a big cathedral or at least a church of respectable size, in proportion to the importance of the town and to the number of Christians in the surrounding areas. The gathering is generally less uniform. It may use different languages in the same service or may have different gatherings for different language groups at different times or in different places. In the metropolitan cities one finds Christians from practically all states and castes of India. They may or may not have close social attachments—this depends on the history and sociology of the place. But theirs is not just a family gathering, or a clan or caste get-together. Something beyond caste, class, language and occupation unites them. They meet, in the full sense of the word, at the point of deepest faith that we shall later analyse.

Similar gatherings take place regularly in all denominations or different churches—we shall speak about them in chapter five. The languages may change, the styles vary, but the essence remains very much the same. Similar meetings are also witnessed at St Peter's in the Vatican or at St Paul's in London, at St Patrick's, New York, or at Notre Dame of Paris, indeed in all cathedrals and other churches, whether in Durban or Buenos Aires, in Tokyo or Beijing, in Bangkok or Melbourne, in Karachi, Dhaka or Colombo. In all churches, Oriental, Occidental, Catholic or Protestant, the same get-together takes place regularly on Sunday. The celebration is called the Eucharist, the Mass, the Lord's Table, the Lord's Supper or generally the Sunday service. The ancient Greeks and the churches in east Europe call it the *syn-axis*, the 'con-verging' or coming together. Alluding to this celebration, a Christian letter written about 55 CE uses this verb three times in two lines! It is this weekly or less frequent celebration, and not ethnic relationship or caste affinity, that gives the sense of community and internal cohesion to Christians.

Such gatherings have been the most constant mark of Christian communities throughout history. They are celebrated today as they were in the time of the Reformation in the sixteenth century, in the medieval cathedrals, in fifth-century North Africa, in Rome or in Santa Sofia of Istanbul. We even have references to and accounts of the celebration in the very first century of the Christian era. In the letter alluded to, St Paul, one of the earliest converts to Christianity, describes and, as we shall see, also criticizes the Sunday gatherings at the Greek city of Corinth.

What do Christians do at such gatherings? They certainly come to worship. They pray to God in thanksgiving; they pray in adoration; they pray for blessings and for their needs and those of their family members and surroundings and the world; they pray also for forgiveness of their sins. They come to somehow experience the divine power which, like most religious people the world over, they are convinced underlies their day-to-day lives. They open up the closed roofs of their existence to discover their communion with the Infinite Existence, which they experience as Infinite Love. They may sing their prayers, using traditional hymns in the various languages of the community, or the psalms of the Bible; they may recite them aloud; they may also pray silently in their hearts.

They also listen to selected readings from the Bible. Generally an ordained minister or priest, but also at times a lay member of the community, comments on the readings and explains their relevance to the present situation, personal or collective, national or international. Christians find in such readings and comments light to understand themselves and the world by seeing everything on a broader canvas than the often-narrow limits of their daily lives. They are able to see their own history in the wider context of human history and perceive divine guidance at the heart of this history. They may also receive encouragement in moments of crisis and difficulty, and strength to continue their lives guided by the higher ideals of honesty, justice and love of themselves and their neighbour, strengthened by divine presence.

However, the gathering does not consist only, or even primarily, of prayers, readings and sermons. The gathering is essentially a *memorial meal*. It is a symbolic community meal where the memory of Jesus becomes so alive that his mystical presence is felt in various ways. As mentioned above, around 55 CE, St Paul wrote a letter to the Christians in Corinth about the abuses in their Sunday gathering and reminded them of what he had taught them in his earlier visit, around the year 50. It is one of the earliest pieces of evidence of Christian activity that we have, from less than twenty years after the death of Jesus. Paul himself had learned this from the other disciples of Jesus, and recalls a meal that took place at the end of the life of Jesus, which we now call the Last Supper. Paul says:

> For I received from the Lord what I also handed on to you, that the Lord Jesus, on the night when he was betrayed, took a loaf of bread, and when he had given thanks, he broke it and said, 'This is my body that is for you. Do this in remembrance of me.' In the same way he took the cup also, after supper, saying, 'This cup is the new covenant in my blood. Do this as often as you drink it, in remembrance of me.' For as often as you eat this bread and drink this cup, you proclaim the Lord's death until he comes (1 Cor 11: 23–26).

In the Sunday gatherings of any city or village of India, as in the rest of the world, Christian communities do what the Lord told them to do on that night. In doing so they relive so to say their own birth. They come in contact with him from whom they receive their inspiration. As they gather together Christians also affirm their belonging to one another, and at the same time experience their oneness with the Lord Jesus, because it is not just bread that they eat together or wine that they drink in community, but sacred signs and symbols of his body and blood, that is, of his person present to them in the celebration. For them, as believers, it is an experience of oneness with the Source. Like Judaism, Christianity is a religion of memory, and therefore of history. It lives by the memory of the historical man Jesus Christ.

At the same time the community does not cut itself off from the rest of the world. An essential part of the service consists of prayers on behalf of those in need in the larger community around and even across the world. They pray that the healing touch of the Lord may bring peace and understanding between individuals and groups. They pray for gifts of 'salvation' for everyone. At the end of the service they are reminded to go out and 'serve' the world, for they have remembered him who, in his own words, 'came not to be served but to serve, and to give his life a ransom for many' (Mk 10:45).

This memory is also 'thanksgiving', which is the original meaning of the Greek word *eucharistia*. The thanksgiving is addressed to God, whom Christians primarily understand as the Father of our

Lord Jesus Christ and Father also of the whole of humanity. The community thanks God first and foremost for the gift of Jesus to the world and for his life, death and resurrection. There is an ancient saying among Christians that it is not so much the Church that 'makes' the Eucharist, but the Eucharist that makes the Church! This means simply that out of these gatherings Christians experience their community, their oneness with the Lord and the sense of mission to serve others, which is the Lord's legacy to them.

Not all churches celebrate the Eucharist every Sunday: some may celebrate it once a month or a few times in the year. Most celebrate it weekly, if possible on Sunday. Others celebrate it even daily, for those who have time and want to participate in it. The frequency depends on various historical traditions. But what is celebrated in a real Eucharist is the meal described by Paul (and other New Testament writers). When celebrated, the meal is clearly the most important moment of the gathering. It is not an ordinary meal as one understands this word today. In the earliest times it does seem that the Eucharist was part of a full ritual meal. Nowadays on some very important feast days some communities may add a community meal to the religious celebration. But the Eucharistic 'meal' consists of simply eating a small wafer of bread and drinking a few drops of wine. Over both elements the words of Jesus are repeated, and so Christians know that symbolically they are 'in communion' with the Lord, or 'eating' the 'body' and 'drinking' the 'blood' of Christ. For them, the memory of Jesus, which has been recorded in the Bible and kept alive in the community's faith, becomes a *living* memory, a real presence, in the meal they share together.

Rivers of ink have flown throughout Christian history trying to offer an 'explanation' of these words of Jesus, 'This is my body' and 'This is the cup in the new covenant in my blood.' The nature of this 'is' has given birth to many volumes of metaphysics. Generally these discussions do not interest the believers who come to the Sunday gathering. They know they come into a real spiritual contact with the Lord present to them in the celebration.

The ritual celebrated by Jesus must be placed in the historical context of the Jewish people. Jesus had that Last Supper around the Jewish feast of the Passover (which Christians now call Easter). Of course Jesus and all his disciples at that time were Jews. The Passover recalled the foundational events of their existence as a nation, their deliverance from slavery and their being made a people by the gift of the 'Law' which they saw as coming from God through the agency of Moses. The 'Law' was their 'Constitution' that made them a nation. This whole process took a long time to be recorded, but there was underlying it the memory of a freedom struggle. Some of their ancestors had been slaves in Egypt, and their collective memory told them that around the twelfth century BCE they were led into freedom under the leadership of Moses. It was at that time, so the Jewish scriptures (or the First Testament, often called the Old Testament) tell us, that God made a 'covenant' (the word used by Jesus) with them. A 'covenant' was an agreement of protection and loyalty, generally entered freely between a strong raja and a small chieftain. God (the name given to him at the time was Yahweh, later corrupted into Jehovah in Old English!) entered into a covenant with this people of slaves and promised to lead them to an independent land where they would be free. That covenant of the twelfth century BCE was sealed with a ritual meal where the blood of the sacrificed animals was sprinkled on the people and poured at the altar. (One may say in passing that this very ancient memory is at the root of the modern conflict between Israel and Palestine. The Jews claim a right to the land on the basis of their covenant with God and their ancient occupation of the land. The Palestinians answer that the Jews had deserted the place, and since it had been occupied by people of Muslim culture for many centuries, the Jews now have no right to it.)

More than a thousand years after the liberation from slavery and the foundational covenant, Jesus in his Last Supper still celebrates the Passover (Easter) but as a 'new covenant'. This is no longer God's covenant with an ethnic group, but the 'new' covenant with humanity. The seal of this covenant is the blood of Jesus which was to be shed on the cross a few hours after the Last Supper. His new community is now liberated from the slavery of 'sin'. Sin is any attitude of the mind or heart that diminishes human beings. Sin is any form of injustice to oneself or to others. Sin is any false views about God as if God's love was restricted to one nation or one people and God was not the 'Father' of all, without discrimination and beyond frontiers, the God who in Jesus leads believers to a deeper religion of service in love.

One may say that this meal symbolizes the deepest reality of Christians, whether in India or anywhere else in the world, the way they understand themselves. The inner intention of the symbol is clear, even if the concrete communities do not live according to it as they should. The Eucharistic 'meal' is first and foremost an 'in-gathering' of people from many social and geographical corners of the earth into one community. Their financial, cultural or ethnic status matters little. They are united by one factor: the faith in Jesus and in his work on earth. The old word for this gathering was *ek-klesia*, a Greek word meaning 'the summons' of people from various places. Southern European languages use modern variations of this word to signify the Church (*église* [French], *chiesa* [Italian], *iglesia* [Spanish], *igreja* [Portuguese], which have become in Hindi *girja* or *kalisiya*, meaning the Church). Northern European languages generally use another word derived from an old qualifier of *ekklesia*, that is, *kyriake* meaning 'Lordly' or 'of the Lord' (*Kyrios*), a title generally denoting Jesus Christ, but which may also allude to God the Lord and Father of all. From this Greek adjective we have *kirche* (German), *kirk* (Scot), *church* (English).

The point of reference for the Christian community is clearly Jesus Christ. In chapter two we shall see how Christians see him. But in our context now it may be significant to point out that the Eucharist consists of the sharing of the body and blood of Christ. This living memory of Jesus Christ finds its focus not only in re-enacting the Last Supper of the Lord with his disciples before his death but also the very passion and death with which his service to the world was concluded and his resurrection, about which we shall speak at length later. The meal is a memorial of the death and resurrection of Jesus, and thus an experience of his presence in the community. We cannot therefore reduce the relation of the Christians to God to a relation of a bhakta to the divinity. The Christian believer is in contact with the historical reality of Jesus as a human being, to his life and death, not merely with his metaphysical divine essence. The *human life* of Jesus ('body and blood') and his role in history are at the core of the Christian experience. These are as important, one may dare to say, as his divine nature. More of this in the next and the last chapters.

THE BIBLE

Christians love the Bible. For them it is a book of prayer, a book of wisdom, a book that gives answers to the basic questions of life and guidance in difficult moments. Old Christians used to call it God's Book (tenth century) or 'the Good Book' (nineteenth century)—as if by comparison no other book was good! Devout Christians live by it. Many people from other religious traditions also read it and find spiritual sustenance in it. The Bible is surely the most widely read book in history. To understand Christians we must know how they see the Bible and what inspiration they get from it.

The word 'bible' derives from the Greek plural noun *biblia*, originally meaning strips of papyrus. Soon it meant the place where, once written on, the papyri were kept (library), or simply the 'books'. The Bible is really a collection of sacred books, or writings, gathered into two unequal collections: early Jewish writings, which Christians normally call the Old (or First) Testament, and writings of the early followers of Jesus, the New (or Second) Testament. 'Testament' means the same as 'covenant' or 'agreement' between two parties; in so far as 'covenant' are recorded in writing, we have the First and the Second, or the Old and the New, Testaments as the collections of these writings.

Although written in very different times and circumstances, these writings are generally published together as one book, and Christians see in them a spiritual unity. The collection of the Second Testament, or the specific Christian part of the Bible, has twenty-seven writings in all the Bibles of the world. The collection of the First Testament has thirty-nine writings common to all Bibles. The Bibles used in Catholic and Orthodox churches (see chapter two) have ten additional writings: seven new 'books' and some additional matter in three other books. These additional writings are often printed as appendices and called 'Apocryphal' writings in the Protestant Bibles. Catholics call them 'Deuterocanonical' books, that is, books included in the 'second list'. The historical reasons for this disagreement among the churches are not of particular relevance here.

In one of the printings of the New Revised Standard Version in modern English the whole Bible has 1334 pages, of which 1073 cover the First Testament and 261 the Second. The proportion of the two parts is therefore about four-fifths to one-fifth of the whole text. Sometimes people believe that the Bible is the classical text of English literature. It is true that the translation done under the auspices of King James I of Great Britain (1566–1625), first published in 1611, remains an English classic, but one should not forget that it is a translation, not the original nor the first or the only English translation. The original text of the Bible antedated the very existence of the English language by many centuries. The First Testament was composed mostly in Hebrew, with a few portions in Aramaic and in Greek. The dates of composition must be left rather vague, as a number of the writings arose from oral traditions and it is difficult to decide when a tradition became a fixed text and when it was written down. In general scholars tell us that the actual composition of the texts we have now must be placed between the eighth and the second century BCE (roughly contemporary with the Upanishads and the early Indian epics). The Second Testament was composed in the community of the disciples of Jesus within more or less one century, between 50 CE and 150 CE. Some of these texts too resulted from an evolution of traditions that lasted a few decades. All the writings of the Second Testament are originally in Greek.

Being a collection of writings, like the Guru Granth Sahib and other scriptures of humanity, the Bible does not have a single author. Each writing may be the work of one or several authors, sometimes collected along a number of years. Some authors like St Paul have contributed several writings. Many of the books are anonymous, and some are attributed to important figures from Jewish or Christian history but were certainly not written by them. For Christians who read the Bible the concrete human author is less important than what the text actually says and what it means for us today. The order in which the books are printed in our Bibles is not the chronological order in which they were written, apart from the general division between the two Testaments. In fact the order of the writings included in the Bible is not uniform in the various traditions. Though containing the same matter, the Bible printed by the Jews generally has a different order of 'books' from that followed in the First Testament printed by Christians.

What kind of writings do we find in the Bible? There is a great variety of styles and literary genres. The kind of literature and the style depends on the particular cultural interest and capacities of each author or authors, and of the concrete community which they were addressing. In a way reminiscent of the three 'baskets' of the Buddhist Tipitaka, in the First Testament it is customary to distinguish three broad categories of writings: the narrative books, the prophetic books and the wisdom books. The narrative books tell us stories. Some of the stories are clearly mythical, for instance the creation stories or the story of the Fall, well known the world over, especially through their impact on English literature (for example, Milton's *Paradise Lost*). Other narratives are more of the epic type, offering a glorified memory of the early history of the nation as remembered through its celebrations, ballads and stories.

The most important group among the narrative books are the first five found in all the Bibles, which the Jews call the Torah or the Law and consider the most sacred of all the books, the foundation of their faith. Christians give them a collective name of Pentateuch, originally a Greek word meaning '[the book of] five volumes', namely, Genesis, Exodus, Leviticus, Numbers and Deuteronomy. The best-known part of the Pentateuch are the popular creation stories and the story of the Fall of Adam and Eve, found at the beginning of the Bible in the book of Genesis. The story of the flood that follows the creation and Fall account was derived from the literature of Babylon, in present-day Iraq, where a number of Jews were exiled between the eighth and the sixth centuries BCE. The same story travelled east of Babylon, to India, where it became the source of the matsya avatar myth.

The actual heart of the Pentateuch and of the First Testament is the book of Exodus. It reconstructs a prehistory of the Israelites that links with the saga of the Patriarchs in the last part of the book of Genesis. The Israelites or Jews are now working as slaves in the construction fields of the Egyptians, and the book describes in some detail their oppression and miserable life. In the midst of their misery there arises a charismatic leader, Moses, whom God chooses to convince the Jews of the need to escape with him and embark on an adventure of returning to the land of Palestine from where four centuries earlier their ancestors had migrated to Egypt. This independence movement or the escape from Egypt, the 'freedom struggle', and its success form the theme of much of the Jewish part of the Bible. (The Second Testament makes use of the same themes and symbols.) The other three books of the Pentateuch develop the story of the journey across the desert and the structures the people developed during that period and in subsequent centuries. One of the main ideas is that God made a covenant or agreement with this people: they would be faithful to God whom they had experienced in the success of the exodus and follow God's teaching given through Moses. 'Their' God would be the God of liberation. On his part God would protect his people. This rather parochial understanding of God would be slowly modified in later portions of the Bible till it came to the discovery of the universal God of all humanity. This is explicitly and clearly taught in the New Testament. The frequent recounting of the Exodus story among the Jews makes Judaism essentially a religion of memory.

Another kind of narrative found in the First Testament follows the story of the Jewish nation once it is established in what is today Israel and Palestine. (The Jews include these narratives among the prophetic books. Christians treat it as part of the 'historical literature'.) The books of this group are called Joshua, Judges, 1 Samuel, 2 Samuel, 1 Kings and 2 Kings. Some books can also be seen as 'historical literature' which the Jews classify as 'Writings' or Wisdom, narrating further stories about the people or of some of their popular heroes: Ruth, Esther, Esdras, Nehemias, 1 Chronicles and 2 Chronicles. To these may be added the writings of Tobit, Judith, 1 Maccabees and 2 Maccabees. The order of the various writings of the Bible is not chronological: some of the prophetic writings were written before the creation accounts in the Book of Genesis, although the oral myths on which the latter are based may be much older than the written accounts themselves.

The second collection of narratives in the First Testament goes under the title of 'The Prophets'. As just mentioned, the Jews actually place in this group many of the narrative books of their later history apart from the Pentateuch. The most characteristic are the writings either in prose or in poetry of the great religious figures who appeared in the history of Israel, especially at the time of crisis, called the prophets. The prophets were individuals who came from very different backgrounds mostly between 800 and 500 BCE (roughly the time of the early Upanishads in India). The prophets felt impelled to go to the people and the kings and demand from them, in God's name, a greater fidelity to the ideals invoked at the time of their liberation, a greater obedience to the demands of the God with whom Israel had made a covenant. The most characteristic trait of the prophets is their sharp moral sense against injustice and corruption in public and in private life. They criticize very strongly the religious life of their contemporaries when it was divorced from justice, a fact they consider infidelity to God, 'idolatry' in their language. Many of their utterances were also a criticism of society and its leaders, especially their treatment of the poor. They appeal to the original inspiration of the nation to be an alternative society based not on a pyramid of power and wealth, as most of the surrounding societies were, but on a sense of equality and dignity of all its citizens. Few writings in ancient religious literature vibrate with so much power and indignation against oppression as the writings of Isaiah, Jeremiah, Hosea, Amos and other prophets. The prophets, one might say, represent the moral conscience of the Israelite nation and continue that function among Christians today. They are also at the root of the social orientation and of the self-critical tradition found in Christian history. They call the people to constant renewal of life. No wonder that they were often unpopular, and many died a martyr's death in the hands of their own people. Jesus was treated as a prophet.

The third collection of narratives in the First Testament is often designated by the general term 'wisdom literature'. The Jews call this collection simply 'The Writings'. It consists of an odd mixture of heterogeneous books. There is first and foremost the book of Psalms, 150 poetic prayers, individual and collective, which were often used for temple worship and personal prayer. They were often composed during moments of individual or collective distress. The sentiments of the psalms, at times very strongly worded, find an echo in the hearts of most Christians. They use these prayers as Jesus and his early disciples used them. The psalms can be compared to many of the poems of our bhakti authors, or more remotely to the Therigatha and Theragatha of the Buddhist Tipitaka (translated by Mrs Rhys Davids precisely under the titles *Psalms of the Sisters* and *Psalms of the Brethren*). The biblical psalms are as much in use today as they were in the times of the First Testament and the early Church.

Another important book of the 'wisdom literature' is the Book of Job. In it Job wrestles with the perennial problem of evil, especially of innocent suffering. How is it that the just and good people are often seen to suffer, while the oppressors and obvious sinners seem to lead a comfortable and successful life? This is not a philosophical problem for Job: it affects him personally, and in the story of the book he and his friends discuss it at great length. They do not reach any intellectual solution, but at the end of the book Job falls prostrate to the ground with a deep sense of awe and reverence for the Transcendent God whom no human mind can ever comprehend. Indians may be reminded of the prostration of Arjuna before the Lord at the end of the *Visvarupadarsanam* in the eleventh chapter of the Bhagavad Gita. Job is one of the most metaphysical and at the same time most existentialist books of the Bible and has even generated commentaries by Hindu authors, for example Sitaramayya 2001.

Other interesting writings in this last basket of the First Testament are the collections of proverbs and popular sayings, representing the wisdom of the simple people accumulated through the centuries. They have a certain similarity with the collections of *subhashitas* found in Sanskrit literature. There is also a poem about the love of man and woman, the Song of Solomon (sometimes called the Song of Songs or Canticle of Canticles), which had a great influence in the Middle Ages of Europe as a symbol of the love between a human being and God. Some passages of the Krishna bhakti literature have been compared to this poem. (The Jews include in this third 'basket' some of the later narrative literature regarding their history like Chronicles, Esdras and Nehemias, some hero literature like Ruth and Esther, and the Deuterocanonical Judith and Tobit.)

The Second or New Testament consists exclusively of Christian writings, most of them with a direct reference to Jesus Christ and composed within about a century, beginning about twenty years after the death of Jesus. We can divide these writings into four parts.

In the first we have the four Gospels attributed to Matthew, Mark, Luke and John. Although Matthew and John are names that come up among the earliest disciples of Jesus, the books attributed to them were probably written by others, perhaps their disciples. 'Gospel' is an Old English translation for *eu-angelion*, a Greek word meaning 'good news' or 'good tidings'. The 'gospel' is a specific kind of literature created by the disciples of Jesus. It is not a biography of Jesus in the modern sense of the word. A Gospel collects the oral memories and traditions that were floating in the community of believers about the founder of Christianity during the thirty to fifty years after his death. Each of the four authors organizes the material available to him (they were almost certainly men) according to his own purpose and the insight he had into the work and person of Jesus. In the first three Gospels there is a fair amount of overlap, but also much that is proper to each writer. The Gospel of John, written towards the end of the first century, is a much bolder interpretation of Jesus. The Christian faith generally amalgamates the data of the four Gospels and other data of the New Testament to create a 'composite' picture of who Jesus was.

After the four Gospels the Second Testament includes one quasi-historical book called Acts of the Apostles, which narrates how the Christian community emerged and organized itself in the thirty or forty years after the death of Jesus. During this time the community was transformed from an ethnic religious movement within Judaism into a multi-ethnic and multicultural community. The two main heroes of this 'history' are St Peter, the leader of the twelve main disciples of Jesus, and St Paul, an early convert from Judaism whose dramatic change from persecutor to disciple of Jesus is recounted three times in this book. Most of the narratives in the book of Acts are woven around the preaching and travels of these two leading figures of early Christianity.

Next in the New Testament comes a collection of letters written by or attributed to the earliest disciples of Jesus. Thirteen are by or attributed to Paul and are written to Christian communities in different parts of the Roman empire or to individuals. The usual titles are *Romans, 1 and 2 *Corinthians, *Galatians, *?Ephesians, Philippians, Colossians, 1 and 2 *Thessalonians, 1 and 2 Timothy, Titus and *Philemon. (Today scholars generally accept that those marked with an asterisk are authentically by Paul; others were written later. There is hesitation about Ephesians.) To this collection is also added a long doctrinal text called the Letter to the Hebrews, which is certainly not written by Paul. Other letters are attributed to other early disciples of Jesus, that is, James, Peter, John and Jude.

The last book of the Second Testament is called by the Greek word 'Apocalypse' or its Latin equivalent, 'Revelation'. The book is quite different from all the others: it is a symbolic writing about the spiritual fight between God and the forces of evil (Satan) written in the context of the persecutions suffered by the early Christians mostly at the hands of the authorities of the Roman empire. The writing is meant to encourage Christians to hope and constancy in their faith. This book became a great treasure trove for literary symbols in the middle and modern ages of Western literature, but to understand the book one needs the key to the symbols used, and that key is not always available. In spite of this, for believers the book contains magnificent insights into history and the place of Jesus Christ in the world of politics, as seen from the perspective of the Christian faith.

THE HOLY BIBLE AS SACRED BOOK

Like any work of literature, the Bible may be studied from various points of view. But for Christian believers it is not merely a book of literature. They consider it a book wherein God speaks in a special way. However, except for very fundamentalist Christians, the Bible is never considered a book 'dictated' by God. It has human authors, some known, many unknown. It carries within itself all the marks of human books. It is at times very inspiring in its religious and poetic peaks, at times quite prosaic and uninspiring unless read in the light of faith. It has the imperfections of human writings, and although it contains deep spiritual truth, rare errors of fact or understanding may have crept in in its composition (and not merely as a result of the imperfect transmission of the text).

Yet, in spite of its human face, Christians both in private and even more as a community 'hear' the word of God in the Bible as a whole, more powerfully in the New Testament. They realize how God accompanies the history of the people and how the infinite and eternal God is concerned about the well-being of the human community. Perhaps one of the best ways to speak of this 'inspired' and 'inspiring' character of the Bible is to recall the Indian literary tradition of *dhvani*. Any poetic work, our ancient scholars tell us, besides its direct or verbal meaning and its indirect or implied meaning, has the power of a 'suggested meaning' (at times called *dhvani* or *vyanjana*). This meaning is the source of beauty and produces an aesthetic experience. Christians would say that the Bible besides offering (at times) a powerful 'aesthetic' meaning, creates an experience of bhakti or faith. The 'Word of God' 'resounds' in the human words of the authors, as the Second Vatican Council of the Catholic Church (1962–65) puts it—a resounding that recalls the function of *dhvani*. This is why the Bible is so loved by all Christians all over India, whatever community they belong to. Although in its external expression it is written in a different culture from ours, it still speaks to the human heart in all situations, because in it the word of God resounds. The Bible is the source for the bhakti and the knowledge of all Christians.

THE BIBLE IN INDIA

For a reliable history of the English Bible one may consult *The Cambridge History of the Bible* (1963–70, three volumes), Cambridge University Press (with many reprints). As we shall see later, the great pioneers of Bible translation in India are the Protestant churches. Of special interest is the work done by the trio of Serampore (Srirampur) in Bengal, William Carey, William Ward and Joshua Marshman, who soon after their arrival in India in 1793 organized Bible translation in Asian languages on a large scale. For this work they employed the services of many pandits and scholars, Christian or of other religions. The translations are therefore mostly Indian products, although done under the supervision of the missionaries.

However, the first Bible published in India came not from Serampore but from South India. The Lutheran mission started in 1706 published a Tamil New Testament in 1715 and a full Tamil Bible in 1726. We must also acknowledge that the Gospel of Matthew had been translated into Tamil earlier and published in Sri Lanka in 1688. Other translations flowed rapidly from Serampore: Bengali

(1801–09), Urdu (then called Hindostani) (1805–43), Sanskrit (1808–22), Marathi (1805–19), Oriya (1809–15), Hindi (1811–18), Punjabi (1815–26), Assamese (1810–33), and the New Testament in Telugu (1818), Konkani (1819), Gujarati (1820), Nepali (1821), Marwari (1821), Kanarese (1822), Pali (1935). At present the Bible is available in full in about fifty Indian languages and the New Testament in eighty. Parts of the Bible are available in about fifty other languages or dialects (www.bsind.com).

2

Who Is Jesus Christ?

Jesus known in India ~ Testimonies of national figures ~ Jesus in Indian art ~ Did Jesus come to India? ~ The Christian perception of Jesus ~ The search for the historical Jesus ~ What do we know about him historically ~ Why history is important ~ Historical background ~ Life and teachings of Jesus ~ Jesus' passion and death ~ The aftermath ~ The experience of Jesus

When Christians meet together on Sundays or read the Bible at home they especially recall the person of Jesus Christ. He is indeed central to their faith. To be a Christian is not primarily a matter of a specific ethical code or even of an understanding of God and his creation, but first and foremost to be a disciple of Jesus Christ, and to relate to God 'the Father' as Jesus related to Him. Jesus is not merely the teacher of the Christian doctrine or the guru who leads us to enlightenment, but the heart and centre of the Christian existence. Without Jesus Christ there is no Christianity. We shall look at him from an Indian perspective.

Jesus is not unknown in India. One might dare say that he is better known and loved in this country than in much of the Western world. He may be even better understood here. For was he not an 'Oriental', an Asian born in Palestine around 4 BCE? Was not his bhakti towards God, whom he called Father, closer to the models of Indian bhakti than to those of the playful Greek mythologies or the Roman religion? Was not his moral teaching closer to the Gita than to that of the teachers of Greece or Rome? Many Indian devotees, and not only Christians, have a deep respect for and trust in Jesus Christ. Many like to pray to him, or through him, and his picture is revered in many an Indian home. Yet perhaps his personality is overlaid with presuppositions coming from the avatar theologies of India, which veil something of the historical reality of the man.

INDIANS SPEAK ABOUT JESUS CHRIST

Let us hear some Indian voices on Jesus.

Perhaps the best-known 'vision' of Jesus Christ in India is the one attributed to Shri Ramakrishna Paramahamsa, who is said to have passed through the various religious experiences available to humanity. It seems that around 1874 when visiting the house of his friend Sambhu Charan Malik, Ramakrishna was struck by a picture of the Madonna with the Divine Child. Suddenly he felt that rays of light were emanating from the figures of Jesus and Mary and entering into him. This experience brought him to a period of intense reflection on Christian life.

> He saw the vision of Christian devotees burning incense and candles before the figure of Jesus in the churches, and offering unto him the eager outpourings of their hearts. For three days those ideas held sway in his mind. On the fourth day, as he was walking in the Panchavati, he saw an extraordinary-looking person of serene aspect approaching him with his gaze intently fixed on him. He knew him at once to be a man of foreign extraction. Ramakrishna was charmed and wondered who he might be. Presently the figure drew near, and from the inmost recesses of Ramakrishna's heart there went up the note: 'This is Christ who poured out his heart's blood for the redemption of mankind and suffered agonies for its sake. It is none else but the Master-Yogin Jesus, the embodiment of love.' Then the Son of Man embraced Ramakrishna and became merged in him. At this the Master went into samadhi and lost all outward consciousness (Diwakar 1956, 143).

Seventy-five years later a fellow Bengali, also a mystic but a philosopher as well, Sri Aurobindo Ghose, would reflect on Jesus in his great poem *Savitri* (Book 6, Canto 2) just before he died:

The Son of God born as the son of man
Has drunk the bitter cup, owned Godhead's debt,
The debt the Eternal owed to the fallen kind
His will has bound to death and struggling life
That yearns in vain for rest and endless peace.
Now is the debt paid, wiped off the original score.
The Eternal suffers in a human form,
He has signed salvation's testament with his blood:
He has opened the doors of the undying peace.
The Deity compensates the creature's claim,
The Creator bears the law of pain and death;
A retribution smites the incarnate God.
His love has paved the mortal's road to Heaven:
He has given his life and light to balance here
The dark account of mortal ignorance.
It is finished, the dread mysterious sacrifice,
Offered by God's martyred body for the world;
Gethsemane and Calvary are his lot,
He carries the cross on which man's soul is nailed;
His escort is the curses of the crowd;
Insult and jeer are his right's acknowledgment;
Two thieves slain with him mock his mighty death.
He has trod with bleeding brow the Saviour's way.
He who has found his identity with God
Pays with the body's death his soul's vast light.
His knowledge immortal triumphs by his death.
Hewn, quartered on the scaffold as he falls
His crucified voice proclaims, 'I, I am God!'

                    (*Birth Centenary Library* 29: 445–46)

The high regard Mahatma Gandhi had for Jesus Christ is well known. In *The Modern Review*, October 1941, Gandhi wrote that Jesus was '[O]ne of the greatest teachers humanity has ever had', and that he, more than anyone else, expressed the spirit and will of God. Gandhi believed that the presence, actions and words of Jesus had touched the lives of all human beings in some way or the other. 'And because the life of Jesus has the significance and the transcendence to which I have alluded, I believe that He belongs not solely to Christianity, but to the entire world; to all races and people, it matters little under what flag, name, or doctrine they may work, profess a faith, or worship a God inherited from their ancestors.'

Jawaharlal Nehru had his own perception of Jesus. Writing to his daughter, Indira, in 1932, he says:

> The Jews expected a messiah, and perhaps they had hopes of Jesus. But they were soon disappointed. Jesus talked a strange language of revolt against existing conditions and the social order. In particular he was against the rich and the hypocrites who made of religion a matter of certain observances and ceremonial. Instead of promising wealth and glory, he asked people to give up even what they had for a vague and mythical Kingdom of Heaven. He talked in stories and parables, but it is clear that he was a born rebel who could not tolerate existing conditions and was out to change them. This was not what the Jews wanted, and so most of them turned against him and handed him over to the Roman authorities (1949, 85).

Keshub Chander Sen was known as a fiery leader of the Brahmo Samaj out of which he founded his own 'Church of the New Dispensation'. He remained a faithful Hindu to the end but found in Jesus Christ a great spiritual inspiration. He sees him as a friend, a living presence in his life, and at the same time the light that enlightens him and the joy that gives meaning to his life. In 1879 he delivered a lecture under the title 'India asks: Who is Christ?' He described him as a Yogi, a Hindu. He also said:

> The time has come when you can no longer be inimical or indifferent to Christ. Say unto Christ, as unto your best friend,—Welcome! I say emphatically, and I say before you all, that Christ is already present in you. He is in you, even when you are unconscious of his presence. Even if your lips deny Christ, your hearts have secretly accepted him. For Christ is 'the light that lighteth every man that cometh into

the world'. If you have in you the spirit of truth, and filial
devotion and self-sacrifice, that is Christ. What is in a name?
My Christ, my sweet Christ, the brightest jewel of my heart,
the necklace of my soul,—for twenty years have I cherished
him in this my miserable heart. Though often defiled and
persecuted by the world I have found sweetness and joy
unutterable in my master Jesus (Scott 1979, 217).

The above testimonies are from Hindus who had come to know
about Jesus through various sources. We add to them an English
version of a Sanskrit poem in praise of the Incarnate *Logos* ('Word'),
Jesus Christ, written by a Bengali patriot and freedom fighter,
Brahmabandhab Upadhyay, and published in January 1901 in his
own weekly paper, *The Twentieth Century,* ten years after his
conversion to Christianity. The various stages of the 'existence of
Jesus' as found in the Gospels and the Christian tradition are alluded
to with the help of Indian similes, and the poem ends in his victorious
resurrection:

> Transcendent Image of Brahman, blossomed and mirrored
> in the full to overflowing, eternal Knowledge, Victory to
> God, the God-man (*jaya deva narahare*)!
> Child of the golden Virgin, Mover of the Universe, Absolute
> but charming with relations, *jaya deva narahare!*
> Ornament in the assembly of the learned, destroyer of fear,
> chastiser of the spirit of wickedness, *jaya deva narahare!*
> Dispeller of spiritual and physical illnesses, servant of all,
> whose very play and games are sanctifying, *jaya deva
> narahare!*
> Offerer of your own agony, your very life is sacrifice,
> destroyer of the poison of sin, *jaya deva narahare!*
> Tender, beloved, charmer of the heart, soothing pigment of
> the eye, crusher of fierce death, *jaya deva narahare!*

It is obvious that all these Indian reflections on Jesus Christ are
conditioned by the particular context in which they were written.
The political context of all of them was the British Raj in ferment,
challenged by the freedom struggle. At that stage Jesus Christ was

very much present in the public consciousness of India. Some saw him as the Divinity of the West and therefore to be rejected. The question of his divinity was prominent especially in Hindu writings both as a reflection of and an answer to the missionary propaganda. Others spoke of him as the Oriental or Asiatic Christ, at home in India for centuries, who could empower the national longings for full political freedom. But even then the human reality of Jesus had little interest. Jesus was seen primarily as a divine figure.

JESUS IN INDIAN ART

Indian artists have also appropriated the figure of Jesus to some extent, and not only, or even principally, Christian artists. Very little of the art production of the earliest Christian communities in India has resisted the vagaries of time. The earliest and best attested Christian symbol is the so-called cross of St Thomas, with a number of Indian variations of the theme deriving from West Asian traditions. This motif dates from the seventh century and is still popular in India. The message of this beautiful piece of art is clear: the cross where Jesus was crucified is the source of life. Everything around the cross suggests life. The cross itself sort of flowers at its corners. Seated on a throne, the cross reigns. From the throne life sprouts in abundance. The Spirit of God descends on the cross and points to the mysterious fruitfulness of the supreme sacrifice of Jesus. The body of Jesus is not represented in this ancient symbol.

Hindu and Muslim painters in the Mughal court were busy for centuries reproducing paintings brought from outside India and giving them an Indian setting and an Indian message. A fair number of these paintings, mostly miniatures, are found even today in museums in India and abroad. Jesus appears at home in the Indian colourful settings, with their lush vegetation and exotic fauna. The miniatures brim over with life. The Indianness of Jesus is stressed, for instance, in a Last Supper scene where Jesus and his disciples wear Eastern garb—except for Judas, who is presented in Portuguese clothing! The composition suggests the confrontation between the two visions of life.

The most creative Indian art about Jesus probably came from the Bengal school of painting that flourished during the Bengal renaissance of the nineteenth and twentieth centuries thanks to the efforts of the Tagores and others. Nandalal Bose (Basu), Jamini Roy, Nikhil Biswas and Arup Das are well-known Bengali painters of this school. But its influence reaches beyond, with K.C.S. Paniker and M. Reddeppa Naidu in the South, K.H. Ara and the Parsi Chiavax D. Chavda in Mumbai and the Muslim S.Y. Malak in Nagpur. More recently Krishen Khanna also created a number of paintings of Jesus Christ, often in settings of political conflict. The crucifixion and the sufferings of Jesus are very common themes of many modern Indian artists. Richard Taylor (1975, 98–99) comments:

> When they painted Christ most of the leading painters painted his sufferings. They did not paint much about his life and teachings. But they speak about his life and teachings leading to his suffering. They also speak about his suffering service. At their best they take the great-Man-ness of Jesus utterly seriously. Often they see this as leading to his agony— which in some sense is prototypical of our life in this present world too. They dwell on the angularity of Jesus. He is strange, awkward, unloved, difficult, misunderstood—and probably he is so just because of his great (perhaps perfect) love and understanding. His angularity is, I dare say, precisely the other side of his idealness as a man.

Thus Biswas finds Jesus 'the most maladjusted man in history—the greatest and most maladjusted'. Or rather, he adds, 'we are all non-adjusted to him. Jesus was relevant, or is relevant, but we do not recognize this, or we do not accept him' (ibid., 79). Christ is often surrounded by human misery, and the darts or arrows of opposition often surround him. One gets a similar impression from Khanna's paintings.

Christian painters in India generally soften his angularity. Perhaps an unconscious apologetic drive leads them to show Jesus as better fitted to the Indian milieu. Often he is the guru, the teacher and the way to God. Like in ancient Western art he is also the Good Shepherd, or indeed his Indian counterpart, the cowherd. Jyoti Sahi has portrayed Jesus with the help of traditional Indian symbols:

even on the cross he is a Nataraja, a 'Lord of the Dance', or he is the serene face of the Trimurti of Elephanta caves, facing the worshippers and enabling them to have a true darshan of the mystery of the Divine Trinity. Indian Christian artists have also painted in abundance Madonnas and Nativity scenes in Indian settings, mostly for devotional use.

Also directed to devotional use is the popular bazaar art which produces the most often bought and used reproductions of Indian gods and goddesses and their various mythologies. Part of their mass output consists in the reproduction of many of the Western pictures of Jesus Christ in the gaudy colours of bazaar art, and without much search for inner authenticity. Even then, some are pretty pictures that adorn many living rooms all over the country. A popular theme is Christ in agony in the garden of Gethsemane just before his death. The figure of Christ with the heart seen in his chest, as in the modern Western tradition, is a very common picture—and rightly so, for love is surely the centre of Jesus' personality.

DID JESUS COME TO INDIA?

So familiar is Jesus in India that not seldom has literature been produced to 'prove' that Jesus lived in India and perhaps learned from India the wisdom that he later preached in Palestine. Our dailies or weeklies regularly bring the theme to public notice, often as if this were a recent discovery of 'science' or of the most recent 'American scholars', when the 'discovery' dates from the nineteenth century! Two recent publications that expound the thesis will suffice for our information: Kersten (2001) and Benjamin (2001.)

There are two variations of the Jesus-in-India thesis: one says he came to India, specifically Kashmir (Punjab and Tibet are also mentioned) between the age of twelve and thirty, a time about which the Gospels give us no detailed information except that 'the child grew and became strong, filled with wisdom; and the favour of God was upon him' (Lk 2:40). The second hypothesis, not necessarily excluding the first, affirms that Jesus did not die on the cross but fainted; when put in the tomb he revived under the effect of the aromatic spices used in his burial and managed to escape the guards and then ran away, perhaps with some disciples, to India, and that he died in Kashmir, where the tomb with his name Yus Asaf is still preserved (the name could be a variation of Joseph rather than of Jesus). The tomb, called Rauzabar, is situated in Khaniyar in the northern part of Srinagar. Other local traditions also claim to have the tombs of Mary and Moses.

There were many variations of the name Jesus among Jews and other Semitic people: Joshua, Joses, Josu, Isa . . . the last (also spelled as Issa) being of course the Muslim version of the name of Jesus of Nazareth, occurring twenty-five times in the Koran. In ancient Israel and the surrounding cultures the name was rather frequent. There could have been in India at some time or other some ascetic with the name of Yusuf and perhaps also with the name of Issa, either Muslim or pre-Muslim, possibly with Jewish connection. One cannot deny the possibility of some Isa in India. In the absence of any contemporary evidence it is difficult to identify any such mention with Jesus of Nazareth, unless other proof is given.

One of the sources of such speculation, mentioned by most if not all writers, is a Russian journalist and traveller, Nicolas Notovitch, who in 1894 wrote a book in French, published in English in 1895 titled *The Unknown Life of Christ*. He bases his thesis on the claim of a Pali manuscript he discovered in the Buddhist monastery in Himis or Hemis (south of Leh in Ladakh). He said that the monks translated the important parts of that manuscript to him when he was in their monastery convalescing from a fracture. Later he published the notes he took at the time in the form of a book. He records the life of 'Issa' who at thirteen escaped his parents' house to avoid marriage and came to Sindh and Punjab and Rajasthan where he met Jains. He learned spiritual practices from the Buddhist monks and went back to his country where he was crucified. In this account Jesus does not travel to India after his death, but his disciples spread throughout the world with the good news. The manuscript as reported by Notovitch ends thus:

> And the disciples of Saint Issa abandoned the land of Israel, and scattered themselves among the heathen, preaching that they should renounce their errors, bethink them of the salvation of their souls, and of the perfect felicity awaiting humanity in that immaterial world of light, where in repose

and in all His purity the Great Creator dwells in perfect majesty.

The pagans, their kings, and their warriors listened to the preachers, abandoned their absurd beliefs, and forsook their priests and their idols, to celebrate the praise of the all-wise Creator of the universe, the King of kings, whose heart is filled with infinite mercy.

Notovitch's report was not well received by scholars. Max Müller criticized the book as fiction and Notovitch tried to defend himself in the English edition. In his new apologia he clarifies that the passages he quoted may not have come from one Pali manuscript but from various sources and that he merely put the themes together. He also admits the possibility that they may have been memories either of Indians who travelled to Palestine during the life of Jesus and came back to their countries, or of the preaching of St Thomas in India! He merely wants to reaffirm the existence of the manuscript(s), questioned by Max Müller, and the conformity of the teachings of Jesus found in them with those found in the Christian scriptures. At present the name of Notovitch hardly appears in any encyclopedia or dictionary.

Another source of the 'Jesus-in-India' thesis is a fairly long Sanskrit text describing the life and teaching of Jesus found in the 1897 edition of the *Bhavisya (Maha) Purana* published by the Srivenkata Press in Bombay. Already in 1903, Theodor Aufrecht unmasked this publication as a 'literary fraud' (see Winternitz 1927, 1: 567, note 1). The passage about Christ does indeed refer to Jesus of Nazareth, but it is the composition of some unknown pandit possibly in Bombay in the later part of the nineteenth century, not an ancient Indian purana.

We may mention in passing here that even today there are claims by Christian apologists that the Vedas contain specific prophecies about the life and especially the death of Christ, with extraordinary detailed descriptions. A careful look at the literature produced in this context shows that the quotations from Vedic literature are taken totally out of their context, are often mistranslated from the Sanskrit and given quite fanciful interpretations. This is of course quite different from the theology of fulfilment as, for example, proposed in the nineteenth century by Krishna Mohan Banerjea, who saw in the sacrifice of Christ on the cross for the salvation of humanity the 'fulfilment' and a full explanation of the Vedic myth of the saving power of the sacrifice of Prajapati.

A third source of the legend of Christ in India comes from a late Muslim tradition, especially as popularized by Hazrat Mirza Ghulam Ahmad (1835–1908), founder of the Ahmadiyya Movement in Islam, in his book *Masih Hindustan Main*, first published in Urdu in 1899 (English version *Jesus in India: Being an Account of Jesus' Escape from Death on the Cross and of His Journey to India*, London: The London Mosque, 1978). The book attempts a reading of some passages of the Bible from the perspective of the Muslim affirmation that Jesus did not die on the cross. It says that after the burial in the tomb Jesus revived and eventually came to India to preach to the ten lost tribes of Israel, which the author identifies with some of the Afghan tribes.

We are therefore left with the impression that the thesis that Jesus was in India, once or twice, has little historical probability. It would not change the Christian faith if it was proved to be true. But it is not proved. And it would indeed be strange that no reference to this contact with India percolated in the whole canonical and non-canonical literature about Jesus emerging in the Mediterranean and West Asian world of the early centuries CE and that this discovery took place only in the nineteenth century. In fact none of the serious historians, whether Jewish or Christian or secular, who have studied the history of Jesus from all available sources gives any credibility to the 'India thesis'.

Let us end this discussion with the words of Jawaharlal Nehru. Writing to his daughter on 12 April 1932, he says:

All over Central Asia, in Kashmir and Ladakh and Tibet and even farther north, there is still a strong belief that Jesus or Isa travelled about there. Some people believe that he visited India also. It is not possible to say anything with certainty, and indeed most authorities who have studied the life of Jesus do not believe that Jesus came to India or Central Asia. But there is nothing inherently improbable in his having done so (1949, 84).

We must not confuse the view that Jesus spent some time in India with the fact that his life and teachings were known in India well before the colonial era. We shall see it clearly in chapter three. Here in the context of the 'strong belief' mentioned by Nehru we may record that in Tibetan and Chinese sources there are some references to the teachings of Jesus and even probably to a teacher Ye su, seen as a Buddhist teacher, 'called Lord of the universe, born in a miraculous way. He wrote a book where he gave his commandments in ten points, as for example not to kill human life, etc.' These words of an eighteenth-century Tibetan sage called T'u'u bkvan blo bzan C'os kyi ni ma are reported in Tibetan and Italian translation and with notes by Giuseppe Toscano in *Il 'Byun K'uns'* (1984, 331). In the early centuries of the first millennium the Christian Church had spread out to central Asia and the record of Jesus was known there. But this does not say that Jesus actually lived in India—or Tibet, for that matter.

In a sense Jesus did come to India, not during his lifetime, but in the testimony of his disciples who brought his memory here. *This* visit of Jesus to India did not stop in the early centuries: it continues in the community of his believers and in the memory of many who through them come into a faith contact with Jesus.

THE CHRISTIAN PERCEPTION OF JESUS

Today's Christians pay much more attention to the human life of Jesus than Christians did in the past. Without denying his divine character, they prefer to see him as the real human being that he was, part and parcel of history. A witness to this could be a rather enthusiastic summary of his life and of the effect he has had in history, written anonymously a few years ago, probably in Spanish. Here is an English version:

> He was born in a small village, the son of a peasant woman.
> He grew in another village, a carpenter till he was thirty.
> Then, for three years, he became a wandering preacher.
> He never wrote a book. Never held public office.
> Never had a family or home. Never went to college.
> Never travelled more than 200 miles from his place of birth.

Never achieved anything that is associated with greatness.
Had no credentials other than himself.
He was only thirty-three when public opinion turned against
        him.
His friends abandoned him.
He was handed over to his enemies, who made fun of
        him at a trial.
He was crucified between two thieves.
And while he agonized asking God why he had abandoned
        him, his torturers cast lots on his garments, the only
        possession he had.
When he died, he was buried in a tomb lent by a friend.
Twenty centuries have passed, and he is the central figure
        in our world, a decisive factor in the enlightenment of
        humanity.
None of the armies that have marched,
        none of the navies that have sailed,
        none of the parliaments that have met,
        none of the kings that have reigned, or even all of them
        together, have changed human life on earth as much as
        this single Life (adapted from Gonzalez Faus 2001).

Is this true? In fact, the first question we ask about Jesus the man is:
What do we really know, if anything, about him? Is not his life
perhaps one of the many myths, built along the centuries, that fill
the religious literature of the world? Is he a construct of a faith
community, rather than their source as a real human being? To these
questions mystically inclined people tend to answer: What does it
matter? Is not the 'myth' truer and more important than whatever
history says? Is it really important to know what kind of life he
lived, what he did, how he died? Is it not his teaching and the
inspiration we derive from his life that matter? In general Christians
think that the reality of the history of Jesus *is* important for their
own faith. Without this historical rooting they would find that their
faith would be nothing but a doctrine, a philosophy rather than the
discipleship of Jesus they experience in their own lives and in the
community.

THE SEARCH FOR THE HISTORICAL JESUS

In the nineteenth and twentieth centuries the Gospels, together with the rest of the Bible, were subject to intense critical scrutiny regarding their composition and their reliability. As a result of this study it was found that the Gospels were not what the simple piety of the earlier centuries had assumed them to be: accurate and reliable biographies of the deeds and words of Jesus written by eyewitnesses who had no reason to create myths. The Gospels were not histories in the modern sense of the word, whose primary concern is accurate reporting. They are rather witnesses of how the first-century Christians in various parts of the Mediterranean world had assimilated the memory and the teachings of Jesus. They indeed refer to a historical person, Jesus, who lived, preached and died in Palestine 'under Pontius Pilate', as the old Creed puts it. But they are documents of the faith of a number of communities that sprang up after the death of Jesus. Their credibility is based on the credibility of the community that produced them, a community which was indeed vibrant with the Divine Spirit and whose writings, we believe, bear the stamp of divine authenticity. Are the Gospels reliable in respect to the historical Jesus?

Their critical study took place at a period when, and in a continent where, modernist thought and dry rationalism were at their peak. It is a firm tenet of rationalism that nothing which cannot be demonstrated scientifically can be true. Accordingly, the cures and other miracles of Jesus must be taken a priori as popular inventions. The result of the work done in the eighteenth and nineteenth centuries regarding a critical study of the sources of our knowledge of Jesus was summarized in a famous book by Albert Schweitzer published in 1906, just before he announced his decision to study medicine and dedicate himself to philanthropic work. The English translation of this work was published in 1910 titled *The Quest of the Historical Jesus: A Critical Study of Its Progress from Reimarus to Wrede*. For Schweitzer the search was futile: it was not historical enough. Each scholar found in the Gospels a projection of his a priori religious categories! The 1952 Nobel Peace Prize winner thought in 1906 that most scholars missed the Jewish religious outlook around the first quarter of the first century CE. That outlook was decisively 'apocalyptic': it expected a clear and final intervention of God to give Israel its leading place among the nations and expected this intervention to take place in the immediate future.

The historical scepticism of the nineteenth-century scholars regarding the historical value of the Gospels seemed to be confirmed by Rudolf Bultmann in the first part of the twentieth century. Bultmann studied the literary pieces out of which the Gospels were made, and because he saw them as faith affirmations, he denied that they can give us a true picture of the history of Jesus. The Gospels tell us about Christianity, not about Jesus. Christianity, according to him, began after the death of Jesus! Jesus belongs to Judaism, but Judaism reports very little about him.

By the middle of the twentieth century, however, the disciples of Bultmann begin criticizing his extreme scepticism about the value of the Gospels and make a wider and more detailed study of all the available data at the time. They begin what has been called 'A new quest for the historical Jesus' (the title of a book by Bishop John M. Robinson, first published in 1959). Highly competent scholars joined in this search and developed criteria of historical credibility to discern what in the Gospel accounts goes back to the history of Jesus and what is the expression of the faith of the earliest Christian communities. Among others, the criteria are multiple attestations of independent sources, discontinuity from what was expected in the Jewish or Christian culture of the time and consistency between the words and deeds of Jesus. These criteria offered sufficient basis to assure us of a basic framework of historical events reported to us from within the faith testimonies of the Gospels, completed about seventy years after the death of Jesus.

This work of scholars coming after the great Bultmann is completed by what has been called 'The third quest' started around 1985, which besides working on Christian documents paid much more attention to the Jewish background of the life and doctrine of Jesus and found support from contemporary literary sources not included in the Bible. It also paid more attention to data coming from the archaeology of Palestine and the Mediterranean world, philology and sociology of the first-century Roman Empire and its dependencies.

The results of the work done during the last century offer us a picture that avoids a fundamentalist and literal reading of the Gospels as simple historical records, but see them as the testimony of a community whose faith was based on the history of a man who had transformed the lives of the believers. The historical event is however recorded in the language of bhakti.

Today most scholars would agree at least on these basic facts about the 'life of Jesus':

- He was born around 4 BCE: he was born before the death of Herod the Great, which occurred in 4 BCE. The birth could have been in 5 or 6 or even 7 BCE.

- His childhood and early adulthood occurred in Nazareth, a village of Galilee, north of Palestine.

- He was baptized by John, a sort of 'charismatic' preacher who announced the imminent coming of the 'reign of God'. Many think that for Jesus this baptism was a transforming event. It was certainly important and marked a new stage in his life.

- Jesus too preached about 'the reign of God' but his interpretation differed from John's: the stress was on God as Father rather than as judge of history.

- Possibly after the imprisonment of John (eventually executed), or perhaps even before, Jesus began to preach in the small villages of Galilee, mostly around the Sea (lake) of Galilee. He seems to have avoided the towns.

- He called some fellow Galileans to be his disciples, some of them fishermen, but together a rather mixed group.

- Unlike John, he not only preached but exercised a kind of charismatic healing ministry that attracted many villagers to him.

- Around 30 CE he went with some disciples to Jerusalem to celebrate the Passover, the most important religious and national festival of the Jews.

- His presence caused a kind of agitation in the city and a disturbance in the Temple area.

- He celebrated an important final meal with his disciples around the time of the Passover festival.

- He was arrested and brought for interrogation to the Jewish authorities, specifically the High Priest.

- His disciples ran away at the time.

- He was executed just outside the city of Jerusalem by order of the Roman procurator Pontius Pilate.
- Some of his disciples somehow saw or had an experience of his living ('risen') presence after his death; the exact nature of this experience cannot be explained.
- They believed that he would come back to inaugurate the Reign of God.
- They formed a community to prepare for his return and to convince others to join them in their faith in him as the Messiah of God (summarized from Vargas-Machuca 2002).

WHY HISTORY IS IMPORTANT

Gandhiji is reported to have said that he did not care at all whether the Mahabharata war took place in history or not. He knew that the Mahabharata is true because it portrays what happens in every human heart, the battle between the forces of good and of evil. In other words the truth of a story that matters is its doctrine, not its factual history. Similarly he also said that it did not matter whether Jesus was or was not a historical person. The Sermon on the Mount remains true in either case. We have to look for the spiritual, not the historical, truth. Hence all the enormous effort summarized above in the search of the historical Jesus would appear to Gandhi and perhaps to many Indians as rather futile work.

There may be some truth in this attitude. From the perspective of spiritual growth history seems rather superficial and irrelevant. Obviously the study of mere historical details of Jesus' life or of any other historical person, for that matter, generally tells us nothing significant about her or him. A person is not primarily determined by where she or he is or by external events of her or his life. Detailed minutiae of the places or time where and when Akbar went or the Buddha spoke do not by themselves enlighten us about their personalities. What matters for us is to know their basic decisions, their attitudes, their relations to their surroundings and their outlook on life as spelt out in their teaching and in their activity.

While all this is true, Christians whether in India or elsewhere know that the full reality of Jesus matters for their faith and their lives. It is not enough just to know what Jesus taught, nor even to put his teaching into practice. Jesus is surely a guru, but also more than a guru. If we may say so, he is much more central to the faith of a Christian than Mohammad is to a Muslim or the Buddha to a Buddhist. Or even more than what Krishna means to a Krishna bhakta.

We explain. In the Gospel of John, Jesus asks us to obey his command—the command of love—and tells us that keeping his commandment will lead to an experience of oneness with him and with the 'Father', that is, God. The Gospel of John reflects the spiritual experience of the early disciples when reporting the words of Jesus. To a disciple who asked how he will reveal himself to them, Jesus answered, 'Those who love me will keep my word, and my Father will love them, and *we will come to them and make our home with them*' (Jn 14:23). A little later in the same discourse Jesus tells his disciples what the disciples had already experienced, 'I am the vine, you are the branches. Those who abide in me and I in them bear much fruit, because apart from me you can do nothing . . . If you abide in me and my words abide in you, ask for whatever you wish, and it will be done for you. My Father is glorified by this, that you bear much fruit and be my disciples' (Jn 15:4–8). This deep sense of union with Jesus as the Son of God, explained by the image of the tree and the branches and their fruitfulness, is central to the understanding of the Christian life. Without the reality of Jesus it would lose its very foundation.

Fifty years earlier, another disciple, St Paul, reported the same experience that followed his decision to change his spiritual outlook from a law-abiding Jew to a faith-relying disciple of Jesus: 'For through the law I died to the law so that I might live to God. I have been crucified *with Christ*; and it is no longer I who live, but it is Christ who lives in me. And the life I now live in the flesh [in weakness] I live by faith in the Son of God who loved me and gave himself for me' (Gal 2:19–20). This is the basic mystical experience which in some form or other Christians strive to attain—to a greater or lesser degree—an experience of being in unison and in union with Jesus Christ and in him with the Absolute Divine Mystery. The concrete person of Jesus is essential for this experience. A myth would not do.

Living in Christ or with Christ does not just mean living in God or with God, as any mystic would do. Living in and with Christ means also living after the pattern of the man Jesus and in union with his risen existence. This is why his historical existence is so important and essential to the Christian faith. Christ is not another name for God. Christ is a qualifier of the man Jesus, who has been revealed to us as the messenger of God.

BACKGROUND OF THE HISTORY OF JESUS

Two words now about the socio-political situation of the time. Palestine, where Jesus grew up and became a public figure of some reputation, had been for a long time occupied by the Roman army. The Roman Empire controlled much of the regions around the Mediterranean Sea, and beyond, to the north and east. Palestine or Israel was divided administratively into different provinces under different forms of authority. Socially it had a powerful but small elite holding whatever power it could wrest from the Romans and the masses of farmers (generally landless), fisherfolk, artisans, petty merchants and public servants who had little control over their own lives. People were heavily taxed, both by the Romans and by the temple in Jerusalem, the central religious institution of Judaism. Except for a few places, the land was not particularly fruitful. Crime abounded.

There were several influential religious groups. There were the priests who relied on the written Torah as the only source of authority and were strict in the interpretation of the penal legislation, which was at least in part their responsibility. Some of them were active in the process that led to the death of Jesus. The aristocracy among them were the Sadducees, who were allied to conservative landowners and merchants. They adapted to the presence of the Roman power and had a great influence on the lives of the people. Jesus would be quite critical of the attitudes of the priests. There were also movements of spiritual renewal and asceticism, some popular and some elitist. Among the latter were the Pharisees, often allied to the scribes or the scholars and intellectuals of Judaism. The Pharisees appealed not only to the written law but also to the oral tradition of the elders. On the whole the Gospels present them as opposed to the positions of Jesus. They may have feared that the doctrine of the new rabbi threatened their position as religious leaders.

But the ordinary folk lived generally by faith and hope—faith in religious traditions, some of which went back 1200 years and kept a memory of having once been slaves and having been liberated by the power of God. They felt 'covenanted' to, or specially allied with, that God, whom they called 'the Lord' or by the 'sacred name of four consonants' (*Tetragammon*) that should not be pronounced aloud or written in full lest it be desecrated: Yahweh. Yahweh was their God; they were Yahweh's people. The prophets had in old times been sent by the Lord to the people (although in the time of Jesus apparently no more prophets were available) and had promised that Yahweh would act decisively so that they would recover the former freedom and the former glory, such as there had been a thousand years ago in the idealized state of David and Solomon. And so the people hoped. And prayed. And paid their taxes!

A good number of popular preachers appeared from time to time. Some were violent extremists, in the line of the old Maccabees who fought futile battles against the Romans. The Zealots, the extremists, wanted to organize similar movements of violent resistance against the Romans. Today they would be called 'terrorists'. At the opposite extreme were people ready to collaborate with the Romans. Some were tax collectors, somewhat similar to our old zamindars, who could extort taxes from the people, a portion of which went to the Roman authorities, the rest to themselves. They were highly despised by the general public. The establishment, priests and scholars, kept aloof but did not generally dare to oppose the Roman military might. The Pharisees strove to lead a pious life by a strict observance of the religious laws found in their Bible, even in a social situation where all its prescriptions could not be kept. And there were the monks, people who withdrew from society to live in separate communities trying to organize themselves into self-sufficient religious groups. Whether these were indirectly influenced by Indian monasticism has not been sufficiently studied.

Israel was not a purely Jewish nation. Apart from the military occupation which generally did not interfere much in the religious sphere, there had been Greek cultural influences for a very long time, and other highly developed nations also brought different values to society. Especially in the north of the country, Galilee, where Jesus grew up and did most of his preaching, people were confused and the foreign influences were strong.

LIFE AND TEACHINGS OF JESUS

It is in this rather depressed and bewildered nation that Jesus appeared and began to preach. According to the Gospel memories, he went first to listen to the message of a religious guru who was in the line of the ancient prophets. He was called John the Baptist and was telling people to get ready for the coming of God's Rule, a God who would judge and do away with the wickedness of the people. Jesus listened to John, and was even baptized in a water ritual to express readiness for the rule of God and the greater purity of life of the new era.

The well-known popular accounts about the birth of Jesus found in the Gospels of Matthew and Luke reflect the somewhat later meditations of the early Christian communities about the meaning and significance of the life of Jesus. They contain the messages of the angel to Mary and to Joseph, the journey from Nazareth to Bethlehem, the birth in a manger for lack of place in the inn, the announcement by angels to shepherds, the arrival of the 'wise men' from the East who had seen a star and come to worship him, the ensuing persecution, all rich in symbolism and spiritual doctrine. They were not written as strictly biographical accounts but as folkloric expressions of faith.

The stories and their symbols are integrated in the Christmas lore, especially in the ever-popular carols, whether in English or in Indian languages. The earliest Gospel of Jesus Christ, St Mark's, starts the account with the preaching of John the Baptist to whom an adult Jesus comes to listen and by whom he is baptized.

All the Gospels allude to a kind of mystical experience of Jesus at the time of his baptism by John. He heard a voice 'from heaven', in the Jewish mind the dwelling place of God, calling him, 'My son, my beloved, in whom I am well pleased.' This experience seems to have given a special quality to the bond between Jesus and God, whom Jesus called Father. This way of speaking about God became central in his teaching. For after his baptism Jesus is said to have spent a time of prayer in the wilderness after which he began the life of a preacher similar to that of John, and yet different. He was itinerant, not bound to a locality or to any ritual like baptism. When Herod, the local raja, imprisoned John and eventually murdered him, Jesus came out more publicly.

What was the activity of Jesus during the short time he acted as a public figure, before he was crucified? The Gospels summarize his life then with three words: he announced, he taught, he healed (healing is often presented as an 'exorcism' or casting out of demons from people). Clearly he had a message about God and the present situation of the people. In line with the theme found in the ancient prophets and taken up by his own predecessor John, he announced the imminent 'Rule of God'. The original Greek expression, influenced by the Hebrew tradition, is generally translated as 'Kingdom of God'. But 'Rule of God' and 'Reign of God' seem more accurate translations. Primarily it was a message of courage and hope to people in a rather depressing economic, political and religious situation. According to the prophets God had promised that he would take care of the people. God would keep this promise, for the primary characteristic of God, already in the First Testament, was fidelity, constancy. This basic characteristic is not far from what the ancient Indian tradition called *sat* or *satya*, an attribute disclosing the reality of Brahman, the Indescribable Mystery surrounding our existence. Satya means permanence, authenticity, truth, fidelity. God is faithful. And his fidelity would be shown in a new initiative: God would manifest what Jesus called God's Rule. This decisive moment had arrived. It was at hand. It was now. It came with Jesus. Things had changed.

Jesus specified the character of the Rule of God. It was the Rule of a Father. He called God by the most intimate word a child could use for his father, 'Abba' (perhaps close to the Hindi 'Bapu'). And because God is a father his strongest characteristic is forgiveness. He receives sinners and forgives and restores them. It is not necessary to be a 'saint' to be accepted by God. One can always trust father! Even the much hated tax collectors and the despised prostitutes could find a place in the new Rule of God. One of the things about Jesus often recorded in the Gospels and which shocked especially the Pharisees was that he mixed with sinners—tax collectors and prostitutes—and even ate with them. Open commensality became the symbol of the new order. All human beings can eat at the same table, because all are equally daughters and sons of God. This does not mean that he did not have a message for the Pharisees and religious people: the contact with Jesus was always a call to repentance, to a change of life.

If God had established his reign, as Jesus said, a response was needed to this saving action. The response is described by a word translated variously in the English language: 'repent', 'be converted', 'change your attitude', or by another word also used by Jesus, 'believe' (at times translated as 'have faith' or 'trust'). Convert and believe: people were being called to new attitudes. The change would be inside, an attitude of the heart that would find expression in forgiveness of one another, for if the Father forgives and accepts all of us, we too need to forgive and accept each other. The change brought in a new understanding of God: rather than a law-giver, God is Father. The change meant also a change in values: wealth, power, learning, even the law and ethics are less important than the straight heart, the humble life, the spirit of compassion. These values are suggested in the famous Beatitudes that open Jesus' Sermon on the Mount, recorded in the Gospel of Matthew, chapters 5–7. Their traditional translation is well known: 'Blessed are the poor in spirit, for theirs is the kingdom of Heaven,' etc. We offer a fresh translation in modern English, first published in 1960:

- How happy are those who know their need for God, for the kingdom of Heaven is theirs!
- How happy are those who know what sorrow means, for they will be given courage and comfort!
- Happy are those who claim nothing, for the whole earth will belong to them!
- Happy are those who are hungry and thirsty for true goodness, for they will be fully satisfied!
- Happy are the merciful, for they will have mercy shown to them!
- Happy are the utterly sincere, for they will see God!
- Happy are those who make peace, for they will be known as children of God!
- Happy are those who suffer persecution for the cause of goodness, for the kingdom of Heaven is theirs!
- And what happiness will be yours when people blame you and ill-treat you and say all kinds of slanderous things against you

for my sake! Be glad then, yes be tremendously glad—for your reward in Heaven is magnificent. They persecuted the prophets before your time in exactly the same way (Mt 5:3–12) (translated by J.B. Philipps).

The Sermon on the Mount offers an inkling of the meaning that 'conversion' or 'repentance' held for Jesus. It meant a real change of outlook. (A shorter redaction of many of the same themes is found in the Gospel of Luke 6:20–49.) It is well known that this sermon caught the imagination of Gandhiji who found in it a powerful confirmation and the spiritual basis for his own teaching of ahimsa:

> You have heard that it was said, 'An eye for an eye and a tooth for a tooth.' But I say to you, Do not resist an evildoer. But if anyone strikes you on the right cheek, turn the other also; and if anyone wants to sue you and take your coat, give your cloak as well; and if anyone forces you to go one mile, go also the second mile. Give to everyone who begs from you and do not refuse anyone who wants to borrow from you.
>
> You have heard it said, 'You shall love your neighbour and hate your enemy.' But I say to you, Love your enemies and pray for those who persecute you, so that you may be children of your Father in heaven; for he makes his sun rise on the evil and on the good, and sends rain on the righteous and on the unrighteous. For if you love those who love you, what reward do you have? Do not even the tax collectors do the same? And if you greet only your brothers and sisters, what more are you doing than others? Do not even the Gentiles do the same? Be perfect, therefore, as your heavenly Father is perfect (Mt 5:38–48).

Everybody recognizes in these words an impossible ideal, at least in its full measure. That was part of the power of Jesus' message: he called his disciples to an impossibly lofty goal. The point was not in reaching the peak, but in striving towards it. And in trusting in the God who called us to it.

Why did Jesus say that the Rule of God or the new society he was announcing was 'at hand'? Was it because a new moral consciousness was breaking into the world to raise its moral standards? Was it because a political crisis was coming to a head that might perhaps overthrow the Roman Empire and allow the smaller nations to free themselves from the foreign rule? Was there a sense of an impending change? It really does not seem so from the historical data we have. The Pax Romana was fairly well established in the Palestinian world at the time of Jesus. There were surely frequent uprisings and protests, but the Roman authorities could deal with them with ruthless efficiency. The Jewish Council, the Sanhedrin, had come to an acceptance of the status quo, and managed to have a limited power in Jewish affairs, at least of Judea. In which way was the Kingdom of God at hand?

For the writers of the four Gospels and other New Testament texts, it was clear that the new Rule of God had dawned with the life of Jesus. For them this new era was obviously related to the existence of this man whom they called Lord and Messiah. From the evidence of the Gospels it would seem that Jesus himself did relate the coming of God's Reign to his person: he was its announcer. His understanding of God started the new era within Judaism, which would soon extend to the world through the announcement of the disciples.

THE SIGNS OF JESUS

It was not merely because of a moral or religious message that the Reign of God started. All the Gospels refer to the 'signs' that Jesus performed, his 'works' as evidence of the irruption of God's Rule. Those who did not have faith found it difficult to accept signs. As the various Gospels record them, the signs were found first and foremost in the new attitudes adopted by Jesus: in his breaking the laws of purity by touching and healing lepers; in the scant attention he paid to external observances of washing before meals and the new stress on the purity of heart; in his giving to every woman, whether a widow, or sick with bleeding, or a known prostitute or even one caught in adultery, the respect and attention she deserves as 'a daughter of Abraham'; or in his receiving children and making them more important for the Reign of God than the learned scribes!

There were other kinds of signs, specifically called wonders or deeds of power. Many have been recorded in all the Gospels. Some may have been added in the course of Christian preaching to those that Jesus performed in his lifetime. For all of them the value was less in the 'wonder' than in the 'sign': what they suggest by way of dhvani about the new Reign of God. The frequently mentioned multiplication of loaves of bread and fish to satisfy thousands of followers suggested that his preaching, and his very person, provided the 'food' people need to live under the Rule of God. Today, when we read the same accounts in the context of the modern situation, many believers read in this 'sign' a pointer to the concern the followers of Jesus must have about the hunger of the world. The account of the calming of the storm contained in itself a message for a budding Christian community expelled from the synagogue or the Jewish establishment and persecuted from many quarters. Equally significant for persecuted Christians would have been the story of the serenity of Jesus as he walked over the waves of the stormy waters of the lake of Gennesareth (called the Sea of Galilee). Sign and message had to go together to be powerful: the sign without the message would be meaningless; the message without the sign would be powerless. Rabindranath Tagore's lines in *Stray Birds* beautifully illustrate this: 'I am ashamed of my emptiness,' said the Word to the Work. 'I know how poor I am when I see you,' said the Work to the Word!' The sign is the fusion of Word and Work.

The most frequent and telling signs in the story of Jesus are his 'healings'. It would be difficult to refer to the life of Jesus without his healing activity which is also reported in the story of the early Church and indeed in many forms throughout the centuries. That the presence of Jesus, his touch, his nearness, brought forgiveness, inner peace and physical healing to many people can hardly be denied. Jesus often attributed these signs to the faith of the people and is never reported to have used any miraculous powers for himself. His charisma was a gift from God and he generously shared it with all who were ready to receive it. It was not meant to ensure his success.

It is not for us to establish here a historical, philosophical or theological inquiry into the reality and value of these reported 'signs'. They form an intrinsic element of the Christian writings of the time, especially of the Gospels so that one could hardly rewrite a recognizable Gospel without them. But they must be read in the cultural context of the times. Since David Hume, modern thought has tended to dismiss all miracles as mythical or impossible. Postmodernism is less dogmatic in the matter. The point is that Christians in India and elsewhere take these signs as a true revelation of what Jesus was and what his message signified. The signs give us the clue; they have tongues, as St Augustine said. Their message is clearly one of fullness of life, of overcoming all anti-life forces operative within each individual and in society in general. When such signs are recounted during the Sunday meetings they are not meant to rouse admiration for a powerful wonder-worker but to convey a message. They tell us in the powerful language of symbols what the Kingdom of God was about.

The healings of Jesus are often interpreted in the New Testament as victories of God over the oppressive powers that maintain human beings in slavery. In their Sunday meetings India's tribal Christians listen with special fascination to the story of Jesus' victory over the world of the spirits. The demons are symbols of all that is against the Rule of God and the authentic freedom of human beings. Demons or devils possess people and enslave them. People need deliverance from such inimical superhuman powers. This symbolic outlook of the Mediterranean world of the first century finds an echo in the twenty-first century in terms of the social, political, economic and psychological forces that keep people in bondage and in a state of inhuman deprivation and utter misery. The liberating action of Jesus, his 'victory' over the mysterious forces, personified as demons in his time, continues today in every human effort to liberate people from the powers that control and diminish their lives. Liberation theology has taken much inspiration in a fresh interpretation of the signs and miracles of Jesus, and sees its programme of action as a continuation of what Jesus did in his own time.

THE DISCIPLES

Jesus did not merely announce God's new rule and demonstrate it through his healings. A great part of the accounts found in all the Gospels is his search for followers to accompany him in his programme of action and to continue it after him. Jesus not only admitted disciples who followed him on their own, at least for some time, but also chose and appointed some of them, as the Gospel of Mark tells us, 'to be with him, and to be sent out to proclaim the message, and to have authority to cast out demons' (Mk 3:14–15). As in the Indian bhakti tradition, the guru called the disciples, not the other way around. Twelve of them are central to his story. They are often called the 'apostles', that is, the 'messengers', 'those sent out'. The number twelve, attested in many writings of the New Testament, had a strong symbolic meaning for the first disciples who came from the Jewish tradition. The Jews, the people of Israel, considered themselves descendants of the twelve children of Jacob, grandson of Abraham. The saga of these 'patriarchs' is recounted in the first book of the Bible, the Book of Genesis. At the formation of the nation of Israel the twelve sons were linked with twelve regions of the nation. This tradition was alive in the religious and national literature. For the early Christians, the twelve 'apostles' symbolized the new Israel, the successor of the old Israel. Christians took the new as the true inheritor of the essence of the divine promises given to the old Israel. But there is a big difference between the old and the new: by the time the Gospels were written, the new Israel consisted not only of ethnic Jews but of people from many nations. The principle of ethnicity, symbolized in the rite of circumcision, gave way to the principle of faith, also symbolized in a sacrament of ritual, baptism. Now the twelve represented the whole world.

Jesus did not have only the twelve apostles as disciples. According to early accounts he chose them out of many others for a special role. But discipleship is a broad concept. It is interesting that it included many women, who followed Jesus where he went and who ministered to him and other disciples in many of their needs. According to the Gospels it was some of these women who, after Jesus died, first saw him alive and who conveyed the great news to the men disciples. Prominent among them was his own mother, who according to the Gospel of St John was with him as he died on the cross and who remained united with the apostles after the death of Jesus. As we shall see, Christians have a special bond of affection for her.

The disciples who followed Jesus during his preaching and activity in Palestine would become after his death the nucleus of the

Church that carried the living memory of Jesus all over the world. According to an ancient tradition, very strong in South India as we shall see in chapter three, one of the twelve apostles, St Thomas, came and preached the Gospel in India in the very first century. The names of the others are worth recalling here because of their importance in Christian history and because the community has perpetuated those names in the personal names given to children in India as elsewhere. The names derive from Hebrew-Aramaic language or from Greek. They are Simon Peter, who was clearly the leader among them, Andrew, his brother, James and John, also brothers, Philip, Matthew, Bartholomew (some say that he too came to India), another James, Simon, Jude Thaddaeus. The last in the list is always Judas Iscariot, who betrayed Jesus and hanged himself in horror of his own deed.

We do not know much about the majority of the twelve disciples and their background. Some of them were clearly fishermen from around Capernaum, the centre of Jesus' activity in the early part of his public preaching, around the Sea of Galilee, in the north of the country. One disciple is said to have been a tax collector. Others were relatives of Jesus, but we do not know their occupational background. We must remember that Jesus himself came from the artisan class. According to the Gospels he was a carpenter or a mistri. He certainly did not come from the intellectual class of Israel.

To the list of the twelve were later added important figures to whom the title of apostle is also at times given: Matthias, the nominated substitute of Judas after the latter's suicide; Nathaniel, who may or may not have been the same as Bartholomew; and two very important figures of the early Church, Barnabas and especially Paul, an early persecutor of Christians who had a unique experience of Jesus Christ on his way to Damascus where he wanted to persecute and exterminate more Christians. So important is the figure of Paul that some consider him the founder of Christianity as a theological school.

We do not know for certain how long this public life of Jesus lasted. The early part seems to be marked by an enthusiastic but often misdirected reception on the part of the villagers of Galilee. According to the account in the Gospel of John the ministry of Jesus could have lasted nearly three years. Some modern authors think, on the basis of the accounts in the other Gospels, that it may have lasted only one year. This is unlikely, for he seems to have created very strong personal bonds with the twelve, and probably also with others, which would have taken more than a year to mature. At any rate what seems important is that towards the latter part of his public life Jesus concentrated more on teaching 'the twelve' and explaining to them his insights into God and God's plan for the nation than in meeting the crowds in the villages. The place of his preaching also shifted from northern Galilee to southern Judea, especially the capital Jerusalem.

In Jerusalem Jesus took a clearly confrontational attitude towards the religious and social authorities of Judaism. He made a solemn entry to the city where he was acclaimed by many fellow Galileans as the saving Messiah. To make matters worse, he created some kind of riot in the premises of the great temple, the religious and political centre of the nation, by throwing out the merchants trafficking there and declaring it a holy place consecrated to God. He defied the authorities when they questioned his activity and showed them up for what they were in a series of parables and public controversies. As the religious authorities had some degree of political power, they decided to do away with him.

JESUS' PASSION AND DEATH

The story of the last hours of Jesus covered in various forms in all the Gospels is well known. After a farewell meal (mentioned in chapter one) Jesus went with his disciples to pray in a garden outside the Jerusalem walls called Gethsemane. There he experienced great anguish and fear and went on calling God as Father.

Soldiers sent by the Jewish authorities, who had been alerted by the traitor Judas Iscariot, found him in the garden and arrested him. The disciples fled. The prisoner was first taken to the Jewish authorities who condemned him to death on charges of 'blasphemy'. Then they brought him to the Roman procurator Pontius Pilate who, probably under pressure, had him scourged and also condemned him to death for claiming to be 'King of the Jews'. He was then taken outside the city with two other convicts and nailed to a cross till he died on a Friday afternoon. Some friends obtained from the procurator permission to get his body and laid it in a built-in tomb of theirs.

The four Gospels mention separately seven different sentences of Jesus which are said to have been uttered by him when he was being crucified or on the cross. Whatever their historical background (they can hardly be 'the very words of Jesus'), they reflect some of the many ways in which the community of his followers remembered and still remember him. We could call them the last mahavakyas of Jesus, which in a way sum up his character and his message:

- The first mahavakya is found in most manuscripts of the Gospel of Luke: 'Father, forgive them for they do not know what they are doing' (Lk 23:34). Later on the first Christian martyr, and many others after him, would die repeating the same words—words of forgiveness.

- According to the same Gospel Jesus accepted the act of faith of one of the thieves who was crucified with him and with great serenity told him, 'Truly I tell you, today you will be with me in Paradise' (Lk 23:43)—a promise of salvation.

- Just before dying Jesus saw his mother and John, his dearest disciple, nearby. Concerned about them, he entrusted each to the other: 'Woman, here is your son,' and to John, 'Here is your mother' (Jn 19:26–27). Many Christians see in this double mahavakya Jesus' 'testament' giving his mother, Mary, as the spiritual mother of all humankind.

- 'I thirst' (Jn 19:28), a word that obviously expresses a physical need. But Christians read a deeper meaning in it: Jesus' longing for love in the world. All the convents of the Missionaries of Charity (Mother Teresa's sisters) have the words 'I thirst' displayed next to the crucifix in their chapels.

- 'My God, my God, why have you forsaken me?' (Mk 15:34, Mt 28:46). Two Gospels report this mahavakya. Both quote it in Hebrew besides giving the Greek translation. The words are the opening line of the well-loved Psalm 22. This psalm describes the sufferings of a just man. Despite the pathos of its opening line, the psalm ends as a prayer of trust in God.

- 'It is finished,' says Jesus at the end (Jn 19:30). A young man in his early thirties, he has accomplished his life mission. His life has been guided by the will of God in all things. His death inaugurates the new life he had announced. This is a victorious word of a mysterious success.

- 'Father, into your hands I commend my spirit' (Lk 23:46)—this last mahavakya sums up the life of Jesus—a life of total trust in God as 'Father', complete faith in God's fidelity and the assurance that his existence will remain permanently rooted in God. It is also part of a prayer of trust of the just person, found in the Psalms (Ps 32:5).

One of the frequent practices of devotion for Christians during the Holy Week—especially on Good Friday, which recalls the death of Jesus on the cross—consists of a three-hour service in remembrance of the three hours during which, according to the traditional accounts, Jesus remained alive on the cross. During the service his last words are repeated and commented upon. The commentary, along with the singing accompanying it, is likely to arouse a great sense of bhakti, piety, devotion, love for the Lord and a desire to shape one's life according to his.

Today scholars discuss the question of why Jesus was put to death on a cross. What were the reasons for his execution? The mode of dying was not special: crucifixion was a common way of execution by the Romans, who borrowed it from the Persian empire (Iranians), although it was considered so cruel that it was used only for the execution of slaves and non-Romans guilty of heinous crimes. (The Jews traditionally executed criminals by stoning.) In the accounts of the Gospels at least two different reasons for his death are intermingled. One was political. Jesus was clearly ordered to death by Pontius Pilate. The executors were also members of the Roman army. Jesus was charged with revolt against the authority of the empire. His being acclaimed as 'Messiah' may have contributed to the fears of the occupation force. Messiah meant a person 'anointed' by the will of God to be a leader of the people. Even if it may primarily have had a religious connotation, the political implications of the title could not be ignored. All the Gospels report that the Romans placed over his head the cause of the death sentence: 'This is the King of the Jews.' Rather than letting things get out of control, it was better to eliminate the source of danger.

The Gospel accounts on the other hand seem to blame the death of Jesus on Jewish authorities, the high priest, the Sanhedrin and influential Jews, like the Pharisees. They would have been threatened by the new vision of Jesus. His way proposed an egalitarian, in some sense a democratic, society, which was a threat to the establishment. Jesus also criticized the ways in which the First Testament was interpreted, and the heavy burdens the religion of his time imposed on simple people. Jesus was a religious revolutionary, although his method had nothing to do with violence. The powerful high-priestly families, the Jewish establishment, would have manipulated the death of Jesus, especially after his expulsion of the merchants from the Jerusalem temple. Pilate just gave in to their insistent demand.

It has been asked in recent writings whether the Gospel accounts are not biased against the Jews and present one side of the case. Were their writers influenced by an incipient anti-Semitism in the Church? By the time some of the Gospels were written the followers of Jesus had been expelled from the synagogue, that is, from legitimate membership in the Jewish religion. Did this create an anti-Jewish feeling in the early Christians? Or, perhaps, by blaming the Jews or their authorities, were the authors trying to maintain good relations with the Roman authorities that, after all, had the political control of the empire? However, we cannot forget that Jesus and all the early disciples were Jews. Can we then speak of an anti-Semitism in the Gospel writers or the tradition creators? It is difficult to pass a definitive judgement on this question. Both factors were probably intermingled, but with the historical evidence available to us we cannot decide which was the dominant factor. But there is hardly any doubt that there was an opposition to Jesus on the part of some people of the dominant Jewish classes. This issue was recently at the centre of the controversies around the film *The Passion of the Christ* by Mel Gibson.

Independently of the political and religious factors at play in the tragedy, Christian believers look at Jesus' death from a deeper perspective. They see it as somehow part of a mysterious 'plan' approved by God himself, a plan not of death but of life (see Acts 2:22–24). The death was only that Life might emerge. God's mysterious design is centred on the way in which Jesus accepted his mission with love for all, including those who crucified him, and did so with courage to the end. According to the Christian faith vision, the obedient love of Jesus as he hanged on the cross and accepted death as the outcome of his mission was the inauguration of the new pattern of life by which humanity could come out of its entanglement with sin. Sin had abounded in the world. But love can overcome sin. This will become clearer in the aftermath.

THE AFTERMATH

One of the strangest features of the Christian world view and perception of Jesus is that his death was not the end. His story continues. After his burial (really an 'entombment' which consisted of placing the corpse within a cave that was then closed), in a mysterious way God made him alive. The earliest New Testament document is the first letter of Paul to the Thessalonians written about 50 CE, scarcely twenty years after the death of Jesus. In it the fact of Jesus being alive is taken for granted and mentioned in passing to provide hope to those who had lost dear ones, 'For since we believe that Jesus died and rose again, even so, through Jesus, God will bring with him those who have died' (1 Thess 4:14). Note that the English 'rose again' is a poor translation of the original Greek word that means literally 'stood up'. The 'again' idea comes from the misleading Latin translation 're-surrection' which probably originated with St Jerome in the fourth century. Practically all the writings of the New Testament speak directly of the 'resurrection' of Jesus, and it had nothing of the 'again' in it: it was the revelation of a new world, a new form of existence. (Many Indian translations repeat the faulty translation of the Latin and English and hence speak of *punar-utthan*—with the wrong 'again' idea). That Jesus emerged alive from the tomb where he was buried and continues to live in his full human (and divine) personality was the central conviction of the first generation of disciples as it is of all Christian believers today.

In the language of the New Testament it is not so much that Jesus 'rose' to new life as that *God* 'raised' him to life in God. The 'event' was really an action of the one Jesus called Father, the God whom the Jews worshipped. As a result of this divine action Jesus 'was seen' by the disciples, and his tomb was found empty. It is difficult to describe the exact nature of the 'sightings' of the risen Jesus. The language of the New Testament speaks of his 'being seen' by the disciples rather than of his 'appearing' to them. The 'sightings' may have been exceptional and given to a few, although around the year 55, that is, twenty-five years after the events, Paul writes in one place of his having been seen by more than 500, some of whom were still alive (1 Cor 15:6). More importantly, there is a common conviction expressed in many ways in the earliest writings that the Lord was alive and very close to the disciples especially in their witness to him. The first Gospel ends with Jesus telling his disciples, 'And remember, I am with you always, to the end of the age' (Mt 28:20). In a kind of appendix to the Gospel of Mark, added rather early, the last verse specifies that the disciples 'went out and proclaimed the good news everywhere, while the Lord worked with them and confirmed the message by the signs that accompanied it' (Mk 16:2). We could cite many other texts revealing the same experience of the nearness of the living Lord.

For Christians this 'resurrection' of Jesus, or his 'being made alive', is not a mere glorification of the spirit of Jesus, a mere bestowal of eternal existence on him. Many religions do believe in some form of eternal existence at least for those whose lives have been praiseworthy. This is the meaning of the veneration of the 'saints' found in most religions. Christians say that the 'resurrection' of Jesus means more than that. It is not, for sure, a 'resuscitation' of the body as might happen either medically after the heart has stopped beating or by the power of God who might bring someone 'dead' to life again. Jesus did not come 'alive *again*' in the sense of entering our world of samsara in the way in which he lived in it before his death. Nor does it mean of course that, being God, Jesus has an eternal divine existence. The resurrection is something that God did to the human reality of Jesus. One of the ways the New Testament speaks of this moment in the existence of Jesus is that he was 'glorified': his human personal existence was transformed in all its dimensions into a form of eternal life that was no longer dependent on the conditioning of time and space. We have no way of imagining what kind of existence this involves, in spite of the many attempts by artists to portray it. We only know that it is an existence fully human and, as we shall see later, fully divine.

Indian Christians have made attempts to interpret this post-cross experience of the disciples in terms borrowed from the Indian tradition. Without trying to be exhaustive we may recall the use of the ancient concept of suksma sarira (subtle body) to somehow represent the mysterious reality of the risen Lord. A Telugu theologian of the early twentieth century, P. Chenchiah, spoke of the risen Jesus in terms borrowed from the evolutionary philosophy of Sri Aurobindo, who speaks of the 'super-Man'. Chenchiah also saw him as the Adi Purusa, which he always interpreted as the New Creation, the New Man, the irruption of the Maha Sakti into our world. None of these explanations, nor any proposed in the West, is fully satisfactory to account for the experience not only of the disciples but of all Christians of all times. When they meet every Sunday for the Eucharist, when they read the Bible together, especially the New Testament, they also meet and hear the risen Lord. They have a collective experience of his presence among them. Otherwise they would not meet. This is why, incidentally, the early disciples chose the first day of the week, Sunday, to meet for worship. It was not their usual holiday: for Jews Saturday (the Sabbath) was, and is, the weekly holiday. The early Christians, Jews though they were, met on Sunday to celebrate the Eucharist because the Lord was known to have risen on that day.

The anubhava of the living Jesus must be supported by glimpses of the risen life in one's own life. These glimpses of Jesus' victory over death are experienced in the power to forgive those who have hurt us deeply, or in the strength of hope even in the midst of repeated failure and in times of despair. However much evil one experiences, in oneself or in the world, we can now always look at the world with hope. The deep certainty of faith even in the midst of constant challenges and intellectual questions, a faith that can be free of exclusivism and fundamentalism, is part of the experience of the risen Christ. Jesus' victory over sin and death is also experienced in every act of love for the poor, the marginalized, the enemy, love of those from whom we expect no reward. Jesus' victory is present in every fight for justice which is impregnated with love, in every act of courage to protest when human beings are trampled upon. The same victory is revealed in every act of hope that God's reign will prevail in spite of the power of evil around us. In other words, the resurrection can be sensed every time we say in truth and from the heart *satyam eva jayate!*

3

The First Christians in India

The great divisions of the Christian Church ~ Orthodox (Oriental and Eastern) and Catholic and Protestant ~ The tradition of St Thomas in India ~ Connection with Syrian Christianity ~ Characteristics of the St Thomas Christians ~ Their social and economic background ~ Their religious system ~ The divisions within the St Thomas community ~ The Mar Thoma Church ~ The 'Latin' Christians of Kerala ~ Influence of the St Thomas Christians in the rest of the country ~ What is the 'Church'? ~ Church and Jesus Christ ~ Church and humanity ~ Community or communalism?

The majority of Kerala's Christians and their descendants recognize themselves as 'Thomas Christians' or Nazaranis, that is, Nazarene Christians. Strangely, the most common epithet attached to their community is that of 'Syrian' Christians, although all of them are Indian. As we shall see, the adjective 'Syrian' is based not on the political map but on the history of the Church.

The Christian movement started by Jesus spread out, after his death and resurrection, first in Asia Minor, mostly in the western part of what is today Asian Turkey, and surrounding areas and islands. In many cases it followed the migration routes of Jewish settlements found in most towns of the Roman Empire. From Asia Minor it spread eastward, covering most areas in West Asia, today's Lebanon, Jordan, Syria, Saudi Arabia, the areas around the Caspian Sea, Iraq and even western Iran. From there Christian communities would eventually spread out in small outposts into central Asia, and even China and Korea.

The contacts of the Christians in India were primarily with these groups of Christians of West Asia. The area around the eastern shore of the Mediterranean was the Roman province of Syria. From this contact Indian Christians in the course of time acquired their name and adopted customs, modes of worship and even the official language of worship of the Syrian churches.

From Asia Minor the Christian faith also spread westward, first into the Greek world and from there to the Roman world in present-day Italy, including the islands of the Mediterranean and the shores of north Africa. From there it went further westward to the French and Hispanic worlds and northward to the Germanic world and eventually to the British Isles. This wide spread into present-day Europe and north Africa gave rise to two basic cultural variations of Christianity according to the two main parts of the Roman Empire: Western Christianity, which eventually adopted the Latin language as its medium of communication, and Eastern Christianity, which in early times mostly used the Greek language.

The East appropriated for itself the term 'Orthodox' (meaning 'right doctrine'), which of course all churches always claim to be. The West appropriated the term 'Catholic', which is also a characteristic all ancient churches attribute to themselves. The Greek word *katholikos* originally means 'holistic' and the implication was similar to that of 'orthodox': the claim that the Church kept the 'whole' Christian truth as derived from Jesus Christ, and did not 'choose' (in Greek, *haireo*) only one aspect, as 'heretics' were blamed for doing. Later 'catholic' came to mean universal, worldwide. In common parlance, however, Catholic with an upper case generally signifies that part of the Western Church that upholds the universal authority of the Pope of Rome over the Christian world. In English-speaking countries it is commonly known as the Roman Catholic Church, while its official self-designation is simply Catholic Church.

The East and the West, Pope John Paul II said recently, are the two lungs with which the whole body of the Church breathes. The metaphor referred primarily not to Asian Christianity but to the former eastern and western parts of the Roman Empire, the former including Greece, Constantinople, Russia and the Slavic world, the latter all of western Europe.

The East is subdivided into two main groups of churches. One is constituted by the 'Orthodox' churches in the countries of eastern Europe, including Russia. The other are the 'Eastern' churches consisting of two historic churches in Africa and three in Asia. These

are distinct from the 'Orthodox' churches on the basis of theological
issues, especially in the interpretation of the Christian faith given
by the Ecumenical Council of Chalcedon in 451 CE. The African
'Eastern' churches are the Ethiopian and the Coptic (in Egypt); the
Asian are the Armenian, the Syrian and the Indian, the last two
having strong liturgical and canonical bonds. In today's more or
less official Christian convention, the European group is termed
'Oriental' (not Eastern) Orthodox Church while the Afro-Asian
group consists of the 'Eastern' Orthodox Church. But the
terminology is somewhat fluid. To these may be added an older
Catholic Apostolic Syrian Church of the East, which broke with
the Western Churches earlier, in the Council of Ephesus in 431 CE.

The ancient Christian communities of western Asia, the Indian
subcontinent and continental Asia are therefore part of 'Eastern
Christianity' and form a separate cultural unit from the Latin, Greek
and Slav worlds. Their traditions are authentically Asian and derive
much of their intellectual and spiritual strength from the
communities of Syria, Armenia, Iraq, Iran and India. Most of these
communities were weakened and many disappeared after the rise
of Islam—but not in India, where Christian life has remained
vigorous for nearly twenty centuries. It is likely to have been
established here much before it was established in many European
countries.

As is well known, after several centuries of cultural and
ecclesiastical distancing from one another the two lungs of the
former Roman Empire divided into separate churches which no
longer accepted participating in each others' official rituals. The
West, centred in Rome, covers the whole of western Europe and its
extensions and was for centuries presided over by the Pope in Rome.
The East consisted of a federation of national churches with a kind
of symbolic centre in Byzantium, or Constantinople, now officially
renamed Istanbul, in present-day Turkey. Other important centres
in this 'Eastern Orthodox' Church were Moscow and Athens. These
churches are autonomous but share much of their spiritual
traditions. Negatively they may be called non-Roman, and are at
times (wrongly) designated non-Catholic. They claim to be 'catholic'
in the original sense of the word.

With the Reformation in the sixteenth century the Western

Church subdivided into the Reformed or Protestant Churches and the (Roman) Catholic Church, which continued to hold the tradition of an authoritative role for the Pope in Rome over the whole of the worldwide Church, whatever the local variations.

To simplify and sum up a long story we may speak of four distinct types of Christian churches that emerged in the course of Christian history. Two belong to the 'East' and are generally termed 'Orthodox' churches: of this the 'Oriental' Orthodox group covers most of eastern Europe. Their doctrinal expressions are based on the Bible and the first four ecumenical councils of the Church, celebrated between 325 and 451 CE. In the other group are the 'Eastern' Churches which do not necessarily accept the doctrinal formulation of the first four ecumenical councils. This group was rooted mostly in north Africa and Asia. The two other groups of churches belong to the West. These are characterized by a missionary expansion that has made many of them worldwide in their influence and presence. Of these two, one goes under the title of (Roman) Catholic Church, unified under the authority of the Pope, and the other consists of various 'Protestant' or 'Reformed' churches that emerged after the Protestant split in sixteenth-century Europe. Like the churches of the East, the Protestant churches tend to be linked with national institutions in various countries of Europe, for example, the Anglicans, Lutherans, Methodists and Calvinists.

This simplified classification needs an important corrective, important to understand the situation of Christians in India. We have classified the Roman Catholic Church as one of the two branches of the Church in the West. And in a sense this is true, especially if we stress the adjective 'Roman'. But the Catholic Church that is presided by the Pope in Rome also claims to be and actually is 'universal', and affiliation to it need not imply that one is culturally part of the Roman (also called 'Latin') tradition. A number of Oriental and Eastern churches, including some in India, are recognized by and claim affiliation to the 'Catholic Church', though they keep Oriental or Eastern modes of worship and culture. In other words, belonging to the Catholic Church need not exclude being in the Oriental or Eastern tradition. It is, however, exclusive of belonging to a Protestant tradition.

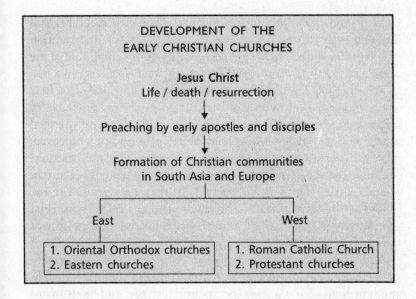

**DEVELOPMENT OF THE
EARLY CHRISTIAN CHURCHES**

Jesus Christ
Life / death / resurrection
↓
Preaching by early apostles and disciples
↓
Formation of Christian communities
in South Asia and Europe

East

1. Oriental Orthodox churches
2. Eastern churches

West

1. Roman Catholic Church
2. Protestant churches

THE TRADITION OF ST THOMAS IN INDIA

It is not known for certain who the first Indian Christians were, although among Christian communities there is no doubt that the Thomas Christians of Kerala are the successors of some of the earliest Christians in the country. Traditions found in the West, West Asia and India say that St Thomas, one of the twelve closest disciples of Jesus, came to India in the very first century, perhaps even less than twenty-five years after the death of Jesus. The place where Thomas first preached in India is also not clear. The 'Malabar' or 'Indian tradition' specifies that Thomas landed in Kodungaloor near Kochi in 52 CE and that he died a martyr's death in Mylapore, now part of the city of Chennai, in 72 CE. His tomb in Mylapore was a centre of pilgrimage well known to Europeans in the Middle Ages, although some traditions say that his relics, or part of them, were carried from Mylapore to Edessa, the modern-day Urfa in Turkey, in 394 CE, and eventually to Ortona, Italy. St Jerome wrote at the end of the fourth or beginning of the fifth century, 'Christ lives everywhere, with Thomas in India and with Peter in Rome.' Many other ancient writers mention India as the place where Thomas brought the Gospel of Jesus after preaching to the 'Parthians' somewhere in modern-day Iran.

The apocryphal *Acts of St Thomas* (possibly composed in the middle of the third century in Edessa) says that Thomas came first to the land of Gondophorus, a Parthian who, numismatic and archaeological evidence shows, ruled over parts of modern-day north-west India and Pakistan. From there he went to Mazday, interpreted as Mylai or Mylapore. The stronger tradition of Kerala, however, affirms that following the maritime trade route he came to Kodungaloor. Kerala was at the time a commercial centre in contact with West Asia and the Mediterranean world. Thomas would first have preached to the Jews settled in Kerala and then to the indigenous population. This tradition affirms that he started Christian communities in seven places: Maliankara, Palayur, Parur, Gokamangalam, Niranam, Chayal and Kollam. It also affirms that he appointed elders (priests) to look after these communities. His death in Mylapore is a common tradition. Kerala and Tamil Nadu were at the time one entity, Tamizham. Whatever the traditions, we know that historically it is in Kerala that a Christian community has existed from very ancient times to our days. This community keeps the memory of St Thomas as their apostle and identify themselves with legitimate pride as the Thomas Christians.

Eusebius, the fourth-century Church historian, mentions that Pantaenus, a Jewish teacher of the theological school in Alexandria, came to India and found a community of Christians that traced their origin to St Bartholomew, another apostle of Jesus, and that he possessed an old copy of the Gospel of Matthew in Hebrew. It is not clear whether the 'India' of Eusebius is the real India or Arabia. The home of that community is called Kalyan, possibly the Kalyan in the area of the modern-day Mumbai, although Kalyanpur near Mangalore in Karnataka is a rival claimant. Some confirmation of this tradition seems to be found in the sixth-century account of Cosmas Indicopleustes, a merchant from Alexandria who claims to have visited India and found Christian communities in Kalyan and Malabar. The Kalyan tradition is certainly weaker than the Kerala tradition; Bartholomew seems to have made no permanent impact on India and probably did not remain here, if he ever came. His place of martyrdom is traditionally identified with Derbent, on the west coast of the Caspian Sea, in Armenia. No historical Christian community claims descent from his preaching.

The case for St Thomas is very different. From the early centuries of the Christian era we have evidence of a vigorous Christian community living in South India, whose traditions refer constantly to St Thomas. This must be considered the first community of Christians in India, at least among all the communities presently alive. About 30 per cent of the Indian Christian population is in Kerala, which in the latest census had 56,22,000 Christians, a little less than one-fifth of the state population. Much water has flown in the Ganga between the time of St Thomas and today. The Kerala Christian community is not uniform either sociologically or theologically. All sorts of influences have added to the simpler faith of the early centuries.

There must have existed if not regular at least sporadic relations between the Christian communities in Kerala and those in West Asia, as there were strong trade relations between the two areas around the Indian Ocean. Two groups of immigrants to India had a significant influence on the Christian community here. The first came in the fourth century from 'Persia', probably in modern Iraq, under the leadership of one Thomas of Cana, whom Christians in Kerala call even today 'Cnai Thomman'. He is portrayed by different sources as merchant, traveller and pilgrim, and the transformation of Kodungaloor into a Christian city is attributed to him. He is said to have brought with him bishops and priests from Syria to take care of the spiritual welfare of the people. He may have been the reason for the contact between Indian Christians and the Syrian Christian community, to the extent that eventually Indian Christians were identified as 'Syrian Christians' and became part of the Syrian Church establishment.

Whatever the historical processes, the fact is that even today there are two endogamous groups among the Thomas Christians of Kerala, the Thekkumbhagar (those of the South) and the Vadakkumbhagar (those of the North). Factors of purity and nobility are associated with this division. The 'southists' call themselves descendants of Thomas of Cana and those who came with him and claim to have kept their racial purity by not intermingling with local Christians. The 'northists' on the other hand claim descent from the Christians evangelized by the apostle Thomas. Thus within the same religious fold there are two social units.

A second immigrant group of considerable importance came directly from the Syrian Church in the ninth or tenth century, and settled in Kollam after receiving grants of land and certain privileges from the local ruler. Two bishops, Sapor and Prot, whom some sources identify as natives of Armenia, were part of the group. (Armenia was the first nation in the world to become officially Christian, in the early fourth century.)

Surely there were other groups of merchants, travellers, perhaps missionaries, who came from different parts of West Asia, at the time deeply Christian. Like other communities outside the Roman Empire, the Indian Christians were part of a general Church organization whose headquarters were in 'Persia', a general term that included the whole region between the Indus and the Euphrates. The principal bishop of this area resided in Antioch, Syria, but eventually the twin cities of Seleucia–Ctesiphon, on either side of the river Tigris, acquired a separate importance. The residential bishop there was called the Catholicos, or general bishop, and he had jurisdiction over the Indian Christians.

SOCIO-RELIGIOUS SYSTEM OF THE THOMAS CHRISTIANS

It is well known that the social status of the Thomas Christians was high. There is a tradition among them that the early converts of St Thomas were Namboodiri Brahmins. In the absence of historical records it is difficult to prove this contention, and perhaps it is even anachronistic. It is not clear if the caste system had spread by that time to the southernmost areas of India, and it is likely that the community of the early Christians belonged to the Dravidian stock. But they surely were, and continue to be, highly regarded by their neighbours of all castes. They lived in the towns of Kochi and Kollam and in certain rural areas like Angamali and Kottayam. Some of them were dispersed in the mountains and forest areas. Their major activities were agriculture, trade and military services. They were organized into families and lineage groups or extended families linked together. This clan-like organization was the basis of their social life.

The link with the East Syrian Church continued for centuries. They followed the customs of that church in matters of theology, ways of worship, and family laws and customs. They were organized in parish assemblies (yogam), where the participation of the laity in church decisions was considerable, and general assemblies (pothuyogam). They received their bishops from the East Syrian Church. The main function of such bishops was to ordain local priests—called cathenars, or elders—who did not have much theological formation. All theological literature, like the public worship, was in Syriac, and the ordinary priests would hardly have had much training in that language beyond being able to read the liturgical books and the Bible. It would seem that the priests were married and heads of families, and the succession in the priesthood passed on from father to son, although they may have required ordination by the bishop.

An important ecclesiastical figure was the archdeacon. Archdeacons were the chief assistants of the bishops in the local administration and according to the canons of the Church of the East they were in the sacred orders inferior to the bishop but superior to the presbyters or priests. The archdeacon of India had thus a great authority and influence in the whole community as he was the leader, the Jathikku Karthavian, and shared the authority of the bishop. He was considered the chief of the priests and his office was for life. He approved priestly ordinations, granted ecclesiastical dispensations and appointed or removed local ecclesiastical leaders. Internal disputes of the community were also referred to him. The succession of archdeacons was in Kerala within a family, that of the Pakalomattams.

The Thomas Christians are part of the Eastern Orthodox tradition, which is shared by most churches in Kerala, some of them with very similar names—giving rise to much confusion, even among Christians. The Malankara Jacobite Syrian Church keeps the traditional links with the Syrian Orthodox Patriarchate of Antioch in Lebanon. This is at times called the Jacobite Church, at times the Orthodox Church of India. There is also an autocephalous Malankara Orthodox Christian Church. Other Eastern Churches are affiliated to the Roman Catholic Church, acknowledging the authority of the Pope, and represent in the community of Catholic

Churches the ancient traditions of the East. They follow the ancient 'rites' somewhat adapted to modern times, especially regarding language. There are two 'Catholic' Oriental Churches in India: the Syro-Malabar Church headed by a Major Archbishop in Ernakulam-Angamali and the Syro-Malankara Church presided by the (Catholic) Archbishop of Trivandrum (Thiruvananthapuram).

There is also among the Thomas Christians an important group that is closer to the Protestant traditions (on which more in chapter five) although it has kept the Oriental flavour. They call themselves the Mar Thoma Church and are highly influential in many parts of the country. The Mar Thoma Church represents the fruit of a reform movement among the Thomas Christians that took place mostly in the eighteenth century, under the influence of the Anglican missionaries in Kerala. The translation of the Bible and of the Syrian liturgy into Malayalam accelerated the movement. Its most outstanding leader was a local parish priest known as Abraham Malpan (1796–1845). Born in the ancient Palakunnathu family, he became a professor of Syriac in the 'Old Seminary' of Kottayam. He was drawn to the ideas of the Anglican missionaries of the Church Missionary Society and introduced them into the tradition of his students and people around him. This resulted in a conflict between the mother church and his congregation. He was excommunicated and hence a new church was formed. Wanting to have for his reformed church the authority conferred by bishops, he sent his nephew to be consecrated bishop by the Patriarch of the Syrian Church at Mardin in Iraq, who returned to India as Bishop Mathew Mar Athanasius in 1843.

The Mar Thoma Church is generally a very forward community of Christians, which took to English education early in the period of British colonialism. Members have established themselves in urban centres, with a strong presence in the liberal professions and in political life. One of its most outstanding members was Thomas Madathilparampil Mammen (1916–96), usually known as M.M. Thomas. He was a thinker, theologian, freedom fighter, political and Church activist. He was an influential moderator of the central committee of the World Council of Churches in Geneva from 1968 to 1975. He was a tireless speaker and lecturer and stimulated the thinking of the Christian churches, not only in India but worldwide, towards an involvement in the social, economic and political issues of the world. Earlier he was associate director and eventually director of the Christian Institute for the Study of Religion and Society (now based in Bangalore), which after independence has had a considerable impact on the thinking of the Indian Christian community and on its orientation towards dialogue and full participation in the national life. The Government of India appointed M.M. Thomas Governor of Nagaland in 1990, but he resigned in 1992 rather than give in to a diktat from the central government which he considered unjust (see Anderson 1998 for details).

In chapter five we shall come back to the history of the St Thomas church especially in its conflict with the 'Latin' Christian community, which was formed in the wake of the missionaries coming from Europe. It does not appear that the St Thomas church was inclined to spread its faith to the rest of the country; it seems to have remained a relatively small, isolated community content to live in fellowship with other religious traditions while keeping its faith in Jesus Christ as a distinctive social mark. Like other Eastern and Oriental churches it tended to be ethnic, confined to the Kerala community. There is no evidence of conflicts or tensions with other communities. After the second spring of Christians in India, following the arrival of the Portuguese and other sailors, and especially in the twentieth century, the Thomas Christians became a great force in the whole Indian church. Many theological thinkers and a great majority of church personnel (bishops, priests and nuns) came out of Kerala and spread not only across the country but also went abroad to announce the Gospel and to help other communities. Their particular forms of worship and of Christian life and church organization are also being spread to other parts of the country, not without occasional tensions with other established communities. In this spread this church tends now to abandon its monocultural and ethnic character in favour of including other communities who want to worship Jesus within this tradition.

To complete the picture of the Christian Church in Kerala we must not forget that a significant portion of Christians there do not derive directly from the ancient traditions of the Thomas Christians but reflect the preaching of missionaries who came to India mostly after the Portuguese and other European merchants arrived and settled in the country. Thus, for example, of the twenty-seven dioceses which the Catholic church has at present in Kerala, eleven belong to what is called the 'Latin' rite, that is, they derive from the traditions of the Western Church, although they have naturally adapted to the country. Similarly most Protestant churches in India have some dioceses or subdivisions in Kerala. (A 'diocese' is generally a territorial division of Christians of one denomination that functions under the leadership of an ordained bishop.)

WHAT IS THE 'CHURCH'?

This may be the right moment to speak about what the 'Church' means to an Indian Christian, and to a Christian in general. Probably few people of other communities guess the density of religious meaning and even emotional load that this simple word can have. We spoke earlier of the etymology of the word. We obviously do not speak here of the church as the building reserved for the collective and private prayer of Christians, and where the Sunday service is generally celebrated. Nor do we give to this word the meaning often found in journalistic literature: the church in the sense of the authorities of the Christians, especially bishops and other high dignitaries. The Church, the 'C' preferably written in upper case, is primarily the community of Christians. But it is not merely a sociological category, a group of people having a sense of unity and having their governing bodies, laws and customs. Nor is it a non-governmental organization of people with a similar frame of mind and a common programme of action to which all members have subscribed. For Christians the Church is an object of their faith, because it is itself related to God's special action in Jesus Christ, who remains present in the community. St Paul called it 'the body of Christ'.

The Church is named in the Creeds—that is, the formulations of Christian faith that come in various forms from the earliest centuries of Christian history. The so-called Apostles' Creed (probably fifth century CE) says it in simple words: 'I believe in the Holy Spirit, the holy catholic Church . . .' The Nicene Creed (381 CE, actually Niceno-Constantinopolitan, named after the two early councils that produced it) specifies it better: 'I believe in one holy, catholic and apostolic Church.' In both cases the Church falls within the scope of faith by which a Christian commits herself or himself to God. Of course the Church is also a sociological reality, but not only that. It is also a reality related to the Divine Presence within history. In this aspect it can only be known through faith ('I believe'), which means through a vision that comes from God.

Perhaps we shall perceive something of what Christians experience when they speak of the Church in this sense from a similar pattern in the Buddhist tradition. This tradition speaks of the 'three jewels' (triratna), specified by name in their initiation ceremony: *buddham saranam gacchami, dhammam saranam gacchami, sangham saranam gacchami,* or its equivalent Pali formula ('I take refuge in the Buddha, I take refuge in the Doctrine, I take refuge in the Community'). The Buddha, the teaching and the community are the triratna, the three jewels that form a whole. They cannot be separated from one another. Each 'jewel' is related and implies the other. The three are goals in which a Buddhist seeks refuge and therefore enlightenment and liberation.

For a Christian the three jewels are Jesus Christ, the Gospel and the Church. The Church fills a role similar to the Buddhist sangha. Perhaps to the Buddhist monk or nun the sangha meant much more than to the lay Buddhist: for them it was their mother, so to speak. The lay Buddhists, men and women, were a kind of associate members. They were indeed part of the 'fourfold sangha', but their belonging to it was dependent on their relationship to the monastic sangha of monks and nuns. At least in the Theravada tradition the laity is somewhat secondary. Buddhism was foundationally a monastic religion. For Christians monasticism came later. Even Church authority is derivative. The community, the Church, the 'sangha', consists of all those who accept the teaching of Jesus and decide to follow his way. There are leaders and elders in the community, no doubt, and structures of authority, but these structures are subsidiary to the egalitarian ethos and are meant for the well-being of the community. The basic idea is the community of believers united as 'one body' with many limbs, a metaphor repeatedly used by St Paul. Or, as a letter attributed to him puts it, 'There is one body and one Spirit, just as you were called to the one hope of your calling; one Lord, one faith, one baptism; one God and Father of all, who is above all and through all and in all' (Eph 4:4–6).

One of the great metaphors for the Church is that it is 'the body of Christ'. This metaphor may seem to have a stoic symbolic meaning. The body politic, for the Greeks, was similar to the human body: composed of many limbs, yet unified. Any organization of people is a 'body' that acts with a common mind. This is only part of the meaning St Paul has in mind when he speaks of the Church as the body of Christ. It is not the whole meaning. For Paul and for Christians in general there is a relation between each Christian and the actual reality of Jesus Christ, his 'risen body', his personality. Through baptism and faith they become one with the risen Lord. Together therefore they are one body (rather than 'form' one body): the body of Christ. This means that the Christian finds Jesus Christ within this body of the community, the Church. The Church has baptized her or him into Christ; the Church keeps and transmits the memory of Jesus; the Church teaches his message and preserves his Gospel; the Church as a community of faith is the sign and symbol of Christ himself.

The traditional terminology reminds us of the theology of Ramanuja. But whereas for Ramanuja the world is the Body of God himself, in the Christian context the community of believers is the extension, the presence, the concrete reality of the *human being* Jesus Christ, who is the source and the head of this Church-Body.

The 1962–69 Second Vatican Council of the Catholic Church recalled an ancient metaphor: it thought of the Church as coming out of the side of Christ as he dies on the cross and his heart is opened with a spear. From it, says the Gospel of St John, flowed blood and water. The ancient mystics saw this as a kind of repetition of the creation of Eve out of the side of Adam in the biblical myth of creation. 'This tremendous sacrament which is the whole Church arose from the side of Christ as he slept on the cross' (Constitution on Sacred Liturgy, no. 5). This text picks up two rich metaphors coming down from the ancient tradition. In one the Church as a community is seen as a female figure, the 'bride' of Christ, as Eve was of Adam. Bride and bridegroom are inseparable.

The other metaphor is that of 'sacrament'. Theologians before the council spoke of the Church as the 'sacrament' of Christ—

sacrament meaning both sign and means of presence. Perhaps symbol would be the better word. The council says that 'in Christ' the Church is 'as a sacrament—a sign and instrument, that is—of intimate union with God and of the unity of the entire human race' (Dogmatic Constitution on the Church, no. 1). These words show that the community of the Church is linked with the human community at large. The Church is a symbol of what the whole human race is, and is meant to become: the body of Christ who makes the divine reality present in the world.

The logic of this metaphor should normally prevent any sense of communalism in the Christian consciousness. The sense of Church is certainly communitarian, but it is not communalist. It should not see the Christian as *against* other communities, but as *related* to them, as symbol and sacrament of the unity of the entire human race. The Christian tradition, like the Muslim and the Buddhist, gives spiritual and religious importance to the community as a means whereby we find God and salvation. This does involve a danger of communalism, or of limiting our sense of belonging to those of the same faith and considering the rest as the 'others', eventually as the 'enemy'. This danger, when found among Christians, needs to be corrected. This is why the council speaks of the Church as a sacrament or sign of the unity of the entire human race. The sign can never be inimical to the thing signified. It leads to it. The meaning of the Church is precisely in being sister to all other communities. Community consciousness may be good, because it relates us to the others. But communalism is bad if it means alienating ourselves from some.

Christians in India have in fact not shown themselves to be particularly communalist. Even during the Constituent Assembly, as we shall see later, they gave up the security of communal electorates: they wanted to be with all other citizens, and vote for the best representatives of the whole people. While reservation of seats for marginalized communities may be justified for a time, Christians did not think it necessary to ask for separate electorates for their community. In the various incidents of communal violence that have broken out in the country in the last centuries, Christians have generally been known to come to the help of the victim community whoever they were. They did not take sides with one community against the other, but helped to reconcile those who were in conflict.

In recent years the consciousness of the community has evolved towards stressing something important in the New Testament, which was largely lost in the course of the history of the Church in the West, though perhaps not so much in India. The important point is that the Christian Church is a Church *of the poor*. By this expression we do not mean that only the poor and the ignorant may be members of the Church. By definition, one might say, the Church can only be an open and universal community from which no clan, tribe, race, class, language or culture is excluded. But Jesus did identify himself especially with the poor and with oppressed peoples: he was born in poverty, lived with the poor and died in destitution. As we saw, the opening of the Sermon on the Mount begins with this startling declaration: 'Blessed are the poor in spirit, for theirs is the kingdom of heaven' (Mt 5:3). This means that in the dialectic of our world between oppressed and oppressors, poor and rich, Christians are called to take the side of the poor. Whether they are personally rich or middle class or proletariat, their options must favour the poor rather than the rich. They have to help fill the gap, shorten the distance between the two poles. How that must be done in concrete circumstances is a problem that must be decided in each case and in consultation with all concerned, including other communities. But the orientation given by Jesus is clear. Only this link of the Church with the poor explains the astonishing work of people like the Missionaries of Charity of Mother Teresa; it alone is the reason for the organized effort of so many Christian communities to make education and social services available to the poor.

We do not pretend that the Church in India or elsewhere has lived consistently according to this orientation. Social analysts and historians can point out case after case when the Church as a community or the Church leadership has sided with the powerful and rich rather than with the poor. For years the Church vehemently opposed the socialist and Marxist movement, not for siding with the poor but for doing it through an ideology of atheism and anti-religious action. The Church failed to see the tremendous importance of the message of Marxism: that society had to be analysed and acted upon from the perspective of the poor. And the fact remains that many Church institutions have eventually served the rich rather than the poor, often against the foundational intention of the institution itself. There is a certain dynamic in the life of institutions that makes them gravitate towards the pole of power and money rather than the pole of deprivation. Christians always need to analyse this dynamic and counteract it in light of the life and the teachings of Jesus.

In 1961 Pope John XXIII, the 'good Pope' as he was called, published a social encyclical (a papal letter meant for all churches), the first words of which call the Church 'Mother and Teacher' (*Mater et Magistra*). This is what for many Christians the Church is. This Church is neither the building nor the authorities of the community. This Church is the community of all, the majority poor and the few rich, a community that acts as 'mother' to the individual Christians because it offers the life that is found in Jesus Christ, and is also the authoritative 'teacher' of his message. Many Christians speak of 'Mother Church'. It must be admitted that this 'mystical' approach to the community as a kind of Platonic essence is very characteristic of the Oriental Orthodox and Catholic churches. The Protestants stress a more personal relation to God through individual faith.

For all Christians, however, the Church has the function of carrying in the world the memory of Jesus Christ. The Church has no special importance in itself, but rather as the body, the manifestation, the bearer of the memory of Jesus. This memory is kept inside the Church community and is renewed at every Sunday service. It is a memory that is also shared with other communities as, we believe, a source of blessing for all.

4

The Second Spring in South India

Arrival of the Portuguese in Kozhikode ~ Reasons for the Portuguese sea enterprise ~ Meeting of Christians with Christians ~ The Kerala imbroglio ~ Role of Padroado ~ Types of leadership among Christians ~ Bishops and the Pope ~ Priests and their formation ~ Deacons ~ Religious ~ New Christian communities in Tamil Nadu ~ The Jesuits ~ Francis Xavier ~ The first Indian Christian martyrs ~ Spread of the Christian faith in Tamil Nadu ~ Roberto de Nobili and his mission to caste people ~ The process of inculturation ~ Spread of Christianity in Andhra Pradesh ~ Reflections on the second spring

The Indian Christians lived their faith for around fifteen centuries, apparently untroubled in their way of thinking and worship distinct from those of their Jain, Buddhist, Hindu and, more recently, Muslims neighbours. They were in harmony with their surroundings; there is no evidence of conflict with other communities. Some have even said that they were so acclimatized to India's social reality that they lost the prophetic power of the Gospel to transform society. (Badrinath 2000 makes this charge against Indian Christianity in general, not specifically about the Thomas Christians. However, see also Ponnumuthan 2003). They were not a large community; sixteenth-century estimates vary between one and two lakh (Thekkedath 1982, 24). But they were large enough to keep continuity in their social life.

ARRIVAL OF THE PORTUGUESE

On 20 May 1498, fisherfolk of Kozhikode in north Kerala, watching the turbulent pre-monsoon sea, witnessed a strange arrival on their shores. People of the sea though they were, the design of the four ships they saw dropping anchor far from the shore was new to them. Out of the main ship a small boat was lowered and in it came a couple of armed, heavily dressed men who introduced themselves as messengers of Emmanuel I, king of a land they called Portugal, in the far west. The fisherfolk could not have known that this moment would radically change their peaceful life.

By the time the boat reached the shore two Muslim Tunisians, then on a business trip in Kozhikode, had joined the group of onlookers. As they could speak Spanish they were asked to meet the young (not yet forty) captain of the float. They addressed Vasco da Gama, for this was his name, aggressively, 'The devil take you! What has brought you here?' to which the Portuguese leader is said to have replied, 'We have come to seek Christians and spices' (Boxer 1969; Schurhammer 1977, 139). This reply has been widely misunderstood, as if the Portuguese adventure in Asia was prompted by a missionary zeal to make converts rather than a simple desire for profit. Actually they came to *find* Christians, rather than to *make* Christians. The purpose of their journey was a political and commercial manoeuvre to break the Muslim monopoly on spices. This does not mean that the idea of making Christians did not soon become part of the imperial ideology: it was clearly so half a century later, when Francis Xavier came to India. The initial motivation is shown in a letter the king of Portugal wrote to his peers in Spain in 1599 (see da Silva Rêgo 1947–57, 3–5). Incidentally, in its transmission in history the famous reply of Vasco became, 'We came to seek souls and spices.' The last avatar of the reply comes in F.A. Plattner's book *Jesuits Go East* (Dublin 1950), where it becomes 'Pepper and Souls'!

Many decades of patient research by Portuguese geographers on the behaviour of the seas around Africa had enabled their men to sail down the western coast of Africa and round the so-called Cape of Good Hope. Vasco da Gama's latest expedition lasted ten months and went further than all earlier attempts. With stopovers in Mozambique and what is now Kenya, he finally crossed the Indian Ocean—it took him twenty-three days of uninterrupted sailing to reach Kerala, bypassing lands and seas dominated by the Muslim rulers of West Asia.

Like other Europeans of the time, the Portuguese were aware

that there were Christians in India. They even thought that there was a Christian kingdom here and wanted to establish relations with it. Reports of medieval overland travellers to Asia like Marco Polo and others had filtered down to the popular culture, and there was an eagerness to find the mysterious kingdom of Prester John who, according to legend, was a priest and king who ruled with justice over a prosperous Christian realm. Some even made him a descendant of the Magi, the three kings who visited Jesus at his birth, according to the Gospel of Matthew! The stories were probably influenced by the travellers' contacts with settlements of Syrian Christians in the heart of Asia and by the aura of splendour associated with the empire of the Mongols, a few of whose royal members had indeed become Christian. In a letter to the raja of Kozhikode the Portuguese king said, 'It has been told to us that there are in those lands Christian people. It will be our desire to establish conversations with them and to profit from them and to help one another with much agreement of love and brotherhood as Christian kings must have among themselves' (da Silva Rêgo 1947–57, 17–18).

The Christians on the shores of Kozhikode were puzzled by the crosses worn by the Portuguese visitors with their official attire, not unlike the crosses they had worshipped from time immemorial. They welcomed the visitors as fellow worshippers and began a joyful period of mutual recognition and acceptance. The Portuguese hoped to use the local Christians as intermediaries to obtain the spices they sought, which of course would also open commercial avenues for the Indian Christians themselves.

The Portuguese adventure and their later behaviour in India must be placed against the background of the strong animosity between Christians and Muslims prevailing in fifteenth-century Europe. For more than half a millennium the Iberian peninsula, of which Portugal was a part, had been ruled by Moorish overlords who had established a brilliant civilization made up of Muslims, Jews and Christians, controlled by the caliphate of Cordova. However the local Christian populations had slowly organized themselves and succeeded in not only stopping the victorious Muslim armies but also in pushing them back out of their territories. Granada, the last bulwark of Iberian Muslim rule, fell in 1492, the very year Colombus travelled to America and six years before the first visit of Vasco da Gama to Kozhikode. At sea, the Mediterranean world was a battleground until John of Austria's resounding victory over the Turks in the battle of Lepanto in 1571.

The rivalry between Muslims and Christians extended also to commerce. Many goods from Asia were arriving in the European bazaars through the Muslims who controlled both the land and the sea links between Europe and Asia. Spices were highly valued and, along with precious stones, a lucrative business. By going round Africa the Portuguese hoped to weaken the Muslim power. In this geopolitical context it is not strange that the Portuguese visitors to India were furiously anti-Muslim and more kindly inclined to the Hindus, even if they disliked their religion.

In fifteenth-century South India, the Muslims had almost a monopoly on the sea transportation of spices. When the Portuguese landed, four ports in Kerala were considered important: Kozhikode, Kannur, Kochi and Kollam. The last three had great concentrations of Christians, but the Muslims were undermining their traditional social and economic position. A common faith and common commercial interests ensured an early cordial relationship between the Thomas Christians and the Christians from Portugal. Their common rival was the Muslim. As the Portuguese leader of the first expedition went ashore, he first paid his respects to the local ruler of Kozhikode, the Hindu Zamorin, and even struck a friendship with him. He also erected a memorial stone (padrao) as a proof that he had reached India. But, as could be expected, relations with the Zamorin soured soon. Vasco da Gama returned to Portugal (where he received great honours), wrongly convinced that the majority in the land he had finally reached were Christians.

Having discovered the route to India, the merchant-king of Portugal began to send regular naval expeditions in search of pepper and cloves and other goods valuable in the European market. In 1500 the king sent an expedition of no less than thirteen ships to Kozhikode. Tension arose between the local ruler and the new arrivals, resulting in a massacre among the latter. Vasco da Gama returned to India in 1502 and concluded trade agreements with the rulers of Kochi and Kannur, and fortresses were erected in both cities to protect the Portuguese trading outposts (often called 'factories'). There were frequent fights with local rulers until the organizer of the Portuguese enterprise, Alfonso de Albuquerque, who became the Portuguese 'Governor of India' in 1509, consolidated the Portuguese presence by capturing Goa in 1510, a valuable port where the Muslim North and Hindu South met. Goa would become the centre of the Portuguese trading empire in the East. Meanwhile the pepper trade and the greed of the Portuguese officials began to hurt the interests of the Kerala Christians.

THE KERALA IMBROGLIO

The rift between the Indians and the Portuguese widened because of the differences—some true, some imagined—in their religious beliefs and practices. The Portuguese found the Indian Christian rituals unfamiliar, as they were accustomed to the European Latin tradition. For most of them this was the first contact with an Eastern-rite Church, and they thought the differences indicated a degeneration of the 'Catholic' faith. It was for instance quite strange to them that in the marriage ceremony the Christian groom would tie a thali (a small cord) round the neck of his bride, in accordance with the Indian tradition, rather than joining hands and giving a wedding ring. They also found, they said, that the churches resembled temples rather than the churches of Portugal. To top it all, the Indian priests were married! The Portuguese found these practices heretical and decided to bring the Indian Christians to the right path—the Latin way! When they heard their teaching and the name of Nestorius mentioned in their liturgy, they became convinced that these Christians were Nestorians, followers of a heretical doctrine that had been officially condemned in the Council of Ephesus in the fifth century.

Many factors contributed to the tensions between the foreign Christians, especially the clergy who came with them, and the Indian Christians. The first was the lack of knowledge on the part of the Portuguese of the plurality of rites within the Church. A rite is a legitimate Christian tradition of worship, law and spirituality that a particular cultural unit develops in order to live the Christian faith. Even in the Mediterranean world several rites were known and familiar in Rome. But the extreme western part of that world,

Portugal, especially its laypeople, knew little beyond the Latin or Roman rite. Everything outside it seemed wrong.

The second factor was the juridical structure of the Padroado, which we shall see in chapter five. In the fifteenth century the popes had granted to the kings of Portugal and Spain the authority to nominate bishops and other ecclesiastical authorities and to promote Christianity and protect Christians in any part of the East and the West respectively, discovered or to be discovered. Armed with this papal authority, the Portuguese claimed jurisdiction to change things religious in communities that did not follow their rite. They tried to bring all Indian Christians under the bishop of Goa appointed by Rome, though strictly speaking Goa belonged to a different rite, Latin, and had no legal jurisdiction over the Syrians. There followed a long period of 'Latinization' or 'Westernization' of the St Thomas Christians that resulted in splits, quarrels and tensions that have lasted even to our day.

The Padroado would cause problems not only between the various ritual traditions within the Church but in later years even within the Latin rite: when missionaries came to India without passing through the authority of Portugal, their presence caused conflict with those who claimed overall Christian authority in the country based on the clauses of the Padroado. Only in the mid-twentieth century was the Padroado finally abolished.

The third factor that intruded into the relations of the newly arrived priests and laity and the old Christians was doctrinal. For historical reasons the Syrian Church to which the Indian Christians were related was considered in the West a Nestorian and therefore a heretical church. Recent research has sufficiently shown that this accusation was wrong, but the conviction led the European priests to a hunt for mistakes in doctrine and liturgy that resulted in heavy changes of the local Christian culture in favour of Western forms of Christianity. These doctrinal quarrels did not emerge from the laity, who were innocent of theological niceties.

There was much confusion between the sixteenth and the nineteenth centuries among the St Thomas Christians of Kerala. Initially the archbishop of Goa insisted that he had canonical authority over the St Thomas Christians, while the patriarchs of the East Syrian Church in West Asia (by now there were two patriarchs, one in communion with Rome and the other autonomous) continued to send their bishops to supervise the work of the Church. The Portuguese played one against the other and managed for a while to control the Christians of Kerala, for some time using a certain Mar Abraham. He had been sent from the Syrian Church, had publicly renounced Nestorianism and embraced the Catholic doctrine. The Portuguese forced him to convoke a synod of the Church in Angamali. The synod supported the undertaking of 'correcting' the Syrian liturgical texts.

After Mar Abraham's death the local Archdeacon George took charge of the community, but Alexis de Menezes, sent from Portugal to be archbishop of Goa, visited the Christian communities in Kerala and was well received. He then forced the archdeacon to break relations with the Syrian Church and to assist him in convoking a new 'synod' at Udayamperur (known popularly as the Synod of Diamper) (1599) which issued 200 decrees confirming the process of Westernization of the first Indian Christian community. Some modern historians and canonists consider this synod illegitimate.

The next three bishops of this Syrian Church were foreign Latin bishops. But the proverbial straw that broke the camel's back was the arrival of Mar Atallah from the Patriarchate of East Syria (Antioch) at Mylapore in 1605. He was imprisoned and deported by the Portuguese. The local Christians of Kerala thought he had been murdered and rose in revolt. Their socio-religious identity had been denied far too long. A group of them gathered at Matancherry in 1653 and took a solemn oath before a cross never to obey the Paulist Fathers (as the Jesuits were called on account of their headquarters at the St Paul's College in Goa) or recognize the authority of the Latin bishops. They accepted their local Archdeacon Thomas as their leader. There was even an attempt to ordain him bishop (from now on he was known as Mar Thoma). Alarmed by the events, Rome sent a group of Carmelite missionaries, and in 1659 ordained one of them, Father Joseph of St Mary, aka Sebastiani, bishop of the St Thomas Christians. Four years later Sebastiani ordained a well-known priest, Chandy Parampil, bishop and put him in charge of the Church of Angamali. He was a cousin of Mar Thoma who was solemnly excommunicated. Chandy Parampil was probably the first duly ordained Indian bishop.

The community of the St Thomas Christians was now divided into two: one group known as the 'old party' (Pazhayakuttukar) remained in communion with the Western Church and in obedience to the Pope whose authority they recognized in the archbishop of Goa. The 'new party' (Puttankuttukar) stayed with Mar Thoma and eventually came under the influence of and entered into communion with the West Syrian Church of Antioch, known also as the Jacobite Church after an ancient Asian leader, Jacob Baradaeus (c. 500–578). Today the Jacobite Church in Kerala has developed two factions: one that still recognizes the authority of the Syrian Orthodox Patriarch of Antioch and the other which accepts the authority only of the Catholikos cum Malankara Metropolitan of India.

In 1896 the 'old party' regained its basic autonomy within the plurality of the Catholic communion and was recognized as the Syro-Malabar Church. In 1930 a small group of the 'new party' under the leadership of Mar Ivanios and his helper Mar Theophilus entered into communion with the Catholic Church and became the Syro-Malankara Church. Even at that time they were allowed to hold their liturgy in Malayalam, while the Syro-Malabar and the Latin Churches held it in Syriac and Latin respectively, until after the Second Vatican Council in the 1960s. There are therefore even now in India three Churches within the communion of the Catholic Church: the Syro-Malabar, the Syro-Malankara and the Latin.

Outside the Roman communion there are, besides the new party or the Jacobite Church, two other small churches of the Thomas Christians. One is the Independent Syrian Church of Malabar (popularly known as the Thozhiyur Independent Church), established in 1772 by Mar Coorillos, which follows the West Syrian tradition. The other is the Chaldean (Syrian) Church of the East, formed in 1874 by a Chaldean bishop from West Asia, Mar Mellus, which follows the East Syrian tradition.

TYPES OF LEADERSHIP AMONG CHRISTIANS

The imbroglio in the history of Kerala invites us to interrupt the historical narrative and give some idea of the forms of leadership developed through the centuries in the Christian churches. Many kinds of leaders took part in the flowering of the 'second spring' of Christianity in India. Indian Christians are generally acknowledged today as being among the most organized and successful communities in providing for themselves a well-formed cadre of leaders.

Churches that have their roots in the great tradition, whether of the East or the West, generally accept a basic three-layered structure of ordained leadership comprising bishops, priests and deacons. 'Ordained' means that the leader has been officially and ritually empowered by the authorities of the community to exercise a specific role. The community believes that in some way these powers come from God. Being ordained also implies that the community comes first and the leader is meant *for* the community. This fits well with the words of Jesus recorded in various places in the Gospels: 'You know that among the gentiles those whom they recognize as their rulers lord it over them, and their great ones are tyrants over them. But it is not so among you; but whoever wishes to become great among you must be your servant, and whoever wishes to be first among you must be the slave of all. For the Son of Man [Jesus himself] came not to be served but to serve, and to give his life a ransom for many' (Mk 10:42–45). The leader is not above the community. Leadership is service.

History has proved that Jesus' norm is very difficult; authority has been abused in the churches as elsewhere. This may be why some more recent Protestant churches reject any form of ordained leadership and govern themselves through democratic processes. It is not certain that this has removed the dangers of abuse. Most Christians, however, believe that the three-layered ordained leadership belongs to the earliest level of the Church tradition and has to be preserved as it has proved its value through the centuries and ensures the authenticity of the Church.

Bishops, Pope and Archbishops

The bishop is generally the head of a local church, that is, the community of Christians in a specific territory (delimited by Church authority or mutual agreement with neighbouring communities, or both). He has the charge to guide its life, to preach and teach the

Christian message, to interpret it, to organize the community and help it live according to the Gospel and to promote the welfare of the whole population. In many churches the unit under the leadership of a bishop is called a diocese. In the Eastern churches a diocese is called eparchy and its bishop is an eparch, an office that normally carries the Semitic honorific title of Mar ('Lord'). Obviously many different structures of councils, offices and organisms function around the bishop. Each Church has its own particular traditions in this respect and evolves ways and means to see that the authority attached to the office is not abused.

Among Catholics, the bishop of Rome has an additional authority: he is not only the head of his diocese, Rome, but is also the spokesperson for the entire community and the sign and means of unity of the worldwide Church. Popularly called the Pope, his official title is, among others, 'Supreme Pontiff of the Universal Church'. Pontiff (from the Latin *Pontifex*) means 'bridge builder', and this describes fairly well the main function of the Pope: to be the bridge among the various dioceses and the various 'individual churches' (local traditions) that constitute the Universal Church. Thus in the Indian Catholic Church the Pope is the 'bridge builder' between the Syro-Malabar Church, the Latin Church and the Syro-Malankara Church, and between the various dioceses of each of these churches. To fulfil this function he has authority over the whole Church, but his authority does not do away and should not conflict with that of the bishop of each place.

This authority of the Pope has been exercised in different ways throughout history, sometimes in more centralized ways, at others with more local autonomy. At present the Pope appoints most of the bishops in the Catholic Church, or at least approves appointments made by local bodies. The office of a bishop in the Catholic Church lasts from his appointment to the age of seventy-five, when he has to present his resignation to the Pope. The office of the Pope is lifelong, unless he resigns. In other churches the process of nomination of bishops and their term of office is determined by their own laws.

The election of the Pope is done by the College of Cardinals. A cardinal is a person (generally a bishop, rarely a mere priest, and at present not a layperson) nominated by the Pope. Theoretically he is a counsellor of the Pope for important matters, but more obviously, he is an elector of the Pope after his death or resignation, if the cardinal is below eighty years of age. The number of electors does not exceed 120. Cardinals are found in all areas of the Catholic world. At present (2004) there are five Indian cardinals.

An archbishop is the bishop of a diocese that is the centre of a metropolitan province, that is, a group of dioceses of a particular region or Church. The archbishop has only a general supervisory role for dioceses of the provinces other than his own. In some cases he is called metropolitan. Some heads of ancient historical churches are traditionally given the title of patriarchs, the most important, besides the Pope in Rome, being the patriarchs of Constantinople (Istanbul), Antioch, Jerusalem and Alexandria, the last in north Africa. In the Catholic Church the same title is also given as a mere token of honour to the heads of a few important dioceses. In India only the archbishop of Goa is designated as patriarch. A similar function in some churches goes by the name of primate.

Some bishops are not heads of a diocese but function as auxiliaries or coadjutors of the principal bishop, or have other roles in the church, for example, as nuncios or ambassadors of the Pope to different countries.

In India at present (2004) there are 149 bishops or archbishops in the Catholic Church, all of them Indian-born. The bishops are organized in several representative bodies. There is first the Catholic Bishops' Conference of India (CBCI), which speaks for the whole Indian Catholic Church and represents it before the government. The bishops of each ritual church also have their associations: the Conference of Catholic Bishops of India (CCBI) includes all the bishops of the Latin rite, the Syro-Malabar Bishops' Synod those of the Syro-Malabar Church and the Syro-Malankara Bishops' Conference those of the Syro-Malankara (Catholic) Church.

The various Eastern and Protestant churches also have internal organizations where their leaders meet. There is no all-India body of bishops of all the churches, but there is the National Council of Churches of India (NCCI), which in some limited way represents most of the Indian churches, but not the Catholic Church. There is however collaboration between the CBCI and the NCCI and their various organs.

Priests and Their Formation

Priests are ordained members of a church with a role of leadership under the authority of the bishop. Their main function is to lead the community within the portion of the diocese assigned to them, often called the parish. In some churches they are called presbyters, elders or pastors. In many churches priests are addressed as 'father' or by the Hindi derivation of the Portuguese word, 'padri'. There are no 'hereditary' priests in Christian churches. Priests are recruited from volunteers and 'ordained' or 'assigned' after a period of training and probation. Their role is to gather the community and lead it in worship, preach the Christian doctrine, impart the sacramental rites to members at their request, organize the community for various activities and lead the people to greater fidelity in following the teachings of Jesus Christ in their lives of dedication to God and to the welfare of the whole human community. Although they are involved in sacred or ritual actions, this is by no means the only area of their activity. They are truly community leaders and guides. They are the Christian gurus.

At the end of 2001 the Catholic Church in India had 19,811 priests, of whom 8584 were 'religious' (see below). Priests are normally recruited on the basis of voluntary service that is meant to be lifelong. They come from all sections of society. To function as priests they must be accepted and ordained for the purpose by the Church. Bishops are generally selected or nominated from among priests.

One of the characteristics of most mainstream churches is their heavy investment in the education of their leadership cadres, especially priests. They require several years of study before they are allowed to be ordained and exercise their official functions. Most Protestant and Eastern churches require that their candidates follow at least the three or four years' syllabus of studies decided by the Senate of the Serampore College leading to the degrees of bachelor of theology or bachelor of divinity. The Catholic training centres for priests also follow a similar programme of studies that lasts at least six years and covers the main areas of philosophy (Indian and Western), the Bible, other religions, history and systematic theology. All training centres also include the practice of spiritual sadhana as part of their education. Catholic candidates to the priesthood are required to make a public promise of remaining celibates for life. Other churches allow the marriage of their priests; in the Eastern churches it must be before ordination.

Most volunteers who begin their studies for the priesthood may be in their twenties, but there is no upper age limit. Many are university graduates. The minimum age for ordination to the priesthood in the Catholic Church is twenty-five years.

Until recently, the ordained leadership of bishops and priests in the Christian Church was exclusively reserved to men on the argument that the twelve apostles chosen by Jesus, who are the prototype of Church leadership, were all men. Today most Protestant churches have accepted women priests, and a few also women bishops. Neither the Oriental and Eastern churches nor the Catholic Church wants to break with the tradition.

The churches run rather large institutions for the formation of their cadres, priests and pastors. Most of the Protestant and Orthodox institutions are affiliated to the Senate of Serampore, which confers the degrees. The best-known teaching institutions are Serampore College, Serampore, United Theological College, Bangalore, the Bishop's College, Kolkata, Union Biblical Seminary, Pune, Leonard Theological College, Jabalpur, Gurukul Lutheran Theological College, Chennai, Tamil Nadu Theological Seminary, Madurai, Orthodox Theological Seminary, Kottayam, Aizwal Theological College, Mizoram, and Eastern Theological College, Jorhat, Assam. The Catholic institutions confer their own degrees, at times recognized by the Congregation of Catholic Education in Rome, while others are affiliated to Roman Catholic universities. The best-known Catholic centres are Jnana Deepa Vidyapeeth, Pune, St Joseph's Pontifical Seminary, Aluva, St Thomas Apostolic Seminary, Kottayam, St Peter's Pontifical Institute of Philosophy and Theology, Dharmaram Vidyakshetram and Kristu Jyoti College, all three in Bangalore, St Paul's Seminary, Tiruchirappalli, Oriens and Sacred Heart College, Shillong, St Albert's College, Ranchi, St Pius X Seminary, Mumbai, and Vidyajyoti College, Delhi. Some of these colleges have postgraduate and doctoral departments. Priests and nuns also do doctoral work in university departments of religion and sociology.

Deacons

Deacons form the third layer of ordained leaders in the Church. Deacon comes from the Greek word for 'servant' and there is a story in the Bible (Acts 6) on how the number of Christians in Jerusalem began to grow, leading the community to create a group of assistants to help in the organizational tasks, whether material or spiritual. They were called 'deacons' and some became conspicuous for their preaching. In the course of the centuries the order of deacons slowly died out in many churches: part of their role has been absorbed by the activities of the priests themselves or been taken up by non-ordained professional helpers like catechists, teachers, accountants and health personnel. Some churches have always preserved the order of deacons (and deaconesses); others are trying to restore it.

Religious

There is a different form of leadership especially conspicuous in the Catholic Church constituted by what are technically called the 'religious', or more broadly 'consecrated persons'. This form of leadership operates on the spiritual level and is open to both men and women. In the dictionary the adjective 'religious' means something or someone connected with religion. But in traditional Western vocabulary a 'religious' is a woman or man who has renounced a normal autonomous and married life and bound herself or himself to serve God by making at least three lifelong vows, of poverty, chastity and obedience. The most visible religious are nuns, well known all over India by the distinctive dresses (habits) most of them wear. Men religious are often called 'brothers' unless they have been ordained priests, in which case they are called 'fathers' like all ordained priests. India in fact is one of the countries in the world with the greatest concentration of religious: 95,531 at the end of 2001. Many of them have gone to various countries of the world, East and West, to help the Church in various functions. Religious are found not only in the Catholic Church but also in non-Catholic Orthodox churches. A few Protestant and the Anglican churches have in recent years also accepted this kind of 'vocation' or call as a legitimate form of Christian life, although Luther, who had himself been a religious of St Augustine, was critical of this institution.

The religious are organized into 'orders' and 'congregations'. They have evolved in various forms in the Church from the early centuries. The first followers of Jesus were not renouncers as religious are. But at the time of Jesus there were various forms of monastic life, the best known among the practitioners being those that inhabited the caves of Qumran, around the Dead Sea, possibly identified with the Essenes mentioned by Josephus, a contemporary Jewish historian. Whether Indian monasticism (Ajivika, Jain or Buddhist) had any role in the appearance of the monastic ideal and practice in the biblical world is a matter for historical research.

From the second century we find some Christians taking to the deserts of Syria, Egypt and Palestine to lead a life of contemplation and austerity, and in their idealistic belief to prepare for the second coming of Christ. St Antony (251–356 CE) became in early Christianity the model of this type of renunciation. A rich Egyptian, he distributed his lands and wealth and retired to an old burial ground and later to the desert. The ideal was to respond to the inner 'call' of Jesus who had challenged a rich young man to sell his possessions, give them to the poor and follow him (Mt 19:21). Antony and his followers were dissatisfied with the easy life of Christians in the society of the Roman Empire of the fourth century. Like many seekers before and after, they wanted to follow Jesus in a radical way and decided to 'flee, be silent and be calm'. Poverty, meditation (especially on the Gospels) and manual work were the characteristics of this kind of life. Like Buddhist and Jain monks, they had a deep influence on the laypeople around them. These monks were soon organized into groups that evolved their own rules, and became the masters of prayer and spiritual life to many Christians. In the East the best known are the rules of St Basil (329–379 CE) and in the West those of St Benedict (480–547 CE), who was influenced by Basil. The Benedictine monks had an important civilizing role in Europe as their monasteries were centres not only of prayer but also of the arts, music, crafts, agriculture, liturgy and learning in general.

What distinguish the religious from the laity are the vows they take. The vow is a solemn promise made to God. The religious promise to remain celibate for their whole life, to renounce any claim to private property and own everything in community, and to engage in any activity that the community, through its leaders, asks them to undertake. Some religious add other vows: the Missionaries of Charity vow to serve 'the poorest of the poor', the Jesuits to obey the Pope in any mission he may give them. This vow is at times grossly misrepresented, even on the Internet, with fantastic and ridiculous suggestions of macabre fights for the Catholic faith. Significantly such attacks are generally anonymous.

Vows are not taken lightly. There are usually several years of testing of the fitness for this kind of life, the 'probation' time during which temporary commitments may be made before the perpetual vows are allowed and officially recognized in the Church. Besides taking vows, religious are expected to live in communities.

In the Middle Ages new types of religious life appeared in the orders of men and women that grew around the figures of St Dominic (1170–1221) and St Francis (1182–1226), both of whom were highly influential among the people and promoted movements of spiritual renewal among Christians. The Franciscans are especially important for India because, together with ordinary priests, they were the first links between the Indian and the Western Christians. In a letter to the Zamorin of Kozhikode dated 1 March 1500, King Emmanuel of Portugal said, 'We send you religious persons learned in the Christian faith and religion, so that they may celebrate the liturgy among you and minister the sacraments, and you may see the religion and faith we have, which was instituted by Jesus Christ our Saviour' (de Melo 1955, 11). Among those 'religious persons' were priests and Franciscan friars. Later, other religious such as Dominicans, Jesuits, Carmelites and Augustinians came with the Portuguese traders. Initially they looked after the spiritual needs of the visiting traders, but they soon extended their ministry to the local Indian population, many of whom were attracted by their concern for the community's welfare.

CHRISTIANS ON THE COAST OF TAMIL NADU

The Pearl Fishery Coast, which the Portuguese called the Pescaria, extends from Kanyakumari to Rameswaram and from there to

Mannar off the coast of Sri Lanka. In these coastlands lived Paravars, deep-sea fishermen and pearl divers. The sea bottom of this coast was rich in oysters. In the sixteenth century the Fishery Coast consisted of twenty-two villages, politically divided into three groups under three different rulers: the raja of Kollam in the south, the raja of Kayattar in the middle and the Thambichchi Nayak in the north. The last two were vassals of the Vijayanagar Empire.

Pearl fishing was an important source of income for the Paravars, but this wealth attracted rival groups and middlemen. Arab merchants, who were also involved in horse trade with the rajas of South India, had over the previous centuries settled in the coastal areas and developed into powerful Indo-Arabian communities, establishing a monopoly of seaborne trade on both the west and the east coasts. They obtained from the raja of Kollam a lease of pearl fishery, and from then on, they dictated terms to the fishing community. The fisherfolk became day labourers and were like slaves under them.

In the early sixteenth century the Portuguese developed an interest in this region. They wanted to take over from the Muslims the maritime trade and the control of the pearl fishery. In 1523 Joao Flores arrived at the Fishery Coast as captain of the Portuguese fleet. Sensing trouble, the Muslims gathered together and a fourteen-year war started between the Muslims and the Portuguese, with fluctuating fortunes. Meanwhile on land the tension between Muslim traders and local inhabitants increased, reaching a peak around 1535. Records speak of bloody conflicts in which both communities suffered losses. While the traders had political and economic clout, the impoverished local inhabitants were at the receiving end from both Muslim merchants and Hindu rulers.

At this point in time came an Indian horse dealer, John of the Cross from Kozhikode, who as a young man had converted to the Christian faith. In Kanyakumari he heard of the plight of the local population. He spoke to them of the Portuguese and the protection they could offer, and how Jesus Christ was 'a powerful God'. The people were impressed by the information John gave and decided to send to Kochi fifteen pattankattis, or leaders of the community. In Kochi they asked for baptism, for priests to take care of them and for Portuguese protection. Their request was willingly granted in principle, but the captain, Pedro Vaz, wanting the whole caste to be ready to accept Christianity, required a more representative delegation. In a short time seventy people came forward to be baptized. Christian sources say that Muslims tried to bribe the Portuguese not to baptize the Paravars, but Vaz is reported to have replied that 'heaps of gold would never make me desist from the purpose'. Besides commercial and political interests, the Portuguese kings at the time had deep Christian convictions about their role in the maritime enterprise.

The vicar general, or bishop's assistant, of Kochi baptized the Paravars who sought help. In the ceremony the new converts adopted Portuguese surnames, which their descendants use even today. A common faith and seafaring activity cemented the relations between the new Indian Christians and the Portuguese merchants. Now the Muslim traders were their common enemy.

In February 1536 a fleet left Kochi for the Fishery Coast with the vicar general of Kochi, four other priests and the Paravars baptized in Kochi. The priests baptized more than 5000 people on the coast, and in 1537 the rest of the community embraced Christianity. This conversion was not well received by the Muslims or rajas, and there was a spate of reprisals. The new Christians stood their ground with the support of the Portuguese, who restored their pearl-fishing rights to them. In spite of their changed names, the Paravars maintained their cultural identity. Later they would hardly mix with Christians of other groups.

The quick conversion of this group presented a problem for the Christian leadership: how to ensure better instruction for these new converts? In 1536 the Franciscan Friar Lourenco de Goes sent the first news of this new Christian community to King John II of Portugal. Impressed, the king sent his ambassador to Rome to inform the Pope. Just then a new order called the Society of Jesus was being formed in Rome, and the king was advised to ask the Pope to send the order to India. Thus the initiative of a few Paravars in Tamil Nadu in 1536 brought Francis Xavier to India in 1542 and after him innumerable other Jesuits from all over the world.

THE JESUITS: FRANCIS XAVIER

The Society of Jesus emerged in the 1530s out of the friendship of an international band of students at the University of Paris, gathered round the leadership of a Basque Spaniard, Ignatius Loyola (1490–1556). Popularly known as Jesuits (originally a nickname), their reputation in Western literature is, to say the least, ambivalent. The order grew and spread rapidly first in Europe and then in the Americas, Asia and Africa. In 1549 Ignatius designated 'India'—the whole of Asia—the third province of the Society of Jesus (after Spain and Portugal) and appointed Xavier as the first provincial superior. Today India has the highest number of Jesuits in the world, followed by the United States and Spain: the Indian Society of Jesus had over 4000 members in 2004. They come from almost all the social groups of the Christian community, but the biggest numbers are from Kerala, Tamil Nadu, Karnataka, Goa and the tribal groups in central and North-East India.

The Jesuit who introduced the Society of Jesus in India was Francis Xavier (1506–52), after whom dozens of educational institutions in India are named. Like the founder he was a Spaniard, from Navarre, who became a disciple of Ignatius in Paris, and eventually his closest friend. When the Pope, urged by the king of Portugal, asked Ignatius to send missionaries to India, only two were available to Ignatius: the Portuguese Alphonse Rodrigues and Ignatius's personal secretary, Francis Xavier. Even before the official papal approval of the new order (27 September 1540), Ignatius sent the two of them to Portugal to embark for India. Rodrigues remained in Portugal and never made it to India, but Xavier embarked with some other priests and two non-priest companions. He arrived in Goa, the headquarters of the Portuguese trade in Asia, on 6 May 1542, forty-four years after the landing of Vasco da Gama in Kozhikode. He came with the title and authority of a Papal Nuncio, although he did not invoke these privileges and began lodging in hospitals rather than in official Portuguese residences. In October the same year he went to Manappad on the Fishery Coast, accompanied by three young Christian Paravars who had been sent to Goa to study for the priesthood. They would be Xavier's interpreters and catechists. Their role in the further formation of the Christian community has not been properly recorded, but it must have been significant.

On arrival at the coast Xavier baptized the children of Christian families born after 1537, had a small instruction book ('catechism') translated into Tamil and learned by heart a sermon in Tamil which he repeated in every village (it was then explained by the seminarians). He also made the new Christians repeat again and again the common Christian prayers in Tamil translation. The king of Portugal had assigned 4000 fanams each year for Xavier's work, and he made use of this to pay a catechist or headman (kannakkappillai) in each village. The catechist conducted common prayers for the people each Sunday, baptized people when necessary and kept abreast of village happenings so as to help the visiting missionaries in their work for the village people. This structure proved successful and was followed in mission work elsewhere.

Xavier's actual work in India went beyond helping the community of fisherfolk in South India, whom he visited and stayed with for some months, ensuring what was for him the most important thing: the instruction in the faith of the new Christians. Besides Goa and Tamil Nadu his outreach included Kerala and the area of Vasai near the present-day Mumbai, and indeed many places of Asia, for he visited what are now known as Sri Lanka, several islands of Indonesia, Malaysia and Japan. He died in 1552 in a small island off the coast of Canton in China. The remnants of his body are even today the object of much veneration in the Basilica Church of Bom Jesu in Goa, a protected monument.

THE FIRST INDIAN MARTYRS FOR THE FAITH

The confluence of the political, military and religious powers was a costly affair for all communities concerned. In 1544 the raja of Jaffna had a grouse against the Portuguese because the previous year they had forced him to pay a tax in the Neduntivu or Cow Island. He was displeased on hearing that many of his subjects in the Mannar Island had embraced Christianity. These new Christians rejected the raja's order to return to their ancestral faith. Six hundred of them were massacred; the rest fled to their relatives in Vedalai on the Indian mainland. These 600 Tamils may well have been the first Indian martyrs to die for the Christian faith.

It was precisely in Vedalai where, five years later, the first Jesuit martyr was also killed. His name was Antony Criminali and he was only twenty-nine years old. He was martyred in the company of a Tamil 'new Christian', whose name the European records have not cared to preserve. Here too a colonial injustice was the remote cause of this tragedy. The Portuguese had imposed a toll on the narrow passage from mainland India to Ramanankovil or Rameswaram Island, which innumerable Hindu pilgrims passed every day for the sacred bath. Thirty to forty soldiers under the Portuguese controlled the toll and kept the pass open during the day. Contemporary records say that the greedy soldiers said something highly injurious to the Brahmins. The Brahmins of the temple sent a complaint to their raja of Ramnad, who in anger sent 7000–8000 of his own soldiers to attack the Christians of Vedalai. Criminali was then instructing a number of families in the Christian faith. Seeing the soldiers come, the villagers took their goods and fled to their boats, but the women were slower and Criminali refused to embark until they were saved. The soldiers arrived, killed the young Christian Tamil and eventually speared Criminali. The martyr had been the first missionary to read and write Tamil. As happens often in such cases, the raja's quest to avenge an injury got the wrong man. For, as Xavier had written to Ignatius just before this event, on 14 January 1549, Criminali was 'a holy man and most suited for this region, and he is greatly loved by the local Christians, the Gentiles and the Muslims!'

Henry Henriques was a friend of Criminali. He was a Portuguese 'new Christian' (that is, from Jewish or Muslim stock) who learned Tamil very well, composed a Tamil grammar after the model of Latin and Greek grammars and wrote and translated books in and to Tamil. He won the respect of both Hindus and Muslims, and it is said that when he died in 1600 Muslims fasted for a day and Hindus fasted for two days and shut their shops. His life interests us here mostly for the fine compliment he left about the quality of Christian life of a group of helpers and leaders among the new Christians of the Fishery Coast. On 12 January 1551 he wrote from Kochi to his companion Simon Rodrigues in Portugal:

They show a great desire to serve God and they do this every time in a better way. They are quite ready to obey the Fathers, as if they lived under obedience, and they are quite ready to die for the love of Christ Our Lord. You may believe that one of the great consolations which we, Fathers and Brothers, have here is to see these men, or better *these brothers of ours,* because we consider them as such for their great virtue and for the deep friendship they have with us. And it is certain that in some of them we notice such virtues that we would be very grateful to God our Lord if he would grant them to us. Such men edify the people very much by their good life, free from all self-seeking. And so, after they are placed in the various villages, by the goodness of God a very different fruit is produced in those places compared with the earlier times [when only foreign missionaries worked there] (Wicki 1950, 155).

Paternalistic, no doubt, but not an insincere tribute to an incipient Christian group. One year later Henriques again wrote about this community, now to Ignatius Loyola in Rome:

These people live in the various villages teaching the Christian doctrine and helping us . . . I already wrote about them. Now I cannot add anything but that they persevere doing a great service to God and helping their neighbours. We, the Fathers here, are very consoled and have a holy envy of them, as we see that we lack some of the virtues that shine so splendidly in them. We feel that in this way Christians will profit much from them as we see that in fact they do. We have a great confidence in God that in this way and other ways we have here with this people, if Our Lord for our sins would permit that in these parts of India there would be no Portuguese, these Christians would among themselves carry on the Christian movement, a thing that we think in few places of India could be carried on (ibid., 301).

In fact an official of the Jesuits, Alessandro Valignano, in his report on the Indian Province of 1579-80, averred that the children of the Fishery Coast knew the catechism of the Christian faith better than children in Europe!

Nor was the fervour of the Christian community restricted to the first generation, as illustrated by an incident that took place nearly 200 years later. Eustache de Lannoy was a Catholic from Belgium, an admiral in the Dutch army. The Thiruvithancoor (Travancore) raja Marthanda Varma's army captured him. But the enlightened raja made him the Valia Kapithan of his own army and sought his help to reorganize it according to the European model.

In this capacity Lannoy came into frequent contact with Neelakandan, a Hindu Nair soldier in the raja's army, who hailed from Nattalam, about 25 kilometres north of Nagercoil. When Neelakandan told Lannoy about the heavy loss of money and landed property he had recently suffered, Lannoy spoke to him on the uncertainty of earthly riches and advised him to put his trust in God. He also narrated the story of Job, who in the midst of similar losses and other trials kept his trust in God. Job's story gave Neelakandan great relief. They continued to meet and discuss religious matters. Eventually, inspired by the truth and value of Christian religion, Neelakandan decided to embrace the Christian faith.

Lannoy sent him to Father Buttari, the Catholic parish priest at Vadakankulam, but Father Buttari was hesitant to baptize him immediately; he wanted more details on the man's motives. Neelakandan told him, 'There is no cause for delay. This is no compulsory baptism. I came here to receive the sacraments not by force, but by my own free will and desire. I shall even give up my life to maintain the Truth of which I received the light and of which I am convinced.' Seeing his firmness of faith the priest baptized the officer in 1745, changing his name to Devasahayam, which means 'God's help'. Devasahayam advanced in Christian piety, preached the Gospel to others and was instrumental in bringing his wife and some other members of his family to Christianity (Agur 1990, chapter 5).

The news of his conversion and its effects on others reached the administrative circles of the Thiruvithancoor government and caused much resentment. Devasahayam won the personal displeasure of the diwan of Thiruvithancoor, and the two had a discussion on Christianity and Hinduism. The diwan was already much prejudiced against Christians; now, when he threatened to expel all the Christians from Thiruvithancoor, Devasahayam said, 'You may start with me.' Fearing the worst, friends advised Devasahayam to go into hiding elsewhere, but he refused. On 23 February 1749 he was arrested. During the trial Devasahayam was told that if he renounced his Christian faith he would be freed. He refused. He spent about three years in captivity, subjected to torture, deprivation and humiliation. On 13 January 1752 he was shot dead at the hillock near Aralvaimozhi about 12 kilometres east of Nagercoil. His mortal remains now rest in the cathedral of Kottar (Nagercoil). He was forty when he died and had been a Christian for seven years, of which he passed three in captivity.

News of the martyrdom of Devasahayam reached Bishop Colaco of Kochi, who was then residing in the coastal village of Anjuthenku. He had a solemn service of thanksgiving (the singing of the Latin hymn *Te Deum*) in the 'cathedral' for the gift of an Indian martyr to the world. Devasahayam's memory is kept alive in the folklore in the form of natahams (dramas) that were composed soon after his death and enacted in the villages. The 'Devasahayam Pillai Nataham' continue to hold the village people in thrall. The dramas, enacted over a span of several days, spread the fame of the martyr far and wide. The dramas bring out emphatically the reasons for which Devasahayam was killed: his conversion to Christianity and his disregard for the rigid caste distinctions of society, giving up the rights of his noble birth by identifying himself with the outcastes and the marginalized. Two hundred and fifty years after his martyrdom he still lives in the hearts of the people, as they continue to flock in large numbers to his place of martyrdom in Aralvaimozhi, his grave in the cathedral of Kottar and his birthplace Nattalam.

SPREAD OF THE CHRISTIAN FAITH IN TAMIL NADU

The birth of the Christian community in Kanyakumari is also closely linked to the political history of the district. It took place among the caste of the Mukkuvars, who had been impressed by the way in which their neighbours the Paravars had acquired social strength and protection by becoming Christians. In 1544 the rajas of Kollam and Thiruvithancoor, the Varma brothers, wanted the protection of the Portuguese in their struggle against the Pandyan raja. The Portuguese Governor of Goa agreed and in gratitude the Varmas gave permission to their people to become Christians if they so wished. Many did, especially because of the reputation Francis Xavier had among them of being a saintly man. They were baptized, but two years later the Varmas changed their position because the Portuguese refused further help. Their harassment of the Mukkuvars did not undermine the decision of the new Christians to remain in their faith.

A good number of missionaries came to India during the second half of the sixteenth century and the following centuries. Eventually groups of religious women also arrived. They all worked with the local priests who had been trained either in the traditional community of St Thomas Christians or in training centres ('seminaries') opened for the purpose by the newly arrived missionaries. Gradually the Church in Tamil Nadu organized and divided the work of all these volunteers. The religious and priests worked with the local Christians. The local Christians were the direct link with the non-Christian population and through them the Christian faith began to extend to others. The 'second spring' of Indian Christianity flourished not only on the Fishery Coast but also in some of the interior regions like the area around Madurai, and eventually the interior regions of Karnataka and Andhra Pradesh as well. Evidently they were everywhere a minority, but they were a specific community with its own modes of self-understanding and of worship, a community spread over a good many villages and a few towns where Christians had not been known earlier.

ROBERTO DE NOBILI AND HIS MISSION TO CASTE PEOPLE

Something new happened in Europe's attitude to Asia in the second half of the sixteenth and in the seventeenth centuries. Consider the following names and dates: Alexandro Valignano (1539–1606),

Thomas Stephens (1549–1619), Matteo Ricci (1552–1610), Roberto de Nobili (1577–1656), Alexander de Rhodes (1593–1660) and a little later Constanzo Beschi (1680–1747) and Hyppolito Desideri (1684–1733). Perhaps none of these names is familiar to the general public, but they brought a new era and a new way of understanding the Church. That they were all Jesuits may or may not be relevant. More interesting is that, apart from the Englishman Stephens, they all came from Italy (Rhodes actually from Avignon, now in France but then part of the Papal States). They were all champions of the need to learn and understand Asian cultures. They became experts in Sanskrit, Tamil, Konkani, Chinese, Tibetan, Vietnamese and other Asian languages. Some wrote highly valued classics in these languages. All initiated the policy of dialogue as they understood it at the time. Was there a reason for this sudden interest in Asia? Was it the repercussions of the European Renaissance being felt at the outer frontiers of the Church?

The Renaissance was a European humanist movement that made people open to the treasures of human cultures, mostly the classical cultures of Greece and Rome but also the 'others'. The missionaries mentioned above stressed the need to study the classical texts of the countries that received them. They felt the need to meet the scholars of the cultures of which they were guests. From then on, dialogue between religions was part of the Asian Christian existence. The Indian (or Chinese, etc.) religions were an intrinsic element not only of the national culture of Asian Christians but also of the official work of the Church. Their lesson has not been fully assimilated even now. But those missionaries, the forerunners of the Orientalism that would develop one or two centuries later, introduced a new self-understanding in the Church too.

Roberto de Nobili came to Madurai, the centre of Meenakshi worship, in 1606, when the only Christians in the Pandyan capital were either Portuguese merchants or low-caste Paravars from the coast, who had been under the care of a classical Portuguese missionary, Father Gonçalo Fernandes, for a dozen years. The First Oriental Scholar, as the title of S. Rajamanickam's book (1972) calls de Nobili, wanted to establish contact with the Brahmins who were in the temple town in large numbers. He realized that as long as he was identified with the Portuguese and the low castes who, from the Brahminic point of view, had impure eating and living habits, there was no chance of a contact in depth, in fact of any contact at all. No Brahmin would want anything to do with a pharingi, a foreigner who by definition and way of life was a mleccha, a barbarian. If Christianity had to be present in the heart of the Hindu world its representatives had to accept the cultural conditions that the place demanded.

de Nobili left the mission house of Father Fernandes, built a mud house in the Brahmin quarter of Madurai, allowed there no chairs or other European furniture, got permission to remove his black soutane that identified him as a Christian priest and to wear instead the ochre robe of a sannyasi, became vegetarian in his diet and took meals only once a day. He said he was from a kshatriya background since his Italian family were from the nobility and a sannyasi by choice, who had come to preach the *Sattiya Veda*. All these were not 'tricks' to deceive the Brahmins, but conditions needed for dialogue, and in fact corresponded better to the truth of his life than the image projected by the foreign priests who were unable to establish contact with the culture of Madurai. His small hermitage was a kind of city ashram in the centre of the Shaivite society. Madurai was renowned for its temples and its scholars. de Nobili managed to make friends with a Brahmin who agreed to teach him Sanskrit and the Indian scriptures. Under his guidance he studied Tamil too.

Eventually he convinced some of his companions to follow the same style of life. They did not hide their religious faith or the desire to spread it. But they believed that the Christian faith should not be at odds with the local cultures. They aimed at a cultural pluralism within the Church, beyond the ancient pluralism of various rites or 'churches' united in one faith. The values India had created for itself and defended so tenaciously had to be accepted. These defenders of new approaches had to suffer for their stand. They were persecuted by their own companions even more than by the Hindu world, where they found a place for themselves.

The problem had many ramifications. One was social. Should not all the believers in Jesus Christ worship together? How could they do it in a form of worship that included a symbolic meal, the Eucharist, and therefore table fellowship? The cultural sensitivity of the time did not allow the Brahmin converts to be in such close contact with 'low castes' and even less with untouchable fellow Christians. It is to be noted that the Syrian Christians in Kerala also did not easily allow converts of 'low castes' in their churches. They had them worship in separate churches. In Madurai the problem was 'solved' by assigning different places in church, and even different entrances, for different castes. The 'low castes' received Holy Communion after the Brahmins. The 'solution' of worshipping in the same place but separately seemed at the time a reasonable compromise. Much later, even a few Protestant churches adopted it. However, this issue was at odds with the basic egalitarian ethos of Christianity. It created tensions and drew strong criticism from some missionaries.

Apart from the caste question there was a larger area of 'inculturation'[1] where de Nobili's creativity had an impact. He did not want the converts to adopt Latin or Portuguese names. He gave Tamil names. He also 'christened' the local harvest festival of Pongal and other symbols. He had in mind the formation of an Indian clergy based on Sanskrit studies. He had no objection to Brahmins continuing to display the traditional marks of their caste, including the sacred thread. This led to serious conflicts.

The wearing of cultural signs that identified members of other religions bothered the theologians. The problem travelled from Madurai to Kochi, and from there to Goa, where de Nobili had to face the Inquisition and was asked to explain his style of life. From Goa the problem went to Rome from where Cardinal Robert Bellarmino, an uncle of de Nobili, wrote a sad letter bemoaning his nephew's betrayal of the Christian faith. Many of the accusations were trivial. But they had to do with the cultural identity of the new Christians. Could they preserve their social place in the Indian cultural set-up, or had they for all practical purposes to change

---

[1] 'Etymologically, "inculturation" means the process of insertion of new values into one's heritage and world-view. This process applies to all human dimensions of life and development. Within contemporary Christianity, inculturation signifies the movement which takes local cultures and their values as the basic instrument and a powerful means for presenting, reformulating and living Christianity' (Lossky et al. 1991, 506).

their loyalty to the Portuguese culture? Could the Brahmins keep their uncut tuft of hair, the kudumi, and wear the sacred thread of the twice-born? de Nobili studied the Hindu shastras and discussed the problems with the pandits. He came to the conclusion that these symbols were primarily social, not tied to any specific faith, and that a believer in Jesus Christ from the 'high castes' could and even should keep his cultural identity. In Rome, after a long discussion on the matter, including the written defence de Nobili wrote of his policy (see de Nobili 1971 and 1972), Pope Gregory XV decided in 1623 to approve de Nobili's approach.

Other missionaries began to move into cities like Tiruchirappalli and Salem and adjoining rural areas to spread the Christian faith there. But the role of the Tamil Christians in this movement was most important. Yesu Adiyan, a Catholic convert of the Vellalar caste, formerly superintendent of the royal gardens in Tiruchirappalli, was instrumental in the conversion of his former guru Muthudaiyan to Christianity. The latter was a Parayar by caste. He had about 2000 disciples and was specially honoured by the Nayak raja of Madurai. Muthudaiyan in turn brought many of his former disciples to Christianity. This infuriated some people, who burnt down the Christian chapel, beat up the converts and had them arrested. Driven out of Tiruchirappalli, the new Christians settled in Karur where they built a church for Parayar Christians. Peter, another Parayar, instructed thirty 'caste people' in the Christian faith and brought them to the missionary for baptism. We know the names of a few other outstanding helpers, or 'catechists' as they were called: Savarirayan, a high caste, probably kshatriya, esteemed by the Nayaks and a man of piety, austere life and a sense of justice; Dhairiam, a yogi of the Nayak caste, well known for his singing; Yesupaten, also a Nayak, who took a vow of celibacy; Mariadas, a Parayar, who was a very faithful preacher for about thirty years; Arulanandam, a poet of some merit; and Gnanamuthu, a catechist of St John de Britto (Thekkedath 1982, 259–62).

A few Brahmins, not many, listened to them and accepted the faith and were baptized, de Nobili's own teacher Sivadharma among them. The high hopes some had placed in de Nobili's new method were, however, not to be realized. The group of Brahmin Christians, sincere and fervent though they were, would always remain small. Some went back to their original faith. Others may have merged with the larger Christian communities, by that time well established in Tamil Nadu; for example, the Christian community at Kamanayakkanpatti records that among their ancestors were two Brahmins who came from Madurai (Sauliere 1995, 425).

However, the basic question was not the number of converts but whether Christianity as it was developing in this 'second spring' was to remain a religion reserved for the Dalits and other backward castes or remain open to any Indian without the loss of cultural identity. de Nobili and the Indian Brahmins who followed him, and other missionaries, wanted to respect India's social identity and thought that the Christian faith was flexible enough to accommodate other traditions. But this problem has remained unsolved in Indian Christian circles. With the demands of the Dalit Panthers in the 1960s in Maharashtra, and the emergence of Dalit consciousness all over the country, including among Christians Dalits, much criticism has been expressed against de Nobili and his followers. In his eagerness to have Brahmin converts the missionary is believed to have compromised the essential element of the Christian faith, which is the equality of all human beings before God and God's own preferential option for the poor as reflected in the Bible.

No doubt de Nobili would have answered and did answer this accusation. He affirmed the dignity of every human being and the basic human equality of all before God. But he also affirmed the dignity of every culture and its right to exist, though after correcting the evils that have crept into it. He treated, perhaps too lightly, caste as a social arrangement similar to class in Western society. He undoubtedly thought that what was not according to the Gospel in this social structure would change under the impact of the Christian faith as lived by the community. He himself was not dogmatic in the matter. He ministered not only to Brahmins but also to outcastes: in fact the first neophyte from among the Parayars, a Valluvan (priest), had read a writing of de Nobili in Tamil and came to him for initiation in the Christian faith. de Nobili baptized him and he became a powerful influence in his district. The whole idea of de Nobili and his companions was therefore to open the Christian community to anyone who was convinced of its value and wanted to follow it—there should be no social impediment to her or his doing so.

The Jesuit annual letters sent to their headquarters in Rome mention many different castes from which Christians had emerged, among others, Paravar, Mukkuvar, Vellalar, Maravar, Parayar, Pallar, Ideyar, Nayakar, Vanniar, Odeagar, Sanar and Sakilier. In some villages Christians of different castes lived together as a homogeneous group. In others they lived separately, and the caste consciousness remained strong among them.

With the arrival of people from different caste groups into the Christian fold, there arose the problem of catering to the spiritual needs of all. de Nobili realized that given the existing system the same missionary normally would not be able to interact with Brahmins and low-caste groups simultaneously. So a system of two classes of priests was introduced, the Brahmin-sannyasis and the Pandarasamis. The former had to study Sanskrit, be vegetarian and lead a life similar to that of de Nobili, looking after the spiritual needs of the higher castes. The latter took care of the others. They were not required to know Sanskrit or be vegetarian. In sheer numbers these proved more 'successful' than the 'sannyasis'. Besides the cultural necessity of this arrangement there was also a legal aspect to the question. When some missionaries tried to bring together people of different castes, complaints went to the civil authorities resulting in persecution of Christians or the expulsion of the missionaries from the region.

Among the Pandarasamis whose name history has preserved, we may mention St John de Britto, who played a leading role in attracting people of Ramnad District to the Christian faith. During his nineteen years of ministry there he was persecuted and expelled several times. One of his converts, Thadiya Thevan, a local chieftain, conformed to the demand of monogamy of the Christian doctrine and sent away all but one wife. One of those dismissed was a niece of Setupati, the ruler of the Marava land. He had de Britto imprisoned and executed in Oriyur, on 4 February 1693. The place has become a great pilgrimage centre. Local legend has it that the red sand of the place is due to the blood of the martyr! Priests of the area even today wear a red sash over their priestly garb in memory of the martyrdom of their beloved Pandarasami. In 1947

John de Britto was declared a saint for the whole Catholic Church.

Beschi, an Italian who came to the mission in 1707, has already been mentioned. Though Pandarasami, he was a great hero of the policy of inculturation. He knew Tamil very well and composed many simple and touching hymns invoking Mary, the Mother of Jesus, and an epic work, *Tembavani*, in honour of Mary's husband, St Joseph. Even today this is studied as a classic of Tamil literature. He ordered a statue of Mary for the church at Konankuppam in pure Indian style, resembling a Tamil woman dressed in a sari, bedecked with jewels, whom he called Perianayaki, the Great Lady, a term borrowed from the local bhakti tradition.

The mention of the missionaries should not mislead us into a false picture of the forces at work in the spread of Christianity. The missionaries were generally few in number and their influence was rather thinly spread in the whole area. The main inspiration for sustaining and spreading the Christian faith came from the workforce normally called 'catechists' in missionary literature, the kannakkappillai in South India. This institution came from the time of St Francis Xavier. The catechists were local laymen known for their piety and fidelity, who were given the task of supporting the Christian prayer life in the villages (these were resident catechists), instruct the children in the faith and perform religious rituals like burial of the dead if the missionary was not available. Other catechists would be itinerant and often work in coordination with the priests. Like the priests they also divided the work according to the castes with which they worked: the upadesiyars for the higher castes and the pandarams for the lower castes.

The institution of catechists has remained a permanent feature of the Church in India. The *Statistical Yearbook of the Church* (2001) published by the Vatican counts 60,144 catechists in the Indian Catholic Church. To these one may add about another thousand laypeople working in autonomous groups less dependent on the priests.

The movement of de Nobili and his Indian and foreign disciples did not result in a mass movement to Christianity but did help to give an Indian cultural face to Christianity in India. Tamil Nadu is perhaps the place where there is greatest affinity between Hindus and Christians. It is also the area from where many of the leading

Christian theologians have emerged in our country, precisely because they have grown in a fairly deep symbiosis of two great religious traditions. Many others have appealed to de Nobili and his group for their own understanding of the Christian faith, notably the Bengali patriot and freedom fighter Brahmabandhab Upadhyay.

India has not forgotten the Roman pioneer of inter-religious dialogue. It has erected at least two statues in public places to the first foreign scholar of Tamil: one on Marina Drive in Chennai and the other in Madurai. There he is recalled by the Indian name he chose for himself, the Tamil version of the Sanskrit word *Tattva Bodhakar,* the Awakener to the Essence of Reality. de Nobili is important to our story not merely for his genuine interest in Indian culture and tradition but because he could enter into a dialogue with and understand the highly educated Indians of the upper castes and enabled some of them to take an interest in the faith of Jesus and to follow him without thereby denying their culture or even, in some sense, their religious roots. They are a small group and cannot be seen as representative of their community. But they were significant because this phenomenon would be experienced throughout the course of the history of Christianity in India.

The second spring of Christianity in India was occasioned by the arrival of priests and missionaries who came with the merchants in the sixteenth and seventeenth centuries. The first to arrive were the Portuguese, but soon the Dutch, the French, the Danes and other mercantile powers arrived on Indian shores. With them a different form of Christianity arose, which we shall see in later chapters. But the method developed in the Madurai mission remained the basic matrix of the Catholic Church. Though the majority came from the Dalit castes, the community remained pluralistic even in terms of castes. The spread of the faith was often along caste lines, one family or group leading others to follow them. The majority of those who promoted new communities were Indian Christians themselves, although they worked in collaboration with priest missionaries sent from the West, especially members of religious orders. Later on, religious women were also sent in significant numbers, and much later lay Christians too came. But their presence in the country would have been fruitless without the work and testimony of the local Christians.

What these Christians could offer to their relatives and neighbours was, perhaps, better organized structures of the community life of faith, a form of communal prayer that fitted well with the strong communitarian sense in village life, a sense of respect for the dignity of every individual, significant attention paid to the poor, the women and the marginal classes, and above all the inspiring figures of Jesus and his mother, Mary, and of important saints of the Christian calendar who appeared very human and close to the people in their concerns and at the same time 'powerful' intercessors with God. There was also the living memory of saints who had blessed the land with their presence, specially Francis Xavier and the martyrs. What most sustained the new communities was the frequent celebration of the Eucharist where the memory of Jesus was constantly renewed.

Another factor that favoured the emergence of Christian groups was that the missionaries would normally contact the local rulers for permission to spread Christianity. Most often the rulers gave permission willingly and at times even facilitated the enterprise by offering land or other facilities. It also happened that rulers either denied permission or revoked it, with occasional scenes of persecution that forced Christians to flee elsewhere. But this was not the general experience.

Pondicherry saw the presence of French priests who developed their mission policies more or less in line with those of the Madurai mission. Mysore also developed its first brand of Christian life thanks especially to the zeal of a Brahmin convert and his wife. However, the first fruits of this effort died under persecution and the mission had to be restarted in the middle of the seventeenth century.

SPREAD OF CHRISTIANITY IN ANDHRA PRADESH

The Christian presence in Andhra Pradesh began in 1530 when a Franciscan priest, Luis de Salvador, was sent to Vijayanagar as ambassador of the Portuguese. He was successful in forging a political alliance between the Portuguese and the Vijayanagar kingdom, and the raja gave him permission to preach Christianity, but in this he was not successful. It is said that Brahmins were against the idea and that a Muslim killed him in Bisnagar in 1570. In 1559 two Jesuits, Simon de Sa and Francis Ricci, met Venkata Devaraya II, the raja of Chandragiri. The raja received them cordially, gave them a plot of land and permission to his subjects to become Christians if they wished to. Sixty-six years later the Jesuits left the place without having set up a Christian community except twelve adults about whom we have no further details. It was only in the eighteenth century that some Christian communities emerged in Andhra Pradesh, organized along the lines followed by the Madurai missionaries. Again there seems to have been a willing acceptance by the political authorities. The faith spread among the respected castes, including Brahmins, kshatriyas and some members of the Reddy caste. About twenty years after some Reddys embraced Christianity many Kammas became Christian. The movement began with the healing of a woman from that caste, who during her baptism took the name Annamma. The story says that in her younger days, when she did not give in to the seduction attempts of one of her relatives, he took recourse to magic to punish her. For many years she suffered from ailments caused by the spell. Since her own religious people could not cure her, she sought the help of Father John Calmette (1692–1739) who exorcized her and healed her of her infirmities. Her husband and daughter followed her example and were baptized (Sebastian 2004, 109–10). Many people of their caste followed her in the faith.

The Christian communities of South India, except for Kerala, were spiritually dependent on the services of the missionaries. There was not yet a local clergy, apart from the Thomas Christians and a few local priests trained in Goa, but we must not forget the role of the auxiliary group of catechists mentioned above and the ordinary Christians themselves. Most of the missionaries were members of religious orders that continued to come regularly to the 'mission field'. In general they were concerned with fostering ongoing instruction in the faith, regular reception of sacraments and the formation of a well-knit community. Rivalry among missionaries based on their national origin was almost inevitable, a rivalry especially felt between Portuguese and Spaniards. But this problem does not interest us here. When the Pope in Rome suppressed the Society of Jesus in 1773 the fathers of the Missions Etrangeres de

Paris took their place in many places in South India and elsewhere. The suppression of the Jesuits by the Pope had been preceded fifteen years earlier by their expulsion from Portugal and all Portuguese territories, including India.

REFLECTIONS ON THE SECOND SPRING

This spread of the Christian faith in the southern states from the sixteenth to the eighteenth centuries touched different communities. A good number were farmers but there were also many fisherfolk. Eventually teachers and leaders evolved from the community. We shall later speak about the Christians on the western coast, who also were part of this second spring but had a different cultural make-up. What is characteristic of the South Indian communities is that they kept their traditional culture. They were at home in Hindu festivals; they did not distance themselves from their neighbours and collaborated in their festivals. In many ways they celebrated their festivals like their neighbours celebrated Hindu feasts. Like their neighbours they publicly celebrated with joy the menarche of their girls. They generally kept indigenous names, although in some areas more influenced by Portuguese presence the adoption of south European names and surnames became rooted in their culture. It may not be possible to give reliable figures of the numbers involved in this movement century by century.

We may ask what caused the second spring. Why is it that now, after more than a thousand years of Christian life in India, there was a movement of revival and expansion? We may think that the *Zeitgeist*, the spirit of the time, produced an effervescence in many places. In India the bhakti movement affected Tamil Nadu and Karnataka, and spread to Maharashtra and the north. It showed a new awakening of the masses that now had other options than the sanatana dharma of the shastras on which to focus their religious and ethical life. There were not only the traditional Hinduism, Buddhism and Jainism but 'modern' dynamic movements like those brought in by Islam and developed in Sikhism.

Internationally there was of course a great movement of voyages of 'discovery' in all continents that brought people from different cultures in contact with one another. For centuries Indians had sailed through the south-eastern seas and had commercial and cultural contacts with the islands. Buddhist monks had crossed the formidable Himalaya to speak of the message of Gautama in languages unheard of in the subcontinent. In its search for India, Europe 'discovered' by chance the existence of America and the sea route to India around Africa.

The Europeans came seeking the commerce of spices to compete with the monopoly of the Muslims. In Asia they did not think originally in terms of land conquest, though they did establish colonies protected by their military power. It would take two centuries before the north European nations actually controlled the policies of many Asian lands. Besides commerce, the king of Portugal and other powers did wish to spread their religion; the new religious orders had awakened in the European population a personal love for Jesus Christ and a desire to carry his name and message to the newly discovered lands. It is difficult to deny a large measure of goodwill in their adventures. Many sincerely thought that by spreading their faith they were bringing 'salvation' to all peoples. In this they were not so different from the Buddhist and Zoroastrian missionaries in various parts of Asia.

The Europeans had very little reliable information about the religions of Asia, and what they had was not favourable. They had of course no atlases of the new lands, no encyclopedias of religions, no dictionaries, no sacred books (apart from the Koran) and no translations to learn from. They did believe that it was God's plan and their own responsibility to spread the message of Jesus to all the nations. Were not the last words of Jesus recorded in the Gospel of St Matthew (28:18–20), 'All authority in heaven and on earth has been given to me. Go therefore and make disciples of all nations, baptizing them in the name of the Father and of the Son and of the Holy Spirit, and teaching them to obey everything that I have commanded you. And remember, I am with you always, to the end of the age'?

Believers as they were in the Bible, especially important for the Protestants, they took advantage of the new openings of maritime travel to spread that which they believed in. It is true that the preachers came with merchants, under the patronage of kings and the protection of soldiers. The society they came from fused religious and political authority into a complex whole, even if the sources of power for each were different. The idea of a separation of church and state was yet to be articulated. Similarly, the modern distinction between spiritual salvation and material well-being was not so watertight as in later centuries. The Gospel came to foster the well-being of the whole person and did not compromise with any form of oppression. What is indeed amazing is that the communities that were formed from the sixteenth to the eighteenth centuries have continued to hold to the Christian faith in spite of an overwhelming cultural predominance of the various indigenous religions. Even when Christian personnel stopped coming from other continents, these communities flourished, and produced their own forms of leadership and theology that have the stamp of Indian culture and are very different from those of the West.

According to the 1991 Census of the Government of India 5.69 per cent of the Tamil population is Christian, and only 1.83 per cent in Andhra Pradesh. These figures refer of course to all the Protestant and Catholic communities.

5

The Western Coast, Akbar's Mission and the Question of Conversion

Variety of styles ~ Portuguese influences ~ Westernization and inculturation ~ The Krista Purana *~ Goa ~ Early Christians ~ 'Rigour of mercy' ~ Azu Nayak ~ Confraternity of the Christian faith ~ Discrimination against Hindus ~ Protest movements ~ The Goan Inquisition ~ Padroado and propaganda ~ Spread of the Western coast form of Christianity ~ Latin Christians of Kerala ~ The Mangaloreans ~ Mumbai and Vasai ~ 'Western' Christians in the East Coast ~ Akbar and the North Indian mission ~ The Armenians ~ Outstanding Indian missionaries ~ Blessed Joseph Vaz ~ Sadhu Sundar Singh ~ St Gonzalo Garcia ~ The problem of conversion*

One of the striking features of the Christian communities of India is their ethnic and cultural diversity. Not only did they inherit different Church traditions but they assimilated them differently and gave new shapes to the same tradition. Thus the Christian communities of Tamil Nadu and those of India's western coast differ considerably even though they developed around the same time. Both were influenced by the presence of missionaries who came to India in the wake of the Portuguese arrival, well before the Protestant Churches emerged in India.

The Christians of the western coast are concentrated mostly around Mumbai, Goa and Mangalore. The contrast between them and the Tamil (and Telugu) Christians is indicated even in their family names. The latter Christians generally use biblical names or names of traditional Christian saints, very often translated into the Tamil idiom: thus Soosai stands for Joseph, Gnanapragasam for Aloysius, Arokiam for Mary as patroness of health, Chinappa for

Paul and Rayappa for Peter. As is well known, most of these communities do not use fixed family or caste surnames. The name of the father is appended to one's personal name for complete identification. We must add, however, that a few communities of the Coromandel coast follow the Portuguese tradition of the communities of the western coast. (The first author of this book is an example of this.) By contrast, members of the Christian communities of the western coast are generally known by surnames coming from the Iberian peninsula, of which Portugal is an important part: we are all familiar with names like de Souza, Fernandes, Gonsalves, Pinto, Menezes, Silva, Alphonso, Coelho, Andrade, D'Sa, Faleiro, Cardoza and Campos.

At times people think that these names indicate mixed parentage of Portuguese colonizers and Indian women. Some may, but by far not all Indian Christians bearing Iberian names are Indo-Europeans by blood. In Goa, and in other areas with a Portuguese presence, there was a tradition of solemnizing the baptism of new Christians by elaborate public ceremonies, for which some important personality, even the Viceroy himself, would be invited as sponsor. His surname would then be inherited by all those of whom he was the 'godfather'; hence after the ceremony there would be one or two hundred more Fernandeses or de Souzas in the colony!

However, the assimilation of Christians of the western coast into the Portuguese system had its own repercussions for their cultural identity. Christians in Goa had to give up their old social customs and adopt the Portuguese way of life, a Westernized culture. Hindu names and family names were given up when taking on the names of the Portuguese godparents. The personal name would be the name of a particular saint, a practice that had been followed in other parts of the Christian world. For the last half century, however, the tendency among many Christians even in this Westernized community has been to use traditional Indian personal names like Ajay, Ashok, Bidyut, Lata, Pushpa, etc. with the result that many of them cannot be distinguished by name from their fellow Indians. Church authorities in general have left individuals and communities free to use any name for their members, as it is not the name that makes the Christian. Some prefer to keep traditional biblical names while others feel more comfortable with traditional Indian names.

Formerly, Catholics were required by law to give their children names of recognized Christian saints. Today the Code of Law for the Catholics of the Western Church only requires that the name not be repugnant to Christian sentiment (canon 855).

The distinctive character of the west coast Christians is not only a question of names. The colonial mentality was especially operative in the places where the newcomers had established their little kingdom. Apart from being separated religiously from their parent religion, Christians in these places were also expected or even forced to conform to Iberian cultural traditions in habits of food, dress, family relationships, language and music. It was most evident in the change of language. Today the west coast community is characterized by a greater familiarity with English than most other communities in India. This is partly explained by the relatively high rate of literacy and education it enjoys, but it is also a consequence of the Portuguese authorities' imposition of Portuguese for official and educational work in their dominions. When the Portuguese influence waned, English substituted for Portuguese as the daily language of the elites of this community.

The Christians of the Konkan also helped to preserve and develop their own original language, Konkani, a twin language of Marathi. Among much production in the line of grammars and dictionaries and other literature, one must mention a masterpiece of early Konkani/Marathi literature, the *Krista Purana*, even if it was written by a foreign missionary, the Jesuit Father Thomas Stephens (c. 1549–1619), the first Englishman to live in India. He arrived in 1579, ministered to the Brahmin converts of Salsette in Goa and wrote a Konkani grammar, a catechism and the biblical epic *Krista Purana* in 10,962 stanzas, first printed in 1616 and reprinted a few times later. In times of persecution, this was one of the books that sustained the faith of the Christian communities of western India.

The Westernization of the elites in these areas did not affect other Christian communities, nor all the layers of the local Christian population. Many groups remained deeply Indian in culture and language, although distinctively Christian. This is true of the old St Thomas Christians and also of the older Tamil and Telugu communities. It is also generally true of tribal communities in central

India. By contrast, the small Anglo-Indian communities in the major metropolises and railway colonies were totally anglicized; to a lesser extent this also happened to the tribals of the North-East. Today, of course, Westernization has spread well beyond Christians to a great many Indians among the elite. It is partly fostered by the great attraction that migration to Western countries holds for many people, whether educated or less educated.

In response to the problem of the Western face of some Christian communities of India there has been since the twentieth century one countermovement called 'inculturation'. The metaphor behind this word is that of seeds cultivated in different fields. As they grow and produce fruit the seeds draw from the riches of the soil where they are planted. Basmati rice is different from other varieties that grow in different geological and atmospheric conditions. Similarly the 'inculturation' movement wants to ensure that the Christian faith in India preserves or acquires the cultural and even religious characteristics of the place where it is lived. Inculturation works at many levels, some more successful than others. It is found in food, dress, language, architecture, house decor, music, arts, hobbies, culture, worship and symbols. One thing cannot be doubted: by and large, Christians in India deeply feel their Indianness and want to merge it with their faith. A sign of this national spirit is the high representation of Christians in the defence services, where many have courageously laid down their lives for the country.

GOA

The Portuguese came to the East to initiate trade relations. To safeguard their trade routes they established themselves in key posts under their military and political domination. They used to be called 'factories', though they were not centres of production but deposits of goods for trade. Governor Alfonso de Albuquerque (1453–1515)—called Alfonso the Great—set out to implant such outposts in west Africa, the Persian Gulf, India and South-East Asia. He was a genial colonizer and administrator. He studied well the western coast of India as he had studied the coast of Africa and would later study the islands of South-East Asia. He decided to transfer the centre of the Portuguese presence from Kochi, where it had been established in the first decade of the sixteenth century, to Goa.

Goa consisted originally of five islands in the present state of Goa, which at the time fell practically at the junction between the Muslim kingdoms of the north and the Hindu Vijayanagar kingdom in South India. In 1510 conditions inside Goa were favourable for a conquest. Albuquerque entered into an alliance with Hindu feudal lords of the south and in a military action took the islands of Goa from the control of Adil Shahi, the Muslim sultan of Bijapur, one of the five sultanates into which the Bahmani kingdom split up at the turn of the sixteenth century. Many Goans resented the rule of the Adil Shahis, for they had increased the land revenue to double the amount collected by the rulers of Vijayanagar who had held Goa from 1336 to 1472. When Albuquerque captured Goa in 1510 the mostly Hindu inhabitants welcomed him as liberator from the oppressive Muslim rule. A counteroffensive of the sultan in the same year, helped by some Muslims in the city, failed and the Portuguese maritime power recovered the Goan islands. At the beginning they promised a liberal policy of allowing each one to practise his or her religion. But because some Muslims had sided with the forces of Adil Shahi in his counterattack, Albuquerque reacted by brutally massacring the Muslim population and destroying Muslim monuments. The crusade spirit was strong among the Iberians! Muslims were considered the arch-rivals: 'I am determined to permit no Muslim to live in Goa,' Albuquerque wrote to King Emmanuel (or Manuel). By contrast, the early attitude of the Portuguese soldiers towards Hindus was of religious tolerance. They were not enemies to be conquered; on the contrary, they were needed for efficient administration. However, they were still seen as 'pagans' and 'idolaters' who needed to be brought to the 'true religion'. The Portuguese hoped the Hindus' conversion to Catholicism would make them allies in the struggle with Islam.

From 1510 (till 1961) the Portuguese were in effective control of the islands and a little later of some of the surrounding mainland. It was not until 1530, however, twenty years after the conquest, that the Portuguese transferred the capital of their Asian outreach from Kochi to Goa, and placed it under the leadership of the Governor or Viceroy. Goa thus became the principal focus of the new Christian presence in the western coast and came to be known as 'the Rome of the East'. In 1533 it became a diocese with its own (Portuguese) bishop and in 1557 an archdiocese with Kochi and Malaysia ('Malacca') as subordinate dioceses. We have abundant information about the history of this Christian group especially from Portuguese records and from sources of the various religious orders that became established in the area. The local population was initially partly Hindu and partly Muslim. Some welcomed the Portuguese power as it liberated them from the tyranny of the sultan. The colonizers tried to set up in Goa a cultural replica of the society they knew in Europe, even if adapted to local circumstances.

For some time the policy of tolerance if not equality of religions was followed, although sati was immediately forbidden. The 1526 Charter sanctioned the authorities in the villages to bestow lands to temple servants and regulated the inheritance laws in polygamous marriages. But the Portuguese did not keep their promises of freedom of conscience for long. Partly because of the ideological faith of the king of Portugal, partly through pressures of ecclesiastics in Goa itself, they became obsessed with making Goa a Christian land. The first means for this was allowing and encouraging the Portuguese soldiers and other adventurers to marry local women, whom, incidentally, they found highly attractive. The Christian legislation on marriage was still rather loose and it tolerated a lot of concubinage.

The first group of Christians in Goa was formed through marital alliances—the marriage of Portuguese soldiers and sailors to Muslim women captured in the battles of 1510, and to Hindu women. For political reasons the Portuguese king was in favour of interracial marriages. The progeny was bound to be attached to and defend Goa as their motherland. Another early group of Christians were former slaves. By law a baptized slave could no longer belong to a Hindu master. He had to be bought by a Christian and was often freed. Former slaves began to work in and around warehouses as free persons.

Interracial marriages and the Christianization of slaves led only to individual conversions. The Portuguese sought to promote group conversions so that the traditional family networks might be kept up after conversion to Christianity. In 1517 a group of Franciscans led by Antonio de Louro came to Goa. They began to take care of the pastoral needs of the Portuguese and other Christians and began to preach the Gospel to Hindus. Thanks to their efforts, by 1539 there were small and large groups of Christians spread throughout Goa. Many villages had churches. Despite these conversions, Goa was still mostly Hindu a quarter of a century after its occupation by the Portuguese, but this was going to change.

'Rigour of Mercy'

The European missionaries were accustomed to the maxim *cuius regio eius religio* ('the religion of the people must be the same as that of their ruler'), an equivalent of the ancient Indian saying *yatha raja tatha praja*. They found it difficult to accept that Goa, now no longer a mere factory like Kochi, but a colony of the Christian king, should still remain largely Hindu. Since Portugal was a Catholic country, the colonies belonging to it should also have Catholicism as the official religion. The idea of a secular state had not yet been born in Europe. The clergy, especially, found it difficult to see strange gods and goddesses publicly displayed in a 'Christian' land, sacred cows roaming in the streets, sacred stones with red cobras painted on them, the Shivalinga, sacred trees and pools, and countless monks and sannyasis. They thought Christianity deserved a more determined effort to be implanted there. So they opposed the policy of religious tolerance practised by the administration.

Under pressure from the higher clergy the Portuguese authorities changed their policy around the year 1540. Inanely, they defined the new policy with an oxymoron: the 'rigour of mercy'. The Catholic faith had to be imposed on the population through all sorts of pressures short of physical violence. How unjust and unwise this policy implemented mostly in the sixth and seventh decades of the sixteenth century was can be extracted from many contemporary documents. We quote two of them that show that the policy of forcing conversions was not really necessary but rather a block to a true growth of the Church which had begun well without it. The first document was written in 1595 by Francis Pais, when he was giving an account of the rents of the temples in the islands of Goa. He shows that the ideology of the conversion of India had by then been established in official circles. Among other things he says:

Since the goal of the conversion of infidels was the most important incentive that led the King our Lord to conquer these parts of India, once the island of Goa was conquered and its inhabitants at peace and accepting to be his vassals, the king sought to bring his holy intention to execution. He was informed that many inhabitants of the island were already Christians, but that the rest remained strong in their pagan faith. This was because they had been allowed to perform their rites and ceremonies to the idols they adore. The king therefore ordered that these idols be destroyed and that none would exist in the island of Goa and within its boundaries, and that in the lands under his dominion no pagan worship would be allowed. The purpose was that with this rigour of mercy (*rigor de misericordia*) they would forget their pagan cult and be converted to our holy faith, as already many had accepted and continue to accept conversion. In the fulfilment of this holy decision in the year [fifteen] forty the above mentioned idols were broken and destroyed (Wicki 1948, 759).

That many conversions were actually taking place on the island before the policy of the 'rigour of mercy' is confirmed by an earlier document. It comes from a learned Hindu in the crown's employment, Azu Nayak by name, who from Vasai, near present-day Mumbai, wrote in 1549 a forthright letter to the king of Portugal. The king had suggested to him that he become a Christian, and he replied that it is not for the king to make any such suggestions. He showed a remarkable understanding of the difference between religion and politics, the state and the Church. The letter is worth quoting at length:

For there is one only God in whom all believe, and He is indeed very merciful to those whom by His grace he wants to lead in the way of truth, and this belongs to Him alone . . . When the territories of Your Highness are well peopled and developed by native inhabitants, they are a source of profit and revenue: and it is out of this that India and the churches are maintained. There is a great difference between a Friar's life and work and that of a King. There is a similar difference between civil government and ecclesiastical affairs. For the main thing is the taxes that are realized from these lands and are paid by the inhabitants of the place: out of these, as I say, churches are maintained. The King's Government ought to take care of such people, and neither allow nor authorize any violence or injury against them. Rather, favour should be shown to them and authorization given to reside there secure in their customs. And he who freely wishes to become a Christian will do so as has been happening all along till now.

Your Highness should not wish to have everything accomplished in one hour. For in Rome, where the Holy Father is, he permits in his lands all kinds of people, nor does he send them away thence if they do not want to become Christians. Since this is so, why should they act in Goa as they do?

Let none tell Your Highness that if the leading persons are expelled from Goa the others will become Christians. For by this time many people in Goa have become Christians, and some of them are related to these leading persons, who never hindered them. And day by day more people do so, because they live among Christians. If they are expelled, they will have no more dealings and contacts with Christians and Portuguese, and so will never become Christians. And if the leading persons are expelled the people will perhaps follow them.

If the slaves of Christians are not freed on becoming Christians, but remain whose slaves they are, why should Gentiles and Muslims lose their money? Granted that they cannot retain them as slaves for being Christians of Your Highness. You want them to be free. Then order compensation to be paid, or let them be sold to Christians and the price be made over to the donors.

Not all agree with the novel thing that is being done in Goa. For all think that what is being done is neither unto God's service nor that of Your Highness. It is only the Bishop [who wants it]. And he has no concern for the territories, since neither he nor the other Fathers have to take to arms and fight in defence of the lands. Neither do they contribute to the revenue of Your Highness, but rather eat it up. And the Governor agrees to this policy lest they write ill about himself to Your Highness.

We all hold that there is to be only one Law, and at present I see none to which all can turn except that of the Christians. But the time of realization has not yet come. From now on till then, people will become Christians little by little, and since the Lord God has willed to grant this interval, Your Highness should not exert pressure either (da Silva Rêgo 1961).

This serene and wise letter gives us much information. First, the king was personally interested in the conversion of those he considered his subjects by right of conquest, some of whom actually were active in his service. He tried to influence Azu Nayak to become a Christian, but Azu refused without any sense of endangering his position. Second, there was a movement in Goa of what we might call 'cultural conversions': a number of leading citizens were embracing the religion of the new rulers. From a large number of individual accounts, it is clear that many of them were sincere, their Christian life rich in spiritual gifts and generous outlook. It is also clear that the official policy of the colonizers was changing from one of respect for the religions of the local people to one of strong pressure to force the whole population to become Christian. Such pressures included the legal prohibition of any other worship, the expulsion of Hindus from the civil services of the government, interference with the laws of inheritance and the personal law of the subjects, imposition of taxes of various kinds and even dispossession of lands and other properties. One might say that within its logic, the policy of forced conversion was successful. After an intensive campaign in the second half of the sixteenth century Goa was, at least for a time, a Christian colony. However, slowly the original faiths revived in the course of subsequent centuries and according to the 1991 Census Christians are less than 30 per cent while Hindus are nearly 65 per cent and Muslims above 5 per cent.

Even at that time the new Portuguese policy was criticized by some missionaries. One ferocious criticism came from a rather unbalanced Jesuit who eventually returned to Portugal and was expelled from the order for other reasons. But this criticism was quite balanced and there is no reason to deny the basic veracity of his report:

> With regard to the propagation of Christianity, the manner of it was so outrageous that it could not but cause scandal throughout the whole of India. We claimed that we did not force our religion on anyone. But in practice they saw us forcing our religion on the inhabitants of our territories, after we had stated, and made an agreement with them, that they would be allowed to live without constraint and in peace (Neill 1984, 1: 228).

This letter shows that the policy of freedom to accept or not accept the Christian faith was seen as the right one but was not practised. Seven bishops in Portugal protested to the crown against what was going on in Goa, and Rome itself in the person of the superior general of the Jesuit order criticized the practice prevalent then (ibid.). Today all churches condemn such flagrant violations of human rights.

The Confraternity of the Holy Faith

If the 'rigour of mercy' was the negative side of the Portuguese effort to Christianize Goa in the sixteenth century, an institution was created in 1541 to hasten the Christianization of the population in a more positive manner. Called the 'confraternity of the holy faith', it was conceived by two important clerics in Goa, Michael Vaz and Diogo Borba, and its members were some leading clerics and laypeople from the local Portuguese government. They would work for the spiritual and material welfare of the people, especially those who wanted to convert to the [Christian] faith and those who had already converted (Wicki 1948, 777).

The Confraternity also promoted the understanding of their faith among the new Christians especially through the 'College' of St Paul. The Confraternity was responsible for maintaining churches, helping Christians in lawsuits, endeavouring to get Christians preferred in government appointments, visiting the sick and the abandoned, helping the poor, taking care of orphans and providing the rites for the dead. It helped Christians in need and ensured that they got adequate jobs. It helped Christian girls to get good partners in life and arranged for their marriage.

It also assumed the negative role of seeing to the implementation of the 'rigour of mercy': it stopped Hindus from constructing new temples and repairing old ones, punished those who molested Christians, forced Hindus to provide for their relatives who became Christians, prevented Jews and Muslims from buying Hindu slaves, diminished the burden of taxation on Christians and made it heavier for Hindus (da Silva Rêgo 1961).

Clearly the ideal aim of the Confraternity was the establishment of a Christian state in Goa. It also wanted to counteract the influence of powerful people, especially Brahmins, who prevented people from becoming Christians. There is little doubt that the Confraternity was a powerful influence, for good and for evil, not only in the legislation that emerged from new government sources but also in the practice of Christian life. It was a factor responsible for the policy of the 'rigour of mercy' in the ensuing years.

But the most important work of the Confraternity in Goa was 'an institution for the education of Christian boys from all over the East with a view to ordaining them priests and sending them back to minister to their own people' (D'Costa 1962). The Confraternity raised funds for building a college in which Indian and East Asians could be educated for the priesthood. This was the renowned College of St Paul, which one year after its foundation became the first Jesuit school in the world. At the beginning it was no more than what today would be called a seminary for young boys preparing for the Christian ministry, either as priests or as catechists. Out of this institution, however, the educational structure of the Jesuit order and of the Catholic Church in general developed. One of the contributions of the College of St Paul was that it became the site of the first printing press in India. The press was originally meant to help the work of the Jesuits in Ethiopia (Abyssinia), but it somehow found its way to Goa. The first books printed in India from 1556 onwards were on religious topics, but already in 1563 we have an interesting book, *Conversations on Indian Plants and Drugs Referring to Medicine in India,* by Garcia da Orta, a resident of Bombay who was a pioneer on Indian medicine and flora. We know of eighteen titles printed in the sixteenth century and twenty-one in the seventeenth. The first publications in Indian script were in Tamil printed in Kollam in 1578. Christians were often the pioneers in printing in many Indian languages even into the modern age (see Priolkar 1958).

A Pyrrhic Victory?

A decree passed by Governor Barreto in 1557 made the open practice of Hinduism more difficult and offered remunerative posts to Christians while Hindus were deprived of them. As a result, the number of Christians grew rapidly and by 1563 Goa had almost become a Christian territory with a Christian population of about 70,000. By the beginning of the seventeenth century Hindus had become a minority group: 20,000 in a total population of about 1,50,000. This does not deny that there were also conversions to Christianity by conviction, based on a true faith in Jesus Christ or inspired by the charitable activities of the Christians, as attested to by some contemporary Indians. But far too much force and inducement was applied to ensure the conversion of practically the whole population at one time.

Two social groups profited much by conversion to Christianity: the peasants and the Brahmins. When the peasants became Catholics they were freed from compulsory labour and they could get the land of the defeated Muslims and also rent lands from Christians for cultivation. The converted Brahmins stood the chance of being given administrative posts. Through these conversions both the peasants and the Brahmins integrated themselves not only in the religious system of the Portuguese but also in their economic, political and administrative system.

Despite their assimilation into Portuguese culture, the Goans did not enjoy all the privileges of the Portuguese. The Portuguese were always 'more equal'. They continued to remain the dominant social group and practised a fair amount of racial discrimination. The Inquisition, established in Goa in 1560, played havoc in the lives of new Christians. Some left Goa for other areas so as to remain faithful to their Goan customs while keeping their Christian faith. The imposition of the Portuguese language was another factor of friction between Goan Christians and the Portuguese. In 1787 a revolt was planned in Goa to overthrow the Portuguese rule. This revolt is considered by historians as the second anti-colonial revolt in modern times, the first being the American War of Independence. Two Catholic priests, Fathers Caetano Francisco Couto and Jose Antonio Gonsalves, masterminded it. But before the date fixed for the revolt (10 August 1787) a clerk at the Aldona Communidade disclosed the plot to the government. The government arrested forty-seven people as conspirators of this plot. Of them seventeen were priests and seven were military officers. Three of the priests were acquitted and the rest deported to Portugal. Of the laymen who were arrested, fifteen were given capital punishment and the rest deported to Portugal. Those who were given capital punishment were treated cruelly in public places—dragged along the streets, hands quartered, heads fixed on stakes and allowed to rot—to discourage any more revolt against the Portuguese government. The way out for those who could not cope with the Portuguese rule was to migrate to other areas under Hindu and Muslim rajas or another European power.

In recent times, and even before Goa was reintegrated into the Indian union in 1961, some Christians of the western coast have tried to recover their pre-conversion family names and a good number adopt personal names clearly of Indian origin for themselves or their children. There has been a slow process of de-Westernization of this community for a fairly long time.

The Goan Inquisition

One of the signs that Goa was considered a 'Christian' state was the establishment of the Inquisition in 1560. It lasted for more than two centuries, till 1774 when it was abolished under the influence of the Marquis of Pombal. Four years later it was restored in a new form to be definitively suppressed after twenty-four years, in 1812. The roots of the Inquisition were of course in European history. It is not our concern here to trace the history of this institution. It came into being at a time when the southern countries of Europe were deeply concerned about heresy, about certain doubtful features that had crept into traditional religion and about the 'new Christians' who, politically forced to convert, secretly continued their old religious practices, generally Jewish or Muslim. The secrecy of this kind of double belonging made the authorities anxious about the loyalty of their subjects at a time when religious authenticity was identified with patriotic loyalty.

The Inquisition, even in Goa, was a 'Christian' institution and it was not in its purview to judge or punish members of other communities, Hindu, Muslim or any other. It was an affair not of Indian Christians but of the Portuguese establishment. Its concern was the authenticity of Christian belonging as understood at the time in both political and ecclesiastical circles. Neill (1984) calculates that in the 214 years of its existence an average of seventy-six Christians a year must have been brought to trial; it is, however, impossible to say what proportion of the cases involved serious 'offences'. Hunter (1886) mentions a total of 4046 people in the whole period sentenced with various forms of punishment, including 105 men and sixteen women condemned to be burnt alive, of which sixty-four were burnt in effigy and fifty-seven executed. In the peak years, between 1562 and 1567, Neill (1984, 230) mentions eleven *autos de fe* (trials of faith): 'These must at all times have been terrifying displays of ecclesiastical power; but the terror was due more to menace than to execution.' The *auto de fe* was the solemn conclusion of a trial where, after a procession, Mass and sermon, sentences were read and executed. 'Those sentenced to death were handed over to the secular power with a formal exhortation to mercy . . . [Officially] execution had to follow in five days' (Cross and Livingstone 1997, 135). Burning alive was very rare.

Padroado and Propaganda

This may be the right moment to explain a conflict that deeply affected the Catholic community, especially in the western coast, from the seventeenth to the twentieth century. It was a conflict between two structures of governance within the Church. These structures did not originate with the Indian Christians but affected them indirectly. Their problem arose from the fact that the role of the papacy in Europe was passing through a period of profound changes.

From the Middle Ages the European culture worked with two basic sources of authority, which at times worked harmoniously, often discordantly. The two sources were on the one hand the emerging dynasties in Europe and, on the other, the Pope in Rome, who from the time of Gregory I (sixth–seventh century) had acquired not only a religious but also a political ascendancy in western Europe. The popes and their legates used the kings and nobility to promote religious activity, and often granted them the rights of 'patronage' (in Portuguese *padroado*), for instance for founding church institutions. The patronage entitled the political person to propose names for appointments in the religious institution in question.

This right became more important at the time of the European expansion overseas and their adventures of discovery. It seemed natural that the Pope would entrust to the states engaged in travels of discovery and commercial and political expansion the responsibility of providing for the spiritual care of the travellers and settlers in new places and for overseeing the Christian works there. Specifically in 1418 Pope Martin V granted the Portuguese crown a long list of privileges in its overseas territories. The system seemed to work satisfactorily—for a time.

Two centuries later it began to show its weakness. On the one hand the Portuguese power had declined with the rise of the Dutch and English maritime strength and the rivalries with the Spanish crown. The work of the mission was being obstructed rather than helped by the political link with the Portuguese crown. On the other hand the Holy See (the papacy) became more aware of its responsibility as the guide of the spiritual life of the church. The long cultural and political journey towards the separation of church and state was just beginning. Many ecclesiastics had already realized that the preaching of the Gospel and the care of new Christian communities were the responsibilities of the Church and not of political institutions. The cross and the sword had to separate.

Even in the thirteenth century, the Catalan mystic Ramon Llull had asked the popes to establish a structure in the Church to assume the responsibility for the spread of the faith. After some tentative attempts, in 1622 when Portugal was under the control of the Spanish crown, Pope Gregory XV constituted in Rome the 'Congregation for the Spread of the Faith', a kind of ministry in charge of all Catholic mission work anywhere in the world. (Unfortunately this institution, still at work, was popularly known by one of the words of the Latin title, 'Propaganda'. In its original context the word does not mean what it does in modern English, a religious advertising agency! It simply means 'spread' or 'extension' of the faith.)

Portugal enjoyed the rights of patronage, which had been given in perpetuity and could not be revoked unilaterally. For a long time it cooperated well with the Roman institution, but tensions between the two bodies soon surfaced. Rome began to appoint 'vicars apostolic', who did not have the full authority of a bishop, to places in Asia which the Portuguese government thought to be under their Padroado. The conflict was most acutely felt in Bombay, originally a Portuguese colony but ceded to Britain as part of the dowry of Princess Catherine when she married Charles II of England in 1661. In 1720 the Portuguese government expelled the Franciscan missionaries from Goa and its ecclesiastical dependencies. Rome then appointed vicars apostolic as substitutes for the bishops it could not appoint under the terms of the existing treaties.

Catholics thus had a twofold channel of ecclesiastical jurisdiction in the same place. For some time the churches in Bombay were divided between the two contending authorities. The division caused endless local tensions, quarrels, lawsuits and even fights both in Bombay and in other territories. The ordinary Indian laity had little say in all these quarrels but were divided among themselves as a result of the rivalries between their priests and missionaries. It was only in 1953 that India saw the end of Padroado, when an agreement was signed between the Holy See and Portugal.

SPREAD OF THE WESTERN COAST FORM OF CHRISTIANITY

The western coast Christians did not exist only in Goa. We find the same kind of Christianity in other parts of India, especially in the cities. This outreach is first visible in the areas where the Portuguese presence had been found: the Vasai/Bombay region, Daman and Diu, Kochi and Bengal. Because this particular Christian community was more obviously different from their neighbours in dress, language, food habits and social conventions, and was more comfortable with Western culture than other communities were, they were somehow taken to be *the* representatives of Christianity, which was thus considered 'Western' as a whole. Christians are thus portrayed in the press, cinema and television as wearing Western dress, drinking foreign liquor, speaking only English and having names such as John, Peter, Albert, Anthony, Mary or Elizabeth. One out of dozens of Christian communities has become the stereotype of all Christians.

Kerala, Mangalore and Others

The Portuguese presence was felt in Kerala before it settled in Goa, though it did not become a real colonial power here. The Portuguese first landed in Kozhikode and soon opened more important commercial centres in Kochi, Kollam and Kannur, and even around present-day Thiruvananthapuram. As merchants, they were interested in good commercial relations with the rajas and other authorities. They encouraged but did not impose conversion to Christianity. They also intermarried freely with the local women and so formed communities of Eurasians. In these places the community of St Thomas Christians was already well established, and the merchants and their priests inevitably came in contact with other local populations, poor and rich, Hindu and Muslim. Out of this contact there emerged a new form of Christian life, for the converts were not integrated into the traditional St Thomas communities.

Besides the Eurasians the new converts came mostly from the Nair, Ezhava and Pulaya castes, to whom one must add a few Brahmins and Mukkuvars and some Syrian Christians. The raja of Kochi resisted the pressure of the king of Portugal to become a Christian and forbade conversions under pain of confiscation of property. But eventually an agreement was reached to allow conversions, especially after the harbour superintendent of Kochi converted with his clan, and other officials showed an inclination to follow the Portuguese whom they admired for their navigation skills. Members of the new community came to be called 'Latin' Christians, because originally their official public prayers were recited in Latin, as in all parts of the Western world, while the older St Thomas Christians prayed in Syriac. Pope Paul IV made Kochi a diocese in 1558. The Latin Christians have remained to this day a significant presence in Kerala, especially among the fisherfolk and other poor communities. Most of them come from disadvantaged castes and communities, even though early Portuguese memoirs record the conversion of some high-placed persons like the king of Kannur and others. Today among Catholics there are eleven dioceses of the Latin rite out of the twenty-seven dioceses in the whole of Kerala.

Just north of Kerala there is a strong Christian community around the city of Mangalore. The Portuguese captured the city in 1568 and constructed a fort there, but, as in Kerala, there were few conversions of the local population. The majority of Mangalore's Catholics came from Goa in the sixteenth and seventeenth centuries, and brought their language with them: even today they speak Konkani, though they write it in Kannada script. Ironically, the religious policies followed by the Hindu rajas of Vijayanagar regarding Christian life were more tolerant than those of the Portuguese in Goa. The Goan Inquisition forbade many Indian social customs connected with the rites of passage—childbirth, marriage, death, burial—and prescribed a dress code in which many simple people felt uncomfortable. It frowned on the use of the local language, Konkani, and tried to impose Portuguese in its place. A number of people refused to give up their ancient (Hindu) customs which they kept together with their Christian faith. When the Goan Inquisition insisted on their abandoning them, they chose to migrate.

Besides, in Goa the many invasions by Marathas, the Adil Shahis of Bijapur and other surrounding powers had a devastating effect on the population. Famine and epidemics added to the misery of the people. Portuguese taxation was also hard on the poor, and culturally the local population was always inferior to the dominant lords. All these factors combined to make a significant number of Christians leave Goa and seek refuge elsewhere.

Many came to the territory ruled by the Nayaks of Keladi. They were welcome: they were hard-working farmers and had a number of artisans like goldsmiths and carpenters. The richer ones among them also brought wealth that they invested in their new home. The Keladi kingdom stood to gain by the immigration and offered newcomers land available for farming. They belonged to different castes but most of them were united by one faith. They kept the community together without mingling too much with their Tulu-speaking neighbours.

If the Goans migrated to escape persecution, their successors would be sorely disappointed. In 1784 a tragedy, which lasted fifteen years, fell on the community. The villain of the story is Tipu Sultan. His father, Hyder Ali, had conquered the territory from the Hindu rajas, but his religious policy towards Hindus and Konkani Christians was liberal. He did not interfere with their practices and even protected the Christians. But when it was reported to him that some Konkani Christians had supported the English in the Anglo-Mysore war he imprisoned their priests, though he did not do any other harm to the community. But Tipu was not happy with this tolerance of Christians. When he came to power in 1782 the second Anglo-Mysore war was on and it seems that the English received help from Christians, some of whom even enlisted in the British army and refused to fight for the sultan. Was this a revival of the old Muslim–Christian animosity?

In 1783 the English army was defeated. After the victory Tipu decided to uproot the Christian community from their place and keep them near him at Srirangapatnam, close to Mysore, so that they would do no more mischief. The eviction order was issued in 1874, and although not all Christians actually migrated—many farmers remained in their lands and others bribed the officials or were spared because of their loyalty—the number that went into exile was considerable, although records give different figures: between 20,000 and 80,000. On arriving at Srirangapatnam, the women were put into harems and the men forcefully circumcised and forced to become Muslims. The priests were sent to Goa. A small community remained faithful to the Catholic religious practice, especially by saying the rosary to Mary and by reciting Thomas Stephens's *Krista Purana* in Konkani. At the end of the fourth Anglo-Mysore war, when Tipu was defeated, the Konkani Christians still in Srirangapatnam moved out and settled in neighbouring kingdoms, especially in Coorg. The ruler of the place, Virarajendra, welcomed the Christians, whom he needed for the prosperity of the land.

North of Goa there was an important nucleus of localities where the Portuguese installed themselves. First there was the fort of Chaul, in Ratnagiri District, which had at one time a strong community of Christians. Eventually they migrated or were reabsorbed into their original religions, Muslim or Hindu. Farther north there were settlements around the present-day city of Mumbai: the islands they called Salsette (Thane District, including Bandra) and Bombay and the fort of Vasai ('Bassein'). Still farther north on the Gujarat coast were the townships of Daman and the island of Diu.

Vasai remains important to this day, especially because many of its considerable Christian population migrated to Bombay, forming there, with other communities, one of the most numerous and important Christian communities of the country. It consists of migrants from other states of India, brought in by the industrial revolution of the nineteenth century. Although there are thousands of Christians from Kerala, Tamil Nadu, Bihar, Andhra Pradesh, Gujarat and other areas, three main blocks constitute the Christian population of the city: those from south Karnataka (the so-called Mangaloreans), those from Goa and the local population from the islands and mainland that adopted the Christian way of life between the sixteenth and seventeenth centuries. This last group is called East Indians, a name they inherited from the East India Company of the early British presence. Their language is Marathi while the language of Mangaloreans and Goans is Konkani.

While the upper classes among the Goans and East Indians partly adopted the Portuguese language, many of these Christians slowly adopted English, when the British Raj established itself from the eighteenth century onwards. English became a link language, the main medium of education and for communication within the Church. To this day the Mumbai Christians are possibly the community most versatile in English, even though new educational policies have helped them to recover the use and appreciation of Marathi and Konkani.

The flourishing Christian community of Mumbai extends to Pune and other nearby cities. Its educational institutions are known all over the country, such as St Xavier's College, Wilson College, Sophia College and many schools. Once the problem of the Padroado jurisdiction was solved and with the advent of Protestant Christianity (about which more in chapter six), the community became quite visible in the country. It owes much to the leadership of its first Indian archbishop who in 1952 became the first Indian Cardinal, Valerian Gracias (1900–78), originally of a humble Goan family settled in Karachi. Under his leadership, Mumbai celebrated a remarkable Marian National Congress in 1954 and in 1964 the thirty-eighth International Eucharistic Congress. For the first time in history a Pope, Paul VI, travelled out of the Mediterranean world and came to India. This event marked a turning point in the activities of the popes who started from then on to visit Catholics and other believers the world over as a means to encourage and unify the various communities. Together with the Third General Assembly of the World Council of Churches celebrated in New Delhi in 1962, the thirty-eighth International Eucharistic Congress gave India a prominent place on the map of the Christian world.

'Western' Christians in the East Coast

The south-eastern coast was much influenced by the style of the Madurai mission created by de Nobili. But the Portuguese methods prevalent in Goa found their way to the Bay of Bengal where the Portuguese sea traders were busy. Thus the early Christianity in Bengal and Orissa was intimately connected with the mission posts in Kochi and Goa. Already in 1574 the Jesuit George de Castro informs us in passing that the vicars (probably diocesan priests) who accompanied the Portuguese ships going to the ports of Bengal baptized local people. These are probably the beginnings of a flourishing community even now bearing Portuguese surnames in Tagore's Golden Bengal, including the present Bangladesh.

In 1576 the Bishop of Kochi sent two Jesuits, Fathers Peter Dias and Anthony Vaz to Bengal to take care of the Portuguese merchants settled there and of the local Christians. They chose Hooghly where they started a school and a hospital. From there the Jesuits moved on to Chandecan, the capital of Jessore. There, Raja Pratapaditya, together with the Portuguese in his service, received them cordially. By 1600 they built there the first church in Bengal. Through the seventeenth century a good number of missionaries went to Bengal, especially Augustinians of the thirteenth-century Order of the Hermits of St Augustine (OSA), which went through a revival in the sixteenth century thanks to its extensive missionary activity in Asia and the Americas. They came to India in 1572 and sent missionaries to Bengal where Jesuits and Dominicans were working with diocesan priests.

Christianity however did not really flourish in Bengal at that time, partly due to persecutions resulting from the war between Shah Jahan and the Portuguese in 1632. Historians record that in 1633, 4000 Christian prisoners were brought to Agra: there the children were circumcised, the women put in royal and other harems and the men asked to apostatize. Many did, though some returned later to the faith. Among the prisoners who died in jail was a Bengali priest from Sripur. In spite of this, the mission was restarted. Bernier (1972, 439) tells us that in 1666 there were 8000–9000 Christians in Hooghly. We have very little historical information about their lives, but an English traveller who went there about 1675, T. Bowrey, writes that most of the 'sons of India were very poor, but they tried to earn their living honestly through hard work. Some were engaged in making silk and cotton stockings. Others baked bread for the English and Dutch factories [settlements], individual families and the fleet. Still others prepared all kinds of fruits: mangoes, oranges, etc., and sold them very cheap. A large number of men found employment in English and Muslim ships' (Thekkedath 1982, 465). Bernier's poor impression about the Christian community in Arakan (1972, 174–75) is confirmed by the report of Msgr Cerri of the Roman Office of Missions written around 1680 (see Thekkedath 1982).

The Christian presence in the eastern coast arising from the Portuguese mercantile enterprise extended to towns in Orissa and the whole of coastal Bengal, including Bangladesh. The village of 'Colicata' had a small church or chapel by 1690. But only in the eighteenth century did the prosperity of the English settlement there bring a large number of people, including Catholics (ibid., 468). In the nineteenth century, thanks especially to the presence of the Protestant churches, Calcutta and Bengal became prominent centres of Indian Christianity and pioneers in the line of inculturation.

In spite of their poor beginnings, Christians in Bengal produced the first printed book in Bengali, a translation of a treatise on the Christian religion and a catechism in the form of dialogue, published around 1599. About eighty years later a Bengali convert from a high caste, baptized as Dom Antonio de Rosario, published a dialogue about religion between a Christian and a Hindu Brahmin, which was later translated into Portuguese and republished with the Bengali text. Dom Antonio and his wife, also a convert, became influential propagators of the Christian message in Bengal (see Hosten 1917–18).

AKBAR AND THE NORTH INDIAN MISSION

The very year Francis Xavier landed in Goa, in faraway Umarkot, Sindh, Mariyam Makani, wife of the deposed Mughal emperor Humayun, gave birth to a baby on 23 November. The baby was named Abu-ul Fath Jalal-ud-din Muhammad Akbar. His father had just lost the throne of Delhi and was trying to keep a hold on Sindh. The baby was the grandson of Babur, and descendant of the great Timur Lenk and Genghis Khan. He was well named for he proved to be the greatest of the Mughals in India, great in many senses. He succeeded his father at the age of fourteen and gradually became independent from the ministers and other influences and succeeded in consolidating and extending his kingdom. By the time of his death in 1605 he had control of most of North India.

Interestingly, Akbar was in a sense the founder of the North Indian Christian mission. His is a rare case in history where a Christian community owes its existence to an invitation from the local authority. The character of this Muslim ruler lends itself to many different interpretations and many have been given. There is no doubt that he had a keen thirst for knowledge. Many think he was dissatisfied with the Muslim doctrine the mullahs had imparted to him and wanted to know what other traditions said about the deeper questions of life. In *Ain-i-Akbari* he says, 'On completion of my twentieth year, I experienced an internal bitterness, and for the lack of spiritual provision for my last journey, my soul was seized with exceeding sorrow' (Neill 1984, 167).

It was part of the court style developed by Akbar to have discussions with different religious leaders—first the Muslim Shaikhs, Sayyids and ulemas, then the Shias and the Sufis, then the Hindu pandits of various sects or traditions, the Jains, whose ahimsa doctrine attracted him, and the Zoroastrians, whose cult of fire was also found in the China of the great Timur Lenk. Akbar readily allowed the practice of other religions around him, and was not even averse to taking part in their worship. This easy fraternization with 'kafirs' could not have been appreciated by the traditional Muslims in his court. His own great translator and historian Bada'uni could make quite critical comments: 'His majesty till now had shown every sincerity and was searching for the truth . . . but when the strong embankment of our clear law had once been broken through, his majesty grew colder and colder, until within the short space of five or six years not a trace of Islamic feeling was left in his heart' (ibid.). This story apparently climaxed in Akbar's attempt to found a new syncretic religion, the Din-i-Ilahi, the divine monotheism. But we run ahead of our story.

The starting point of the sixteenth-century Christian mission in Agra and Delhi was Bengal, where Akbar had gone to consolidate his reign. There was a small Portuguese garrison at Satgaon, on the Hooghly, with some local Christians. As we saw above, their bishop in faraway Kochi asked the authorities in Goa to send two Jesuits to Bengal to minister to the spiritual needs of the Christians there. In their ministry around the year 1578 the Jesuits refused to give the sacramental absolution of sins to Portuguese citizens who were cheating in paying the taxes due to Akbar. This trivial fact was reported to Akbar who, contemporary Montserrate informs us, 'was greatly astonished at the purity and truth of the Christian law, which commands and lays it down that justice is to be observed even in relation to foreigners and to those who live outside that law. This inspired in him such a desire and wish to understand that law that he set himself to obtain all the information about it that he could' (ibid., 170). Akbar arranged for the chaplain of the Christians in Satgaon, Aegidius Eanes Perera, to be brought to the court at Fatehpur Sikri. Akbar told him he wanted to learn Portuguese! At the same time he invited him to participate in the religious dialogues he was entertaining in the court. Father Perera arrived at Fatehpur

Sikri on 8 March 1579. He found himself inadequate to the task of serious inter-religious dialogue. Possibly there was also the problem of linguistic barriers. He persuaded Akbar to send a delegation to Goa and ask two priests from the College of St Paul for this task.

This was not the first information Akbar had about Christians. Back in 1573 a delegation from Goa headed by Antony Cabral had met him in Surat during his military campaign to annex Gujarat. In 1577 he received in his court Pedro Tabares, the commandant of the Satgaon garrison, with his wife. There were also in the court some Christians from Armenia; one of them, Dominic Pires, was sent with the delegation to Goa, possibly as an interpreter but perhaps also a pleader for Akbar's cause.

The firmans the emperor sent to the Viceroy, the archbishop and the superior of the Jesuits in Goa were almost identical and have been preserved in several translations. Here is the translation of the firman sent to the Jesuit Provincial:

> To Father Provincial, in the Name of God.
> The order of Jalal-ud-din the Great (Achebar), King by God appointed. To the Principal
> Fathers of the Order of St Paul,
> Know that I am most kindly disposed towards you. I send 'Abdulla, my Ambassador, and Dominic Pires, to ask you in my name to send me two learned priests who should bring with them the chief books of the Law and the Gospel, for I much wish in my heart to study and learn the Law, and what is best and most perfect in it. And I earnestly request that they may not fail to come with the same my Ambassadors as soon as they arrive there and then bring the books of the Law. And let the Fathers who come know also that they will be received with all possible honours, and their arrival will give me the greatest pleasure. And when I shall know about the Law and its perfection what I wish to know, they will be at liberty to return as soon as they like, and I shall not let them go without loading them with honours and gifts. Let them have no hesitation in coming, for I take responsibility for them. Written ... (Wicki 1950; Maclagan 1932, 24).

Reporting to their headquarters in Rome, the fathers say that the (Muslim?) date corresponds to December 1578. The emperor even sent two mules to ease the priests' journey!

The unexpected letter left the Goan authorities perplexed. The power and influence of Akbar ('Achebar' in their transcriptions) was known to them, no less than his political cleverness. How to interpret this request? The viceroy was suspicious: the emperor might keep the priests as hostages and thus negotiate with the Portuguese authorities for favours. The priests were also cautious, but some were enthusiastic: ancestral memories of Emperor Constantine, the first Christian emperor of Rome in the fourth century, added fire to their imaginations. Would 'Achebar' be the Indian Constantine through whom India would become Christian? Were they on the verge of a great missionary breakthrough in the work of the Church in India begun under the Pope and the Portuguese king about eighty years earlier? After consultations it was decided to accept the request of the emperor. Three priests were assigned to the work: the forty-three-year-old Catalan Antoni Montserrate, the forty-one-year-old Francis Henriques, a Muslim convert of Persian origin, from Hormuz, who could act as interpreter in a court where the language was Persian, and the twenty-nine-year-old Rudolf Aquaviva, an aristocrat born in Naples, who had arrived just that month from Europe and, although the youngest, was made the head of the delegation. Montserrate would leave for posterity the most interesting account of their mission and the life in the court of Akbar and one of the historical sources about the reign of Akbar.

The priests were lucky. The emperor had asked for 'the chief books of the Law and the Gospels'. The Goan college had recently received from Europe 'a huge and sumptuous Bible, well-bound and gilt', in eight volumes, just published by the Belgian firm of Plantin, under the patronage of Philip II of Spain. It contained the Bible in four languages, Hebrew, Syrian, Latin and Greek, in parallel columns (except the Hebrew, printed at the bottom), and is known as the Royal Antwerp Polyglot. Not without regrets the priests decided to send to the emperor this truly royal gift. We are told that on receiving it, Akbar asked the fathers to show in which volume the Gospels (injil) were printed and showed particular reverence towards it.

We may wonder what an eight-volume polyglot Bible was doing in Goa less than ten years after it was published in Belgium. Its presence there is a hint of the serious intellectual life that the missionaries were fostering among themselves and their students in their college. In a chapter devoted to 'Culture and language' Maclagan enumerates some other works that Akbar had in his possession as a result of his interaction with the Europeans, which in 1595 he offered to the Jesuit priests and some of which they took. These included the Royal Bible itself, other Bibles and concordances, the *Summa Theologiae* and other works of Thomas Aquinas, surely in Latin, works of Domingo de Soto, of Antonino Forciglione, *Historia Pontificalis, Chronicles of St Francis, Constitutions of the Society of Jesus* and *Spiritual Exercises* of St Ignatius. Most of them would have come from missionaries. The Jesuits also had with them a Latin translation of the Koran, printed in Basel in 1543. There was a fair amount of exchange of literary works among the nobility at the time, and the College of St Paul in Goa, besides the seminary opened in Kerala, would have been an important centre of culture. We must also record that in China too and in Japan, missionaries were asking for books and paintings to help them in their interaction with the intellectuals of their respective countries.

The mission to the Mughal court failed in its hopes of obtaining the conversion of Akbar. Akbar had never said he wanted to convert but that he wanted to be informed about the Christian doctrine. The fathers may have misunderstood him, and it is clear that as the years followed one another without any growing interest in the emperor for the Christian faith, they were disappointed. They lived in the court, they accompanied the emperor in his shifts of capitals— Fatehpur Sikri, Lahore, Delhi—they had occasional conversations with him and were certainly treated not only respectfully but with affection. They participated in the discussion in court with other religious leaders, as some of the Mughal paintings record. At the time Akbar was only thirty-seven years old. He was extremely cordial with the priests, especially with Aquaviva who was younger than him. We have charming descriptions of the emperor openly walking in his gardens 'with his arm around Rudolf's neck' or walking arm in arm with him (Maclagan 1932, 32; Neill 1984,

174). The emperor also made Montserrate the tutor of the second of his three sons, Prince Murad then thirteen years old, who showed intellectual promise.

The priests however became disappointed with the king's dallying tactics, his loss of keen interest in religious dialogue (although he would occasionally come to them for conversations on Christian theology) and by his increasing assumption of semi-divine prerogatives leading to the establishment of his new syncretic religion, which, like all syncretism, did not last. The priests communicated their impressions to their provincial in Goa, who decided to recall them, but left them the freedom to remain if they thought their presence could be useful. Henriques went back to Goa in 1581, Montserrate in 1582 but as member of a proposed embassy to the king of Spain and bringing with him Akbar's request for another Christian witness for his court and for more books on the Christian faith. The embassy to Spain failed to materialize and Montserrate remained in Goa. The last to return was Aquaviva, who travelled with regrets in 1583. A few weeks later he would die a martyr at Cuncolim, in Salsette near Goa, as a result of a serious misunderstanding between the missionaries and the local population.

One of the reasons Aquaviva was reluctant to leave the capital Fatehpur Sikri is, as he said, that 'we have discovered a new nation of heathen called Bottan [actually Tibetans] which is beyond Lahore, towards the river Indus, a nation very well inclined and given to pious works. They are white men and Mahommedans do not live among them, wherefore we hope that if two earnest Fathers are sent thither, a great harvest of other heathen may be reaped' (Maclagan 1932, 38). Eventually the revived Mughal mission would in the following years be the stepping stone of an enterprise in Tibet the like of which has not been repeated since. However its success was certainly not in the line of 'a harvest of souls', to use Arun Shourie's phrase, but a first encounter between Christianity and Tibetan religion and the beginnings of a Tibetan Christian literature by the hand of Hyppolito Desideri (ibid., 97).

Perhaps the encounter of the Jesuits and the Mughal court was less of a failure than many take it to be. In fact, though the official presence of priests ceased in 1583, seven years later Akbar again asked the Goan authorities to send some fathers. Two priests and a brother were sent, but they seemed to have met with strong opposition in the court. They returned to Goa the same year. Four years later, in 1594, Akbar dispatched yet another message through an Armenian Christian to the Viceroy of Goa asking for learned Christian theologians to be sent to him. The Jesuit authorities in Goa were hesitant, in the light of the previous failures. The Viceroy, probably for political reasons, insisted on the opportunity the mission offered. The superior general in Rome had also been favourable to the mission. This time a forty-four-year-old grandnephew of Francis Xavier, known as Jerome Xavier (1549–1617), was chosen leader of the expedition. Like his granduncle, he was born in Navarre, northern Spain. He had come to India in 1581 and worked in Kochi and Goa. This time the mission was more successful: it remained for more than two centuries. It changed its character, of course, and passed through many vicissitudes depending on the emperor who occupied the royal throne; its focus was no longer the conversion of the emperor but simply to maintain a presence in the court and provide spiritual help to those Christians gathered around the court. Jerome Xavier managed to master enough Persian to write some books on Christian topics in that language. Geographical and astronomical interests occupied the attention of the fathers. They were involved in the observatories put up in Jaipur and in Delhi. Sharma (1995) contends their influence was negative, as they rejected, for dogmatic reasons, the Copernican revolution already accepted by scientists in Europe.

One of the reasons for Akbar's insistence on having Christians in his court was perhaps his cultural and artistic temperament. One of the unexpected results of the presence of the Jesuits was the cultural enrichment of the courts of Agra and Delhi. As mentioned above, books were sent in abundance, many with illustrations. Even more important were the pictures produced or printed in Europe which found their way to the Mughal court. In a fascinating book on the theme Bailey (1999) says that Europeans visiting Mughal India between the 1590s and 1660s were surprised to see mural paintings depicting Christ, the Virgin Mary and Christian saints adorning the palaces and tombs of emperors. Christian subjects were also used in miniature paintings, jewellery and sculptures, some of which were used as devotional images. 'The catalyst for this extraordinary episode of cultural convergence was the Society of Jesus, whose Mogor mission facilitated what may well have been the most reciprocal artistic dialogue of any of their world missions' (ibid.).

What is more interesting for us is that Hindu and Muslim artists creatively reproduced the European paintings and enriched the cultural patrimony of their country. Some of their names have been preserved: Kesu Das (flourished c. the 1570s to 1590s), Manohar (c. 1582–1620), Basawan (c. 1560–1600), Kesu Khurd (c. 1580–1605), Miskin (c. 1580–1604) and Husain (c. 1584–89). Bailey affirms that 'by the turn of the century, paintings and drawings in which Christian devotional images were the primary subject represented a major share of Mughul artistic production' (ibid., 119).

The interest in artistic production was inherited by Salim, Akbar's son, who became Jahangir. He emulated his father in the technical knowledge of painting and his production was by any account astounding. One must admit, indeed, that art was not the only motive that inspired this artistic creativity on the part of the Mughal emperors. As Bailey says, 'the Catholic-inspired images . . . are consonant with the ideology of Din-i Ilahi. They manifest the same blend of Hindu, Muslim, and Mongol traditions, from esoteric Sufism to genealogical symbolism' (ibid., 140). The fusion of the symbolic elements of religion with the life of the court would make of the emperor an image of Jesus, a Sufi Shaikh, and therefore as holding a divine authority to which obedience was due. 'Jesus, the ultimate *pir*, with the apostles as his *murids*, was therefore a powerful and appropriate symbol for this fellowship (of the Sufi elders and their followers, as sought in the Din-i Ilahi), combining fealty with religious devotion' (ibid.).

The atmosphere around the court in the time of Akbar and in most later periods was rather liberal, so that a few conversions whether in the upper or lower classes did not cause undue anxiety. Christians were spread very thinly in North India. With the decline of the Mughal empire the presence and influence of Christians in the court also declined. In the middle of the eighteenth century under the growing influence of the Enlightenment and as a result of a conflict between the government and the Jesuits in the colonies of South America King Joseph I (1750–77) of Portugal expelled the Jesuits from his kingdom and its dominions. A few years later, in 1773, the Pope himself, at the instigation of several European dynasties, suppressed the Society of Jesus, putting an end to the 'Mogor' mission in Delhi. Thus, as someone said, 'a mission founded by a heathen Emperor was exterminated by the Pope'. A few priests remained in the service of the community, no longer Jesuits but just priests. The last two to die were a geographer and astronomer, Father Josef Tieffenthaler, in 1785, and Father Frances Xavier Wendel, a Belgian or German, also something of a geographer and deeply involved in politics, in 1803. That year the English captured Delhi, and for all practical purposes the Mughal dynasty came to an end.

Armenian Christians

The few conversions that the priests made during their stay at the Mughal court may be considered the first North Indian Christians. However, earlier there were a few Christians established there. It is plausible that some St Thomas Christians travelled and remained in North India for various reasons. A community of which we have historical evidence is that of the Armenians. Armenia, north of Iran between the Black Sea and the Caspian Sea, was the first nation in the world to officially accept Christianity, even before the 313 CE Edict of Milan by Roman emperors Constantine (West) and Licinius (East). At the time Armenia's frontiers were larger than they are at present. Indians had settled in Armenia perhaps even before the Christian era. Although in the fourth century they experienced the persecution against all non-Christians, eventually they seem to have merged with the local population, accepting its faith. Armenians were enterprising traders and they came to various parts of India for trade, generally returning to Armenia. They also established trading centres, including an important one in Varanasi. It seems that it was during Akbar's reign and at his invitation that they settled in India, first of all in Agra. The Jesuits at the court ministered to them.

Out of this presence there arose the legend that Akbar himself had a Christian wife, Mariam Zamani Begum, who many believed was an Armenian, although some Portuguese writers claimed she was of Portuguese descent. Contemporary Jesuit sources do not refer to her at all. But there was an Armenian Christian lady in the court of Akbar who was given as wife to Iskandar, a court official. She gave him two sons, Mirza Zu'lqarnain (1592) and Mirza Sikander (1595). The former accepted the faith the Jesuits presented to him and became a Roman Catholic. After the death of his father he was appointed to the jagir of Sambhar, with the responsibility for the collection of salt revenues. He was a faithful and generous Christian. He became the patron founder of a Jesuit college in Agra. The Armenians, though in union with Rome, kept their ancient Church traditions and at least seven Armenian priests are known to have worked in Agra in the seventeenth century (Neill 1984, 386). Some Armenians in the court took an active part in the administration of the state. Armenians were found in many commercial centres of North and South India, had separate churches and even separate cemeteries. Armenian streets still exist at least in Madras and Calcutta.

Another important Christian lady in the later court of the Mughals was Juliana Diaz da Costa (c. 1657–1734), born probably in Agra apparently of parents from Kochi, with or without Portuguese blood in her (irrespective of her Portuguese sounding name) and died in Delhi. 'She seems to have joined the service of Aurangzeb's wife, the mother of Muazzam Bahadur Shah and to have been entrusted with the education of several of the Princes' (Maclagan 1932, 183). Her post was rather high in the court and she protected the interests of the Christians there. Her properties in Delhi near Okhla eventually passed to the Catholic Church, in the locality called Masihgarh, where a church still exists and a Juliana Sarai once existed.

OUTSTANDING INDIAN MISSIONARIES

The word 'mission' does not necessarily indicate the presence of foreign missionaries. Actually, at present the foreign personnel in most Indian churches are minimal, often zero. Evangelical churches do receive more people and finances from their countries of origin, but they are less representative of the typical Christian community.

To the extent that there is mission work at various levels in the country, it is planned, directed and conducted by Indian Christians. It is an expression of their faith and of their contribution to the well-being of the country. Mission includes education, justice, social work, awareness programmes, preaching, worship and other activities. Mission today is not only multi-layered but also multi-directional. Many Indian Christians have volunteered for service abroad in all the continents of the world. By a modest estimate there may be 2000 Christian Indian missionaries in the world. To these must be added the many missionaries involved in the spread of Indian religions in most countries. As in old times the Buddhist monks spread throughout Asia and communicated the message of the Buddha, so also today many monks, nuns and laypeople have gone out of India to announce the religious truths that have gripped them.

This is not a new phenomenon. One of the most outstanding examples of heroic mission is a Goan priest, Blessed Joseph Vaz. He was born in Benaulim in 1651 and died in Kandy, Sri Lanka, in 1711. In the sixty years of his life he revived the Catholic faith among Catholics in Karnataka, reeling under the persecution of Tipu Sultan. But his great work was among Sri Lankan Catholics, then under intense persecution from the colonial Dutch Protestant power. His mission work was not patronized by any political entity. When Catholic priests were expelled from Sri Lanka he smuggled into it in the guise of a coolie, attended the Catholic communities in Kandy and surrounding areas, and revived their faith, always hiding from the Dutch colonial police. Interestingly, he survived there thanks to the protection of a native Buddhist ruler, whose faithful subject Vaz remained for twenty-three years. Vaz devised ways of inculturating the Christian faith in Sri Lanka, promoted local leadership, founded the first fully indigenous religious congregation in the world and founded a hospital in Kandy and an underground network of Catholic schools. He was a mystic, taught the way of meditation and lived by the rules of the Hindu and Buddhist renouncers (Devi 1939, 343). His memory is revered in Sri Lanka and Karnataka where he worked, and in Goa where he was born and educated. On 21 January 1995, Pope John Paul II in a visit to Sri Lanka finally raised Blessed Joseph Vaz to the honour of the altars, an act he said he had greatly desired to perform from the beginning of his Pontificate in 1978. On this occasion he said when he arrived in Sri Lanka:

> Tomorrow I shall gather in prayer with the Catholic community of Sri Lanka to celebrate *the beatification of Fr Joseph Vaz,* a holy man and a man of peace, who won the respect of his contemporaries by his humility, goodness and tolerance. I am certain that in honouring the memory of this saintly priest, Sri Lanka's Catholics will be inspired to continue to work for reconciliation and peace in a spirit of service to all their fellow-citizens and in solidarity with them (*L'Osservatore Romano,* 8 February 1995, 4).

And on the day of the beatification he said:

> Joseph Vaz is rightly considered the second founder of the Church in your country. From his native India he came, a dedicated priest of Jesus Christ, to this land of ancient spiritual traditions, a land steeped in respect for the *sannyasi,* the man of holiness, the man of God . . . *Fr Vaz was a son of Asia who became a missionary in Asia.* He was also a true son of his native Goa, outstanding for its deep Christian and missionary traditions (*L'Osservatore Romano,* 9 February 1995, 6).

Another remarkable Indian evangelist of more recent times is the well-known Sadhu Sundar Singh, born in 1889. This son of Punjab went as a child to a mission school and was quite incensed at the way the missionaries in the school promoted the Christian religion. Such was his anger that one day he took a Bible and burned it in the school, for which his own father, a Hindu, reproached him and told him to respect all religions. Eventually Singh passed through a youth crisis, thought of committing suicide and according to his own accounts one night in 1905 when he had decided to put his suicidal idea into practice he had a vision of Jesus Christ who invited him to follow him. The transformation of the boy was instantaneous. He decided to follow Jesus, left his parental house, adopted the sannyasi's robe and went to live a kind of religious life with a

Cross of St Thomas, *Christliches Indien,*
Aufnahmen von Bernhard Moosbrugger

Statue of Mary, mother of Jesus,
Dhyana Ashram, Chennai. It is
probably one of the earliest Indian
images of Mary, dating back from
about the seventh century CE.

Pre-Portuguese (?) cross, Kanyakumari, called
Cross of St Thomas, *Christliches Indien,*
Aufnahmen von Bernhard Moosbrugger

Descendant of one of the first converts along the
Fishery Coast, Tamil Nadu, *Christliches Indien,*
Aufnahmen von Bernhard Moosbrugger

Women at prayer, Ernakulam, *Christliches Indien,*
Aufnahmen von Bernhard Moosbrugger

People at worship, Cross Maidan, Mumbai, *Christliches Indien,* Aufnahmen von
Bernhard Moosbrugger

Papal Nuncio and Dibrugarh tribals, courtesy Archbishop's House, Shillong

Tribal dance in Assam,
courtesy Archbishop's
House, Shillong

Jesus and the tribals, Marcus Topno, courtesy Art India, Pune

Akbar holds discussions in the 'Ibadat Khana', Akbar Nama, Narsingh, c. 1603–05, CBL In.03.263v, © The Trustees of the Chester Beatty Library, Dublin

Eucharistic meal of Jesus with
Apostles, Angelo da Fonseca,
courtesy Art India, Pune

Christ on the cross, Angelo
da Fonseca, courtesy Art
India, Pune

Pandita Ramabai

Sadhu Sundar Singh

Bishop Azariah of Dornakal

Reverend Jerome D'Souza, S.J. (extreme right), with C.N. Annadurai (second from left) and Pope Paul VI (second from right), courtesy Gujarat Sahitya Prakash

St Mary's Cathedral, Varanasi, courtesy St Mary's Cathedral

missionary friend near Shimla. He even tried to study theology in a seminary in Lahore. But study was not his interest and he decided to be a preacher. He went through the mountain villages of North India telling parables similar to those of Jesus and spreading the message of the Gospel. He used to walk from village to village along difficult mountain paths. According to his account, he even entered the 'forbidden kingdom' of Tibet where he says he found old sannyasis who followed the Gospel of Jesus. It is not clear if he actually crossed into Tibet or remained in the high mountains of Uttaranchal.

Whatever the facts, Singh became an extremely popular preacher in India and was invited by many congregations to give his testimony of conversion and of his highly personal interpretation of the Gospel. His listeners unanimously testify to his utter honesty and spiritual transparency. They considered him a mystic. In 1918 he began to travel and preach abroad, first in Asia (Burma, Malaysia, Singapore, Japan and China), then in Europe, North America and Australia. Ill health and controversies about his stories made his life more difficult, but in 1929 he embarked on another expedition to the northern mountains, his 'Tibet', from which he never returned. The date and place of his death are unknown.

Another Indian missionary remembered by some Christians in India is Saint Gonzalo Garcia. Born in 1557 in Vasai District near Mumbai, either of a mixed parentage or into the family of a local convert, Gonzalo was very good at learning languages, so the Jesuit missionaries (whose outreach went as far as Japan) took him at the age of fifteen to be an interpreter and preacher of the Gospel in Japanese. He became fluent in the language and after six years he applied to become a Jesuit, but his application was rejected. He went into business and worked in Macao and from 1587 in Manila. There the Franciscan order admitted him as a brother and in 1593 he was sent back to Japan to help the mission of the Franciscans and continue his preaching. In a fierce persecution two years later, Gonzalo was imprisoned in Kyoto, was made to join the 'death march' from Kyoto to Nagasaki and there, with nineteen other Christians from Japan and other parts of the world, he was tied to a cross and pierced with a lance. This Maharashtrian Christian was just forty years old when, in 1597, he died in circumstances similar to those of Jesus, who had also died on the cross, at the age of thirty-three. Together with his nineteen Asian and six European companions he was declared a saint by Pope Pius IX in 1862. Even in faraway Cuernavaca in Mexico a stained-glass window in an old Franciscan church has a portrait of the Indian Saint Gonzalo Garcia.

THE PROBLEM OF CONVERSION

Today, no feature of the Christian existence agitates Indian observers more than the question of conversion. The issue has come to occupy a central place even on the national political agenda. It may be useful to discuss the meaning of conversion from the Christian perspective, the mistakes and errors made in the course of centuries, and today's official and general attitude of Indian Christians towards conversion.

The term 'conversion' has been central to the Christian consciousness from the very beginning, but it did not originally denote a change of religious community, at least not primarily. St Mark, the first Gospel writer, sums up in this way how Jesus began his public life: 'Now, after John had been arrested, Jesus came to Galilee, proclaiming the good news of God, and saying, "The time is fulfilled, and the kingdom of God has come near; *repent* and believe in the good news"' (Mk 1:14–15). The verb 'repent' (*metanoiein* in Greek) can also be translated as 'be converted'; hence this text may be seen as the basis of the conversion outlook. But here 'conversion' is not a change of religious affiliation but a call to the listeners to accept the 'news' that God has brought his reign of love on earth in the person of Jesus.

Like its Hebrew background (for Jesus spoke Aramaic, within the Hebrew culture, although the Gospels were written in Greek), this conversion does involve a change, *shub*. But it is a change from 'wrong' personal attitudes to openness to the divine presence in our lives. It is a change away from any form of 'sin' or dehumanizing features in our existence. It is a change towards God's 'Rule', towards a more godlike attitude in life. Author and scholar Nirad Chaudhuri wrote, 'Christianity is not a moral code, but a view of man's relationship with God. The Christian *kerygma* we Hindus completely brush aside', and he adds that 'conversion' will always be a central concept for the Christian as it cannot be for the Hindu (Subramanyam 1970, iv). The implication of this insight is that nobody is really *born* a Christian. One *becomes* a Christian, and this becoming is through 'conversion', that is, through *voluntary* decision.

This is the biblical understanding of conversion. But sociologically most Christians are born and raised within a Christian family; their faith is in this sense inherited, not by birth but by education. The symbol of the 'conversion' required from every Christian is baptism by which a person publicly becomes a member of the community of Jesus. Even when one receives baptism in infancy, as nowadays happens in most cases, a personal decision, a personal 'conversion', is required throughout life. Every year during the Easter celebration Christians are called to renew the 'baptismal vows' included in the ritual of their baptism; when they were infants, the baptismal vows were taken only through the medium of their parents and godparents. The vows remain as guidelines throughout the life of the Christian, and in this sense conversion is central to the Christian faith.

Conversion is also a right that flows from the freedom and dignity of each individual. Religious affiliation must be within the realm of personal choice and not be imposed for life. It can only be a free response to God impelling us to seek the highest good above all human-made structures. The freedom to keep or to change one's faith is not only guaranteed by our Constitution but also a value accepted in any enlightened society. It is also true, however, that all communities put social pressure on their members *not* to change their religious affiliation and tend to consider the 'convert' somehow a traitor to the inherited faith. One needs to assess when such a pressure becomes an unjust denial of freedom.

Of course, by the process of socialization in the family, children are integrated into the religion of their parents. This is normal, as a child shares the whole life of its parents and cannot be deprived of what for many is the most important element in human existence, the religious dimension. The general public understands the baptism of children of Christian parents and their subsequent education in the Christian faith, nor does it object to the baptism of adults who by a personal search have found in the Christian faith the light and truth that can guide their lives.

What many people in India find repugnant is that anyone would *try to convince* another person to change his or her faith in favour of a new one. It is even worse when people are professionally deputed to the work of convincing others. Any organized activity normally requires certain financial underpinnings, and this makes the work of 'fostering conversions' suspect from a spiritual point of view. Everybody agrees, even among Christians, that conversion is a personal decision to be taken freely, a decision in favour of truth, goodness and salvation, not a mere search for financial advantage or social security. Conversion has to do with the ultimate values of life, the sreyas, not the merely pleasing values, the preyas, to use a distinction of the Upanishads. Conversion by allurement, or by fraud, or by force, is condemned by all. Christians do not want such conversions, and one of the duties of any Christian priest deputed to admit a seeker into the community is to screen the candidate and find the reasons for his or her seeking to be a Christian. Mere reasons of social security, job opportunity, improvement of financial prospects, even aesthetic satisfaction, are not good enough. The Christian wants to share the ultimate values— truth, goodness and love—he or she has discovered through surrender to Jesus Christ. Such a sharing can only be by personal witness, not a mere communication of information.

The traditional Christian activity of sharing the faith finds its biblical source and raison d'être in what in the Bible appears to be a clear injunction of Jesus after his resurrection. The most solemn expression of this 'Great Command', as conservative Christians normally call it, is found at the end of the Gospel of St Matthew:

> Now [after the resurrection of Jesus] the eleven disciples went to Galilee, to the mountain to which Jesus had directed them [through his message to the women who saw him alive]. When they saw him they worshipped him; but some doubted. And Jesus came and said to them, 'All authority in heaven and on earth has been given to me. Go therefore and make disciples of all nations, baptizing them in the name of the Father and of the Son and of the Holy Spirit, and teaching them to obey everything that I have

commanded you. And remember, I am with you always, to the end of the age' (Mt 28:16–20).

The traditional end of the Gospel of Mark has a similar injunction. Modern Bible scholars, and all but the most conservative Christians, do not take these texts as word-for-word reports of what Jesus said at the time. They are, however, powerful expressions of how the earliest Christian communities understood that the message of Jesus must spread in the world. These Gospel reconstructions were written after the experience of the early community, which in fact began spreading quite early in and beyond Palestine, the country of Jesus and his first disciples. Whatever their origin, these texts, enshrined in the Bible, have for all Christians a spiritual power and authority that is central to their self-understanding.

Of course, other factors entered the history of Christian missions at various times. One of them had a great influence: the negative attitude that Christian theology developed towards other religions. There was, and there still is, in more conservative Christians a belief that 'salvation' (understood as liberation from a life of 'sin') is possible only through faith in Jesus Christ. The Bible itself tells us that it is only in the name of Jesus that salvation is possible (cf. Acts 4:12). There are other similar expressions in various writings of the New Testament.

Today middle-of-the-road Christian theologians read these texts as saying fundamentally that in the life and death of Jesus God has provided the world not only with a model but with a source of spiritual power, the energy of the divine Spirit, to obtain freedom from all forms of human diminution. This 'salvation' they seek in Jesus Christ is universally available and is not intrinsically dependent on whether individuals know and acknowledge the work of Jesus in the world. 'Salvation' comes to us, as taught also in other religions, by the gift of jnana or higher knowledge, of bhakti or love of God and others, and of karma or active concern for the welfare of all. It is through these, which the New Testament calls faith, hope and love, that the 'salvation' Jesus brought to the world is made personal. The present position of most Christians was well articulated by the Second Vatican Council of the Catholic Church (1962–65): 'We must hold that the Holy Spirit offers to every person the possibility of being made partners, in a way known to God, in the paschal mystery [of the life, death and resurrection of Jesus Christ]' (Document on *The Church in Today's World*, n. 22). Christians today feel that most religions do foster the basic attitudes essential to true salvation.

In past centuries this matter was not seen in the same way. As a result of the struggles of the Israelites with the Egyptians, the Canaanite and other cults recorded in the Bible, many biblical authors developed a negative attitude towards other religions: they saw them simply as *false*, while the cult of Yahweh was *true*. There were indeed a few individuals like the author of the Book of Jonah who were critical of this Jewish self-righteous confidence. Jesus also recognized the value of the faith of non-Jews. But the negative trends continued in the history of the Church, as the result in part of the early Roman opposition to the Christian message and, later, of the political struggle between Islam and the Christian West. Those not in the Christian fold, many Christians sincerely thought, could not attain eternal salvation, or at best could attain it only with great difficulty. This was what impelled many Christians to go and preach the Christian faith to others and even use social, political or other pressures to help them take the step that, in their view, would open for them the portals of salvation. We must not forget the almost total ignorance in medieval countries of the religions and spiritual traditions of the East, not to speak of those of Africa.

Barring extremist and rare positions, the present views regarding conversion among Christians may be summarized thus:

- Conversion is a personal right. Everybody is free to take decisions regarding faith affiliation, if any, and the way in which one wants to serve God. This applies to all: if a Christian wants to change his or her faith affiliation, the community or friends may try verbal dissuasion, but must not prevent him or her by force, and must respect the final decision and continue to treat that person in a friendly manner.
- Everybody has the right to share his or her faith, and even to try to persuade others of its value. This must be done humbly and in a spirit of inter-religious dialogue. The freedom of the

other can never be crushed. No manipulation through inducements or false arguments is acceptable.

- Some Christians feel it necessary to share their faith and would like others to accept it because they find in it a precious and unique value. Basically that value refers to the memory of Jesus Christ, although it is often accompanied by social and emotional conditioning.

- Other Christians feel no urge to share their faith. They feel that God guides people down various paths, and that they should respect God's ways and not interfere. These Christians tend to feel that each religion has its own value and that these values cannot be compared, although we may learn many things from one another.

- Most Christians still think that as a body they and their Church are sent to the world to continue the mission of Jesus. But this mission is often reinterpreted in terms of spreading the message of Jesus about the kingdom of God for this world, a kingdom of justice, equality, love, forgiveness, freedom, respect for one another and friendship. Thus their role and the mission of their Churches is to contribute to the achievement of these ideals in dialogue and cooperation with other believers and with people without religious affiliation but imbued with the same spirit. The mission is a call to dialogue and common action in favour of the higher ideals of humanity.

- Many think that in this common endeavour and mission that belongs to all, different religious traditions can bring values that inspire and give guidance to the common enterprise.

- The official position of mainstream churches is rather inclusive. They affirm the right of individuals to personal conversion, including, if they think this is their call, a change of religious affiliation. They also reaffirm the duty of Christians to engage in mission work. This mission involves all aspects of salvation, beginning with the construction of a world of justice, equality and fraternity. It also includes the announcement that Jesus Christ is the means by which the fullness of divine life reaches us. They stand by the New Testament understanding of Jesus Christ as Saviour of the world.

Indian Christians share in the full spectrum of positions on conversion. Since, however, they have a long experience of living peacefully in a pluralistic society, they tend to stress the importance of dialogue and the promotion of just and harmonious living. Communities that have lived in greater isolation from others, like the tribal communities, tend to identify more easily with evangelistic positions.

6

The Third Spring:
The Protestant Communities

History and nature of Protestantism ~ Protestantism in India ~ South India: B. Ziegenbalg and companions ~ North India: Serampore with W. Carey and companions ~ Earlier Christians in North India ~ Establishment of Christian and governmental educational institutions ~ A. Duff and his influence ~ Some famous converts of the nineteenth century ~ Upadhyay ~ Church organization ~ The Ecumenical Movement and its successes in India, especially in the formation of the CSI and the CNI

Protestantism, one of the main forms of the Western Church, was originally a reaction against the ways in which the popes of Rome exercised their authority during the Middle Ages and the Renaissance, especially in respect to northern Europe. The figure who embodied the earlier protest and gave it a definitive doctrinal and social shape is Martin Luther (1483–1546). Born into a pious Christian family in eastern Germany, he took his master's degree in humanities in 1505, and gave up an offer to study law to enter the Black Cloister, a rather strict monastery in the Augustinian tradition. In 1507 Martin received the order of the priesthood and was soon sent to teach theology at Wittenberg; in 1512 he received a doctorate in theology and was assigned to teach Scripture.

Luther was a person of deep spirituality and strong inner conflicts. He had a terrifying sense of the demands of God on the human creature, and was conscious of the power of sin in life. He searched in vain for inner peace in many old practices of the Christian religion. Reflecting on the teaching of the New Testament in the monastery tower, probably in 1512, he received an illumination that transformed his life: the 'justice' of God of which the Bible speaks is not a condemning justice but—unlike human justice—is totally beneficent and liberating. The inner peace Luther had sought for so long could not be the product of his own work or personal efforts to become just (holy, perfect), but could only come as a gift from God. The inner liberation ('justification') had to be received gratefully, not achieved. The great slogan of the Protestant Reformation was born: *Sola fides*, or 'Justification only by faith, not by works'.

Few people have had such an influence on the Christian Church as Luther. His new insight, articulated in powerful writings, galvanized much of the sentiment of central and north European Christians. They were tired of a religious teaching that seemed obsessed with what people had to do to counteract the terrible power of sin in their lives and the lives of those dear to them, especially those who had died: penances, fasts, prayers, pilgrimages, alms to the poor or to the Church. Luther's new interpretation seemed life-giving, a better reflection of the message of the Gospel. It also freed them from a papal authority that was felt as overbearing and economically oppressive; for decades the popes had made constant demands of money to build or rebuild the great churches of Rome.

An 'indulgence' was a remission of punishment due for one's sins. It was granted by the Church authority in God's name, taking into consideration the good actions performed by the penitent sinner, or the alms given for worthy causes. In a culture strongly marked by the fear of the 'God of Justice' indulgences were psychologically very important. Moreover, the strong medieval sense of human solidarity led to the practice of 'applying' the indulgences one had gained to other people, especially the loved ones who had departed from this life; for, the 'souls' of the dead (particularly remembered on All Souls' Day, 2 November) were thought to be in need of purification through suffering ('fire') before they could enter heaven. The stage of purification between death and entry into heaven was called 'Purgatory'. The Pope and bishops were considered authorized to announce how much 'indulgence' was linked to specific purificatory works, and to issue written certificates testifying to the indulgences gained, for instance, for financial contributions to church building. Naturally this led to a shocking 'sale of indulgences'.

It was the Dominican friar John Tetzel's fiery sermons insisting on the purchase of indulgences that incensed Luther to the point of drafting his famous Ninety-five Theses, which, according to legend, he nailed on the door of the church of Wittenberg. These points challenged the whole medieval Catholic system. Luther gave primacy to the authority of the Word of God, as found in the Scriptures, over human authority within the Church. Thus began what is known in Christian history as the 'Reformation'. Luther also stressed the primacy of the individual, so that the 'we' of the earlier tradition became the 'I' of the reformed Christian. Every Christian has the spirit of God, and is able to read and interpret God's word written in the Bible as it applies to his or her life. Luther protested the imposition of Roman ways on the whole Church, and rejected the authority of the Pope over the councils—thus opening the way for national and local churches.

Luther's protest was successful in central and northern Europe, from which it spread to England and later to North America and the other northern European colonies. Protestantism gave a new face to the Christian tradition. The stress was on personal faith and personal responsibility rather than the saving power of the Church or its sacraments. In his famous thesis *The Protestant Ethic and the Spirit of Capitalism*, sociologist Max Weber reflected on two paradoxical phenomena: that ascetic monastic institutions produced much material wealth, and ascetic Protestant sects were also noted for their economic success, especially in the early phase of industrial capitalism. For Weber, the doctrine of predestination characteristic of the Calvinist brand of Protestantism produced an anxiety about one's future salvation, as one had no control over it. He thought the pastoral response of preachers to this anxiety was to explain that the world is the place where God calls on us to be responsible—with the implication that success in work and frugality in life can be the reassuring sign of divine predestination. Whatever the value of Weber's thesis, it is a fact that industrial capitalism emerged largely at the times and in the places where Protestantism was strongest.

Protestantism stressed a central role for the laity in the Church. It denounced religious orders as not in conformity with the Gospel, and they were abolished in Protestant countries. Luther himself married at the age of forty-two Katherina von Bora, sixteen years his junior. She had been kept in a convent from the age of five, took vows at sixteen, and left the convent in 1523, when she was twenty-five. Two years later, in 1525, she married Luther and they had six children, four of whom survived them. (They also raised eleven orphaned children, a venture that caused them much economic hardship.) The Protestant world therefore has no monks or nuns, although in recent years there have been modest attempts in some churches, including in India, to revive some forms of monastic life, which is seen as a source of spiritual empowerment for the community.

Protestantism has given rise to a great number and variety of churches all over the world. The central and northern European churches generally adhere to the strict Lutheran tradition, while in Switzerland, France and Holland the Calvinist tradition prevails. John Calvin (1509–64) was a French theologian who during his stay in Paris was attracted to the work of Luther and the ideas of the newly emerging humanism. Eventually he retired to Geneva, where he tried to establish a rather rigid and severe theocracy. From the time of Henry VIII the 'reformers' in England followed a middle path between Lutheranism and Calvinism and between Protestantism and Catholicism. They prefer to be called Anglicans. In India they became important streams within the united churches called the Church of South India (1947) and the Church of North India (1970). They also had much influence in the formation of the Mar Thoma Church, adding a strong Anglican flavour to the earliest St Thomas Christian tradition.

Over the centuries many reformed churches gave rise to movements of more radical reform, at times in the form of Puritanism, and from them new churches emerged. In general they tended to object to those traditions of the old Church still followed by the churches of the Reformation. Those who rejected bishops were termed Presbyterians. They attempted new forms of Church organization based on the democratic principle and organized around 'presbyteries' composed of ministers and elders. In the United Kingdom the Methodist and the Baptist churches arose; both were termed non-conformist because they did not accept the structures and doctrines of the officially established national church, the Church of England. Both Methodists and Baptists have an important presence in India.

It is important to distinguish between the mainstream Protestant churches and new religious movements that call themselves Protestant but jettison much more of the ancient Christian tradition than traditional Protestantism does. By its rejection of any authority for its teaching and practice other than the Bible, the Protestant tradition finds it difficult to maintain the basic identity of each church, and hence more and more churches are formed. Some of those that emerged in the twentieth century come under the general title of Pentecostal churches, based heavily on personal experience and private inspiration. In general they are rather small revivalist groups with strong mutual support and great trust in their inspiration, and they proselytize vigorously. Some of their activities and attitudes are at variance with those of the mainstream Protestant, Catholic and Orthodox churches. They tended to be closed to dialogue with other religions and are concerned with individual experience and salvation and group cohesion rather than with the problems of society in general, although in recent years one detects an awakening to social concern. They often have strong financial support, especially from groups in North America.

PROTESTANTISM IN INDIA

In the first century of its existence, Protestantism showed little concern with sharing the Gospel with other people. The Reformers' problem was to establish themselves in the Western world, then dominated by the Roman Catholic Church. Only by the end of the seventeenth century did Anglicans begin to think about their duty to spread the Christian faith and form missionary associations like the Society for Promoting Christian Knowledge (SPCK) in 1698 and the Society for the Propagation of the Gospel (SPG) in 1701. Probably the first Protestant to come to India was the deeply religious Sir Thomas Roe (1581–1644), who came as ambassador from Britain to the court of the great Mughals between 1615 and 1618. He asked as chaplain for himself the Reverend John Hall, a quiet and humble Oxford graduate 'of an unspotted life' as Roe described him (Neill 1984, 365). Hall thus became the first Anglican priest in India. But he died soon after his arrival in Surat. He was succeeded by the Reverend Edward Terry, a good observer who wrote his impressions after his two and a half year stay.

Indian Protestantism began in the eighteenth century, more than 200 years after the arrival of the Portuguese on the coast of Malabar. In the seventeenth century the European sea mercantile enterprise grew considerably. After the Portuguese the following nations came and established temporary settlements in Tamil Nadu: the Dutch in Pazhaverkadu in 1609, the British in Masulipatam in 1622, the Danes in Tarangambadi in 1620 and the French in Pondicherry in 1674. The English East India Company had been founded as a private company for the sake of trade in 1600, the Dutch East India Company in 1602 and the French in 1664. None of the settlements in the seventeenth century had missionary intentions, although the Dutch were strongly anti-Catholic not only because of their Protestant allegiance but because they were fighting against the control of their country by the Spanish crown.

It was only the king of Denmark who, like the earlier Portuguese king, saw his adventure in India as a missionary enterprise incumbent on him as a Christian. For this purpose he hired the services of two young German pastors. In the early eighteenth century the Danish East India Company entered into competition with the Portuguese and Dutch traders who were then governing the seas to the eastern world. A ship of the Danish company took possession of a little port in Tarangambadi, south of Madras, known to Christian history in India as Tranquebar. There began properly the Protestant missionary presence in India. The first missionaries to arrive there, on 9 July 1706, were Bartholomew Ziegenbalg and Henry Pluetschau. They were not very welcome by the authorities of the station but managed to establish themselves and begin learning languages. At the time the common language in trading stations along the Indian coast was Portuguese, so they learned both Tamil and Portuguese.

The first Indians to accept their Christian message were the domestic workers and local helpers and some orphans the missionaries collected for a Tamil and Portuguese school they started. As soon as Ziegenbalg, a quick learner, could speak Tamil he began sessions of religious dialogue with the local population. A foreigner who spoke Tamil on religious matters was a novelty and attracted attention. Soon a little congregation of nine Tamil converts was formed and they were baptized in September 1707. One of the notable early Tamils to embrace the Protestant faith was Kanabadi Vathiar, the son of Ziegenbalg's munshi, who helped the missionaries in their translation work and eventually composed in Tamil a versified version of the 'catechism', a primer of Christian doctrine in question–answer form, and of the Gospel stories which were sung by the children with great delight. Like many other converts, he too had to undergo a fair amount of persecution. The following year he became a Roman Catholic and eventually he returned to Hinduism.

We owe to Ziegenbalg among other things the first Indian translation of the Bible: the Tamil Bible, published in 1714 (Second Testament) and 1728 (First Testament, in cooperation with B. Schultze).

The work of the German missionaries under the auspices of the Danish king faced many difficulties, financial and others. From England the SPCK supported the German work and sent financial help and a press to print their pamphlets and eventually the Bible. The new missionaries benefited from the presence of Roman Catholics, some of whom they converted to their form of Christianity especially by appealing to the Bible. Conversions across denominations were frequent. The work of the Protestants spread to other places of European presence in South India. It went largely to the areas where Roman Catholics were already established. An outstanding Adi Dravida early convert from Roman Catholicism was Rajanaiken, a petty officer in the army of the raja of Thanjavur. He left the army and became a very successful catechist (teacher of religion). One of his disciples was Sattianaden, who was a catechist at Tarangambadi. The first Tamil Protestant to be ordained a pastor (the common Protestant word for 'priest'), in 1733, was Aaron, the son of a Hindu merchant, who had been working as a teacher of religion with the missionaries. The Protestant churches in Thanjavur, Mayavaram, Cuddalore and Ramanathapuram owe much to Aaron. Eight years later a companion of his, Diogo, from a Roman Catholic family, was also ordained and ministered in the villages around

Thanjavur. The number of Indian pastors increased to fourteen in the Tarangambadi mission.

SERAMPORE

Krishna Pal was a simple worker of the carpenter caste in Srirampur (which the foreigners called Serampore), thirteen miles from Calcutta, up the Hooghly river, at that time an impressive town of English gentlemen and ladies. But Krishna had little to do with them. His work was to make low tables for scholars, doors and windows for the fast-growing housing industry and repair all types of wooden objects which townspeople had used for centuries. It was the year 1800 and the sahebs had made a great fuss about the change of the century, a point that made little sense to the thirty-six-year-old carpenter or his family, accustomed as they were to a different calendar. He consulted his guru, Malpara Gosain of the Bhoja sect, who gave no importance to the calendar concerns of the foreigners. His own Bengali panchang marked the current year as san 1207, but he knew that his Bihari neighbours were in the samvat year 1858!

Coming home from a working assignment one evening, he crossed the bazaar and saw three foreigners, Reverend William Ward and two companions, Dr Thomas and Mr Brundson, speaking publicly in hardly intelligible Bengali about Jesus Christ and how he obtains for us forgiveness of sins. Krishna listened, more taken up by the strange Bengali of the foreigners than by the message he hardly understood. After the sermon the street preacher asked the audience where the Brahmin school was. Nobody knew, except Krishna Pal, who may have done some repair work there. 'It is at Balpur,' he said. 'Can I go there and come back in one hour?' Krishna smiled and said, 'No.'

That short conversation was the beginning of a friendship. When days later he dislocated an arm Krishna was taken to the new dispensary, and there Dr Thomas treated him. The theme of the early sermons came back: Jesus could save us from sin. This was something Krishna had not heard from his guru, although he had bathed in the Ganga many a time to get rid of his sins. The friendship deepened and Krishna Pal decided to take the bold step: he would be baptized and thus become a disciple of Jesus. Arrangements were made for a public baptism in the Hooghly before Christmas, in the presence of the Governor and a large gathering. The occasion was worth celebrating, for after their arrival in Bengal's Madnabati five and a half years earlier, and in spite of their intense study of the language, the Baptist Protestants had seen no results of their evangelical work. Now, in Serampore, a town under the control of Danish merchants, at last an Indian was accepting Christ. A few weeks later Krishna Pal's wife and sister-in-law and a neighbouring family were also baptized. Thus began Protestant Christianity in Bengal.

Thus began also the famous mission in Serampore, where even today the Serampore College continues the work started by William Carey (1761–1834). Carey was an unlikely leader. Though born an Anglican, he had been attracted to the Baptist tradition, taught himself geography and European languages, and became a country pastor, supplementing his humble salary by working as a cobbler. He taught himself theology and became a preacher and linguist. He realized that although we depend on God for everything, human responsibility is not thereby taken away. His slogan was 'Expect great things from God and attempt everything for God.' Mission became his passion and he organized what was later known as the Baptist Missionary Society. At the age of thirty-two he sailed with his family but without travel documents from Dover in England to colonial Calcutta and found work on an indigo plantation.

In 1799 he moved with two young recently arrived British colleagues, Joshua Marshman and William Ward, to Serampore. He collected a number of pandits specialized in Indian languages and initiated the translation of the Bible into dozens of Indian and other Asian languages. Carey himself was responsible for the translations into Bengali and Sanskrit. He even became a professor of Bengali and Sanskrit in William Fort College in Calcutta. 'He died a humble patriarch and has been highly revered by generations of Bengalis for his contributions to their culture' (Anderson 1998, 115).

Carey's establishment turned into a college and was eventually given a university charter by the then king of Denmark. At present the secular subjects of the university are affiliated to the University of Calcutta, while the theological section continues to confer degrees not only to its own students of theology but to students at most of India's Protestant theological centres.

Of course Krishna Pal and his family were not the first Christians in North India. Christians from the St Thomas tradition must have travelled north for various reasons. There were the Armenians, mentioned in chapter five; there were diplomats and many foreign traders and adventurers. There were also Catholic communities in Bengal and Orissa, specially Hooghly, Chittagong, Balasore, Calcutta (the last was destined to grow in importance) and Chandernagore as a result of foreign mission work as we saw earlier. These small communities had embraced the faith preached by Portuguese and French missionaries who acted primarily as chaplains of the trading communities settled in those towns but often took personal initiatives for preaching the Gospel. The invasion of Shah Jahan, no friend of the Portuguese, in 1632 was a tragedy for the Christian community of Hooghly. Four thousand of them were taken prisoner and brought to Agra, where the women were taken to various harems and the men forcibly circumcised. Many embraced Islam though some later came back to their Christian faith.

Thekkedath (1982, 442–43) says, 'The majority of the Christians in north India consisted of Indian converts. The greater part of them were of Hindu origin, but there were also converted Muslims among them, specially in the early days . . . The bulk of the converts were persons of humble birth . . . mostly servants of Armenians and Europeans, or also embroiderers and the like. But there were also some persons of importance among them.' Although spread in many towns of the empire, the number of Christians was small, counted in the hundreds. In times of persecution some Christians abandoned their faith in favour of the official religion, but most were steadfast even to a heroic degree.

EDUCATION AND FAMOUS INDIAN PROTESTANTS

If the first form of Indian Protestantism emerged in the eighteenth century out of the contacts of South India with Continental Europe's Protestantism, in the nineteenth North India responded to the presence of the British Protestant tradition with a new form of

Christian faith. Though originally it came from the non-conformist tradition, the political evolution of India in that century ensured a characteristic form of Indian Protestantism more attuned to the Anglican tradition. The impact of this faith on the national scene would come in large part through the great educational institutions the British developed in India. Interestingly, the inspiration for the new era can be traced to what has been called the Renaissance of Hinduism, which originated in Bengal but soon spread in various forms all over India. The movement introduced a fascinating new India, no longer an isolated civilization of high calibre but a cosmopolitan and pluralistic culture wherein all humanistic voices of the world could find an echo. The father of this new India was undoubtedly the great Raja Ram Mohan Roy (1772 [or 74]–1833), a prophetic symbol of a new emergent India. He was a polyglot who learned Bengali in his village of Radhanagar, Persian and Arabic in Patna, Sanskrit in Varanasi, English from his friend John Digby, and Latin, Greek and Hebrew from another friend William Adam, not to mention a bit of French. Such was the robust founder of the new India that was to produce extraordinary people like Mahatma Gandhi, Motilal and Jawaharlal Nehru, Rabindranath Tagore, Ramakrishnna Paramahamsa, Swami Vivekananda, Sarvapalli Radhakrishnan, Jagdish Chandra Bose and many other luminaries of the nineteenth and twentieth centuries.

The early-nineteenth-century debate between those proposing only English education (in the style of Macaulay) and those advocating only traditional education (like William Jones) was eventually solved by adopting an educational model that presented modern thought both in the local languages and in English, though in the early stages the main medium was the Indian languages. The programme tried to harmonize and keep the best of both traditions. Early efforts at presenting exclusively Western education (represented by Calcutta's Hindu College) proved unsatisfactory: it produced men (and eventually women) who delighted in a destructive criticism of the old Hinduism akin to that of some missionaries, but had no cultural roots and no sense of the spiritual values.

Christians in India could not be satisfied with such 'intelligent animals'. Like many Hindus and Muslims, they realized that this education could not give India a credible identity. They gradually developed an educational model that was open to the world of the new science but also kept the deeper values of civilization. One of the great leaders of this educational policy was the Scottish missionary Alexander Duff (1806–78). He 'not only revolutionized Christian propaganda making it a force among educated Indians, but also invigorated public life in every department' (*Indian Christians* 1928, 3–4). He was convinced that any religious or social change in India required a high standard of intellectual education, and this is what he set up to offer with the help of his friend Raja Ram Mohan Roy.

Prominent high-caste people responded to the intellectual challenges offered by Duff and accepted the Christian faith. One of them was Krishna Mohan Banerjea (1813–85). As a young man Krishna came under the influence of the brilliant Anglo-Indian poet H.L.V. Derozio (1809–31), a revolutionary and aggressive agnostic. Banerjea began editing the *Enquirer*, a journal of criticism of Hinduism published by liberal young people. Friends of his seem to have indulged in some disgusting acts in his house. This provoked the ire of his relatives who asked Krishna 'to recant his errors and proclaim his belief in the Hindu faith or else to instantly leave his house and be forever denuded of all the privileges and immunities of caste' (ibid., 6). Krishna chose the latter and in the middle of the night left his house and went to a relative's.

At this stage he came into contact with the young Duff, who proposed to him and other young reformers to test the evidence and doctrines of Christianity. Krishna and some friends were convinced, and were baptized in 1832. This conversion caused a minor sensation in Calcutta society. The friends who sought baptism were Mohesh Chander Ghose, A.C. Mazumdar and Gopinath Nandi, all of whom left a mark in the Christian church. In 1836 Krishna became the first Indian to be ordained into the Anglican Church, and was made a pastor of the newly built Christ Church in Calcutta while he continued his work as a teacher. In 1852 he became a professor in Bishop's College, where he remained until his retirement. In this capacity he contributed to the organization of the Calcutta University started in 1857 and became a member of its Senate.

As a member of the W.W. Hunter Education Commission of 1882, he tried to fight the university's 'neutrality with a vengeance', in which all religions came under attack and atheism or secularism had become the most powerful influence. Krishna Mohan has been considered the father of Bengali Christian literature and may be called one of the founders of Indian Christian theology. His best-known contributions in this field are *Dialogues on the Hindu Philosophy* (first published in 1861), *The Proper Place of Oriental Literature in Indian Collegiate Education* (1868), *The Aryan Witness* (1875) with *Two Essays as Supplements to the Aryan Witness* (1880) and *Relation between Christianity and Hinduism* (1881). Many of his other writings (Philip 1982, 126–28 lists forty-two of them) dealt with education and culture, including the *Encyclopedia Bengalensis* in 13 volumes (1846-47) and editions with notes on the *Kumara Sambhava, Raghuvamsa, Vedanta Brahma Sutras, Bhattikavya, Purana Samgraha,* and two adhyayas of the first ashtaka of the *Rigveda Samhita*.

Another convert of Duff's free school was of humbler origin, Lal Bihari Day (or De) (1824–94), son of a bill collector of the Sabarna Vanik caste. After his father's death he continued his education and was baptized in 1843. Eventually he married a Parsi Christian lady from Gujarat, Miss Bachubai Hormadzi Pestonji, and the two of them had nine children. 'In embracing Christianity he registered the low-caste Hindu's revolt against the tyranny of the upper castes' (Sen 1972–74, 1: 409). In the Church he fought for equal treatment of the Indian priests with missionaries, an equality that was generally denied at least at the level of salaries. He supported the socially progressive views of his time like remarriage of widows, female education and Bengali as the medium of instruction. He tried unsuccessfully to organize the 'National Church of Bengal', edited one of the myriad Bengali journals of the time, the fortnightly *Arunodaya,* and contributed much to the English *Bengal Magazine*. In 1872 he wrote *Bengal Peasant Life,* later elaborated into the classic work *Govinda Samanta*. Charles Darwin, among others, was charmed by Day's vivid description of rural Bengal. His love for the life of the peasant makes his work an outstanding piece in the literature of nineteenth-century India.

The temperamental Madhusudan Datta (1824–73) is a well-known litterateur born of well-placed Kayastha parents in Jessore District of Bengal, now in Bangladesh. His father was a successful pleader in the Calcutta court. In college Madhusudan distinguished himself by his knowledge of English literature, especially Shakespeare. He also studied Homer and Virgil in Greek and Latin and later learned Italian and French; still later in life he learned Sanskrit. In Calcutta he came under the influence of Krishna Mohan Banerjea and at the age of sixteen he decided to embrace Christianity and prefix the name Michael to his personal and family name. During this period he passed through a stage of total rejection of anything Indian, including his mother tongue. He went to Madras in search of a job and remained there for eight years writing in journals and helping in their editing. He became famous as a poet in English. Eventually he returned to Calcutta and found work as a translator and continued to write English but now also Bengali poetry. His drama *Sarmistha* in five acts (1859) drew its theme from the Mahabharata and resembled a classical Sanskrit drama, but breathed the spirit of contemporary humanism. Eventually he went to England to study law and for some time lived with his wife in Versailles, France. Returning to Calcutta, he was called to the Bar but was not successful and lived in straightened circumstances.

> Madhusudan was a child of the Bengali Renaissance in the truest sense of the term. He imbibed within him deep respect for classical studies both eastern and western, a spirit of revolt against orthodoxy, sympathy for progressive social changes like remarriage of widows, female education, etc., and [eventually] love for his vernacular and his mother land . . . Madhusudan was born a rebel and died a rebel' (Sen 1972–74, 1: 394).

Yet another caste convert of the nineteenth century was Kalicharan Banerji (1847–1907), of whom Mahatma Gandhi (1958–94, 48: 15) wrote twenty-four years after his death, 'I have not had the privilege of knowing a purer Indian, [who] was also thoroughly identified with the Congress.' He was actually the Indian Christian whom Gandhi went to consult 'as a seeker' in 1901 in fulfilment of a promise he had made to his South African Christian friends that he would continue his inquiry about the Christian faith. Although Kalicharan did not convince the Mahatma on the Christian credentials, Gandhiji gave several fine testimonies to the human and spiritual qualities of the man. 'His simplicity, his humility, his courage, his truthfulness, all these things I have all along admired' (ibid., 27: 435). He also praised the simplicity of his 'un-Europeanized Hindu' Bengali dhoti and shirt and the simple and scarce furniture of his home. Banerji gave an example of a self-sacrificing life, for he was one of the brilliant lawyers who placed not only his legal ability at the disposal of his countrymen, but also his riches, said Gandhi in 1907, the year Kalicharan died (ibid., 6: 480).

Kalicharan too was under the influence of Duff and had been baptized in 1864, aged seventeen, facing strong family opposition. He became a successful lawyer and a patriot, and soon threw himself into political activism in the company of Ananda Mohan Bose and Rash Behari Ghose. He became a member of the Indian National Congress from its very foundation in 1875 and in the third session of the Congress in 1887 he was appointed to the thirty-five-member committee charged with the duty of considering the constitution and working of the Congress. He often moved progressive resolutions in sessions of the Congress and was elevated to the Legislative Council in 1897 as he could be 'a representative of all communities' and not just the Christian community. Education was one of his main concerns. After his death a memorial seat of stone masonry was dedicated to him in Beadon Square, Calcutta, with this inscription: 'This seat has been erected by the Christian friends and admirers of Kalicharan Banerji, to perpetuate the memory of one who by his high character, great qualities of head and heart, became a prominent leader in all movements intended to further the spiritual and social welfare of his country and whose teaching testified to the truth and power of Christianity' (*Indian Christians* 1928, 185).

It was Monday, 23 September 1907. The city of Calcutta was already preparing for its annual puja holidays in honour of Durga's defeat of the demon Mahishasura. But in its high court there was an air of expectancy. The police force had been deployed in strength. The Chief Presidency Magistrate, D.H. Kingsford, was about to arrive and open the case of sedition against the forty-six-year-old

editor of the extremely popular and radical evening daily *Sandhya*.
He was known as Brahmabandhab Upadhyay and he had faced
this magistrate at least twice, once for failing to notify the change
of place of publication of his daily, the other for defamation of a
Mr Malcolm Robert. 'Mr' Upadhyay was a persona non grata. In
fact Majumdar (1962–63, 1: 63, 2: 87) makes him to be then, with
Bipin Chandra Pal and Suresh Chandra Mukherji, the 'new leaders'
of the Swadeshi movement, especially after Surendranath Banerjea
(1848–1925), a very influential leader, had disappointed the radicals
in the movement by his recommendation of 'patience'. In July 1907
the police had started a campaign of repression against newspapers.
In August 1907 *Sandhya* had published an article in its racy Bengali
entitled 'This time we are caught in the meshes of love'. The article
said plainly, 'Our aim is that India may be free, that the stranger
may be driven from our homes, that the continuity of the learning,
the civilization and the system of the Rishis may be preserved.'
Upadhyay, the author, was by faith a Christian, a Roman Catholic.
By culture he was a Hindu.

After the arrival of the magistrate the court sat and the
preliminaries were gone through. But the accused was kept standing
from 10 a.m. to 4 p.m. The Indian Christian, in plain Bengali dress
and wearing his Brahmin thread, was facing the foreign Christian
in judicial robes. This time Goliath would defeat David—in the
eyes of profane history. Chittaranjan Das, counsel for the defence,
rose and begged permission to read a statement written by his client.
In it Upadhyay accepted the full responsibility for the authorship
and publication of the article. He then continued:

> But I do not want to take any part in this trial because I do
> not believe that in carrying out my humble share in the
> God-appointed mission of Svaraj, I am in any way
> accountable to the alien people who happen to rule over us
> and whose interest is and must necessarily be in the way of
> our true national development.

The magistrate was taken aback. Upadhyay was not begging for
independence. He was denying the very legitimacy of the British
establishment in India. He was telling the judge that he had no

moral or legal authority to judge him. In fact, Kingsford would not convict him this time, for the trial was delayed: Upadhyay was operated upon for a hernia in the government hospital and died of tetanus on Sunday, 27 October 1907.

Such was the untimely end of a brilliant orator, journalist, philosopher, religious seeker and above all one of the great patriots India has seen. Upadhyay had been named Bhavani Charan Banerjea at birth, and was a nephew of Kalicharan, but it does not seem that his uncle had any significant influence in his conversion. Rather it was the Brahmo Samaj spiritual leader Keshub Chandra Sen who inspired his early interest in Jesus Christ. Additional conviction came from reading a solid treatise on the Christian faith which he began while keeping a vigil at his father's deathbed in Multan, Sindh. It was the popular work of Joseph Faa di Bruno, *Catholic Belief or a Short and Simple Exposition of Catholic Doctrine*. The fifth edition published in 1884 was over 400 pages long. This work may have inclined Upadhyay to embrace the Catholic rather than the Protestant form of Christianity, in this an exception, one must say, among the famous converts of the nineteenth-century.

Another outstanding Bengali Christian owed his faith to the influence of Alexander Duff, Sushil Kumar Rudra (1861–1925), who became the first Indian principal of the prestigious St Stephen's College in Delhi. Unlike those mentioned above, he was born in a Christian family in so far as his father had been baptized by Duff a year before Sushil's birth and his mother the year of his birth. His father, Pyari Mohun Rudra, belonged to 'an old-established land-owning family in Bengal' (O'Connor 1990, 43). After graduating from Calcutta University he went to Punjab and in 1886 was appointed to the staff of St Stephen's in Delhi where he became a very close friend of his colleague C.F. Andrews, who was ten years his senior. In 1908 he was appointed the principal and he proved to an unbelieving British aristocracy that an Indian could lead a group of English dons with serenity and authority. While he was principal the college reached one of its highest peaks as an educational institution in North India, and supported the national cause represented by Mahatma Gandhi. The Mahatma revered him as a 'silent servant' and enjoyed his hospitality in his early visits to Delhi. But once Gandhi declared satyagraha against the Rowlatt Act, he was reluctant to stay with Rudra, fearing it might compromise Rudra's position and expose his college to unnecessary risk. To Gandhi's offer to stay elsewhere, Rudra said, 'My religion is deeper than people may imagine. Some of my opinions are vital parts of my being. They are formed after deep and prolonged prayer. They are known to my English friends. I cannot possibly be misunderstood by keeping you under my roof as an honoured friend and guest. And if ever I have to make a choice between losing what influence I may have among Englishmen and losing you, I know what I would choose. You cannot leave me.' When Gandhi still offered resistance, he continued, 'I like it all. I like the friends who come to see you. It gives me pleasure to think that in keeping you with me, I am doing some little service to my country' (ibid., 27: 350–51).

Not all nineteenth-century converts to Protestantism were Bengalis. One of the most renowned was a Maharashtrian pandit in Varanasi, Nilakantha Goreh (1825–95). He was born in a village near Jhansi, where his father had migrated, but one year after his birth the family moved to Varanasi, where they lived in affluence thanks to an uncle who had become diwan of the state. He was educated in the best traditions of Sanskrit learning—the Vedas, Nyaya and Vyakarana—innocent of English education, thinking of Christianity as a primitive religion fit only for the uncouth English. He even dared to write a refutation of Christianity. But the reading of the Bible, especially the Sermon on the Mount, and discussions with missionaries finally convinced him of the truth to be found in it. Yet he would not for a time receive baptism out of deference for his father and relatives who begged him not to take the step. He began however to defend Christianity in public debates with fellow pandits of Varanasi, described in his book *Dwij* ('Twice-born', an adjective normally applied to Brahmins and even to all caste Hindus, but which to the Christian mind meant 'born again' in Christ). Finally on 14 March 1848, he went to the mission centre in Jaunpur and received baptism. He wrote the same day to a friend in Varanasi, 'Through the goodness of God I arrived here safely on Monday and today, Mangal ("Tuesday", but meaning also "gladness"), I was admitted by baptism into the Church of Christ a little after eight o'clock in the morning.' In 1870 he was ordained priest (Paradkar 1969, 1–5).

Among others, Goreh inspired a fellow Maharashtrian Chitpavan Brahmin to accept the Christian faith. Her name was Ramabai Dongre Medhavi, better known to history as Pandita Ramabai Saraswati (1858–1922). Daughter of a wandering reciter of sacred texts of Hinduism, she had learned thousands of shlokas by heart. She was born in South Kannada into a very poor family, and her life was one of deprivation and suffering. She saw her father and mother die of starvation. She however continued the wandering life of her father, reciting shlokas from the epics and Puranas in many places in North India, from Kashmir to Calcutta. In Calcutta she met the powerful groups of reformers of Hinduism and joined the Brahmo Samaj. Its leader Keshub Chandra Sen recommended to her to study the Vedas which she had not done till then, out of deference for the strong orthodox opposition to women studying the *Sruti* (revealed text). In Calcutta Ramabai received the greatest public recognition, the titles 'Pandita' and 'Saraswati' being bestowed on her as an acknowledgement of her learning—a rare distinction indeed at a time when women were not supposed to learn Sanskrit (in spite of the memories of Gargi and Maitreyi inscribed in the heart of the Vedic literature). Ramabai involved herself in the reform movement and agreed to a 'pratiloma' civil marriage, that is, marriage to a man of a lower caste, Bipin Behari Medhavi, who was a Sudra and friend of her brother, Srinivas.

Tragedy struck once again; her brother died of a sudden illness in Bengal, and her husband soon after, within less than two years of marriage, leaving her alone, with a baby daughter, Manorama. Again defying tradition, the widow did not withdraw to private domesticity. She involved herself in the defence of the rights of women, especially widows and even widows of the higher castes. She was experiencing personally the way in which traditional society treated them. The fruit of her experience was her first book in English, *High-Caste Hindu Women*, published in 1887. She travelled to England with the help of some Christian friends to learn English and obtain help for her programmes. Before departing she publicly declared in Pandharpur that she had no intention of becoming a Christian. However the experience of Christian women in Britain who were concerned about and respectful of the so-called 'fallen women' and a prolonged reflection on the writings of Goreh made her change her mind. She was baptized in 1883 in the Anglican Community of St Mary the Virgin in Wantage. She spent three years in the United States, where she received promises of help for her work in India. Returning to the western coast of India she started an institution in Mumbai for the education of young widows. She never officially joined any established Church but was consistently a disciple of Jesus Christ and tried to spread his message, while she criticized foreign missionaries for their lack of understanding of Hinduism.

Another Chitpavan Brahmin to find his way to Protestant Christianity in the nineteenth century was Narayan Vaman Tilak (c. 1862–1919), a distant relative of the more famous nationalist Bal Gangadhar (Lokmanya) Tilak. Like others, he too became an 'intellectual convert' as a result of his reading the Bible and seeking for a 'universal religion'. He was baptized in February 1895 but insisted it should be by an Indian pastor rather than a European or American. Echoes of 'Swaraj is my birthright', made popular by his famous relative, resounded in his message and life. Narayan is mostly remembered for his contribution to Marathi Christian poetry so much so that in the Marathi hymnal of the 1950s out of a total of almost 700 hymns 254 came from the pen of N.V. Tilak. They are still sung, especially in Protestant churches of Maharashtra. In the 1940s he underwent another 'conversion of the heart' and gave away much of his money and possessions. His wife, Lakshmibai, originally Manubai Gokhale, was in despair when Narayan converted and tried with all her might to dissuade him, and even attempted suicide several times. For some time they separated but kept up a correspondence mostly in chaste Marathi poetry. Slowly her anger dissipated and the barriers that separated them crumbled down. She was baptized in 1900 and wrote her autobiography in Marathi (*Smriti Chitre*), eventually translated into English as *I Follow After* (1950) and abridged as *From Brahma to Christ* (1956).

Professor Ramchandra (1821–80) was born in Panipat, near Delhi, in a Hindu Kaeth family. Moved by the faith and devotion of some of his close European friends, he converted in 1852. He entered service as a teacher in the English Government School of Delhi, which eventually became a college. A distinguished mathematician, he wrote books which rediscovered the values of ancient Indian science. For about ten years he was in Patiala as teacher of the prince and servant of the state.

From Patiala came Maulvi Imad-ud-din (1830–1900), a lineal descendant of the well-known Saint Qutub Jamal of the ancient royal house of Persia, famous champion of Islam. Like Professor Ramchandra, he does not seem to have been drawn into the Christian faith by direct contact with missionaries, but came to it as a result of a long search. As a Muslim he had taken part in famous debates held in Agra by missionaries of the Basel Mission Society. The missionaries had first worked in Georgia and had composed three works in Persian. Expelled from Georgia, they came to India and settled in Agra. There they republished their booklets, both in Persian and in Urdu. The publication gave rise to strong reactions among the maulvis of Lucknow, Agra and Delhi, and eventually public disputations were held in Agra, in a peaceful atmosphere of mutual respect, but also of strong faith convictions. Both sides considered they had scored in the discussions. Imad-ud-din had attended these debates. They had him thinking for years about the new faith offered by the missionaries. The conversion of Moulvi Safdar Ali of Jabalpur offered him an occasion to study the New Testament earnestly and he was convinced of the truth of Christianity and received baptism in Amritsar in 1866. He received the priestly order in 1872 and became one of the leading clergymen of his diocese. In 1884 the Archbishop of Canterbury conferred on him the degree of doctor of divinity. He wrote extensively in Urdu and in English, about thirty books, among them a book soon after his baptism, addressed to his former fellow maulvis, entitled *Tahqiq-ul-Iman* (The Investigation of the Faith), partly autobiographical. He also wrote commentaries on the Gospels of Matthew and John and the Book of Acts.

Of similar interest and connected with the conversion of Imad-ud-din was the baptism on Christmas Day 1864 of Qazi Maulvi Sayyad Safdar Ali (c.1830–99), reputedly a descendant of the Prophet, coming from a family of Qazis in the state of Dholpur (in present-day Rajasthan). Like Imad-ud-din he participated as a Muslim in the Agra debates. He had been a searcher for God along the lines of Sufism and was a man of refined spirituality. He has left interesting accounts of the path of his discovery of the Christian faith, and in this he was helped by Nehemiah Goreh, the convert pandit from Varanasi. Brahmin and Sufi discussed their new faith and helped one another to grow in it. After his conversion, Safdar Ali continued in government service and wrote extensively.

This short survey shows that especially in the nineteenth century the Protestant churches attracted a number of intellectuals and high-caste people. They found a special attraction for the person of Jesus and decided to become his followers, often in the face of strong opposition. These were generally individual conversions which at most extended to the family members and descendants of the converts. There were no mass conversions, although some had personal influence on others. However, the spread of the churches was not confined to intellectuals. We shall see in subsequent chapters that the poor too were attracted by the life of the Christians and flocked to the church in groups.

CHURCH ORGANIZATION IN INDIA

As they separated from the medieval Catholic Church, the various Protestant churches tended to organize themselves into national churches, each with particular theological orientations. In this they followed a pattern similar to the Orthodox churches. The national churches tended to continue the structures and ways of operating of the old church, including the use of authority. They also tended to keep close links with the civil authorities. This development within the Protestant ethos naturally provoked movements of protest—'Non-Conformist' or 'Free Churches', which declared an independent existence, generally under the inspiration of spiritual and charismatic leaders. In England these churches included Presbyterians, Baptists, Congregationalists, Methodists and Quakers, all of which have adherents in India.

The older churches—the Orthodox, Roman Catholic and Anglican churches—are Episcopalian, that is, they are ruled by bishops, under whom priests (or presbyters or elders) and deacons (servants) work. In India the Church of South India, the Church of North India, the Lutheran and the Methodist churches are Episcopalian. The Presbyterians do not have bishops and are ruled by bodies or synods where ordained ministers (priests) and laypeople participate. They tend to be theologically Calvinist, with stress on hearing the Word of God. Finally Congregationalist churches want each local congregation to be autonomous and independent, though this does not exclude unions or assemblies of the same tradition. Such are the Baptists Union, the United Church of Christ and the Disciples of Christ. There is a strong democratic sense in this Church organization.

By its tradition of a personal interpretation of the Bible and a general suspicion if not rejection of Church authority, Protestantism tends to divide. The twentieth century saw many new churches in India, especially with the inrush of what are called the Pentecostal churches. These churches stress an emotional experience of God's Spirit, develop a close sense of community and rely on the Bible as the only source of authority. They often organize mammoth rallies addressed by well-trained orators and not rarely appeal to the audience to make an immediate declaration of faith in Jesus and experience 'salvation'. Such 'conversions' tend to be temporary emotional decisions rather than a well-reflected surrender to God manifested in Jesus. Such rallies and other activities are often subsidized from abroad, especially by conservative churches of the US. They have a pessimistic view of the world and of other religions and call on their followers to seek salvation *from* the world rather than salvation *of* the world. They tend to have little concern for public morality and social justice, as individual salvation is their main focus. They also have a very strict moral and pseudo-moral code of conduct in matters of smoking, drinking, sex relations, blood transfusion and violence. There are many such new Christian churches, each one generally small.

The multiplicity of churches in India (and in the world) is felt as both richness and tragedy in so far as they frustrate the desire of Jesus that his disciples 'would be one' (Jn 17:11), as he and the Father were one. Some see division as an obstacle to the main role of the Church, which is to give witness to the good news revealed by Jesus Christ. Hence there have been in the Christian tradition constant attempts, often unsuccessful, to bring together the churches that have separated. This effort is called the ecumenical movement (a word derived from the Greek *oikomene* meaning the whole 'inhabited earth'). An effective worldwide ecumenical movement emerged first in the Protestant world with the World Missionary Conference in Edinburgh, 1910. But it was only in 1948, after the Second World War, that the World Council of Churches (WCC) was established with headquarters in Geneva.

In India the ecumenical movement proper began in 1914 with the establishment of the National Missionary Council of India, to which in course of time other all-India Christian agencies (besides the churches) were associated. In 1923 the council reconstituted itself as the National Christian Council of India, Burma and Ceylon. After independence of each of these nations they formed their own national councils. The National Christian Council of India was renamed the National Council of Churches in India (NCCI) in 1979. Its headquarters are in Nagpur.

Indian ecumenism scored in other fronts. There have been a number of unions of churches in the course of the last century. The two most important unions were the Church of South India (CSI) formed in 1947 out of a fusion of the Anglican, Presbyterian, Congregational and (British) Methodist churches, and the Church of North India (CNI) formed in 1970 out of an ecumenical agreement of the Anglicans, some Baptists of North India, the Church of the Brethren of India, Disciples of Christ, British Methodists (in North India) and the United Church of North India. In 2004 the CSI, CNI and the Mar Thoma Church formally constituted a 'Communion of Churches of India' (CCI) as a common expression of a shared life and witness of Christian faith. Some people hope to one day see a United Church of Bharat or India.

The Mar Thoma Church is another case of ecumenism. It is an independent reformed Eastern Church. As mentioned earlier, it arose in the nineteenth century after the Anglican Church had worked in Kerala among the St Thomas Christians. Some of these Christians were impressed by the theological and devotional tradition of Anglicanism and decided to accept some principles of the Reformation. Abraham Malpan (1796–1845), a priest, translated the Syrian liturgy into Malayalam and thus began to celebrate the sacred rites in the language people understood. He also modified the liturgy to conform to the traditions of the reformers, but kept his spiritual roots in the tradition of St Thomas. Thus this Church shares both the St Thomas and the reformed traditions.

It is natural that churches that belong to the same tradition would somehow unite into wider fellowships or associations of churches. Thus there is an Evangelical Fellowship of India bringing together the more charismatic and new churches. There are Councils of Baptist churches in various regions, and the United Evangelical Lutheran church of India. All the larger and older Protestant and Orthodox churches and many of the smaller churches are members of the National Council of Churches. The Roman Catholic Church is not a member of the National Council but in many matters works in coordination with it. The following may help place the main churches in India in their context.

Christian Churches in India

- **The Orthodox churches**
  These are the churches that derive from the ancient tradition of the St Thomas Christians. The first two are in union with the Pope and belong therefore to the Catholic Church. The others are more directly linked with the churches of West Asia. They are:
  - The Syro-Malabar Church (Catholic)
  - The Syro-Malankara Church (Catholic)
  - The Malankara Syrian Orthodox Church (often called 'Jacobite')
  - The Malankara Orthodox Syrian Church (often called 'Orthodox')
  - The Chaldean Church of the East
  - The Thoziyur Independent Church
- **The Roman Catholic Church**
  Besides the Syro-Malabar and the Syro-Malankara, it includes the 'Latin' Church that arose after the preaching of missionaries from the West and accepts the role of the Pope of Rome as a sign of unity and the highest form of ecclesiastical authority.
- **The Mar Thoma Church**
- **The United Church of South India (CSI)**
- **The United Church of North India (CNI)**
- **The Methodist Church of India**

- **The Lutheran churches**
  - The Indian Evangelical Lutheran Church
  - The Tamil Evangelical Lutheran Church
  - The Arcot Lutheran Church
  - The Andhra Evangelical Lutheran Church
  - The South Andhra Lutheran Church
  - The Evangelical Lutheran Church of Madhya Pradesh
  - The Gossner Evangelical Lutheran Church
  - The North-West Gossner Evangelical Lutheran Church
  - The Northern Evangelical Lutheran Church
  - The Jeyapore Evangelical Lutheran Church
- **The Baptist churches**
  - The Council of Baptist Churches of North-East India
  - The Bengal-Orissa-Bihar Baptist Convention
  - The Council of Baptist Churches of Northern Circars
  - The Baptist Church of North India
  - The Samavesam Telugu Baptist Churches
  - Two or three other clusters of Baptist churches not affiliated to the NCCI
- **The Evangelical churches**
  Pentecostals, Brethren, Seventh Day Adventists, Assemblies of God, Mennonite Churches, the Hindustan Covenant Church, the Salvation Army, etc. Many of them are affiliated to the Evangelical Fellowship of India.

7

The Fourth Spring:
Dalit Christians of North India

Dalits come to the centre of Indian consciousness ~ Dalits in the early Indian church ~ The nineteenth–twentieth century spread of Christianity among Dalits ~ Examples of Dalit movements of conversion ~ Analysis of Dalit conversion movements ~ The predominance of the poor in the church ~ Caste in the Indian church ~ The Dalit Christian protest ~ Political discrimination against Dalit Christians ~ Reservations ~ The burning question of Dalit and tribal conversions ~ The anti-conversion debate ~ Dalit Christian Theology

There have been Dalit Christians in India since very old times. We do not know for certain if the St Thomas Christians had in the earliest times believers from the outcastes or low castes; possibly only rarely. But the later Catholic converts did include a good number of Dalits, especially in Tamil Nadu, and the Protestant churches too attracted them in large numbers. In early colonial times various castes were more or less integrated into one Christian community. The de Nobili method resulted in a number of Brahmins and other high castes of South India becoming Christians, although we do not know how many. Other followers of Jesus at the time came from either the middle or the lower castes, the majority probably from the latter. From the seventeenth century the community was also divided by caste, by rite and by denomination.

In the twentieth century the Dalits came to occupy a central place in the attention of students of the Indian reality. The earlier Orientalists, one must say, concerned with the normative texts of Indian society, showed little interest in them. The British administrators tended to see India as a conglomerate of village republics and of castes, as classified in gazetteers and censuses. They tended to seek a common origin of all Dalits and to restrict their occupation to those few classified in the texts. The reality was far more complex. Evangelists, more in contact with the villages, were aware of the consequences of the caste system on the lives of the outcastes in society. They were the principal agents of a new consciousness arising among the Dalits.

Modern writers on the conversion movements to other religions tend to see Dalits as victims of society, without a spiritual tradition of their own. According to them, Dalits just accepted the religions of those who came to them with money or power or more education; presumably Dalits could only have converted through bribes or force or deceit. Again the reality is far more complex. Recent studies on the origin of various Dalit Christian communities show that very often the movement to Christianity was initiated by the Dalits themselves. They were not passive victims, but agents of a liberation movement.

The movement among the Chuhras in Punjab started in the 1870s with a small-made, illiterate man of about thirty, who traded in hides in his village Shahabdike. We know him by one name only, Ditt. He heard of the missionaries and their new religion from the son of a Jat village headman, and in 1873 took the initiative of going to the headquarters of the United Presbyterian Mission in Sialkot and asked to be baptized. The padris agreed reluctantly and he went back to his village, where there was no mission or missionaries. Three months later he came again to Sialkot, now with his wife, daughter and two neighbours, asking for them to be baptized too. Six months later four neighbours joined, and one of them became an associate of Ditt in his evangelistic work in Shahabdike. And so the movement grew and spread (Webster 1992, 46 ff).

About the same period or a little earlier a similar movement took place among the Madigas in the vicinity of Ongole in Andhra Pradesh. It started with a certain Verramgunthla Periah, leather worker and agricultural labourer. He had joined a local religious movement of reform and was even initiated into Raja Yoga by a caste Hindu, subsequently becoming a teacher of yoga. He heard of the Christian faith from a relative while on a trip to buy hides.

He became interested in what his cousin had said and decided to go and meet the missionary in Ellore. The missionary convinced him. In March 1866 he and his wife were baptized into the Baptist Church and for some ten years the Raja Yoga Dalit guru became also the Christian guru and preached his new-found faith. Eventually the movement became organized into a Church. One must note that twenty years earlier there had been a similar movement into the Anglican and Methodists churches in Andhra among the Mala community, which had not attracted the Madigas. Conversion movements followed along caste lines, even when the missionaries, especially the Protestants, vigorously opposed the caste mentality.

The group from whom English and other European languages borrowed the word 'pariah' as a designation of all outcastes is the Parayars of South India. The name derives from the Tamil word *parai*, drum. The Parayars were originally 'hereditary drummers' hired for the rituals of the higher castes, although they also had less noble caste obligations. It must be remembered that the traditional drums consisted of one or two skins of animals at the end(s) of a cylinder and that the skin of dead animals was considered impure. Hence the social need of drum music for festivals could only be fulfilled by people of an 'impure' caste. Some Dalit Christians especially in South India have now adopted the 'humiliating' drum as a basic symbol of their faith, and see Christ, whom the Bible calls the Word of God, as the drum of the divine and saving presence in the world (cf. Clarke 1998).

It was a member of this group, in the subcaste of the Valluvars, who on 31 July 1626 went to meet the new foreign swami who had appeared in the temple city of Madurai and went by the name Tattvabodhakar, better known in history as Roberto de Nobili. The Parayar asked to be informed about the new religion and eventually to be accepted in the Church. This was not at all within the plans of the Roman nobleman, who had decided precisely to concentrate his activity on the higher castes, in the belief, right or wrong but shared by later missionaries, that if the higher castes received the Christian faith it would percolate to the whole Hindu society. Seeing the sincerity of the Parayar, de Nobili decided to instruct him. He was baptized a few months later with the Tamil name of Muttudayan.

Two or three centuries after de Nobili members of the Parayar castes requested many other churches for admission. Many found their way to the Christian communities of the Church of Scotland, the Methodists, the Reformed Church, the Anglicans and the Salvation Army. Detailed studies show that it was not so much that missionaries sought the outcastes; rather, in the nineteenth and early twentieth centuries a new social situation had been created by the colonial presence. New possibilities of employment in trade and the army challenged the stable structures of village life and brought in more mobility and new opportunities. There was also a considerable spread of education, to which the older churches and the colonial government contributed. Even before the colonial culture had spread, and even before the British came, many panths of the bhakti movement in North India had challenged the Brahminic structures. Now among other new possibilities there was the chance of joining one of the many new churches present in the continent. It is not strange that a number of people suffering under the caste system would opt out of it in favour of the churches which offered a new teaching and a protective community atmosphere.

A similar story comes from Bihar of the twentieth century (see Prakash 2000, 117–52). Sixteen men of the Ravidas caste in village Ondha decided to become Christians and asked a distant relative who was employed in the work of the mission to send a priest to the village for instruction and eventual baptism. They were landless agricultural labourers, most of them in the employment of the upper-caste Bhumihars. When the priest visited them a few weeks later they all expressed a desire to be baptized. As per custom, instruction in the faith took a substantial amount of time, but as they did not waver in their determination the priest arranged for their baptism and incorporation into the Christian community on 27 May, five days before Pentecost Sunday, which is the day Christians celebrate the beginning of the church as described in the Bible (Acts 2). On that day about thirty or forty men of the Bhumihar and Kurmi castes appeared in the village, lathis in hand. Sensing a threat to their lives and their families, four of the sixteen fled the place before the baptism ritual started. The other twelve stood their ground and asked the priest to proceed with the service. From then on, this church has lived on, growing in strength in Barbigha and surrounding areas.

Analysing the reasons for their decision, Prakash makes the following points:

- Caste and feudal oppression had a cumulative effect, culminating in the search for emancipation among the Dalits.
- There were increasing opportunities for upward mobility for the Dalits; they had only to grasp them.
- The spread of education sharpened the general awareness of the injustice of the situation.
- Conversion to Christianity widened the horizons of the world Dalits.
- Conversion is a form of social protest (ibid., 146–48).

Were there religious factors underlying the decision of Dalits to join Christian churches? Undoubtedly the missionaries made a serious effort at education in the faith, as they explained the teachings of the new sacred book, the Bible. They taught the neophytes to read its powerful message for personal profit. There was also a new experience of a common worship of God the Father and the attractive figure of Jesus, whose fate was not so different from that of the Dalits. Besides the message of the missionaries and catechists, there was the experience of being a community of faith. The celebration of the Eucharist, the partaking of the same bread and cup, recalling vividly the memory of Jesus, the sense of belonging to the Lord, all were factors that went deeply into the consciousness of these people. A new world, which brought a fresh outlook to their religious beliefs and practices, was open to them.

It is not possible here to describe the emergence and the growth of each community of Dalit Christians. Many Dalits are obviously part of multi-caste Christian communities. In villages many remain in exclusively or mostly Dalit communities, although forming part of a wider Church. From the sixteenth to the eighteenth centuries Dalits embraced the Christian faith mostly in South India: present-day Tamil Nadu, Kerala, Andhra Pradesh and Karnataka. From the nineteenth century onwards, under the spur of the Protestant and Catholic movements, they emerged in Punjab, the Gangetic plain, Madhya Pradesh, Rajasthan, Gujarat, Maharashtra and a few in Orissa although there the tribal movement seemed stronger. We are not aware of reliable statistics on the proportion of Dalits proper (that is, not including tribals) in the various churches and regions of India, although the general belief is that, together with the tribals, they are a clear majority of the total Christian population.

Some of these new Christian communities belong to more fundamentalist and radical new churches or sects. Others are part of the mainstream Protestant churches or the Catholic Church. The churches generally make an effort to provide these new disciples of Jesus Christ, brothers and sisters of the older communities, facilities for growth at the various levels, including religious instruction and assistance, educational facilities, health services and human development opportunities.

However in their own localities the Dalit Christians are a tiny minority when compared with the large number of Hindus, Dalits or others, and of Muslims and Sikhs. Dalit Christians may tend to live in autonomous communities with little interaction with other Dalits. A number of them, though not all, have profited considerably from the educational and social structures that the churches provide. They are sustained in their minority status by a new sense of human dignity which their faith brings, the strength derived from the common reading and explanation of the Bible and by participation in the Lord's Supper, and by a sense of belonging to a larger community that at least theoretically acknowledges them as equal brothers and sisters. Moreover, the practice of the Christian faith frees them from a number of other traditional practices in which they were often economically exploited by religious figures of doubtful authenticity.

In spite of the etymological meaning of the word, rarely is the conversion of these groups to the Christian faith an instantaneous and radical break with the past. There are generally years of preparation before an individual, a family or a group is accepted as a full and baptized member of the Christian community. Often enough, the break with the past is not, nor need be, a radical abandonment of the entire previous religious tradition. Dalits, like other converts, often seem to belong to two religious traditions simultaneously, although the ongoing Christian teaching will help them abandon practices or traditions which are at odds with the Christian message. At the same time a synthesis of the old perceptions and the new faith may also slowly emerge, a truly new Christian way of life. Individuals as well as groups grow very gradually, and the divisions and definitions on paper do not apply so neatly to reality. The leaders of the Christian community are faced here with the task of sifting what is valuable from what should be discarded.

Webster (1992) distinguishes three moments in the history of Dalit conversions. First comes the initiative taken by one or a group to inquire and join one of the churches. Then begins a movement as a result of the first conversions. After this the churches enter into contact with the villages concerned and organize the new Christians into local churches, find local leadership and incorporate them into the larger community. We may add that most movements reach a saturation point after which expansion slows down or stops, and internal organization and development of the community become the main concerns.

Regarding the motivation for the individual or family or group to embrace a new religion, Webster (1992, 57) says, 'There now appears to be scholarly consensus that the underlying motivation was the search for improved social status, for a greater sense of personal dignity and self-respect, for freedom from bondage and oppressive owners.' Missionaries were no opportunists, says Webster, pointing out that they were reluctant to baptize in time of famine. Neither did they have enough resources that would make a drastic change in the living standards of the Dalits who approached them. 'Moreover, the persecution which Dalits faced upon conversion involved not only physical violence but also economic deprivation. The epithet "Rice Christian" thus flies in the face of the facts Dalits had to confront' (ibid.).

One must be cautious about the expression 'mass movements', made popular by the Texan J.W. Pickett (1933). There hardly seems to be any evidence of an organized movement whereby a great number of people led perhaps by some eminent personalities would be converted in one celebration, as happened with the conversions of Dalits to Buddhism in 1956. Many of the Dalit conversions to Christianity occurred in limited areas over a few dozen years, normally along caste and family lines, and responding to a generally felt desire for a change in the social situation. Though the presence and influence of missionaries at some early point in the period cannot be ignored, the main agents were local 'catechists' and recognized leaders of the community.

CASTE IN THE INDIAN CHURCH

There is in many Christian communities in India a strong tension between the caste tradition and the ethos of the biblical faith. It is well known that, like many reform movements within other religions, the Christian faith rejects the division of believers into higher and lower, pure and impure. It wants to be a community of equals. The earliest expression of this egalitarian ethos comes from St Paul in a letter to Christians in Galatia, where some were acting as if the Christian community was two-layered: the higher one being made out of those of Jewish descent, the lower one of Christians coming from the 'pagan' world. Paul attacks furiously the 'foolish Galatians' for tolerating such attitudes. He reminds them of the picture of the rejected man: 'It was before your eyes that Jesus Christ was publicly exhibited as crucified!'—crucifixion having been for the Jews the sign not only of impurity but of divine curse! Jesus crucified was the starting point of the Christian faith! 'As many of you as were baptized into Christ have clothed yourselves with Christ. There is no longer Jew or Greek, there is no longer slave or free, there is no longer male and female, for all of you are one in Christ Jesus. And if you belong to Christ, then you are Abraham's offspring, heirs according to the promise' (Gal 3).

Of course there are and there have always been offices within the Church, as we saw in chapter four. There are even lifelong offices, or ordained ministries. But on principle there are no castes, for offices do not make one a higher Christian, and there are no inherited privileges. An office is a call to serve the community in a specific function, which may involve authority to a higher or lesser degree. But it may be conferred to any deserving member on whom the community has trust and it is not tied to the so-called purity of blood or racial considerations. On principle there is no place for caste within the Christian community, for caste goes against the equality of all believers.

Yet it happens with Christians, as with other religious groups in India, that the caste mentality has slipped into the community and has been kept alive, in some places more than in others. At the beginning of the colonial mission, the second spring, missionaries admitted indiscriminately into the community people from any origin, ignoring the sociological reality of caste. Although the Christian ethos did bring about a new sense of equality, the old mentality was not abolished. Whatever the doctrine in the Church, Christians of higher castes would not mingle socially with those of the lower strata.

de Nobili soon perceived that the cultural strength of Indian society derived in great part from the wisdom it had created in the sacred books and their commentaries and the social institutions it had established for itself. His effort was to learn from this wisdom. He realized that the people to whom his brother priests were ministering in coastal Tamil Nadu came from the middle and lower castes, including outcastes. He also saw that, given the prevailing mentality, as long as missionaries were in contact with outcastes, the Brahmins and other high-caste members would neither communicate with him nor be attracted to the Church.

He interpreted the caste system of India as a social institution, not primarily a religious one. He thought it could be tolerated in the Church, with the expectation that the Christian faith would slowly exorcize the caste mentality from the community, if not from the whole country. He advocated a policy of cultural adaptation and acceptance of caste signs like the sacred thread, the kudumi, the various forms of ornamentation of the body, dietary prescriptions and other such 'social' customs. His submission was that if the Church had lived in Europe with the old stratification of aristocrats, burghers and plebeians, it could also tolerate in India the caste system until it would drop by itself by the impact of the Christian faith. He did not deny the equality of all before the Lord, but permitted either separate churches or separate places in the church, and even in cemeteries, for different castes. Lower-caste Christians, if in the same church, were also expected to approach the sacrament after the high castes had done so.

It is for this 'defence' (or tolerance) of caste that present-day Dalit Christians mostly blame de Nobili. They think that he is responsible for introducing the spirit of caste in the Church, a spirit that denies Jesus' original egalitarianism.

But the complaint is not just about the past. There is in today's Dalit Christian writing a bitter indictment against the Church not only for tolerating clearly discriminatory practices of the past but even more for practising a hidden caste discrimination within the Church. This is especially perceptible in the choice of members of the higher Church leadership. For example, from about the 150 bishops at present in the Catholic Church in India one can count on one's fingers those of Dalit origin, though the majority of Indian Christians appear to originate from this stratum. (By contrast, there are easily over a score of bishops of tribal origin.) Similarly in the recruitment of priests and in the appointment to leadership roles in religious congregations Dalits feel that they are not sufficiently noticed and chosen. Such feeling gave rise to many protests in the 1990s in the Catholic and other churches. Whatever the objective foundation of this feeling and the reasons for such apparent policy, there is bitterness among Indian Christians about the situation.

Through the nineteenth and twentieth centuries Christian groups discussed the question of how to tackle the caste mentality. Some churches tolerated it. Others opposed it vehemently as totally alien to the Christian spirit. The topic was a frequent point of debate in the meetings of missionaries. Indian Christians were generally comfortable in keeping the traditions of their castes that permitted them social exchange with their own former co-religionists. At any rate, the expansion of the churches, even in those churches which most opposed the caste spirit, took place along caste and clan connections. It is only late in the twentieth century that the Dalit movement, with Dalit Christians in it, provided a strong Indian protest to the caste factor in the Church. Today no Indian Christian thinker would approve or even speak of tolerating the caste reality. There are many, however, who live in it.

Christian Dalits handle their past in two different ways. One consists in cutting themselves off from their Dalit roots. They see themselves now as 'a new creation', in the language of St Paul, and hence they do not belong any longer to the Dalit community. If possible they even abandon occupations which society has considered as the root of their impurity. They may tend to assume the mentality of the caste people vis-à-vis their former brothers and sisters. They want a clean break with the past, thus creating a deep spiritual and social cleavage between them and their former colleagues.

The other group remains and wants to remain in solidarity with all the Dalits, whatever religion they may profess, and wants to affirm the equal dignity of all and the rights of all Dalits to the positive protection of the Constitution. It is not by denying their sociological roots that they want to transcend the Dalit mentality but by affirming them and claiming for them the positive recognition of society. Some Hindu Dalits have converted to other religions, Buddhism or Islam, as a sign of protest; others affirm their traditional religiosity and say that they belong to a different genre from that of the 'Manuvadi' Hinduism. Dalit Christians have joined in this general protest against the caste mentality and support the upsurge of the Dalit world.

POLITICAL DISCRIMINATION AGAINST DALIT CHRISTIANS

Dalit Christians suffer not only from the social discrimination common to all Dalits in India but also from a discrimination within the Church, open or subtle, as mentioned above. Considering that many had hoped to escape the experience of social opprobrium by joining the Christian Church, their unrest is not only understandable but justified and righteous. Added to this double discrimination, social and Christian, there is a third form, legal or political. One of the great merits of the Indian Constitution is that it allows for compensatory discrimination in favour of Dalits in the form of reservation of jobs in government and other offices, special concessions to obtain educational opportunities and reservation for political representation in the legislative bodies.

The Constitution provided (1) reservation for Dalits and tribals in the Lok Sabha and Legislative Assemblies; (2) reservation of jobs for Dalits, tribals and 'other backward classes' in government services (later interpreted as including promotion); (3) reservation of seats in educational institutions with provision of financial assistance. The Constitution gave the President of India the responsibility of specifying 'the castes, races or tribes which shall for the purposes of the Constitution be deemed to be Scheduled Castes' and allowed Parliament to add or to delete from the President's list. A few months after the establishment of the Indian Republic on 26 January 1950, the President's Constitution (Scheduled Castes) Order No. 19 of 1950 was issued in which the list of the scheduled castes was announced, but it added a note 3 to say that 'Notwithstanding anything contained in paragraph 2, no person who professes a religion different from the Hindu religion shall be deemed to be a member of a Scheduled Caste.' Thus religion was made a criterion for disqualification of people from the policy of protective discrimination. This seemed to be at odds with the spirit of the Constitution, which requires an equal treatment of all religions.

Strangely, in 1956 the Order was amended to make the Sikhs entitled to reservations. In 1990, to 'celebrate' Ambedkar's birth centenary, the Buddhists were also declared entitled to reservations. Dalit Christians have consistently demanded equality in this area, but their demands have fallen on deaf ears, in spite of promises made by several political leaders.

Already in the late 1950s Nehru had replied to a representation made to him, saying that the limitation of protective discrimination for Dalits to only those of the Hindu fold applied only to the question of separate representation, not to other compensatory means outlined in the Constitution (that is, nos. 2 and 3 above). However, in practice this distinction has been ignored by most state governments as it depends on them to determine who falls under the category of Other Backward Classes.

Webster (1992, 141) concludes his fine summary of the legal aspects of this question with the following words:

Thus, while Independence and the 1950 Constitution inaugurated a new era for India and a new stage in the Dalit movement, it is clear that competitive, communal viewpoints, more appropriate to the politics of number than to a secular democracy, were not only carried over into the new era but also allowed to shape the Constitution, its interpretation and implementation. This can be seen in the very different ways in which the Congress and the courts treated 'Hindu' and Christian Dalits. Whereas the former became automatic beneficiaries of compensatory discrimination, the latter were left to fight their way into the many State lists of beneficiaries as members either of a Scheduled Caste or of a Backward Class.

The argument now most used in this debate is that as the Christian doctrine does not recognize the existence of caste, caste does not exist in Christianity. The argument is still alive in the recent debate. Vasudha Dhagamwar (2003) uses it cleverly if only in passing, when she dismisses the expression Christian Dalits as 'an oxymoron if ever there was one, as Christianity does not recognize caste'. She continues the approach of the old administrators: Don't look at the Dalits; look at what the books and censuses say. That they suffer within the Church is for the Church to correct. It is true, indeed, that the Church must repent for its wrong discrimination. But even if the Church did stop discrimination, the fact is that Dalit Christians are not islands. They live in a mixed society that practises a wide and constant discrimination against all Dalits, regardless of religion. Being Dalit does not flow out of a personal religious attitude, but from the surrounding society that 'crushes' (*dalit* means that!) some members because of their birth and assigned fate. The Dalit Christians are demanding that the state be impartial and give to them also the constitutional protection. Otherwise the secular nature of our political life is in practice negated.

All protests by the churches and by the Dalits themselves and all attempts to remove this anti-constitutional discrimination have met with what can only be interpreted as a fixed prejudice against Indian Christians on the part of those responsible for the public policies of the country. Some Dalit Christians think that the official churches have not worked with sufficient vigour to remove this discrimination that deeply affects their lives. All efforts in the matter have so far failed.

THE ANTI-CONVERSION DEBATE

We have already offered in chapter five an explanation of what conversion means from the Christian faith perspective. Here we look at this burning issue with reference to Dalits and tribals. Since the rise of the Hindutva movement from the middle of the twentieth century, particularly vociferous in the last two decades, the most prominent argument reflected in the media is: In recent decades conversions are known to happen only among Dalits and tribals; the only explanation for this is that missionaries or Christian agents exploit their poverty and ignorance to entice them into the Church.

We have seen how fallacious the argument is and that many conversion movements started from Dalits themselves. We have also seen the importance of the desire of the discriminated people for a new social order, a legitimate aspiration. The evolution of the country from the nineteenth century presented numerous new possibilities of upward mobility. It is not strange that some Dalits and tribals should choose change of religion as the road to a fuller human life. Since this point is at the heart of the passionate conversion debate in our country it is necessary to reflect on the question with serenity and objectivity.

Most people in India, Hindus, Christians, Muslims and others, accept on principle the right of every individual to live by the religion he or she chooses, without pressures and interference from others. Most of us live by the religion we have inherited from our family traditions and may be satisfied with what it offers us in terms of social cohesion and spiritual inspiration and help. But we do recognize the right of any adult to change his or her religion, although we may judge that decision is spiritually useful only if the reason for such a change is based on a personal conviction that the religion one embraces is more inspiring than the one left behind. We consider unhealthy, for example, a decision to change religion taken exclusively for the sake of financial advantages. However, we respect the freedom of the individual to make such a decision even if *we* may consider it unwise.

We also respect the decision of some people, either sudden or gradual, to abandon religious beliefs and practices altogether and to take to a secular view of life. Whether such a decision is for the enrichment of the person or for her or his impoverishment depends on one's perception of the value of religion. Our Constitution respects the freedom of the individual to take decisions in matters of religion, subject to the demands of the rights of others and of law and order, and does not impose any specific belief system on anyone.

All religious groups, whether at the family or at wider levels, protect their adherents and try to keep them within their religious communities and dissuade them from abandoning the religion practised, perhaps for centuries, by the family. This too is legitimate provided it respects the ultimate freedom of the adult individual to take decisions in the matter, whatever be the view of the community. There have been practices in all religious groups that violate the freedom of the individual. The Inquisition was a notorious example of this. Modern versions may be found, for instance, if Christian parents threaten to disinherit the son or daughter who abandons their church to either join another church or a different religion. Similar illegitimate family interference is found in most, if not all, religious groups.

In 1965 the Second Vatican Council of the Catholic Church took a firm step in this direction, correcting wrong attitudes of the past when it made a declaration which most people and religious groups today accept as right:

> The Vatican Council declares that the human person has a right to religious freedom. This freedom means that all are to be immune from coercion on the part of individuals or of social groups and of any human power, in such a way that in religious matters no one is to be forced to act against conscience, or is, within just limits, to be hindered from acting in conformity with conscience, whether privately or publicly, whether alone or in association with others . . . This right of the human person to religious freedom must be recognized in the constitutional law governing society in such a way that it becomes a civil right (*Dignitatis humanae*, n. 2).

Indeed our Constitution had already recognized this in 1950 and the UN Declaration of Human Rights has also affirmed this basic tenet of modern life.

However, the problem of conversion is not just a question of human rights. What many people are suspicious of is the activity of religious groups throughout history and in our time to induce others to change their religion. This is nothing new. Every person convinced of something valuable wants to share it with others. Every political leader does it. Philosophers have always propagated their insights. King Janaka, Yajnavalkya, Socrates or the Buddha, all shared something that they found very valuable and were convinced was valuable for all human beings. The same of course is true of Jesus Christ. This is why the Gospels portray him as sending his disciples to go and preach the good news to all nations, inviting them to enter into the new movement through a religious rite of immersion in water called baptism.

We all have a right to share or 'propagate' our religious views, and this is recognized in the Constitution (Art. 25) and forms part of the packet of religious freedom. Of course nobody has the right to use foul means in this activity of sharing one's convictions. Any fraud in this matter, any form of threat or bribery, is wrong and should be punishable. This applies to any area of human activity: whether in business, politics, teaching or sport, any form of threat, bribery or fraud must be denounced and duly punished. Equally punishable should be any activity that uses fraud or force or bribery to *prevent* people from adopting a particular religious view. The right to religious freedom must be protected on all sides.

The Supreme Court has made a distinction between 'propagating' one's religion, a right enshrined in the Constitution (Art. 25), and 'converting', which is deemed to 'impinge on the freedom of conscience' of another, and which the Constitution would not entitle us to. There may be here a misunderstanding of what 'converting' means for Christians. In no way can it limit; rather it broadens the freedom of conscience. Conversion *presupposes* the freedom to accept a particular view. Without it, there is no conversion. In reality nobody converts another: conversion can only be a personal decision, in the making of which only divine grace may be operative in the heart of the convert. Others can at best try to 'convince' by citing their own experience. The right to 'convince'

others is the keystone of all democratic political debate and surely the Constitution will not forbid us this right?

One of the objections Christians have about the 'anti-conversion' laws, officially called Freedom of Religion laws, is that they give government officials authority to issue prior permissions for what is a personal decision and make them judges of whether the decision is made in freedom. It would seem that the converts themselves would be the judges of the case and they could hardly get from an outsider an impartial judgement in a matter of conscience. It is strange that no prior permission is required for transactions in business, politics, teaching, etc. where only an a posteriori denunciation of foul play can legitimately bring about governmental or judicial action. Why is the area of religious freedom singled out for special control?

A number of people think that special legislation on conversion is necessary because they think that organized conversion activity of churches and religious groups is directed mostly at Dalits and tribals, whose educational and economic status makes them more vulnerable to enticement. Such decisions on their part could not come out of inner freedom but out of sheer necessity. This was the argument of Mahatma Gandhi and of many intellectuals today. They ask Christians why they do not concentrate their propagating activity on adults of the higher and educated classes.

This complex question needs unravelling by degrees. First let us quote the instructions of Jesus which seem to address this problem. According to the Gospel accounts, while he was preaching his doctrine about the Rule of God in human society he sent his companions ahead of him to contact the villagers of Palestine and give a preview of his message. But he laid down the conditions of their preaching:

> As you go, proclaim the good news, 'The kingdom of heaven has come near.' Cure the sick, raise the dead, cleanse the lepers, cast out demons. You received without payment; give without payment. Take no gold, or silver, or copper in your belts, no bag for your journey, or two tunics, or sandals, or a staff; for labourers deserve their food (Mt 10:7–10).

This significant instruction has been an inspiration for the best missionary activity of Christian history. In the Middle Ages it was summed up with the words 'To preach in poverty'. In poverty meant, first, a concern for the poor, the sick, the lepers, those made slaves by social or political forces. Jesus went to the extreme of saying that the Rule of God belongs to the poor, and unless one becomes a poor person one cannot enter into the new world he was preaching. 'Becoming poor' may have many dimensions; in many ways it comes close to the ideals of total detachment preached by the Gita and other religious classics. 'Becoming poor' means also to be on the side of the poor, in solidarity with their suffering and their struggles against injustice.

To preach in poverty is also to use means consonant with the economic status of those to whom the Gospel is preached. The purpose of this instruction is precisely to protect the freedom of the poor in their reception of the Gospel: they must not be manipulated into acceptance by the glint of gold or its equivalent in modern culture. The Christian missionary enterprise in India can be blamed for not keeping in line with this instruction of Jesus. Some missionaries seem to have inexhaustible resources and spend lavishly on propaganda. Indeed, this is a temptation for preachers, especially missionaries from rich backgrounds, and for churches, especially the sectarian groups whose only concern is to report success in number of converts. Indian Christians generally have less access to foreign money, and to preach in poverty.

However, the Gospel is not a purely spiritual message that ignores the world of the body, of disease, food and justice. Jesus himself showed a practical concern for the concrete realities of life. He tells the disciples to heal, raise to life, cleanse lepers, etc. This enterprise, if taken seriously, requires money. There is also need to help those forgotten in the economic structures to develop and acquire the skills necessary to cope with modern life. There is need to awaken the sense of human rights and coordinate activities in favour of justice for all, especially the poor. There is need of education. Such activities should of course be open to all the needy, irrespective of their religious affiliation. No Christian hospital can make acceptance of Jesus a precondition for healing. And the same can be said of schools and other means of promoting human well-being. The wealth spent on such activities is money of the poor and for them. It cannot be spent to 'buy conversions', an activity repugnant to any Indian of whatever persuasion. Political parties may or may not buy votes. Christian preachers may not. If they do, they must be blamed.

Neither the teaching of the Gospels nor the practice of the Church has ever meant that the Gospel must be preached *only* to the poor. Jesus himself spoke to people of the upper classes, such as Nicodemus, Zacchaeus and Simon. The Church has announced its message to all. It is, however, a fact of history that while the poorer sections of society have paid attention to that message and received it in joy, the dominant classes were often too concerned with their vested interests to even consider a new doctrine that might threaten them. This happened in ancient Roman society and the experience has been repeated in history.

The poor have discernment. This needs to be affirmed clearly. Some people presume implicitly that the poor are stupid and that they are easily deceived. Gandhiji's famous comparison with the cow is well known. You cannot preach to a cow, he said, sacred and venerable as she is for a Hindu, because the cow has no intelligence to judge religious doctrine. Similarly the Harijans, for all the respect they deserve, cannot grasp the truth of a religion proposed to them (Gandhi 1941, 98–105). While it cannot be denied that there are simple people among them, as also among the affluent, as a whole the society of the uneducated is no less perceptive of authentic values than the society of the learned. Every political party knows that the poor cannot be swayed easily. The leaders among them, the more alert, will raise the voice of warning against any unfair manipulation of their plight. Even if they are not educated, they can discern signs of authenticity in the messages they receive.

It must also be remembered that for many first-generation Christians from the poor classes, the adoption of the Christian way often mean dispossession, rejection, persecution, even death. They are often outlawed by their caste groups and have to grope in the darkness. Eventually they do find support in the new community, but at the much cost.

Some social analysts feel that the movement to make conversions illegal or difficult is motivated by a fear that the lower classes may enter other religious movements because of the upward mobility they offer. New choices, whatever they are, always break the social pattern and the roles assigned by society and culture. The lower classes claim the right to freedom and equality that the Constitution promises them. This frightens the dominant classes, as was evident during the anti-Mandal agitation of the 1990s. They are afraid they will not have a subservient class to support their style of life and they will have to compete with those who until now were their servants.

This raises the question whether the chance of upward social mobility is a valid argument for a change of religion. Isn't social mobility an issue that belongs to the political level? Is it not part of the realm of economic and social structures rather than religious allegiance? This question might be valid if we are able to dissect clearly the political, the social and the religious. But these areas are intimately interlocked. Many Christians find the deepest root of their new social courage precisely in the sense of having been liberated by Jesus from the burden of sin and of the accumulated karma of the past, and in their experience of Jesus as their brother, giving them a new sense of being children of God, created in God's image. They resonate with the modern expression of God's preferential option for the poor, which draws from the Bible, from the stories of liberation brought to slaves and from the wholeness of life accorded to outcast lepers and sinners. This deeper religious consciousness, strengthened by the Eucharist, prayer meetings, sermons, reading of the Bible, hymns and festivals, enters into their liberation struggle even at the political level. Some Christians are convinced that here they have a message valuable for the poor and are not ashamed of it.

It may be important in this sensitive area to make a distinction between the various churches in India. The ancient churches of St Thomas in general did not indulge in spreading their faith to other groups. They were more closely bound to the social and ethnic structures of the country and to the caste system, and they may thereby have missed some of the liberating power of the Gospel, as Badrinath (2000) has claimed. The churches that came in the early period of mercantile colonialism did indulge for some years in unfair practices of discrimination by offering political opportunity to those who opted to convert and oppressing those who did not. This policy did not last and has long been condemned officially and abandoned in practice. That in later centuries the poor found in conversion a source of liberation and social support that they lacked in their earlier social setting is also true, and they suffered for their new freedom.

In the twentieth century we have seen aggressive forms of proselytism, with condemnatory attitudes towards other religions and much use of the media and propaganda leading more to indoctrination than to conversion. These are the activities of what are called Christian 'sects' or new churches. Most mainstream churches distance themselves from these activities. They cannot in any way be blamed for what small but vociferous fundamentalist groups, supported by foreign money, do. They do not agree with it, and at any rate the results are generally marginal and temporary. But their loud propaganda is picked up by the media and it disturbs the general public.

At present the conversion of new Dalit families is practically at a standstill. The few conversion movements that exist are among tribals, about which we shall speak in chapter eight. Whether such minor changes in 'religious demography' should be of concern to politicians is a matter of opinion. Politics should perhaps be concerned not with what people believe or do not believe, but with how people act and contribute to the overall prosperity of the country.

DALIT CHRISTIAN THEOLOGY

One of the most significant movements started in the last decades of the twentieth century is what is known as the Dalit Theology movement among Christians, especially of Tamil Nadu but also in other parts of India. The movement derives from two or three traditions. In India there was the Dalit Panther movement of the 1960s, partly influenced by the Black Panthers of the US, which strengthened the social protest of the Dalits of Maharashtra spearheaded by Jotirao Phule in the nineteenth century and Baba Ambedkar in the twentieth. From the Christian South American world came the Liberation Theology which in many senses protested against and revolutionized the theological thinking and teaching till then prevalent in First World countries. There was also an East Asian version of it, the Minjung Theology developed in Korea, which looked at the situation of the powerless people at the margin of society. These movements met in the EATWOT, the Ecumenical Association of Third World Theologians, founded in Dar es Salaam, Tanzania, in 1976. The movement had a great influence among Indian Christian theologians, as was evident when it celebrated its Third International Conference in New Delhi in 1981.

It was in this cultural atmosphere that Dalit Theology emerged. Its leaders were first from the Protestant churches, men like M. Prabhakar, James Massey, K. Wilson and Arvind Nirmal, and a few Catholics like Maria Arul Raja. Influential theologians of non-Dalit origin also joined in the articulation of Dalit Theology, people like M.M. Thomas and Samuel Rayan. Much institutional support for the movement came from the Madras-based Lutheran College of Theology, the Bangalore-based United Theological College and its neighbour the Christian Institute for the Study of Religion and Society, and the Madurai-based Tamil Nadu Theological Seminary. They have produced a respectable volume of sociological and theological literature which has influenced other countries too.

Basically, Dalit Theology reflects on the Christian message in the context of the experience of the Dalits. It seeks to find the social and religious causes for the poor plight of this community all over the country and proposes to understand the Christian faith as a powerful means whereby this community can overcome this plight and contribute to the welfare of all. Dalit Theology, however, is not a carbon copy of the Liberation Theology of South America or of the Minjung Theology of Korea. Its starting point stresses not just the problem of poverty linked to the means of production (Marx) or the powerlessness of the common people (Minjung) but the denial of basic human dignity to a group of people because of their origin and occupations, which all agree are necessary and beneficial to society. The basic sin it opposes is the idea that the Dalit is ritually, socially and spiritually corrupt and corrupting. Ritual purity being an essential element of the caste system as traditionally lived in the country, Dalit Theology must reject the caste mentality and the caste division of the country. It is along these lines that the Dalit theologians strive to make their fellow citizens aware of the ideological roots of their plight and unite them for a new vision of themselves and society.

8

The Fourth Spring Continues:
Adivasis in the Church

The tribals enter the Church ~ The nature of the tribal reality ~ Their place in the Indian society ~ Chotanagpur Christians ~ How central Indian Christians came to know Christ ~ The early arrival of the Protestant missionaries ~ Lievens and Hoffmann ~ Why many accepted Christianity ~ The Adivasi struggle for land, water, forest protection ~ Human promotion ~ The Chotanagpur Land Tenancy Act ~ The struggles for Jharkhand ~ Chhattisgarh ~ The North-East Christians ~ Their special situation ~ The early contacts, the Protestant Churches among them ~ The late re-entry of the Catholic Church ~ Impact of education and health services ~ The story of Mizoram

We must now tune in to another side of the fourth spring of Christianity in India that occurred in the nineteenth and twentieth centuries: its birth and growth among what we call the Adivasis or aboriginal peoples of India, most of them known in the Constitution as scheduled tribes. Many of them claim that they are the indigenous peoples of India, but the government has so far denied them this title contending that their sociological place in the life of the nation is not isolated and does not correspond to that of indigenous peoples as defined by international conventions. In recent times there has also been an effort on the part of certain ideological sections of the media to change their common designation from *adi-vasis* ('original inhabitants') given to them at least from the 1950s into *van-vasis* ('inhabitants of the forests') or even *girijan* ('people of the mountains') to rhyme with Harijan! The 'tribals' themselves reject these new attempts to define them and are generally satisfied with the designation of Adivasis or even tribals, although

202 Christianity in India

often it is obviously necessary to name individual tribes.

There is no need in this book to explain what the Adivasis represent in India. There seems to be a general consensus that whatever their origins, and they obviously come from different stocks, they represent some of the most ancient roots in India's ethnic soil and constitute about 9 per cent of the total population. Within the country they have often been migrants. In historical times they have been associated with the forest, clearing it for cultivation, living on it, finding in it their cultural and symbolic habitat. Their religiosity has, in various degrees and at various times, been influenced by new movements and the cultures around them. There has been a process of Sanskritization or Hinduization of a number of these tribes. However many have retained their primeval ethos based on a sense of the numinous character of nature, especially the forests, mountains and rivers and a belief that spirits, benevolent and malevolent, inhabit and influence their world. By any standard this religiosity is different from the main trends of the Vedic religion and from the great cults of Shiva and Vishnu and his avatars, which characterize what later came to be known as Hinduism.

In the decades when the British Raj was established in India many tribes were concentrated in the forests of central India, in and around what came to be known as the Chotanagpur plateau. Many others were found in North-East India, beyond and around Bengal. These two groups have produced new and lively Christian communities, first in the area of central India now covered mostly by Jharkhand and Chhattisgarh, and surrounding areas, and then in North-East India. We will treat the two areas separately as they are different in character.

CHOTANAGPUR CHRISTIANS

The remote cause of the birth of local Christianity in what was then called Chotanagpur is to be sought in a minor but significant decision by a woman in faraway Myanmar (then called Burma, part of the British Raj). A missionary couple was serving the tribe of the Karens (in north Burma). The husband, 'a physician of considerable scientific achievement', was murdered by some tribesmen. The widow took 'a merciful revenge' by preaching her faith to those who had murdered her husband and sent a letter to Berlin to the Reverend John Evangelist Gossner, a former Catholic priest who had joined the Protestants and started a mission organization. Gossner interpreted the widow's letter as a call of God to him to send missionaries to Burma and assigned four men for the job, with instructions to first go to Calcutta and then proceed to Burma or, if this was not possible, to Kotgarh in the Himalayan region. Eventually they went to neither.

While the impatient missionaries were waiting in the then capital of British India, Calcutta, they saw a number of Kols from Chotanagpur, distinctively different from the Bengalis both in colour and in psychological attitudes, and decidedly poor. They were attracted to them and accepted an invitation to go to Chotanagpur to minister to them. They arrived in the outskirts of Ranchi in November 1845. They opened primary schools and orphanages in four places but received an indifferent response from the local population. For five years no seekers turned up. Discouraged, they asked permission from Berlin to change their mission field. Permission was denied. Then a breakthrough occurred.

The Adivasis had not been deaf to the preaching of the newcomers. They had listened and kept silent. At night, in their village huts under the light of hurricane lamps, they discussed among themselves the words of the missionaries and their way of life. There was certainly no bribe offered to them, nor was any deceit or fraud perpetrated. One day four Uraons from around Ranchi, Nabin (or Doman) Pore from Hethakota, Bandhu and Kesho from Chitakoni and Guran from Karand, knocked on the door of the mission house. They were tribals but had recently joined the Kabir Panth under the inspiration of a guru named Iccha. They wanted to see Jesus, about whom they had read in a Hindi pamphlet (extracts from the New Testament) that the missionaries had distributed in the bazaar. The missionaries invited them to the evening prayer service of their little community and a few orphans. They found it interesting, but wanted to *see* Jesus. They could not conceive of anyone adopting a new panth without seeing its leader. They went away disappointed, even angry.

One week later they went back to the Ranchi bazaar and

courthouse, and to the missionaries. They joined them in an experience of prayer, in Hindi and in English. Then they understood that the missionaries were not hiding anything from them but that the 'darshan' of Jesus was possible only in faith. They decided to ask for baptism and initiation into the new panth. It still took three months of intensive instruction and inquiries into the new faith, and then on 9 June 1850 the first recorded adult baptism of Indian tribals took place. A new Christian community was born in India. Other Uraons and Mundas would soon follow, and later other tribes, including Kharias, Santhals and Hos. The next century would see one of the most astonishing and rapid growths of a Christian community in history.

The moment was favourable for change. It has been called 'Crisis in Chotanagpur'. Even before the discovery of abundant underground coal and minerals, this fertile portion of India was seen as potentially important. After the defeat in 1765 by the forces of the British East India Company, the Mughal emperor had ceded to the victors the diwanis of Bengal, Bihar and Orissa. Most of Chotanagpur was inhabited by three main tribes who had cleared the forests with their hands, started cultivation there and settled to a form of tribal life based on common ownership of the land and village administration with ancient democratic traditions. The tribes were the Mundas, the Uraons and the Kharias. From old times a raja of Chotanagpur, possibly of Munda descent, had a somewhat supervisory role over the autonomous village administration. When the Mughals imposed their rule in the area, the raja acquired greater authority and the village power diminished. As early as this, the tribals realized that more and more dikkus (outsiders) were entering their territory and claiming property and other rights.

The real disturbance came with the British administration and their misunderstanding of the traditions of the land and the people. The East India Company consisted essentially of traders interested in revenue, and they squeezed all they could from the villages. The British government that followed pursued a similar policy. But they wanted to reform the administration after the pattern of what they knew, the British law, based largely on private property and on documents as the legal basis to claim property. This was not at all how tribal society had functioned. Even the much-acclaimed and

apparently impartial British system of law in practice worked against
the Adivasis, who had had little access to education, could not
understand the language of the courts and to whom receipts and
other documentary evidence had little significance. Not surprisingly,
outsiders saw an opportunity to profit from this situation, the more
so when the British made the zamindars, tax collectors under
Mughal dynasties, the landowners, often with full proprietary rights.

In the confusion of the time a real clash of civilizations was
taking place: on the one hand was the ancient tribal culture that
had produced its own form of democratic administration based on
the consensus of all village adults and on the other was the Mughal
culture with the monarch as the all-important figure and a
widespread administration needed to run an empire. To these two
was added the British system, whose most important doctrine was
that of private ownership of the land as it was known in Britain,
with documentary evidence as legal proof. The tribals realized that
their culture needed updating and that they could not cope with
the new situation without changes. A number of them had accepted
some of the traditions of Hinduism. Some entered movements that
affirmed a third way between the contenders in the subcontinent,
the Muslims and the Hindus. The Kabir Panth was one such
movement of purification of religious ideas and reform. It is not
without significance that the first tribal Christians had adhered to
the Kabir Panth before their conversion to Christianity.

It was only a quarter of a century after the baptism of the first
tribals that Roman Catholic missionaries appeared on the scene of
Chotanagpur, at a time when the Christian movement was already
advanced. Their presence gave a powerful impulse to the movement
in such a way that the so-called Roman Catholic Church became
the predominant presence in the area, without superseding other
churches, Lutheran and Anglican, which had already been in the
region. It is necessary at this moment to mention two foreign-born
missionaries who identified with the problems and the needs of the
tribals and helped enormously in strengthening the Christian
movement. They are Constant Lievens (1856–93) and John Baptist
Hoffmann (1857–1928).

The Belgian Lievens came to Chotanagpur in 1885 and joined
the group of missionaries in their task of teaching the Christian

faith to tribals who were asking for it in increasing numbers. He had learned enough Mundari and Uraon (or Khurukh) to communicate with the people. He and his companions provided elementary educational and health services. Lievens soon saw that the tribals were losing their lands in most of their court cases because they were not trained in legal matters, and that they practically became serfs because of the high rates of interest demanded by moneylenders. His main contribution to the Christian work in the area was the study of the history of land possession and of British law, and his personal defence of the poor in the courts of justice. Amazingly, he was a great legal success and the people came to trust his word and his judgement. He asked them to do the customary services they had rendered and to pay the customary rents but to demand a receipt from the officers for every payment made. In his hands, these receipts became the charter of liberation from much oppression. Naturally the activity of Lievens alienated many of the powerful lobby of moneylenders and even government officials. They denounced his activities as detrimental to the Raj. Strangely, even the Archbishop of Calcutta, Mgr Paul Goethals, under whom he was supposed to serve, considered his work as 'an imprudent, dangerous and money-wasting business' (Tete 1990, 71). He was sent back to Belgium 'to recover his health'; within one year he died at the age of thirty-seven.

Hoffmann was a German who joined the Belgian Jesuits and came to India in 1878. He too was a great organizer but in a different style from Lievens. In 1909 he started the Catholic Cooperative Credit Society (CCCS), the first of its kind in India, popularly known as 'The Catholic Bank'. It is not a commercial bank but a savings society where individual tribals deposited whatever savings they had, receiving a moderate rate of interest, and from which they could make small borrowings for their urgent needs also at moderate rates of interest. The cooperative was run by the tribals themselves, who saw to it that the return of money was done promptly and according to the law. It ran as a parallel organization to the parish and used the parish infrastructure to ensure smooth administration. It was a great success, a means of liberation from the traditional moneylenders and other forms of extortion then prevalent. On 31 March 1998, the CCCS had 62,268 members to whom it had given a total credit of Rs 1,17,69,898 and had total assets and deposits of Rs 13,87,13,672 (Ekka 1999). The poor had found effective friends to help them organize and beat their own problems.

A few years later the 'grain bank' (dhan gola) was added wherein the paddy collected at the time of harvesting was kept for sale during winter when the prices would be more beneficial to the farmers. It also ensured that grain for sowing would be available in the new year.

Hoffmann also worked on the first draft of the Chotanagpur Tenancy Act, which became the law of the land in 1908 and for years regulated the transfer to tribal lands in the area, preventing expropriation of land by non-tribals. Hoffmann helped also in the planning and publication of the *Encyclopedia Mundarica* in 15 volumes (1929–79), which helped the tribal world to recover their cultural identity.

An important factor in the growth of this Christian movement was that the laity soon organized themselves for social and political action. As early as 1898 there was a Christian association for the promotion of education. From 1912 the Chotanagpur Charitable Association tried to raise funds for tribal students. The Chotanagpur Unnati Samaj was started in 1916 and became a feeder to different organizations, culminating in the Adivasi Mahasabha of 1938. Colleges meant specially for the tribal population were started from 1944. The influence of education and of the Christian presence in the Jharkhand movement has been widely acknowledged.

With the passing of the years other tribes in the area joined the movement with greater or lesser enthusiasm. The Santhalis (the biggest tribe in India), the Hos, and other smaller tribes around the Chotanagpur plateau became interested in becoming Christians. In their cultural perception, the 'spirit' of Jesus had proved itself more powerful than the spirits they had been worshipping. The belief in the spirit world was thus a factor in the conversion of many to Christianity. Beyond Jharkhand, similar movements started among the Bhils in Rajasthan and Madhya Pradesh and south Gujarat, and some smaller tribes in Orissa. In South India the spread of Christianity among tribals has been less remarkable, perhaps because of the stronger presence of other older Christian communities. The tribals are today the only sociological group in which one can speak of a movement of conversion, although no longer with the dynamism it had in the late nineteenth and early twentieth centuries. As elsewhere the success of the mission stops its numerical growth and greater interest is taken in matters of internal organization and improvement of the community.

It is not surprising, however, that conversions have taken place among them, because, whether people like it or not, the tribal world *will* convert—either to Hinduism or to Islam or to Christianity or to an ideology like Marxism. Their culture, precious as it is in itself, needs to change if it has to cope with the basic demands of modernity. Malevolent and beneficent spirits have unavoidably been superseded by medicine, science and psychology. It is true that people need to relate to the transcendent even in a secular world; it is true that our relations to our ancestors are important even in modern and postmodern society—why would we otherwise celebrate so many anniversaries and centenaries, erect statues and buildings in honour of famous people and record their biographies? The tribals expressed the need to relate to the past mostly through ancestor worship. Today we need other forms of remembrance. Whatever laws we pass, conversions to alternative views of life will continue among tribals. The only question is in which direction.

We must remember that conversions of tribals is not conversion from Hinduism, but from forms of religiosity that Hinduism has in part assimilated. It is also worth mentioning that the 'outsiders' who supported these movements were hardly ever from nations that had colonial links with India: neither Belgians nor Germans nor Italians are known to have had any colonial designs on this country. They often conflicted with the authorities of the Raj, who were not too happy by the changes education brought to the people they governed.

Education, culture, economic self-sufficiency, health, equality, liberation, all are interdependent values integral to the concept of salvation found in the Bible. These values as proposed and upheld by the new Christian communities in Chotanagpur had a point of reference in the Christian message. Because the tribals heard this biblical message explained in their own languages, because they saw it embodied in the first tribal Christian communities and realized the universal character of the message, and because they saw it socially organized in a number of churches which generally coexisted peacefully, they were attracted to it. Moreover, their society was organized around the tribe, which was not only endogamous but also limited in its contact with outsiders. The tribe influences its members differently from the caste. There was no ritual purity involved, and relations with other groups are easier than in caste society. If in Hinduism conversion appeared a betrayal of the caste, among Adivasis it was not a betrayal of the tribe or the tradition. The tribal bonds were generally kept after conversion. In their society decisions are surely taken in consultation with the group, and public policy runs on the basis of consensus. But for questions of a private character, whether marriage or transactions or religion, there is less rigidity than in the caste system. Conversions do not cause deep consternation.

CHHATTISGARH

News of the success of the Lievens movement spread to fellow tribals living across the Sankh River, in what is now Chhattisgarh. In 1889 a delegation of three people from the Jashpur princely state—Budhu and Goddo from village Kharkona and Raghu from Benjora— undertook on foot an eastward journey of 175 kilometres all the way to Ranchi to ask the Christian missionaries for instruction in the Christian faith and catechists and priests to visit them. The entry of outsiders into the princely state was not permitted. Soon about 600 tribal delegates tried to go to Ranchi, but the feudal rulers thwarted them. In January 1890 forty-four of them managed to meet Father Lievens in Ranchi. The rulers persecuted those who had received instruction in the Christian faith. No priests or catechists were allowed in. This initial move by the people thus received a setback.

In 1905 despite continued opposition from the feudal rulers and the brutal use of police force, a large number of Oraons went over to Jharkhand, received instruction and became Catholics. In the ensuing years many more embraced Christianity and this had its impact on the neighbouring principality of Udaipur. The rulers there too vehemently opposed conversion to Christianity, and forbade missionaries to enter their area. Despite these hurdles many tribals in Udaipur became Christians. The same surge swept over

Surguja, another neighbouring princely state.

One could call Christianity in Chhattisgarh a people's movement, a movement that grew in number and fortitude despite heavy odds against it (or perhaps *because* of this persecution). The initiative to get to know and then to embrace Christianity came from the people. They went in search of missionaries and catechists to instruct them in the new faith. What happened to their fellow tribals living across the border of their states inspired them to take the bold step. It was only after Independence that they could call catechists and priests to their places.

The stiff opposition, however, continued. Even as free citizens of India having the right to profess, practise and propagate their religion, the tribals had to face the opposition of many officials. On 14 April 1954 the Shukla government in Madhya Pradesh appointed a six-member committee under the chairmanship of B.S. Niyogi to inquire into certain allegations and counter-allegations about the Christian missionaries in Raigarh and Surguja districts. Two years later the Niyogi report was released, based largely on hearsay and sometimes false propaganda. (See a rebuttal of the same in Soares 1957.) Though officially this report was shelved on 19 September 1968, the Madhya Pradesh Dharma Swatantra Vidheyak (The Freedom of Religion Bill) was passed. The anti-conversion law was soon made operative, selectively. As a result, the local Catholics and the missionaries had to face legal hurdles. But the flow of the Christian movement in Chhattisgarh continued. Their problems are not over. Trumped-up charges continue to be made against the priests, nuns and laypeople. Sometimes they are imprisoned. But, as elsewhere in the past, a persecuted community has not only survived but has grown.

THE NORTH-EAST CHRISTIANS

One of the facts of modern history that disturbs many Indians, especially in the majority community, is the 'changes in religious demography' that have occurred in the north-eastern states of India over the last two centuries. Popular writers even present the region as 'lost' to Christianity, a Christian world within the mainstream religious culture of India. Here a certain mirage of numbers is at play. It is caused by ignoring the facts about the two most heavily populated states: in Assam with its 22.3 million inhabitants only 3.32 per cent are Christians, and of Manipur's nearly three million, Christians are only 1.68 per cent (well below the national average). While it is true that in three of the seven states, Nagaland, Mizoram and Meghalaya, Christians are a majority, these three states have a total population of less than four million. According to the 1991 Census statistics, about 76 per cent of this population is Christian. Taking the whole of the North-East, Christians are less than one-eighth of the population.

Another popular misunderstanding is that the separatist tendencies in the region are largely due to their Christian allegiance. This is not so. If anything, as a whole the Christian ethos has rather tended to integrate them into the national life. We must remember that the region was not part of any overall Indian political establishment till the British East India Company and eventually the British government took control of it, as a result of the Anglo-Burmese treaty of Yandalo in 1826. Even the Mughals had controlled only a small part of the region, the Assamese valley up to Guwahati or a little beyond. The hills and the rest of the valleys were always autonomous. In fact, the separatist tendencies are felt as much among Christians as among those who have retained their original religions.

The situation of these tribes is very different from that of central India. Ethnically they belong to a large extent to Mongolian racial stock. The hill communities have not been much influenced by the main religious tendencies of Hinduism or Buddhism, not even the bhakti traditions. (In the plains, on the other hand, there is a large mass of Hindus, influenced by tantrism and the Vedantic philosophy of Sankaradeva.) Moreover, the peoples of the North-East have a tradition of violence: some were formerly headhunters. The Christian influence mitigates and controls this tendency. Finally, many of the tribes have a tradition of great autonomy at the village level, with little overall political organization.

There were a few Christian settlements in the North-East in the seventeenth and eighteenth centuries, partly due to the presence of Mughal power that brought with it a number of experts from many quarters, partly due to early Portuguese trade settlements in the area. However, none of these early communities survived for long, and when Protestant missionaries entered the region they could not find any local Christians. Actually the first Christian missionary there was an Indian, Krishna Chandra Pal (1764–1822), the first convert of the Serampore mission. Pal was sent to Pandua, in the kingdom of Cherrapunji, and there in 1813 baptized among others two Khasis, U Duwan and U Anna, and an Assamese. These were probably the first local Christians. However, this venture was not fruitful either, so the Christian movement started in earnest only in the 1820s and 1830s. Meanwhile the Protestants prepared translations of the New Testament into Assamese and Khasi. The opening of schools in the following decades led to a snowballing movement that attracted most of the Khasis and later the Mizos and the Nagas. Two main churches were present in the area. The Baptists of Serampore eventually merged with the new missionaries and formed the Baptist Missionary Society, largely influenced by the American Baptists. They were most successful in Nagaland. In the south, the Welsh Presbyterian Missions worked more successfully with the Mizos and Khasis and formed a very strong local Church. The Roman Catholic Church joined the work later. According to Downs (1992) in 1990, 43 per cent of Christians of the North-East were affiliated to the Baptist tradition, 26 per cent to the Catholic, 23 per cent to the Presbyterian and 8 per cent to other churches. These figures include a high percentage of tribals from the Chotanagpur area who in the nineteenth and twentieth centuries migrated with their families to the newly opened tea plantations in search of employment. They form a considerable proportion of Christians in the Assam valley and they are found in large numbers in the plantations of north Bengal too.

Contemporary missionary literature, not surprisingly, gives us colourful pictures of the sufferings and persecutions the new Christians had to undergo to remain steadfast in their faith. There is no reason to take all this literature as fiction, but one needs to realize that its purpose was to elicit support from the home constituency for the mission work, and it would not be surprising if the historical memories were embellished to suit the need. Thus John Hugues Morris's *The History of the Welsh Calvinistic Methodists' Foreign Mission to the End of the Year 1904*, published in Welsh in 1904 and in English in 1910 (reprinted in 1996 in the NEHU History Series, no. 7), covers sixty-three years of the Presbyterian mission in the Khasi and Jantia hills and Mizoram and recounts the dramatic story of the earliest converts. Ka Nabon, for instance, was withdrawn from the Cherra Christian school as soon as she expressed her desire to become a Christian. She was kidnapped, taken prisoner, threatened with death by her mother and surrounded by mobs angry at the idea of her becoming a Christian. Questioned by a government official, she replied amid general consternation and protest, 'I want to return to the Mission Station, for it was there I found God's Word, which has told me of a precious Saviour.'

In the mid 1870s, according to the book, U Borsing, a cousin of U Ramsing, the raja of Cherra, heir to the throne and already addressed as 'rajah' for his political involvement during the reign of his cousin, became a Christian after his wife had accepted baptism. On the death of his cousin he was called to the throne on condition that he would revert to his ancestors' religion. He replied, 'I can throw off my cloak or my turban; but the covenant I have made with God I can nowise cast away.' His nephew was then called to the throne, and U Borsing was stripped of all his properties. But he remained steadfast in his new faith to his death in 1888.

MIZORAM

Let us see in greater detail the emergence of one of the most enthusiastic Christian groups in the North-East, indeed in the whole of India. The Mizos or Lushai, a total population of about seven or eight lakh, inhabit the state bordering Myanmar. They are Tibeto-Burman-speaking people, who used to build their villages on the crests of hills and practised slash-and-burn cultivation. They absorbed many of the Kuki clans. In 1890-91 the British occupied Mizoram. By 1894 the whole district of Mizoram was formally annexed by the British Indian government. It took away all the firearms the Mizos possessed, and the chiefs who challenged the British authority were arrested and deported for punishment. Not strangely, the British came across to the Mizos as dangerous white men.

During these politically troubled times two very different white men appeared on the scene. They carried no guns. They preached and sang in the villages about a man called Jesus. They were first known in the villages as 'the two white fools' or 'the white vagabonds'. Their reference to sins and to Jesus as a Saviour from sin was quite foreign to the Mizo culture. They had no sense of sin and felt no need of a saviour. In course of time the love and concern that the people experienced from the 'white fools' made people call the missionaries affectionately 'Mizo Sap' or 'Zosap' (literally 'the Mizos' white people'). Acceptance of the message followed, and a Christian community began to emerge. In the beginning the number of Mizos who embraced Christianity was small. But within about sixty years of the arrival of Christian missionaries to Mizoram almost the whole of the Mizo people embraced Christianity.

The 'change of tempo' (Lloyd 1991, 86) began sometime in 1906. The change was due to the revival movements, something unique in the history of Christianity in India. In the revivals people of all ages experienced spiritual awakening or reawakening in a form 'accompanied by diverse manifestations of emotional outburst' (Lalsawma 1994, 219). The revival movement in Mizoram hills in 1906 had its origin in the Khasi hills. Some Mizo Christians came to know from Khasis residing in Aizawl that an outpouring of the Spirit was expected at the annual meeting in March 1906 in the small village of Mairang. They decided to go. Three women and seven men went as delegates to attend the assembly. At first they were astonished to see the way in which the Khasi Christians acted. Soon the astonishment led to appreciation as they themselves felt affected by the revival atmosphere. During one of the meetings the Mizo Christians were asked to stand in front on the platform, and the whole gathering prayed for them and their land. The Mizos experienced the outpouring of the Spirit on them. 'We stood there weeping and trembling. None of us remained unaffected,' wrote Thanga, one of the ten Mizo delegates who came for the meeting (Lloyd 1991, 92).

In April 1906 in Aizawl during one of the prayer services started by a woman named Hlunziki, individuals, one after another, made spontaneous confessions of their sins and asked the congregation's prayers for forgiveness. The meeting lasted six hours. They agreed to meet again the same afternoon. Similar meetings were held in other villages too. Acceptance of one's sinfulness, asking for God's forgiveness and experiencing it were the major themes of the revival. Compared to later revivals the impact of this first one was less. Still its influence was significant. Many Christians were confirmed in their faith. Many others joined the Christian community.

After the revival of 1906 the young Mizo Christian community went through difficult times. Persecutions broke out in certain villages. After the famine of 1913, Christians experienced one more revival. This revival lasted for about two years and spread to many parts of Mizoram. The third revival which began in 1919 was the greatest. It led to the conversion of the whole Mizo society to Christianity. It sprang simultaneously in three distant villages, several days' journey from each other—Nisapui, Thingsai and Zotlang. But all of them had a single theological theme: the cross of Jesus Christ and its redemptive suffering.

In Nisapui the revival began thus: on the evening of 26 July 1919, three girls were praying and singing in a house. Suddenly they became aware of the depth of the suffering of Jesus Christ. They were moved and wept in deep sorrow. Next day they gathered again to pray in the same house. Their singing attracted others from the village. Many people joined them and the crowd became so big that they had to hold the prayer meeting in the open air. The congregation that gathered was so moved that they continued to sing and dance through the night and the meeting went on for three days. To share their experience with others, the Nisapui Christian community, led by its evangelist, went to the surrounding villages and kindled revivals there. Within a short time, thanks especially to the itinerant preachers, it reached all corners of Mizoram and Mizos living in the neighbouring states of Manipur and Tripura.

The revivals not only led to the conversion of the Mizos to Christianity but also created a distinctive Mizo Christian identity. 'A major contribution of the revivals, especially of the third revival, was its influence on the interweaving of Christianity and the Mizo cultural ethos,' says Pachuau (2002, 131). Three typical elements of Mizo Christian worship show how the Mizo cultural identity was integrated into their Christian identity: the traditional drum, locally composed Christian hymns sung to indigenous tunes and the revival dance. By nature Mizos love singing, and dance accompanies all their feasts.

The drum is a central element in all traditional Mizo festivals. The most celebrated public feast, Khuangchawi, derives its name from khuang (drum). Following the European tradition, the missionaries and the early Mizo Christians had kept the drum away from their worship, as it was associated with pre-Christian feasts. But as local hymns rose from the people's hearts and came into use in Christian worship, the drum too re-entered the community as a means to express the people's deepest faith. For the Mizos, singing has to follow the rhythmic beat of the drum.

In the beginning the missionaries forbade Christians to take part in the traditional dances. In the first revival meetings the Mizos followed the Khasi revival dance by stamping their feet on the floor. But slowly this form of dance began to change. By the third revival it was a common practice to come out to the front of the pews and dance in ecstatic spiritual joy. The Mizos clap and wave their hands, sway their bodies and move in circles to the drumbeat. This dance is similar to their traditional Tlanglam dance.

The three traditional cultural symbols had a deep influence on the new religion of the Mizos. 'The revivals turned Christianity into a people's movement transforming and assimilating the society within its folds. In the process, Christianity was also forced to embrace the people's values, worldview, and ethos. Thus, we see a mutual internalization producing a new and distinctive church of the "transformed" people' (ibid., 142).

At present the work of the churches in the North-East is primarily to foster a sense of brotherhood and sisterhood beyond the tribal lines, and to diffuse the bloody rivalry between groups. Education and health services are the main contributions of Christians to this society; the local Christian community has been especially keen to foster vocational education in trades and skills so that the tribe can face the modern world. Strangely enough, though these Christians have kept much of the ancient tribal customs, they have generally adopted English as their language of education because they have an extremely large variety of languages, almost one for every village, and they need one link language for their political and other activities. (Hindi, they feel, has no affinity to their culture.) The leadership of all the Churches is in the hands of Indians, with no foreign missionaries left. It has been the tradition of the Baptist churches to be congregational: decision-making is mostly at the local level, and the life and preaching of the church is supported by the people. Christians are also heavily involved in the politics of their states and in national politics.

In the area of inculturation the Adivasi churches are now in a stage of recovering the basic myths of each tribe and giving them a reinterpretation in the light of their faith in Christ. There is also a conscious effort to stress the importance and the centrality of symbols in the primeval world, offering a perception of the faith different and in some senses richer than that which comes from concepts. In this way they rescue ancient celebrations of local festivals and art forms, especially the dances. For years they have integrated tribal dances in their Eucharistic and other Christian celebrations. The respect for nature, central to the modern ecological consciousness, finds a strong ally in the tribal consciousness and it is not surprising that tribals have been in the forefront of the battle to protect forests and rivers and to stop the massive interference with nature characteristic of capitalist culture. Many people think that tribal Christianity is destined to become a leading force in developing an ecological theology so needed in our times. Starting from the meaning of celebrations and symbols, there is an incipient effort to articulate a tribal Christian theology. Its expressions are less polemic than those of Liberation Theology, and more unified by a deep experience of harmony in nature.

9

Smaller Christian Communities

*The Bettiah Christians ~ Immigrants from Nepal ~ The Anglo-Indians
~ A waning influence ~ Sardhana ~ Begum Samru ~ The Basilica ~
Clarinda ~ The Tirunelveli community ~ Bishop Azariah of Dornakal
~ The YMCA and YWCA*

The story of Christians in India could go on and on. Each state,
each church, each ethnic group and each institution has
interesting memories of its beginnings, growth, influential people
and obstacles overcome. Within the limits imposed by the nature of
this book, introductory in character, we have only reported a few
of these stories. Others could be told about Christian beginnings in
Gujarat, Orissa, Kashmir, Leh, Darjeeling or Sikkim. As samples of
other types of story we offer here a few subsidiary narratives that
may help fill in the general picture and make the reader better aware
of the complex reality of the Christian communities of India.

A HINDU RAJA STARTS A CHRISTIAN COMMUNITY

Not all Christians in recent centuries emerged out of the deprived
castes or the tribals. An example of a different group is generally
known as the Bettiah Christians. This community has established
itself in North India and has preserved its specific identity for the
past two and a half centuries.

There was during the eighteenth century an effort at organizing
the mission work done by Catholic religious orders. A branch of
the Franciscan order called the Capuchins was assigned the task of
taking the Christian message and influence to Nepal and Tibet, and
although they were few in number, their presence and influence
extended to much of North India. Patna became a stepping stone

in their long journeys to the Himalayan countries, and by 1714 there was a Capuchin mission residence in Patna.

Around 1740 an outstanding thirty-one-year-old priest of the order, Joseph Mary of Gargnano (1709–61), by birth Count Bernardino Bernini of Italy, was resting in the city before the last stage of his journey to Lhasa. By chance he met Dhurup Singh, the Rajput raja of Bettiah, in the Champaran District of north Bihar, who had come to Patna for business with the agents of the East India Company. The two became friends and the raja invited the priest to his small capital. Joseph Mary accepted the invitation and visited the raja at least seven times. He was competent in medicine and successfully treated the raja and some family members, including his wife, in their sicknesses.

Father Joseph Mary lived like a sannyasi and the raja was impressed by his lifestyle and that of other priests who passed on their way to and from Nepal. He wanted to have such priests permanently in his kingdom. The priests said that only an order of the Pope could bring the Capuchins to stay in his capital. A man of quick decisions, the raja wrote to the Pope, obviously with the help of the Capuchins. His letter is interesting and translates thus into English:

Your Holiness:
I have heard that the missionary fathers are sent out into the world to do good to all people. To make sure of this I called them into my presence. Having ascertained that their statement was true and that their work consisted entirely of doing good to every human being under the sun, I ordered them to remain in my kingdom. But they told me that they are unable to comply with my order unless they are commanded to do so by the High Pontiff. I therefore request Your Holiness to kindly send more missionary fathers to my kingdom. I shall esteem this as the highest favour.
Given at Bettiah in the year 1741 and in the month of Busadabi.
Dhurup Singh. Be it so.

The Pope replied with a lengthy letter signed on 1 May 1742 willingly acceding to the royal request. Two Capuchin priests were assigned to the work, but actually neither made it to Bettiah. Instead, Father Joseph Mary and a Nepali Catholic called Michael started the mission on 7 December 1745. They built a small chapel with the generous help of the raja and opened a dispensary and an elementary school. They were allowed to preach freely to everybody, which they did, and by 1751 there were about ten Catholics and about forty others under instruction. Among those who accepted the faith were farmers, various types of artisans like goldsmiths and some petty merchants. This new community organized itself with its own panchayat. 'Some time between 1761 and 1768 they decided of their own accord to abolish caste distinctions among themselves. It can be fairly surmised that this capital decision pointed to inter-caste marriages as well' (Hambye 1997, 447). The subsequent history of the community is the usual story of alternating persecution, especially from local Brahmins, and tranquillity.

Twenty-three years after the mission started, on 17 February 1769, about sixty travel weary people entered Bettiah. Their leader seemed to be familiar with the town. 'The local agent of the John Company accepted the travellers without questioning. They were refugees. They were 57 Nepali Catholics, all Newari, men, women and children of 14 families' (ibid., 448). Like the Parsis 800 years earlier, these Nepali Christians sought and found in India refuge from discrimination and an uncertain future in their country after the abolition of the Malla dynasty. They were settled in the village of Chuhari, 9 kilometres north-west of Bettiah. In course of time they seemed to have merged with the Christian population of Bettiah. Today Bettiah is a diocese in the Catholic Church with only a few thousand Catholics, but many Christians from there have spread out in towns of North India and elsewhere. Besides their own bishop they have provided also the archbishop of Patna and the bishop of Muzaffarpur in north Bihar.

THE ANGLO-INDIANS

Another relatively small community, thinly spread out in most towns of India, very visible in the Churches and in the country until 1947, were the Anglo-Indians. With the departure of the British administrators their importance has naturally diminished. There has also been a significant migration of this community to the UK and its former colonies. The word Anglo-Indian is a misnomer. The Constitution of India, Article 366 (2) defines the Anglo-Indian as 'a person whose father or any of whose male progenitors in the male line is or was of European descent but who is domiciled within the territory of India and is or was born within such territory of parents habitually resident therein and not established there for temporary purposes only'. The Anglo-Indian therefore need not have any connection with England: she or he may have ancestors in any European country. At one time they were also called Eurasians, but the word acquired a pejorative connotation and was abandoned in practice. The majority of the Anglo-Indians do of course descend from British or Irish administrators or soldiers who married Indian women. Most of them have been baptized into one or other Church according to the family tradition. The early generation that descended from Portuguese soldiers or administrators have generally been absorbed into the Goan or East Indian Christian community.

It is natural that by affinity the Anglo-Indian community would have had importance in the country, including its political life, during the Raj. In the churches also they had influence especially in the great metropolises of Calcutta, Bombay, Madras and Delhi and a few places in Kerala and North India. Not allowed to own land, they used to cluster around towns and in cities and developed their mechanical and trading skills. Their level of education was above the average, but not many pursued university education. Being generally at home both in the local language and in English, many found employment in government services and business. Culturally they have tended to follow the British traditions, but adapted to the local situation. They may be said to be bi-cultural. They have been also effective in the field of sports and have propagated 'Indian' sports like hockey in Australia and New Zealand. For some years even after Independence they had a preferential right to employment in the Railways, postal and telegraph services and in customs, and they still have a special representation in Parliament and some Legislative Assemblies.

Anglo-Indians have generally been very attached to the Church and supported its activities. They have been able to mix comfortably with the general population, both Christian and others. Although the general public saw them exclusively in terms of favouring and being favoured by the Raj, one must not forget that 'there were people like Henry [Lui] Vivian Derozio, a radical revolutionary, who influenced a whole generation of the Bengalis through the Young Bengali Movement and in a way initiated the Nationalist movement in the country' (Singh 1998, 1: 97). Derozio was a free thinker and a severe critic of the priesthood. A poet and teacher who lived a short life (1809–31), he influenced many leaders in Bengal.

Another significant member of this community was Lawrence T. Picachy, S.J. (1916–92), who eventually became archbishop of Calcutta and the fourth Indian cardinal in the Catholic Church.

SARDHANA: A ROMANTIC STORY AND A BASILICA

One of the curious stories in the history of Christian India is the short-lived 'vicariate apostolic of Sardhana' and the reign of the Catholic Begum Samru. The story begins with a Luxembourg Catholic, probably born around 1720, named Walter Reinhardt, an adventurer who joined the army of the French East India Company. He was in Chandernagore when Clive seized the French settlement in 1757. The French called him 'le sombre', the 'sad one', because of his appearance. 'Sombre' became in Hindustani Samru, the name by which he passed into local history. After many adventures in the east of India Samru came to the area of the present Uttar Pradesh, where he gathered an army of mercenaries exclusively officered by Europeans. He put the army at the service of Najub Khan, the Persian nobleman in charge of Delhi, against the would-be usurper Zabta Khan. Having won the battle, he was given a jagir between the Ganga and the Yamuna, going from Muzaffarnagar to near Aligarh. Samru chose a central village, Sardhana, near present-day Meerut, as the capital and ruled from there from 1773 till his death in 1778.

In Delhi, in 1765, Samru fell in love with a fifteen-year-old Muslim dancing girl, Farzana, daughter of Latif Ali Khan of Arabian origin, who had settled in Katana, 50 kilometres from Meerut. She was educated and carried herself with great dignity. Samru, already married to a Muslim lady (who was insane until her death in 1838), decided to marry Farzana in the Muslim rite. For all practical purposes she became the begum and accompanied Samru in his campaigns and wanderings. Samru died and was buried in Agra. Farzana became the begum and ruled over Sardhana for fifty-eight years. Her rule was no sinecure. She had 4000 soldiers and eighty-two European officers under her, whom she often led into battle. She had to negotiate with neighbouring rajas, the Marathas, the Sikhs and the British. Contemporary drawings show her, the only woman, smoking a hukka surrounded by a group of male ministers and advisers.

Two years after the death of her husband, Begum Samru decided to adopt his Catholic faith, for reasons unknown to us. Surely they could not have been threat, fraud or bribe. She was baptized in 1781 and took the name of Johanna. She continued to rule the jagir with good political sense, ensuring the cultivation of the land, and when needed led the army, which still kept its original mercenary character. For a long time she played the Scindias, the local rajas, the Mughals and the Britishers one against the other, according to the convenience of the moment. There was also a torrid love affair with a young French officer, Le Vaisseau, whom she married in 1793 in preference to another admirer among the officers, the Irish soldier George Thomas (1756–1802), who left her to join the army of the Scindias but was eventually reconciled with her. Her second marriage was not a success and was most unpopular. It led to a revolt during which she and Le Vaisseau were taken prisoners. Le Vaisseau shot himself and she stabbed herself but not fatally. For some time prisoner of the revolting soldiers, she was finally saved by a counter-revolution inspired by her Irish admirer, George Thomas, and led by his friend the Frenchman Saleur. She was then restored to Sardhana where all the European officers took an oath of allegiance to her.

She resumed the name of her first husband and used her talents and energy to administer her territory. She became very rich but was also very generous with her money. The Mughal Emperor Shah Alam II who had proclaimed her successor to Samru in preference to Samru's son, gave her the title of Zeb-ul-Nisa, literally 'The Jewel of Her Gender' because of favours she rendered to the emperor. 'Her subjects belonged to all creeds and they were free to practise the religion of their choice. Besides her European officers, Sardhana had then a Christian population of about two thousand' (Nair 1963, 29).

Well into the nineteenth century she decided to build a large church worthy of divine worship that would be the attraction of the region. It was built, probably on the advice of her Italian Capuchin missionaries, by the Italian officer Antony Reghalini, who was inspired by no less a model than St Peter's Basilica in Rome. The begum requested the Pope to appoint Father Julius Caesar Scotti bishop of Sardhana. In a letter of 17 September 1734 the Pope was pleased to accede to her request and appointed Scotti bishop of the Titular See of Amathunta and vicar apostolic of Sardhana. During the life of the vicar the church was called the Cathedral of Sardhana. But the vicar apostolic had no successor and the church ceased to be a cathedral. In 1961 Pope John XXIII declared it a minor basilica in recognition of its local importance.

It does not seem that the posting as vicar apostolic agreed with the character of Julius Caesar Scotti. At the death of the begum in 1836, the British government annexed her principality as per agreement with her in the last years of her life. Msgr Scotti left in a hurry for Europe, without appointing a priest to be in charge of the vicariate in his place. He claimed to have received insults and humiliations in the vicariate. Eventually the vicariate apostolic of Sardhana was merged into that of Agra.

Today the Basilica of Sardhana, originally dedicated to the Blessed Virgin May, Mother of God, is an important pilgrimage centre not only for Catholics of the region but also for many Muslims and Hindus who flock to the place to obtain special favours, especially in the months of March and November. The basilica falls within the Catholic Diocese of Meerut, created in 1956, which consists of about 25,000 Catholics. It has been renamed the Church of Our Lady of Graces. For the Basilica has now a special shrine housing an image blessed by Pope Pius XII and by the much-loved Italian Capuchin priest Padre Pio (today a saint), an image with a popular reputation of being miraculous.

The testament of Begum Samru who died at eighty-six after ruling for fifty-eight years may give us some inkling of the deep charitable and ecumenical spirit of the begum. It decrees the following legacies:

For the Supreme Pontiff	Rs 150,000
For the poor of Sardhana	Rs 100,000
For the Catholic Seminary in Sardhana	Rs 100,000
For maintenance of the Catholic Church in Sardhana	Rs 100,000
For Catholic missions in Calcutta, Bombay and Madras, in equal parts	Rs 100,000
For the mission of Agra	Rs 30,000
For the maintenance of the Catholic Church in Meerut	Rs 12,000
For the Anglican-Protestant Archbishop [sic] of Calcutta	Rs 50,000
For the Anglican-Protestant bishop of Calcutta to be used for the poor and indigent	Rs 50,000
For the same, for the use of the mission and works of mercy	Rs 100,000
For Colonel Clement Brow, executor of the Testament	Rs 75,000

Total: 14 lakhs and 67,000 rupees (Hartmann 1939–48, 1: 792)

THE WELL OF THE BRAHMIN MOTHER AND CHRISTIANS IN TIRUNELVELI

Another interesting case of an unexpected growth of a Christian group is associated with 'Clarinda', the widow of a Marathi Brahmin in the service of the raja of Thanjavur. Tradition says that a British army officer, Henry Lyttleton, saved her from the funeral pyre of her husband. As may have been the custom of those days, she decided to live with him. He instructed her in the Christian faith, and inspired by its teachings she wanted to become a Christian. But the missionary Frederick Schwartz (1726–98), whom she approached, refused to baptize her on the grounds that she was living with Lyttleton in an irregular union.

When Lyttleton was transferred to the garrison of Palayamkottai (near Tirunelveli) she went with him. In the new place, although not baptized, she began to share with others her Christian faith. Slowly a small group of people belonging to different castes accepted her teaching and became Christians. She built for them a small chapel and dug for them a small well which even today is popularly known as the Pappattiyammal kinaru, 'the well of the Brahmin Mother'. When Schwartz came to Palayamkottai in 1778 he was informed by the people about what the Brahmin widow had done for the spread of the faith. He was also told that Lyttleton had died. When the widow approached him for baptism Schwartz accepted her as a full member of the Christian community. At her request she received the name Clarinda. She came to be commonly known as Rasa Clarinda ('Royal Clarinda'). She continued to work for the spread of the Christian faith. In 1780 the Christian community acquired an organized structure and a small congregation was formed in Palayamkottai. The Tirunelveli mission register has the names of this community with Clarinda heading the list. At the time this congregation was the only (Protestant) Christian group in the area and the number of members enrolled in it was forty.

In response to Clarinda's appeals, the Tarangambadi missionaries sent two catechists or instructors, Visuvasi and Gnanapragasam, to minister to the budding community in Palayamkottai and the neighbouring areas. Clarinda continued to be the benefactor of the Christian community and helped the poor and those in need. In course of time the community Clarinda had fostered became part of a wider Christian community in the Tirunelveli area.

Another interesting story is that of Sundaranandam, belonging to the Nadar caste, who ran away from his home in the village of Kalangudi and went to Thanjavur. There he became acquainted with Christianity and was baptized around 1795. He was given the name David. In 1796 he was employed as assistant to Satyanathan, the pastor of the church at Tirunelveli. David was instrumental in initiating the mass movement to Christianity in the Tirunelveli area. He formed a Christian group among his relatives and friends. Since most of these Christians faced stiff opposition from their relatives they moved to settlements of their own, such as Mudalur ('First

Town', 1799), Jerusalem (1802), Bethlehem (1802) and Nazareth (1804). Thanks to the missionaries like James Hough, the chaplain at Palayamkottai from 1816 to 1821, and Indian pastors like Visuvasanadan and Abraham at Nazareth and Mudalur, the Tirunelveli mission continued to gain momentum. Apart from the Nadars, who formed the majority of converts to Protestant Christianity at the time, Parayars and a few from other castes also embraced Christianity. The main motivation for the movement was the change of status in the caste-dominated society. By the end of the nineteenth century Tirunelveli had more Christians than in any other district in Tamil Nadu.

One of the most outstanding Christians of this community was Vedanayagam Samuel Azariah (1874–1945), who became the first Indian bishop ordained in the Anglican Church, and the only one until his death. He was influential at the national level as secretary of the YMCA (1895–1909) and founder of the Indian Missionary Society and the National Missionary Society. He played a leading role in the preparation of the Church union resulting in the formation of the Church of South India two years after his death. He supported the movement of indigenization of the Church and Gandhi's freedom movement, although he had lively discussion with Gandhi on the question of mass conversions.

The main work of Azariah was, however, the development of the diocese of Dornakal in Andhra Pradesh where his saintly personality (he was affectionately known as Thandrigaru, 'father') propelled the conversion of about two lakh Malas, Madigas, tribals and members of low castes into the Christian fold. He insisted on a solid instruction of the converts and inspired them by his own life of intense prayer, Bible study and simplicity.

THE YMCA AND YWCA

The Young Men's Christian Association (YMCA) and its counterpart for women, the YWCA, are very visible and influential movements in India. Although bearing the Christian name and inspired by the Christian faith, the movement is interconfessional. It is 'a worldwide voluntary organization of young men [and women] which renders yeomen service to the people, irrespective of caste or creed. It is ecumenical and nonsectarian in its character and is dedicated to bring about international understanding and cooperation' (Kanakaraj 2000, 9). The movement is not a Church and not attached to any Church, and has remained from its beginnings essentially lay. It started in the mid nineteenth century when a number of groups emerged in Europe and eventually in the US concerned with the moral education of youth. The first typical YMCA group was formed on 6 June 1844 when twelve young men belonging to four different Protestant churches but working in a cloth shop in London started 'a Society for improving the spiritual conditions of Young Men engaged in drapery and other trades'. Soon they renamed it YMCA and its scope was enlarged. The YWCA was started in 1855 and is entirely separate from the YMCA, although both bodies are at times referred to collectively as the 'Y'.

The 'Y' first came to India in Calcutta in 1854 and more definitively in 1857. Today it can be seen all over the country, and although originally it was basically an urban movement, in the early decades of the twentieth century under the leadership of K.T. Paul it spread considerably in the villages, especially in South India where its impact in helping villages to socialize across castes and religions and to take collective responsibility for their environment met with considerable success. Another characteristic of the Indian 'Y' is that it has broadened the scope of the association to include not only Christians but young men of other religions as full-fledged members, by focusing its aim at contributing to 'God's design for the world' based on equality, justice and peace, rather than on promoting the Christian religion. The 'Y' stresses activity rather than doctrine and has contributed much to the ecumenical movement in India and elsewhere.

The 'Y' aims to foster a fellowship of all based on mutual respect and seeks to offer a welcoming environment especially, though not exclusively, for youth activities to help them develop in body, mind and spirit. It is known first by its wide network of safe and affordable accommodation for travellers, and it provides education, sports and leisure activities, training, counselling, summer camps and support. In Indian villages it has provided 'light houses' or centres of development, cooperative activities and rural reconstruction.

10

Christians in the Life of the Nation

Absence of historical traces ~ Indian Christians and Sanskrit ~ Sanskrit grammarians ~ Educational services ~ Value education ~ Social services ~ Health services ~ Three levels of social concern: development, justice and dignity of women ~ 'Breast-cloth' agitation ~ Social teaching ~ Christians and the freedom struggle ~ Nationalism within the churches ~ The Congress Party ~ Opposition to separate electorates ~ Brahmabandhab Upadhyay ~ Menezes Braganza in Goa ~ Rajkumari Amrit Kaur ~ J.C. Kumarappa ~ The Joseph Brothers ~ S.K.George ~ The Church in Indian politics ~ Indian Christian theology ~ Nineteenth- and twentieth-century theologians ~ Liberation Theologians

Christians have been in India for nearly twenty centuries. Their presence has generally been discreet. In fact for over three quarters of this time they have hardly left any trace of their existence in the sands of history. A few theories have been raised about Christian influences, particularly in the early Tamil sangam literature, or in the bhakti movement or in the philosophy of Madhva, but fair-minded historians are sceptical of the evidence. Classical Sanskrit literature offers no name that can be identified as Christian, and literature in other languages too has few traces of Christian output except in the last three centuries. The only sure traces of their early existence come from within the community itself, from some copperplates relating to grants to the community, from allusions of a few foreign travellers to India before 1498, and a few artefacts that have survived to our times. The early Christian community lived in symbiosis with its neighbours without drawing much attention to itself; it is not strange that general historians would bypass them. Yet the community as a whole was not alien to literary activity.

CONTRIBUTIONS TO INDIAN CULTURE

There are some indications that in Kerala the first Indian Christian community participated in the culture of its neighbours. They continued to practise the Hindu rituals connected to learning and early schooling. Some Christian families seem to have maintained a keen interest in the various branches of Sanskrit lore, and we can record a Sanskrit literary output from this community. There is, for instance, the *Kristu Sahasranama* by I.C. Chacko, published first in 1914, a poem of 101 stanzas in the stotra genre in honour of Jesus Christ. In 1977 Professor P.C. Devasia published from Thiruvananthapuram the *Kristu-Bhagavatam*, a mahakavya of thirty-three cantos and 1581 stanzas. Incidentally, members of other communities have also produced Sanskrit literature about Jesus Christ: in 1974 Thekkumcore Soma Varma Rajah published from Kochi *Sri Yesu Saurabham*, a kavya in four cantos and 344 stanzas, and in 1976 was published *Mahatyagi*, a Sanskrit translation by K.P. Narayana Pisharote of a Malayalam poem by M.O. Avara, an account of the passion of Christ in 163 stanzas. For earlier output in Sanskrit literature by Christians in the eighteenth and nineteenth centuries one may consult Amaladass and Young (1995). Of special interest may be the *Sri Krista Sangita* apparently to be attributed to W.H. Mill. The Sanskrit hymns to the Trinity and to Christ incarnate composed by Brahmabandhab Upadhyay have come to form part of Christian worship. As mentioned earlier, the Bible was published in Sanskrit from 1808 to 1822 and from 1841 to 1872. And of course many Christians from all nations have specialized in Sanskrit and taught it in universities.

It is not surprising that Catholic missionaries were the first to write Sanskrit grammars in the European form. They had been trained in the classical tradition that included the study of Latin and Greek. They soon discovered the similarities between the European classical languages and Sanskrit, and naturally composed the grammars in the format they knew. Such grammars are at the root of the modern Sanskrit grammars which have served well the new generations of students both abroad and in India. The first such grammarian was the German Jesuit Heinrich Roth (1620–68), who from 1660 to 1662 wrote in Latin the *Grammatica Linguae*

Sanscretanae Brachmanorum Indiae Orientalis (printed, however, only in 1988, in Leiden). It was probably based on the *Sarasvata Vyakarana* of Anubhuti Svarupacarya and perhaps on Vopadeva's *Mugdhabodha*. To Roth we also owe the first Devanagari script in a printed book, published in A. Kircher's *China Illustrata* (Amsterdam 1667). Another German Jesuit, J.E. Hanxleden (1681–1732), wrote a grammar which has been lost, but was probably the basis of the first printed Sanskrit grammar, *Sidharubam seu Grammatical Samscrdamica* (Rome 1790), by the Croat Carmelite Filip Vesdin (or J. Ph. Vezdin or Weszdin) better known in history as Paulinus a Sancto Bartholomaeo (1748–1806), for some time a missionary in Kerala and later a prolific writer on Indian culture in Rome. Fourteen years later, he published a larger grammar under the title *Vyacarana seu Locupletissima Samscrdamicae Linguae Institutio* (Rome 1804). Soon followed the grammars of European Protestants like H.T. Colebrooke (in 1805), W. Carey (in 1806) and C. Wilkins (in 1808). Many more would be published in Germany, France and the United Kingdom in the course of the nineteenth century.

SOCIAL AND EDUCATIONAL SERVICE

Though the community as a whole led a rather peaceful neighbourly life with other communities, its influence from the eighteenth century has been mostly through its services. As Panikkar (1963, 48–49) acknowledges:

> Especially their educational institutions introduced a new spirit of understanding, a better appreciation of life in the community and gave an added impetus to a rethinking of values: men like Dr William Miller of the Madras Christian College, C.F. Andrews of St Stephen's College in Delhi and numerous less-known personalities all over India helped to bring up generations of students to whom the dedicated lives of their teachers became shining examples of service. In the field of social service also the foreign missions [read Christian institutions] have a fine record of achievement. The inspiration of many activities, notably of the advocates

of social reform both in their desire to raise the moral standards of the people and in their narrow philistinism and intolerance, can be traced directly to the missionaries.

Panikkar gives as examples of social reform movements the agitations against child marriage and the devadasi system in temples, and the agitation to allow the freedom of second marriage to widows. He considers these on the whole positive social influences of the Christian teaching in India.[1] But he also points to the philistinism of missionaries in respect to Indian dance, art and the classical literature of the Puranas.

Already in the second decade of the sixteenth century there functioned in Goa and other places of Portuguese influence a Confraternity of Charity to take care of the poor. It collected money from the well-to-do members of the community and used it to help the needy in many ways: giving alms, providing shelters, giving medicines and clothes to the sick or prisoners, giving dowries to poor girls at the time of their marriage, giving ransom of captives, rescuing shipwrecked goods of the neighbours, etc. By the end of the sixteenth century there were hospitals in Goa, Kochi, Manappad, Virapandianpattinam, Punnaikayal, Thuthukudi and Vaippar. A leper hospital was functioning in Goa by 1531.

Both education and social services provided by the Christians were addressed in great part to the lower classes and castes, the existence of high-class colleges and schools in the big cities notwithstanding. There was far more investment in helping the lower classes than the elites. In fact many of the present elite institutions started as services meant for the poor who, however, were gradually pushed aside and out of them by the influence and power of the rich. Today Christian authorities are blamed for having allowed this to happen. But undoubtedly the change in the concept of education from being a privilege of the elites to being the right of all

---

[1] For a comprehensive survey on the history of the contribution of Christians to solving the social problems of India see Fernando 2001, 142–79. For other data and statistics on Christian contribution to India see *Communalism Combat* 8(64): 25–55.

citizens owes much to the Christian inspiration, although other cultural factors also influenced the process.

The extent and breadth of the educational effort of Christian agencies in India in the last two centuries may have no parallel in any other country. Unfortunately comprehensive statistics are not easily available. But the following statistics may give a glimpse of the effort done all over the country. The latest *Statistical Yearbook of the Church*, which includes only data from the Catholic Church, offers the following staggering statistics for 2001: for the sake of comparison we give the figures of the same services of the Church in the Philippines, which has about four times as many Catholics as India does:

Service	India	Philippines
Kindergarten schools	7218	863
Students in kindergarten schools	8,25,339	98,168
Primary schools	9779	680
Students in primary schools	30,19,094	4,00,228
Secondary schools, junior and senior	4727	1048
Students in secondary schools	28,45,889	6,10,082

The yearbook does not offer data on the number of institutions of higher learning, but only on the number of students in these institutions which for India is 3,28,358 in 'higher institutes' and 51,029 in 'universities', without counting 27,421 students pursuing Church studies at university level. (The Philippines has 3,91,219 in 'higher institutes', 2,55,036 in 'universities' and 268 in Church studies.)

The *Directory of Church-Related Colleges in India* published in 2001 by the All India Association for Christian Higher Education in India (AIACHE) completes and specifies the above statistics, covering all colleges related to all Christian churches and gives the historical and statistical data on each of them. There were at the time 271 Church-related university colleges in India (of which 161 were Roman Catholic), and they had a total of 3,53,683 students.

The colleges were established between 1817 and 1999, but 200 of them were started after 1947, the year of Independence. From 1993-94 to 2000-01 forty-five colleges were started, an increase of 20 per cent, but the number of students increased only by 3 per cent, while the number of Christian students decreased by 3.65 per cent.

It is also well known that the Christian community took a lead in the education of girls and women. Interestingly, today the proportion of girl students to boys is higher in Christian colleges: 56 per cent as against 45 per cent. Of all students in Church-related colleges only 35 per cent are Christian. The colleges employ 16,776 teachers of whom 60 per cent are Christian. The directory gives a break up of these colleges by state. They are affiliated to fifty-seven different universities, although nineteen are autonomous colleges (out of a total of 127 in India). All except one of the nineteen autonomous colleges are in Tamil Nadu or Andhra Pradesh, the one exception being in Uttar Pradesh.

The vast majority (193) of the colleges are co-educational, but there are seventy-three women's colleges and only five men's colleges. In 2001 Christian colleges educated 27,603 students from the scheduled castes and 18,478 from the scheduled tribes (7.8 per cent and 5.22 per cent of their total students, respectively).

These bare statistics give some idea of the huge investment Indian Christians have made in education. It is commonly acknowledged that many Christian institutions are forerunners in quality education. This is clear, for example, from the surveys published yearly by *India Today* on Indian colleges: nearly a half of the ten best are generally Christian in inspiration or foundation. More importantly, Christians are greatly involved in running teachers' training colleges or institutes, knowing that the quality of teaching depends mostly on the quality of the teachers. Thus thirty-two colleges offer special courses for teachers' training. Another common characteristic of the Christian education has been the importance given to value education as essential to an overall understanding of life. In older times this value education was based primarily on the Bible classes offered to all students. Today value education is provided through other avenues. Several series of textbooks on value education for schools and colleges have been produced under Christian inspiration. The growth in understanding the scope of education has been fostered by many educational structures, particularly the AIACHE and its journal *New Frontiers in Education*, started in 1971.

Christian education tries to be student centred. One of its important contributions has been the creation of student hostels. This alone has made education more accessible to girls. Students from the lower strata of society have also benefited much from hostels. They provide not only board and lodging but remedial classes and humanistic formation which at times could not be provided in the schools.

Christian education has also fostered the formation of student movements which have had an impact in the universities. The Students Christian Movement, affiliated to the World Students Christian Federation started in 1895, and the All India Catholic University Federation founded in 1948 are the best-known student movements that have added much dynamism to the processes of higher education. These movements have often been imbued with a strong social concern.

Social services and social service camps have also been a regular feature of many Christian colleges and the ideas of education for service have been a regular inspiration for many of them.

Apart from education, the most important contribution of Christians to Indian society has surely been health services. We remember how much the preaching of Jesus himself was linked to a ministry of healing, as a sign of the new life God was offering to humanity. The Gospels speak constantly of the concern of Jesus for the sick. From the beginning the Christian movement had a special concern for the sick and many hospitals and health services in Europe started with the services of people committed to the Gospel. In this they followed a pattern already marked by Buddhist monks long ago, who were also known for their concern for the sick all over Asia.

But health is not only a question of physical healing. Recent trends have put more stress on social health, improving the situation especially in villages and slums, and on spiritual-psychological health, providing means for interior healing and for outside counselling. Not strangely, yoga, vipassana, Zen and other methods of inner healing have had a growing influence in some health services run by Christians.

To give an idea of the scope of social services run by the Christians in India we again take recourse to the statistics of the 2001 *Statistical Yearbook of the Church*. We shall again compare them with those of the Philippines with its much larger Catholic population, to show the extent of the effort of Indian Christians in this direction. There were 737 hospitals and 2429 dispensaries in India, as against fifty-eight and ninety respectively in the Philippines. The yearbook records in addition 248 leprosaria in India, whereas the Philippines had only seven. The Catholic Church runs 865 homes for the aged and the 'differently endowed', 2112 orphanages, 2021 nurseries, 587 marriage counselling centres, 4969 special centres for social education and re-education, and 694 other institutions— a total of 14,672 institutions related to health! Behind these cold numbers there are of course the lives of innumerable Christians and others who devote time, energy and love to the complete health of their fellow human beings.

There is no doubt that, like some educational institutions, health centres run by Christians originally meant to serve the poor have in the course of time become elite. Also a number of them are dependent on foreign funds. This awareness has led some groups like the Medical Mission Sisters to hand over well-equipped hospitals in big towns to other agencies and engage in outreach programmes in villages and slums. Their stress is now on preventive health care and holistic improvement of village life. Emphasis is also on small-sized and mobile institutions to reach rural areas more easily.

In the area of social concern there has been a clear development in the Christian understanding about the kind of service involved in the search for social justice. There was first the approach of beneficence, especially important in times of crisis. Together with others, Christians have been in the forefront of relief activities in times of natural or human-made calamities: during floods, earthquakes, famines, riots or wars they have gone by the hundreds to offer immediate relief to those affected or in danger. For instance, they were there by the thousands when ten million Bangladeshis crossed our borders escaping war and persecution at the time of the birth of their nation in 1971-72. Christians have been able to utilize resources at the national and international level so that help would reach the victims in the shortest possible time. Their contribution has been widely acknowledged by the nation at large, even if not by everybody. There are always those who choose to see such activities through the prism of concern for conversions. No numerical facts of significance are put forward to justify this interpretation, except in cases of fringe Christian fundamentalist groups.

Apart from these 'emergency situations' the Churches have structures of beneficence to reach out to lonely widows, abandoned old people, poor families with no means of income and other extreme cases of necessity. One of the regular structures in many Catholic parishes is the St Vincent de Paul Society, a lay organization founded in Paris in 1833 by Anthony Frederick Ozanam (1813–53) and young Catholic students. Its main concern is the relief of the poor of the locality through help collected from members of the community or elsewhere. This society has been active in India since 1863. It is not a mere social service organization: the stress is on personal contact between the members of the society and the people they reach out to. Their weekly meetings devote a good deal of time to prayer, followed by a revision of the visits and other activities carried on over the week, and the needs to be covered. According to the *New Catholic Encyclopedia* (2003, 12: 594), 'The fundamental work of the society is the visitation of the poor in their own homes. Other activities of councils and conference include hospital and institutional visitation on a regular basis, ministry to immigrants and refugees, social outreach to the homeless, summer camps for needy children, guidance programs for young men, work with delinquent youth, visitation of prisoners and work with probationers.'

It is well known that the church known as the Salvation Army has a great history of work of beneficence. Similarly, most churches have their organs for helping those in need, either temporarily or permanently. The Indian religious congregations— whether those well known like the Missionaries of Charity or others less known— devote much time and energy to the work of assistance in crisis situations.

But beneficence, though always required, is not sufficient. As the Chinese proverb has it, better than giving a hungry man a fish to eat is to teach him how to fish (though if he is extremely hungry he may need to eat a fish before learning how to fish!). Development is an important ingredient of social concern. Many social services of the churches today are oriented towards enabling the weaker sections of society to develop their potential so that they find employment or other means of livelihood through their own efforts. This bestows on them a sense of self-confidence. Most churches run schools for crafts and professional training. as well as home science or grihini schools, agricultural schools, technical schools, adult and rural education programmes. Social service centres work with the ideals of development, that is, helping people to help themselves. Some religious congregations, like the Salesians of Don Bosco, specialize in providing vocational training of this sort. Employment bureaus run by many dioceses also work towards promoting self-help.

By itself development does not reach down to the root of injustice and of the poverty in the country. Injustice is the fruit of unjust structures which need to be uncovered, denounced and eradicated. This is what Liberation Theology has learned and taught Christian churches everywhere. One of the tasks demanded by social concern is to awaken the awareness of people and enable them to analyse their problems, seek the causes of injustice and find solutions, if necessary through the power of common action. This help to the poor is what Latin American sociologists have called 'conscientization', that is, making people conscious that poverty and the conditions under which they suffer are human-made and can be unmade. The poor have to discover the structural roots and the ideological and social conditions that generate enormous inequalities in wealth and power and then organize in such a way that they transform society into a more equitable family. Although no statistics can be given, today many lay Christians, young and old, married or unmarried, nuns, religious men and priests work in groups in villages and cities to help the poor become aware of their situation. Much of the work of adult literacy is connected to the ideal of conscientization. Unless the unjust structures of society are changed, justice cannot triumph, and the reign of God will not manifest itself.

This level of social concern also involves spreading a social teaching that stresses the primacy of the person over profit and the need of ensuring for all a fair share in the economic production of society. 'Justice' is the first goal articulated in the Preamble of our Constitution, and in the text it takes precedence over the three ideals of the French Revolution, liberty, equality and fraternity. Justice has surely been the cry of all progressive movements in the last two or three centuries. For Christians justice is a leitmotif of social concern, for although the central theme of the Bible is love, the litmus test of the authenticity of love is the concern for justice. In recent years the concern for justice has acquired clear objectives in many Indian groups: it focuses on Dalits, tribals, women and unorganized labour.

Conscientization is not a new venture for Indian Christians. This is clear from the famous 'breast-cloth' agitation in Travancore in the early nineteenth century, which met with a measure of success. At the beginning of the nineteenth century, the Nadars lived in Tirunelveli District and in the South Travancore state (now Kanyakumari District of Tamil Nadu). They were engaged in cultivation and tapped the high palmyra palms to make jaggery and extract toddy. The Nadars of South Travancore were economically more depressed and suffered greater social degradation than those of Tirunelveli. Defiled by the ritually impure occupation of toddy-tapping, they suffered the social disabilities of a low, almost untouchable, community. In Travancore the low castes were forbidden to come near people who claimed a high-caste status, and the distances permitted were fixed according to each caste: Nadars had to remain thirty-six paces from Namboodiri Brahmins. They were forbidden to carry umbrellas, wear shoes or put on gold ornaments. Their houses could not be higher than one storey. They were not allowed to milk cows. Nadar women were not permitted to carry pots of water on their hips, as was the custom among the higher castes, nor were they permitted to cover the upper portions of their bodies. By tradition in Travancore, the breasts of men and women were bared as a symbol of respect to those of higher status!

The dress the Nadars were allowed to wear consisted of a single cloth of coarse texture, to be worn alike by males and females no lower than the knee nor higher than the waist. The Christian missionaries objected to this dress code for the Christian Nadar women. This style of dress was declared incompatible with the modesty and decorum of Christian women, many of whom had received a good education and were taught to appear decent in public (Agur 1990, 935).

As early as 1812, Colonel Munro, the British Resident of Travancore, issued an order that permitted 'the women converted to Christianity to cover their bosoms as obtained among Christians in other countries' (dated 19 Dhanoo 988 [1812], see ibid., Appendix 1). In pursuance of this order, the government of Travancore issued a circular order permitting female converts of the lower classes to cover their bodies with a short bodice or jacket, as was worn by the women of the Syrian Christian and Muslim communities. They were not, however, permitted to wear the upper cloth in the manner of the higher castes: the Nadar women were not allowed 'to wear cloths on their bosoms as the Nayar women' (circular order from Colonel Munro dated 7 Yadavam 989 [1813] see ibid., 1: iii).

The missionary wives stitched a loose jacket for the women of the mission. This jacket satisfied the sense of modesty and decorum of the European ladies. But it did not meet the social aspirations of the Nadar women. As the Nadars of Tirunelveli wore the breast cloth freely, the women of Travancore would have nothing less. So, in addition to the prescribed jacket, they increasingly adopted the use of the upper cloth, such as was worn by the women of the higher castes. The dominant caste groups in South Travancore vehemently opposed this move and in October 1828, 'the women were beaten in the public bazaar for wearing the upper cloth over their bosoms, and the clothes were stripped from their bodies' (see Hardgrave 1979, 21). Christian institutions were also attacked.

The missionaries asked the Resident of Travancore to intervene, as the local government had taken no action to prevent unruly behaviour or to punish those who had started the trouble. The government issued a royal proclamation on 3 February 1829: 'As it is not reasonable on the part of the Shanar women to wear cloths over their breasts, such custom being prohibited, they are required to abstain in future from covering the upper part of their body' (see Agur 1990, 1: vii).

The proclamation eased the tension, but the Nadar Christian women continued to dress like the Nairs, as was their custom. Increasingly the women of the Hindu Nadar community in South Travancore adopted the upper cloth as well. The Nairs held the missionaries responsible for the spread of the upper cloth, which had become the symbol of change in South Travancore. Their antagonism towards the Nadars was heightened by the anxiety following the abolition of slavery in Travancore in 1855. The Nairs saw Christianity as threatening the social order and the long-held traditions of Travancore. Riots broke out in October 1858. In a village market, a petty official, declaring that he had been empowered by the government, stripped Nadar women of their breast-cloths. The incident sparked twenty days of rioting in the district, which soon spread to other districts. Houses were burned and looted, and on 10 January 1859, the thatched bungalow which was reserved for the Resident when he was in Nagercoil was destroyed by fire. Between October 1858 and February 1859, nine chapels and three schools were burned, though there was no loss of life.

After consulting the maharaja, the diwan wrote to the British Resident that 'His Highness now proposes to abolish all rules prohibiting the covering of the upper parts of the persons of Shanar women and to grant them perfect liberty to meet the requirements of decency any way they may deem proper, with the simple restriction that they do not imitate the same mode of dress that appertains to the higher castes' (see Aiya 1906, 1: 530). The British accepted the concession, and a royal proclamation was accordingly issued by the state of Travancore on 26 July 1859: 'We hereby proclaim that there is no objection to Shanar women either putting on a jacket, like the Christian Shanar women, or to Shanar women of all creeds dressing in coarse cloth, and tying themselves round with it, as the Mukkavattigal low caste fishermen do, or to their covering their bosoms in any manner whatever; but not like women of high caste' (see ibid., 531).

The proclamation satisfied the demands of 'decency' but not the social aspirations of the poor. It did little to change the situation. Christianity now provided an organizational base for unity in the whole Nadar community, which they had lacked earlier. In each village or cluster of villages a unified structure was established in the form of a village parish. Each village parish was then linked to the others through the hierarchy of the church organization. With this structure the Nadars were for the first time brought into association with each other over a wide area. The unity extended beyond the Christians and reached out to the whole Nadar community. The relationship between Christian and Hindu Nadars continued and served to draw the Hindus within the sphere of Christian influence. Many Hindu children began attending Christian schools. Though belonging to a different religion, the Hindu Nadars shared with their Christian brothers/sisters a consciousness of the unjust caste system. The breast-cloth controversy served as the catalyst of increasing community awareness.

Buoyed by that initial taste of success, the Nadar community has come a long way. In about 150 years the upward mobility of the Nadar community has accelerated so much that in contemporary Tamil Nadu they now have a high status and power. The missionaries' sense of decorum indirectly helped the movement. But the courageous and unwavering will power of the Indian Christian women and men, who demanded equal status in an unjust society, led them to achieve almost impossible goals. In this march towards freedom they did not walk alone. Their Hindu sisters walked with them.

The three levels of social concern—beneficence, development and conscientization—are not exclusive of each other, and in fact the three are necessary in all societies. The important point is that the first two do not block the way of the third level, while obviously the third level cannot deny the importance of the other two. In the Christian church the total commitment to the work of justice and charity finds many different supportive structures. Among Catholics there is a coordinating agency at the level of dioceses and at the national level, linked with an international network. It is called Caritas India. In the Catholic Bishops' Conference of India there is a commission for justice, development and peace (under which Caritas India operates), besides the commissions for scheduled castes and tribes and other backward castes, for labour, for health and for women. Other churches have similar or parallel organizations, like the Christian Agency for Social Action, Relief and Development (CASA).

More important than organization is the commitment of the Church to what is called in a general way the 'social problem'. In our times this is often spoken of as *the* central concern of the Church, and the enormous social injustice of the world, both at the local level and at the world level, is seen as the gravest manifestation of sin which Jesus came to overcome and directed the disciples to fight against. In the spirituality and the ideology of the Church this orientation has now taken the shape of a necessary 'option for the poor' on the part of all Christians and churches. This goal has nothing to do with a glorification of poverty. Nor is it a denial of the universal scope of Christian discipleship. All peoples, rich or poor, are welcome to it, but discipleship will imply 'becoming poor' in the sense of accepting solidarity with the victims of society and doing what one can to change unjust structures.

The 'option for the poor' is also a rallying call to focus the spiritual, cultural and physical energies towards saving society from the injustice it perpetrates on a great number of people—on all condemned to remain in inhuman poverty at the bottom of the social scale because of economic, social and religious structures of the present or of the past. The 'option for the poor' is the perspective through which many Christians today look at the Gospel and at the life of Jesus. For this cause, many are ready to offer their lives. It has become the inspiration for all mission work. To the extent that this option touches the areas of conscientization, it is also a political option. To politics we now pass.

CHRISTIANS AND THE FREEDOM STRUGGLE

It should not surprise anyone to learn that India's Christian communities as a whole were not enthusiastic about the freedom movement in its earlier phase. The presence of a 'Christian' government in the country was for many an assurance of survival amid an otherwise massive Hindu population. In the ever volatile tension between the two main religious bodies, Hinduism and Islam, which according to the 1901 Census of India formed 72 and 20 per cent of the Indian population respectively, many, and not only Christians, thought that the presence of the Raj contained the promise of an impartial arbiter. In the early years of the renaissance of Hinduism, after the first freedom struggle of 1857, quite a few patriots of all religions still spoke of the British presence as beneficial to the country, a door to modernization. Even when they eventually aspired to control the political affairs of the country, they spoke more of 'dominion status' than of independence.

The mood changed considerably, however, after the partition

of Bengal in 1905. From then on more and more Indians, including Christians, entered the freedom movement, and resistance to the colonial set-up found new expression. An important cultural and political instrument in the search for autonomy and eventual independence was undoubtedly the Indian National Congress. Pune had been planned as its birthplace, but because the city was at the time in the grip of a cholera epidemic, the first Congress meeting took place in Mumbai on 28 December 1885. It defined its aims as:

(a) The promotion of personal intimacy and friendship among all the more earnest workers in our country's cause in the different parts of the Empire;

(b) The eradication, by direct friendly personal intercourse, of all possible race, creed, or provincial prejudices among all lovers of our country, and the fuller development and consolidation of those sentiments of national unity that had their origin in their beloved Lord Ripon's ever memorable reign;

(c) The authoritative record, after this has been carefully elicited, by the fullest discussion of the matured opinions of the educated classes in India on some of the more important and pressing of the social questions of the day (Zaidi and Zaidi 1976, 1: 46).

The minutes record that besides 'Hindus of many castes, high and low' and 'Mohammedans', there were 'Christians, both native, Eurasian and Europeans' (ibid., 41–42). Among the Europeans a prominent place is to be given to the one who for many years was general secretary of the Congress, Allan Octavian Hume from Shimla. Another prominent member was D.S. White, president of the Eurasian Association. In the third Congress in 1887 there were fifteen Christian delegates, not counting twenty more British or Eurasian Christians (Thomas 1979, 88). The presidents of the fourth and fifth sessions of the Congress, in Allahabad and Calcutta respectively, were Christians, and by the sixth session in 1890 there were fifteen Christian delegates. From the beginning the Congress assumed a pluralistic and secular face. N. Subramanyam, a Christian municipal commissioner in Madras, said in the third session that though Congress delegates came from different parts of the country, spoke different languages and professed different religions, 'all come together with one desire—to consider and discuss questions affecting the welfare of this common country, our common motherland' (ibid.).

As mentioned earlier, one of the prominent reformers and political leaders in Bengal was the Reverend Kalicharan Banerjea (1847–1907), 'a Brahman convert to Christianity, [who] has taken a prominent part in all social, religious and educational movements of the day' (Buckland 1906, 26). A member of the Congress from its very inception, he soon became one of the prominent leaders of the party. When he was elevated to the Legislative Council in 1897 as representative of the Christian community, the orthodox Hindu vice-chancellor of the University of Calcutta Gooroodas Banerjee said, 'It is a mistake to think so. Mr Banerjea is a representative of all communities' (*Indian Christians* 1928, 181). He was described as 'perhaps the finest orator in the whole assembly'.

One of the major contributions of the Christian community to the freedom struggle and the subsequent Constitution of India was to renounce and even oppose the idea of separate electorates for separate religious bodies and reservations on the basis of religious affiliation. Such experiments had been tried during India's gradual transformation from a mere colony to an independent nation. But soon many prominent Christian nationalists decided to work for a truly democratic nation based on mutual trust. This opposition to the British decision of separate electorates was already expressed in the 1922 All-India Conference of Indian Christians, and eventually it influenced the Indian National Congress too (see Jayakumar 1999).

The speech of Reverend Jerome D'Souza, S.J., another prominent freedom fighter, in the Constituent Assembly on 18 May 1949 further illustrates this attitude. Addressing the president of the assembly, Dr Rajendra Prasad, he said:

> Sir, I know that in thus giving up what seems to be the last vestige of a safeguard on which the Christians and other minorities had counted . . . it is not we who are taking the risk. I venture to say that the national leaders and the majority community are undertaking a responsibility the

gravity of which I hope they fully realize. In very grave and solemn words Sardar Patel has emphasized the responsibility of the majority community. From this day it is up to them to see that men of all communities, provided they have personal worth, provided they are socially and politically progressive and acceptable to their association or to their organization, receive a fair chance in the selection of candidates, and are given a fair deal in the course of the election . . .

They [the majority community] are willing to accept it [this responsibility], if I can judge from the attitude of this House. We are willing and glad to accept their assurance, that to the best of their ability, they will stand faithful to the spirit of this pledge, and to the spirit of this compromise, so that we and they may join together today in celebrating the end of a political experiment which has meant so much unhappiness for our people and which is, at last, being ended by the free and willing vote of the elected representatives of Indian democracy. (Cheers)

I shall not say anything more than this. I hope and pray that the spirit which has inspired the utterance of Sardar Patel and the reaction of this House will continue to animate the political leaders and the majority organizations and the public of our country; and that along the lines of secular democracy, wisely and firmly traced out by our great leaders, this country, without distinction of caste and creed, will bring to the service of the motherland all the treasures of character and strength which each community possesses by virtue of its traditions. In this way Muslims and Christians, Hindus and Parsees and Anglo-Indians, will stand shoulder to shoulder and work out the prosperity and happiness of all our people, and lead the new Democracy of India to the glorious triumphs which Providence has in store for her (quoted in Sundaram 1986, 196–97).

The national sentiment had already been felt within the organization of many churches. By the middle of the nineteenth century many Indian Christians wanted to be in charge of their affairs and develop forms of Christian life and worship consonant with the cultural traditions of the country. While not noticeable in the Christianity of the west coast until later, in the early period this was strongly felt in Bengal and Madras, two of the most lively centres of Christian presence. Thus in Tirunelveli, Tamil Nadu, in reaction to the CMS missionaries, the local Nadar Christians formed the Hindu Church of the Lord Jesus (1858). Lal Bihari Day suggested in the late 1860s the founding of a National Church of Bengal. In 1868 the high-sounding Bengal Christian Association for the Promotion of Christian Truth and Goodness and the Protection of the Rights of Indian Christians was created, with Kalicharan Banerjea as the leader of the radical group. Again in 1884 the Calcutta Christo Samaj (Church) took its stand on 'substantive Christianity' without its historical accretions, influenced by the Brahmo Samaj. Already then women were allowed to preach in it. In 1886 S. Parny Andy, aka Poulney Andy, formed the National Church of Madras, based on a rather liberal theology and aiming at financial self-sufficiency. It sought to uncover the 'Asiatic face of Jesus Christ'. None of these movements lasted long, but they are an indication that the Christian communities were in sympathy with the incipient national sentiment. Later similar movements arose elsewhere.

In the early part of the twentieth century we find a more articulate search for an authentic Indian Church, Indian in theology and organization ('Faith and Order'). One of the significant movements was the 'Rethinking Christianity in India Group' formed by prominent thinkers of Andhra Pradesh and Tamil Nadu, especially P. Chenchiah, V. Chakkarai, Dr Jesudasan, E. Asirvatham and M.A. Sundarisanam. It advocated a dialogue between Hinduism and Christianity and the secular mission of the Church in a spirit of self-forgetting love, essential in the task of nation building.

BRAHMABANDHAB UPADHYAY AND OTHERS

Of great significance for the nationalist movement was Brahmabandhab Upadhyay. His friend and contemporary Rabindranath Tagore (they were born the same year) described him as 'a Roman Catholic ascetic yet a Vedantin—spirited, fearless, self-denying, learned and uncommonly influential' (Thakur 1934, Preface).

Upadhyay studied in Calcutta during the time of the revival of Hinduism. He was an admirer of Keshub Chander Sen and a member of his Church of the New Dispensation. He was also a friend of young Narendranath Dutta, better known as Swami Vivekananda, and the group of Ramakrishna's devotees. A man of deep religious convictions and a patriot from his youth, he was determined to free India from the yoke of foreign rule and foreign culture. As a young boy he tried, unsuccessfully, to join the army of the maharaja of Gwalior, in the hope of throwing the British out of the country through military action. On his return to Calcutta he took to teaching and journalism as the fields where he could contribute to India's freedom from foreign rule.

After his studies he volunteered to serve in a new school started in Sindh with some friends of his. Already an admirer of Jesus Christ when in the circles of the Brahmo Samaj, Upadhyay became more fascinated by him. Convinced of the truth of the Christian faith, he asked for and obtained baptism from an Anglican priest, but refused to join the Anglican Church. A few months later he joined the Catholic Church, where he remained somewhat uneasily to the end of his life.

His contribution to his times is now receiving recognition. He was a pioneer in the programme of inculturation of the church. He was pained that the church appeared as a European institution to his fellow citizens when it is in fact universal in character, always able to adopt the culture of the different places where it functions. He was a pioneer of the double-belonging idea nowadays being mooted, like that of the double nationality. Upadhyay said he was 'A Hindu by birth, a Christian by rebirth (=baptism)'—or a Hindu by culture, a Christian by faith. He kept his allegiance to the samaj dharma (cultural way) even as he took Jesus Christ for his sadhana dharma (way of growth). He even started, unsuccessfully, a local order of Christian sannyasis to follow a way of living the religious life and preaching more in consonance with the ancient Indian traditions. He continued doing what he had done since his youth, publishing and editing journals, and spoke about the need for the Church to be Indian.

At a more general level he worked for the reform of education along the lines of Indian culture as he understood it. He helped

Rabindranath Tagore found what would become the Santiniketan institution in Bolepur. Upadhyay was the first to acclaim Tagore, as early as 1900, as a 'world-poet' and reviewed some of Tagore's work with great warmth. A year later, on the occasion of the establishment of Tagore's new school at Santiniketan, he gave Tagore the title Gurudev, an epithet that stuck throughout the poet's life. In Santiniketan the ideals of education developed separately by Tagore and Upadhyay merged into a new venture. The first pupils of Santiniketan came from a school run on 'Aryan' lines which Upadhyay and his friend Animananda had started in Calcutta. Animananda became the first teacher in Tagore's establishment, but had to resign a year later because his openly professed Christian faith made Tagore's father and other members of his family uneasy. Upadhyay continued to spread ideas about a new form of education in continuity with the Indian cultural tradition.

In the last years of his life (he died at forty-seven), he entered into more clearly political journalism. He founded an evening daily paper in Bengali, *Sandhya*, where in a very popular Bengali style he abused the colonial presence in India and aroused the political consciousness of the popular classes. His political writing became more and more aggressive. His place was not among the 'moderate' nationalists: he was an 'extremist'—belonging to the *garam dal*, not the *komal dal*. By 1906 he was under constant vigilance of the police. On 3 September 1907, he was arrested with Haricaran Das, the printer of *Sandhya*, and released on bail. (The manager, Saradacaran Sen, had been arrested and given bail four days earlier.) We saw in chapter six the development of the trial against him for 'sedition'. At the outset he challenged the very authority of the English magistrate to try him.

Upadhyay was not the only Christian freedom fighter. In spite of misgivings about the fate awaiting minorities in a potentially Hindu-dominated country, many Christians did long for and fight for freedom. During the freedom struggle nationalist sentiments were freely expressed in the theological journals of the time, for example, the *Guardian*.

Among other adherents to the political freedom ideology was K.T. Paul (1876–1931), a moderate leader who was concerned with the rural reconstruction programme and believed that persuasion rather than agitation would lead India to political and social freedom. He represented the Christian community at the first Round Table Conference in 1930. Joseph Baptista (1864–1930), better known by the mill-workers of Mumbai as Kaka Baptista, was a friend and adviser of Lokmanya Tilak. He organized the mill-workers and led them to strike for the sake of their rights. He also organized the first all-India postal strike. He persuaded the freedom fighters to form the Indian Home Rule League of which he became the first president in 1916. He was bolder than Paul but he also put his main trust in constitutional methods. Lokmanya Tilak sent him to England in 1917 to contact the Labour Party and persuade them to adopt Home Rule for India as part of their political programme. He addressed the party at its conference in Nottingham. The resolution was adopted unanimously and bore fruit in 1947.

Outside British India and in spite of the Catholic government in Portugal, Luis de Menezes Braganza (1878–1938), who for a time had studied for priesthood, fought for political liberties and for autonomy for Goa. He was a born journalist and as early as 1900 he founded the first Goan Portuguese daily, *O Heraldo*, where he criticized the Portuguese ecclesiastical establishment for making Goan Christians their slaves. In 1911 he started *O Debate*, and later wrote more in *Pracash*, a paper in the local language. In 1920 he founded the Goa Provincial Congress to agitate against the oppressive regime. His popularity is reflected in the title O Maior de Todos (The Greatest of All [Goans]) given to him by friends and foes alike and by the renaming in 1963 of the Vasco da Gama Cultural Institute after him. His words in the Council of the Government are worth remembering: 'Portuguese India refuses to renounce the right, given to all nations, to attain the fullness of their personality when they are able to constitute units capable of guiding their own destinies, since this is an inalienable birthright' (Sen 1972–74, 1: 231).

About the many Christian sympathizers and helpers of Mahatma Gandhi and his movement we may recall the friendship between C.F. Andrews and the Mahatma, and Andrews's support for the national cause and the Indian labourers in other colonies. A man with a socialist heart, Andrews came to India as an educationist missionary and taught in St Stephen's College, Delhi, where he promoted the candidature of S.K. Rudra as the first Indian principal of the prestigious college. Like Rudra later, he was a close friend of Gandhiji and his collaborator in the freedom struggle, which at times put him at odds with his British compatriots in India. He was also an intimate friend of Tagore. His contribution to the freedom movement has been studied in his many biographies. His main concern was the future of the working classes and the poor: not for nothing did Gandhiji give him the epithet din-bandhu, 'friend of the poor', and said of him, 'He preaches through his life as very few do, and he preaches the purest love' (ibid., 1: 60). Rajkumari Amrit Kaur (1889–1964) was a daughter of Raja Sir Harnam Singh Ahluwalia, of the Kapurthala ruling family. Her father had converted to Christianity in his youth and, at the death of his brother, the heir to the throne, became the manager of the Oudh estates (rather than the state Kapurthala). Sir Harnam Singh led an exemplary quiet life within the British establishment. His daughter, however, affirms that 'the flames of my passionate desire to see India free from foreign domination were fanned by him'. She entered public life through social welfare activities and concern for women's uplift. She was secretary of the 1930 All-India Women's Conference and later president of the All-India Women's Association. She served as Mahatma Gandhi's secretary for sixteen years and was one of his closest collaborators. She was lathi-charged and imprisoned in Kalka during the Quit India movement of 1942. In 1947 she became the first health minister of India under Jawaharlal Nehru's premiership and remained a champion of female education and the uplift of Dalits.

Another close collaborator of the Mahatma was Joseph Chelladurai Kumarappa (1892–1957) coming from a middle class Christian family of Thanjavur. He gave up the study of capitalist economics in favour of the Indian economic problems. 'Kumarappa's scholarly thesis on the economic exploitation of India by the British through their taxation policy won the admiration of Mahatma Gandhi who published it in a series in his Young India' (ibid., 2: 375–76). Later Kumarappa would edit Young India in the absence of Gandhi, and in 1931 he was arrested for his writings there. Gandhiji's influence on him was profound as he changed his Westernized and capitalistic style of life for a simple Gandhian style in dress and food. Intellectually he gave a scientific interpretation of the Gandhian economic ideas, interpretations which were not, of course, accepted by the capitalist establishment. His thought gave rise to a new School of Economics of Non-Violence and logically led towards the economic views of Amartya Sen.

Two brothers who at one time collaborated with Gandhiji deserve mention here: George Joseph (1887–1938), by profession a lawyer, and Pothan Joseph (1894–1972), who for more than half a century 'edited more newspapers and journals than any editor of repute, living or dead, in the world', according to V.N. Narayan (ibid., 2: 253). In 1917 George joined Annie Besant in her movement for Indian Home Rule and later joined the Indian National Congress under the inspiration of Gandhi. Motilal Nehru persuaded him to take up the editorship of the *Independent,* a daily published in Allahabad. After a term of imprisonment he edited Gandhiji's weekly *Young India.* Disappointed by a split of the Congress Party in the early 1920s and by Gandhiji's suspension of the political programme of non-cooperation, George abandoned politics in 1925 and returned to legal practice in Madurai, only to re-emerge in the politics of Travancore in 1932. He presided over the deliberations for the formation of the 'Catholic Congress', which seemed to many a departure from his non-communal politics. In politics he and his wife supported the weaker sections of society. He led a simple and unostentatious life. He was a habitual wearer of khadi, in whom 'religious conservatism and political radicalism were harmoniously reconciled' (ibid., 2: 249). Pothan remained all his life a nationalist journalist of great influence.

S.K. George (1900–60) was born in Kerala to a very pious Christian family. He was a lecturer in Bishop's College, the theological centre of the Anglican Church in Kolkata, when in 1930 Metropolitan Foss Westcott, while sympathetic towards the national aspirations of India, disapproved Gandhi's civil disobedience movement on theological grounds. S.K. George challenged the archbishop, and found the metropolitan's reply to J.C. Kumarappa 'very unconvincing'. In the tension that followed the lecturer eventually felt obliged to resign his post and explained his decision thus:

Believing as I do that the Indian *Satyagraha* is the Cross in action and that it gives Jesus Christ His greatest opportunity to enter the hearts of a remade India, I held it to be my highest duty both towards the College and the Church in India to identify myself with this non-violent movement, based absolutely on Truth and seeking solely to establish Peace on Earth and Good Will among men. But such an attitude on my part was regarded as disloyalty to the College and therefore I had no other alternative but to leave the College to follow my own conscience at this time of my Country's need and my Lord's opportunity (quoted by Studdert-Kennedy 1998, 126 from Bishop's College Archives).

These courageous words led George into a life of commitment to the national cause, but also a life of privation and poverty.

Pandita Ramabai (1858–1922), whom we met in chapter eight, was one of the most outstanding Christians to support the national cause and Gandhiji's way of life. She was a woman of great influence.

By the later phase of the struggle for independence, many Christians supported the national cause, some in the political field, others as journalists and opinion makers. Many more served the nation then and after independence in other fields: defence, administration, the judiciary, diplomatic service, sports, science, literature and theatre in many Indian languages and English—there is hardly a field of human activity where one cannot draw a list of Indian Christians who have visibly contributed to the welfare of the country. Whatever the political options of individuals, the Christian community as a whole lived in the past and lives its present as an integral part of the complex reality that is India.

THE CHURCH IN INDIAN POLITICS

There is a fear among politicians (not just in India) that the Christian churches, with their influence on people, interfere in the field that belongs to the political establishment and even seek advantages for their members to the possible detriment of other communities. It has indeed taken a long time for the Christians to formulate their proper role in the political reality of their nation and of the world. Today India's churches are generally satisfied with the theory and practice of the separation of church and state, although this phrase is perhaps too negative; one would rather speak positively of the relation between the two spheres.

Of course the relationship between religion and politics is not contentious for Christians alone. All religious movements with a wide influence, whether Hinduism, Buddhism, Islam or Sikhism, have at various times in their history met the problem of the interface between their sphere of influence and that of the political power. In Hindu theory it takes the form of the relation of the Brahmin and the raja or kshatriya. Both politics and religion appeal to the loyalty of human beings. Politics deals essentially with power and how the collective power has to be shared and exercised. Religion deals essentially with the deeper self-understanding of individuals in the large world of history and the cosmos, and with the values deriving from that understanding, which are wider and superior to power: the world of ethics, of relations between individuals and groups, the field of transcendent reality or the destiny of human beings, whether one calls it salvation, moksha, nirvana, the Kingdom of God or heaven.

Like other citizens Christians accept the importance of the political society and its role. Its specific role is decision making in what concerns the welfare of all. *Niti*, the Hindi word for politics, means 'leading' (from the root *ni*): political activity leads us to decisions we take in common and commit ourselves to. Religion is a darshan or a drsti, a vision that should *guide* decision making. Without the vision the decisions will be blind. But without the political commonwealth, the vision cannot 'lead' to decision. Like other religions, Christianity does not replace the political establishment. But at the same time it does propose an understanding of the human being and of human society which it finds wholesome and valuable, and wants politics to take into account this understanding and the values it invokes. The vision may at times involve a prophetic critique of what society at large does or the political establishment decides. Such criticism is part of the democratic life and must be acceptable to all. As the American revolutionary Thomas Paine said, 'It is the duty of the patriot to protect his country from its government.' Cooperation and criticism can go hand in hand and in fact criticism is at times the best way of cooperation.

At times people seem to perceive Christianity in India, and particularly the Catholic Church, as a 'branch' of a foreign world body. And it may be true that, in the past, priests in Christian 'missions' were excessively controlled by the mission boards of their respective churches abroad. Today we regret such overdependence on others. We do not deny our deep communion with all Christian communities everywhere in the world, and Catholics do affirm their loyalty to the sign and symbol of the unity of the Church, the Pope in Rome. But this does not make the Church in India a 'branch' of a multinational society. This is not our self-understanding, in this country or elsewhere. Each Christian community presided over by a bishop, living its faith in solidarity with Christians elsewhere and led by the light of the sacred Scriptures, is created by the presence of the risen Lord in its midst. It is in itself authentic and complete. Our communion with other churches elsewhere is simply an affirmation of our common fidelity to the message of Jesus Christ.

INDIAN CHRISTIAN THEOLOGY

From this self-understanding derives the need for all churches, especially the churches living in different cultural units of the world, to develop from within, as it were, though always in communion with other churches, new ways of articulating, expressing and celebrating their Christian life. At the end of the twentieth century the Church in India rejoices that especially in this century there has been a rich growth of what we call Indian Christian theology. Such theology is of course a complex and multiform undertaking, responding to the complex reality of India. But it is an undertaking that is taken seriously by all the churches in the country and by their organs of reflection and decision.

Indian theology begins with the lives of ordinary life: their hymns in the local languages, their symbols and their use of the cultural elements proper to each region are the seeds of Indian theology. The inculturation discussed earlier leads to new ways of celebrating the Eucharist—the integration of bhajans into the service, the use of tablas and other musical instruments of our tradition, Indian ways of performing the namaskarams, the practice of arati to welcome the Lord in our midst, the profuse use of incense and flowers, all are non-verbal expressions of the 'Indian theology'. Tribal dances will be different from Dalit dances and both different from Bharatanatyam and similar cultural forms. The use of colours changes according to local culture. The hours of worship are in continuity with the ancient customs. These cultural expressions of Christian life demand new Indian ways of speaking about our faith.

At the level of conceptual articulation, the Indian Christians must acknowledge with gratitude the help received from our Hindu brothers and sisters in particular, who expressed their understanding of Jesus Christ when they came across him. At the beginning of chapter two we mentioned in passing some of their views on Jesus. Without necessarily representing the Christian perception, their expressions have helped Christians to speak about Jesus in ways that draw meaning and significance from older Indian traditions. In the nineteenth century three names are particularly important: Krishna Mohan Banerjee, who spoke of Jesus as a Christian believer in the context of the significance of the cosmic sacrifice in ancient Indian culture. For him the sacrifice of Christ somehow explained and gave meaning to the Vedic theme of the creative sacrifice of Prajapati. Brahmabandhab Upadhyay reinterpreted and gave new meaning to the Christian faith in the Trinity by his celebrated hymn *Vande Saccidanandam*. We have recorded his stotra in honour of the Word Incarnate. In the previous section we have also recorded some of his rich reflections on the meaning of the Christian faith in India: he wrote much insightful material, now available in two volumes published by the United Theological College, Bangalore. A third important name in the nineteenth century is the Chitpavan Brahmin Nilakantha Goreh (1825–95), who converted to Christianity in 1848 and became a kind of apologist for his new faith against the attacks of his former colleagues in Varanasi. He may be the first to have articulated the orthodox Christian faith as developed by the traditional church in the cultural terms and context of Brahminic Hinduism. Though critical of his former traditional sources, he recognized the values in them, as when he wrote in 1887 in a letter to Pandita Ramabai:

> Providence has certainly prepared us, the Hindus, to receive
> Christianity in a way in which, it seems to me, no other

nation—excepting the Jews, of course—has been prepared. Most erroneous as is the teaching of such books as the *Bhagavadgita*, the *Bhagavata*, etc., yet they have taught us something of *ananyabhakti* (undivided devotedness to God), of *vairagya* (giving up the world), of *namrata* (humility), of *ksama* (forbearance), etc., which enables us to appreciate the precepts of Christianity (quoted in Boyd 1989, 55).

The Varanasi Pandit, Father Goreh, as Ramabai referred to him, embodied in his saintly life those virtues of ananyabhakti, vairagya, namrata and ksama.

In the twentieth century Indian theology came into its own. The popular preacher Sadhu Sundar Singh from Punjab wanted to present his new faith as 'the water of life in an Indian cup'. He is famous for his use of Indian parables and similes in presenting his message about Jesus. A.J. Appasamy (1891–1976) from south Tamil Nadu was inspired mostly by the bhakti tradition and wrote *Christianity as Bhakti Marga* (1927) and *What Is Moksha?* (1931). About the same period we find the members of the 'Rethinking Group' mostly from South India. Their theology had a sharp nationalistic edge. The name of the group comes from the book they published jointly in 1938, on the eve of a meeting of the International Missionary Council in Madras, rejecting the views regarding the Indian Church offered by the then famous European theologians Hendrick Kraemer and Karl Barth. One of the members of this group is Pandipeddi Chenchiah (1886–1959), from a Telugu family settled in Madras. He practised law and became a judge in a small state. Converted with his family in 1901, his thinking about Jesus Christ as the Adi Purusa or a new creation was much influenced by the *Integral Yoga* of Sri Aurobindo.

Vengal Chakkarai (1880–1958) came from the Chetty caste of Tamil Nadu and was the brother-in-law of Chenchiah. He was converted when he was twenty-three. Like Chenchiah he was a lawyer but left the practice to join Gandhi's freedom campaign and later the labour movement. He was elected mayor of Madras in 1941. He published *Jesus the Avatar* (1927) and *The Cross in Indian Thought* (1932). Another influential Madrasi theologian was Paul David Devanandan (1901–62) who became professor of philosophy and religions at United Theological College in Bangalore and eventually the founding director of the Centre for the Study of Religion and Society, now based in Bangalore and New Delhi. In this task he was helped by M.M. Thomas, and together they started the journal *Religion and Society*, focusing on dialogue and the secular meaning of the Gospel and the tasks of religion in the social sphere.

Perhaps the greatest name among Indian theologians in the field of inter-religious dialogue is Raimundo Panikkar (b. 1918), a man of rich experience of cultures. He was born in Barcelona of a Hindu father and a Catholic mother and was baptized a Catholic in childhood. He embodies thus the Hindu–Christian dialogue in his flesh, but has added to it much wisdom from his study not only of these two traditions but also of Buddhism, science, phenomenology, existentialist philosophy as well as Marxism. He has lived and worked in Europe, India and the US. Among his many publications the best known in English are *The Unknown Christ of Hinduism* (1964, revised ed. 1981), *Christianity and World Religions* (1969), *The Intra-Religious Dialogue* (1978), *Myth, Faith and Hermeneutics* (1978), *The Vedic Experience* (1979), *Blessed Simplicity* (1982), *The Silence of God* (1989, Spanish ed. 1970), *Cultural Disarmament: The Way to Peace* (1993), *Invisible Harmony* (1995) and *The Cosmotheandric Experience* (1998).

Another widely read Indian theologian was Father D.S. Amalorpavadoss (1932–90), founder director of the Bangalore-based National Biblical, Catechetical and Liturgical Centre and later of the Anjali Ashram in Mysore. He too worked for the dialogue of the Church with Indian religions and cultures, fostered Indian forms of worship and had a strong influence in the later part of the twentieth century on the transformation of the Catholic Church into an open church. Among his publications are *Gospel and Culture* (1978) and *Integration and Interiorization* (1990). Amalorpavadoss must not be confused with Michael Amaladoss (b. 1936) whose reflection has been more on the theoretical analysis of culture and its relation to religion and social justice. He has also endeavoured to reinterpret the significance of Jesus in a world of many religions.

Anthony (Tony) de Mello (1931–87) became a world-famous guru who applied the wisdom of Eastern sages and modern psychology to lead people closer to God and to open their minds to broader horizons than those of their narrow religious formation. His books, such as *Sadhana*, are mostly in the form of wisdom literature leading people to discover themselves and the divine dimensions of life. He has also written beautiful passages on Jesus Christ and what inspiration he received from him. Like his presence during his lifetime, his writings have the quality of freeing people from within.

While the group so far mentioned (many others could be added) draw inspiration from the mainstream Hindu theological and spiritual tradition, in the last decades of the twentieth century there emerged a powerful group that preferred to seek inspiration from the protest movements of India and from a critical analysis of Indian culture. They have created what may be called the Indian version of Liberation Theology. While M.M. Thomas worked in that direction, perhaps the most articulate author in this line is Sebastian Kappen (1924–93). The back cover of the two volumes of his collected works (*Jesus and Culture* and *Jesus and Society*, Delhi, ISPCK 2002) rightly says, he moved 'along the boundaries between Christian faith and secular ideologies [and] developed theological perspectives which open wide horizons for the understanding of the message of Jesus in a pluralistic context.

'A critique of religious fundamentalism and cultural imperialism runs through all these pages.' Kappen gave great importance to the work of the Buddha in this critique. He also made a serious study of Karl Marx, specially the younger Marx.

Samuel Rayan (b. 1920) is also associated with this liberation trend and draws much inspiration from the Indian literary tradition. George Soares-Prabhu (1929–95) was a great biblical scholar and supplied a solid scriptural basis to the liberationist interpretation of the Christian faith. We have elsewhere spoken of Dalit and tribal theologies. There are many other living theologians who continue to develop Indian theologies, articulating the Christian faith from the cultural and sociological reality of India.

The written output of Indian theologians is considerable. One of the main themes of Indian theology has been a new reflection on how Indian Christians view their faith in the context of the pluralism of India and Asia in general. It is clear that the old opposition to other religions as false or evil has been abandoned in the last two centuries. There is now no polemic against them. There is of course a criticism of religion to the extent that it has failed to consider the social issues of justice and has remained enclosed in an individual spirituality, but this criticism is addressed to all religions, including Christianity (for example, on the issue of caste). There is a general sense among Christians that religions often represent not only one of the finest endeavours of human culture but also a sign of the presence of the divine in each particular culture.

Some Indian Christians embrace what is called a pluralistic view of religions, according to which all religions are equal in so far as they are paths leading to the same goal of salvation or union with the divine reality. One outstanding Indian Christian who has propagated this view is S.J. Samartha (1920–2001). He was for ten years (1971–80) the first director of the sub-unit for Dialogue with People of Living Faiths and Ideologies in the Geneva-based World Council of Churches, where he had great influence on many churches all over the world. He stresses that the Divine Mystery is the absolute reality, and all religions are distinctive responses to that mystery, responses that are, however, inter-related. He wrote, among others, *Courage for Dialogue: Ecumenical Issues in Inter-religious Dialogue* (Geneva: WCC 1981) and *One Christ—Many Religions: Towards a Revised Christology* (Maryknoll: Orbis 1991).

However, many Christians find the pluralism of many-rivers-flowing-to-the-same-sea a simplistic solution to a complex question, and feel it does not fit their own Christian experience. For them, Jesus Christ did not come to abolish other religions, but he cannot be considered just one of many gurus. He is on a different level. Nor is he just an avatar of the divine, descended to give us an enlightening teaching or an individual salvation. For those Christians who remain within the parameters of the Christian faith as articulated thus far in history, Jesus Christ is the goal of human history, in whom the divine and the human become one: he is the point of arrival in whom all human endeavours towards the true, the good and the beautiful achieve their fulfilment. There is still no unanimity among Christians on how to reconcile Jesus Christ with the many religious endeavours of humanity. There is, however, a clear rejection of negative attitudes, a positive acceptance and gratitude for the many insights and paths religions have offered to peoples in all cultures, and a desire to find expressions wherein Jesus Christ does not appear as a threat or a fighter against religions but rather as a symbol of divine acceptance.

11

A Day in the Life of an Indian Christian

The morning prayers ~ Relationship to Mary ~ Marian sanctuaries in India ~ The rosary ~ The saints ~ Canonizations ~ Indian saints ~ Saint Buddha ~ Angels and devils ~ The Christian calendar ~ Christmas ~ Easter ~ The ordinary times and its Marian feasts ~ Food and drink ~ Friends and relations ~ Christian communities ~ The priest as father ~ Rites of passage ~ Baptism ~ Confirmation ~ First communion ~ Education in the faith ~ The girl child ~ Boys and girls ~ Marriage and sexual morality ~ Interfaith marriages ~ Celibacy ~ Attitudes to other religions ~ Change in the meaning of mission ~ The last rite of passage: death ~ The final destiny

THE MORNING PRAYERS

How does the average Christian live in India? In many ways very much like his or her neighbours of other communities, yet with a distinct consciousness and outlook in life. Like most Indians, the average Christian gets up early in the morning. They have been trained at home and in school to start the day with a thought about God or a short prayer. Before or after the ablutions they may take time for morning prayers. Catholics often open the prayer time with the simple gesture of tracing the lines of a cross with the hand on their bodies and saying at least mentally, 'In the name of the Father and of the Son and of the Holy Spirit, Amen.' This simple ritual sums up the Christian consciousness. The tracing of the sign of the cross may externally look like an adaptation of a tantric rite in which the body is 'sanctified' or consecrated to God by touching different parts with the invocation of a divine name. For the Christian the gesture recalls the consecration of her or his person to Jesus Christ in the rite of baptism. The symbol of the cross of course recalls the death of Jesus who died in love for the sake of humanity. It is necessarily linked with his resurrection. The invocation of the Trinity sums up the basic core of the Christian faith, as we shall explain in chapter twelve.

The morning prayer that follows the sign of the cross depends on the various Church traditions. Protestants especially, but other Christians too, include reading a text from the Bible and reflecting over it and praying for strength to live the teaching in the daily life. Often the Lord's Prayer is included, that is, the prayer St Matthew's Gospel says Jesus taught his disciples (cf. Mt 5:9–13). Its most important words are the first two, 'Our Father', calling us to relive in our daily life a relationship to God similar to that of a child to its loving parent. But everybody is included in that prayer: 'Our Father', not 'My Father'. The prayer will of course be said in the language of the family, which may be any of the eighteen official languages of India or any of the many tribal languages or dialects. There is no language more sacred than others: not Latin, not Greek, not Hebrew, nor, of course, English! In some families prayers are said in English, either because this has become the language of the family or because the members have been educated in this language. The traditional English version of the Lord's Prayer most used is a somewhat archaic translation: 'Our Father who art in heaven, hallowed be thy name, thy kingdom come, thy will be done on earth as it is in heaven. Give us this day our daily bread, and forgive us our trespasses as we forgive those who trespassed against us. And lead us not into temptation but deliver us from evil. For thine is the kingdom, the power and the glory for ever and ever, Amen.' Other more modern translations are also in use. The last sentence is not in the Gospel text but is a widely used conclusion of praise. The 'Amen' that closes most Christian prayers is an ancient Hebrew word to express assent, commitment, acceptance, faith.

If the Christian belongs to the Catholic tradition, he or she will often pray to Mary, the Mother of Jesus. The most frequently used prayer, sometimes repeated three or more times, is the 'Hail Mary', an ancient composition of a few words from the Bible referring to Mary and an ancient prayer addressed to her. The prayer reads, 'Hail Mary, full of grace, the Lord is with you, blessed are you among women and blessed is the fruit of your womb, Jesus. Holy

Mary, Mother of God, pray for us sinners, now and at the hour of our death, Amen.' The relationship to Mary is very central to the Catholic and the ancient Orthodox and Oriental traditions. The expression 'Mother of God' seems to raise Mary to the status of a goddess, but this is not the Christian consciousness of Mary. 'Mother of God' is a paradoxical expression. The eternal God does not, of course, have a mother: God indeed is the Mother of everything that exists (although Christians in general do not use feminine pronouns to refer to God, except in the modern feminist movement. God is beyond sex and gender distinction, but the linguistic tradition has been from biblical times to use the masculine when referring to 'God'). To say that Mary is the 'Mother of God' is a shortcut to saying that she is the mother of the human individual called Jesus, whom the Christian professes to be united in a single person to the eternal Son of God (see chapter twelve). 'Mother of God' was a defiant title given to Mary in the fifth century to reject the views of some heretics who in their explanations split the personality of Jesus into a human person and a divine person. It indirectly affirmed that in Jesus divinity and humanity were united in a single personal reality.

Whatever the historical and theological background, Christians of the older traditions have no problem in invoking Mary in this way. They know that she is not a goddess, but in her personal role as a human being she shows us a beautiful way of relating to God in our lives. As Catholics read them, the Scriptures present her as the perfect believer. That is why the title 'full of grace' found in the Gospel of Luke is imbedded in the popular prayer. The Gospel of John tells us that on the cross just before expiring, Jesus 'gave' his mother to the youngest of his disciples, John. Catholics have assumed from ancient times that John was a symbol of each believer and that somehow Jesus wanted his followers to take Mary as their mother in the life of faith, she who was his biological mother. Some Catholics may invoke and relate to Mary more often than they do to Jesus or to God. They have been told that Mary leads 'automatically', so to speak, to the Son of God and therefore to the Father. For believers Mary is not just a historical reality of the past: she is alive and in faith we communicate with her. She somehow reflects to us the feminine face of the divine, a theme generally weak or missing in the Semitic traditions.

The many sanctuaries of Mary that dot the map of Christian India are expressions of Marian bhakti. The most famous is surely that of Our Lady of Health in Vailankanni, Thanjavur District. It is a shrine to which devotees of all castes and communities come for help, not only from the south but from the whole of India and even from South-East Asia. Vailankanni is thus a bridge that spans rich and poor, city and village, Hindu and Christian, sea and land, heaven and earth. 'Vailankanni appears to be a calling port or resting place where people come with their needs and return recouped with new strength. A lot of depressed youths come here and go back with peace in their hearts. Reconciliation between members of a family is prayed for and obtained. Those suffering from sickness . . . are cured and brought back to full life. Those who had been leading a life away from God and people, seek pardon . . . and vow to start a new life' (Leonard 1985, 41).

The Catholic population of Vailankanni proper is very small, around 4000, counting the many outsiders settled there. Local traditions say that the place used to be a sanctuary of a local goddess which has been transformed into a Catholic centre. The legends speak of three different apparitions of Mary here during the sixteenth and seventeenth centuries. The first two were seen by local Hindu boys who came to recognize the identity of the apparition through their Catholic friends. These visions resulted in the building of a thatched hut used as a chapel. The third was seen by a group of Portuguese sailors in danger of shipwreck who were brought safe to port in Vailankanni on 8 September, the day Catholics celebrate as the birthday of Mary. In Vailankanni one can directly see the fusion of Hindu and Catholic traditions into one popular festival of chariots. It is interesting that many towns in India have a sanctuary or church under the title of Our Lady of Health, as they call her, often making explicit their dependence on Vailankanni.

There are other Marian sanctuaries in the country, including Our Lady of Bandel outside Kolkata, Our Lady of Carmel in Mount Mary's, Bandra, Mumbai, Our Lady of Snows, Thuthukudi, Our Lady of Graces in Sardhana, near Delhi, the Dhori Mata Tirth in Jarangdih, Bokaro, popular with the Christian tribals, and Unteshvari Mata Mandir in Mehsana District, Gujarat. Many ordinary churches are also dedicated to her; from them she presides over the prayers of Catholics and other visitors who turn up to pray there. Following a south European tradition, in many churches and shrines the month of May is celebrated with special prayers to Mary.

The rosary is a popular prayer in which the worship of God and devotion to Mary are integrated. Many families still keep the custom of gathering together to say the rosary every day or some days a week. The prayer essentially consists in recalling twenty significant moments in the story of Jesus, moments mostly connected with Mary, and while mentally reflecting on it vocally or silently one repeats a prayer consisting of one 'Our Father', ten 'Hail Mary's' and one 'Glory be . . .' This last is an ancient doxology or sukta of praise that reads: 'Glory be to the Father and to the Son and to the Holy Spirit, as it was in the beginning, is now and ever shall be world without end, Amen.' The twenty 'significant moments' (usually called 'mysteries') are divided into four sets of five, and different days of the week individuals or the family will say one or the other set. In order to count the prayers, the faithful often use a mala or a string of beads called a rosary (bouquet of roses). Scholars think that the use of the mala travelled from India, where it was used by monks and sadhus, to the world of Islam and hence to the Christian world.

THE SAINTS

The Christian religious world is 'crowded'. Strict monotheism is not incompatible with the existence of the world of the Spirit. For besides God, there is Jesus, 'a man like us in all things but sin', and there is mother Mary, and most Christians also have a tradition of invoking saints. Jesus is of course unique in that he shares both the human nature and divine status. Apart from him all other creatures whom Christians may invoke or venerate, whether Mary or any of the saints, are never called God. They are spiritually outstanding persons whose lives reflect a high degree of the ethical and spiritual values of the Christian faith. Although in the present time they are not visible to us, they are believed to be close to us and seen as models and helpers. We live in the hope that one day we shall form an eternal company with them. The most venerated saint among all Christians is of course Mary, the mother of Jesus. Her husband, St Joseph—though not Jesus' biological father, since Jesus is believed to have been born of the 'virgin Mary' by God's power—is also, to a lesser extent, venerated by Christians, especially Catholics.

The twelve apostles or closest disciples of Jesus, most of whom are believed to have died a martyr's death, have been venerated from the earliest times by all churches. For Indian Christians, Thomas has a special significance. But the most important among them was Peter. The ancient tradition has linked Peter and Paul, who was one of the first converts after the death and resurrection of Jesus, in a single celebration. Besides the apostles many of the ancient Christian martyrs for the faith are remembered every year in most Christian communities. The Christian calendar is not merely a record of seasons, months, weekdays and holidays, or of the phases of the moon and the rising and setting of the sun. The calendar is primarily a reminder of the saints who have lived among us. Most dates have the memory of one or more saints linked to them, often because it was the day of their death. The Christian somehow lives in their company. The official Catholic prayer for the Eucharist, addressing God the Father, says on the feasts of the saints:

In their lives on earth you give us an example.
In their communion with them, you give us their friendship.
In their prayer for the Church you give us strength and protection.

This sense of communion with the saints is particularly attuned to the tribal religious sense of communion with the ancestors. In a broad sense the saints are our ancestors in the faith. They are near us. Many Christian families or groups may be particularly fond of one saint or another, according to their traditions and often because there is a public shrine in their honour in the vicinity. We shall presently mention also the sense of fellowship Christians have with relatives and friends who have 'departed' from this life. They too are alive to God and to us.

Most churches hold the ancient saints in reverence, either because they are mentioned in the Bible or are early martyrs for the faith venerated in the whole church, or particular important bishops and theologians like St Augustine, St Ambrose, St Anthony, St Basil and St Chrysostom. In the Oriental churches the declaration of saints is usually made by the synod of bishops of a particular Church. After the break-up of the churches in the sixteenth century, however, the Protestant churches stopped the custom of declaring more saints. However in its annual almanac, the Church of North India does include the 'commemoration of notable Christians for optional observance locally'. It includes Samuel Azariah, Devasahayam Pillai, Roberto de Nobili, N.V. Tilak, Kalicharan Banerjea, Imad-ud-din, Dhanjibhi Naoroji, Sadhu Sundar Singh and Krishna Pal, Indian converts, evangelists, martyrs, persons 'who have demonstrably inspired others to holiness'. They do not include any Christian who died less than thirty years ago.

The process of the declaration of saints is most legislated in the Roman Catholic Church. The process takes a long time. It cannot begin, except by special permission of the Pope, before five years after the person's death. When a bishop decides to propose a person of his diocese for sainthood he appoints a number of commissions to study her or his life, writings if any, relations with the community and influence on others. During this period of inquiry the future saints are called 'Servants of God'. Of popular interest are the 'miracles' that a person is reported to have performed when his intercession has been invoked (usually cures that are medically difficult to explain). Nobody can be declared saint while alive; Christians have a strong sense of human fragility and how every human being has 'feet of clay', that is, anyone may fall.

The dossier prepared in the diocese on a particular candidate is sent to Rome where there is a permanent office of canonizations (that is, making of a saint—putting the name of a person in the 'canon' or list of saints that may be invoked). If the life is proved authentic and inspiring, its effect on people positive, the writings orthodox and at least one 'miracle' proven to be true, the office proposes the candidate to the Pope first for 'beatification'. Beatification is a preliminary step in the process of canonization and allows local worship of the candidate where she or he is known. At this stage she or he is called 'Blessed', not yet 'Saint'. Only another 'miracle' after beatification and a further inquiry about the influence of the person will enable the candidate to be enrolled as a saint, and his or her veneration will be recommended throughout the Church. In the Catholic Church only the Pope has authority to declare a person Blessed or Saint. John Paul II, the present Pope, has become a specialist in this task: in the twenty-five years since he was elected Pope he has beatified 820 men and women and canonized 283. Catholics believe that the declaration of sainthood gives a certainty to the community that the person has reached full salvation and is for eternity in communion with the divine. They also believe that they can spiritually communicate with the saints.

Indian Christians have been for most of their history only indirectly connected with Rome, and so they have only one officially canonized saint and four blesseds. They have been mentioned earlier: Saint Gonzalo Garcia (1557–97); and Blessed Joseph Vaz (1651–1711), Kuriakose Elias Chavara (1805–71), Sr Alphonsa (1910–46) and Mother Mariam Thresia Mankidiyan (1876–1926). The last three were members of the Syro-Malabar Church in Kerala and religious in vows. Though not an Indian by birth but one by nationalization, the most well-known of all the blesseds is undoubtedly Mother Teresa of Calcutta, beatified on 19 October 2003, in the celebrations of the twenty-fifth anniversary of the election of Pope John Paul II.

SAINT BUDDHA

A curious fact in the official list of saints of the Catholic Church is the cryptic presence of one who is perhaps the greatest Indian saintly figure of all time: Siddhartha Gautama, the Buddha, the 'Awakened One'. His presence in the Catholic book of saints is hidden under the name of Saint Josaphat. Surely, he is not in the Christian calendar because the Church explicitly acknowledges the saintliness of the founder of Buddhism; only Christians are included in the liturgical list of saints. The Buddha is there because of the story of 'Barlaam and Josaphat', an ancient version, probably originating in Tamil Nadu, of the renunciation of the Bodhisattva or Bodhisat. The story, incorporated in the *Lalitavistara*, travelled from India to central Asia and hence into Arabic literature where the Manichaean *Bodisaf* became *Yudasaf* (perhaps because of a confusion in the written vernacular initial), and hence into Georgian literature and to Greek and Latin writings where the name took the form of Josaphat, and hence to the vernaculars of all Europe. In the late sixteenth century the popes had the ancient official book of saints or martyrology revised. It was published by Pope Gregory XIII in 1584. Cardinal Baronius, who had a leading part in the revision, incorporated in the book the legend of the Indian prince converted by the monk Barlaam and turned into a Christian! The monk Barlaam was an addition to the original story introduced somewhere during its long journey to the West. Baronius was keen on purifying the martyrology of apocryphal legends but accepted this story on the authority of the writings of St John Damascene (c. 657–749 CE) who often mentioned the two ascetics. The entry in the martyrology, 27 November, reads, 'In the Indies, bordering upon Persia, Saints Barlaam and Josaphat, of whose wondrous deeds St John Damascene has written.' After the enormous modern research on this story, St Josaphat is likely to be dropped from the martyrology in the next revision—a pity! At the moment the Buddha is still officially, even if cryptonymously, celebrated in the Catholic Church (see Smith 1981, 6–11).

ANGELS

We said earlier that the Christian world is crowded. Effectively, a New Testament text says that we are in a huge and cosmic stadium, 'surrounded by a great cloud of witnesses' (Heb 12:1), the saints, all of them alive to God and our companions, seeing how we 'run the race'. But we can count also on the spiritual services of innumerable 'angels'. Angels are popularly believed to be non-human spiritual beings created by God, and therefore finite, who are in God's service and act as his messengers. They are benevolent spirits, and although bodiless, artists portray them imaginatively as having human bodies with wings. Angels are mentioned in the Bible with various shades of meaning, sometimes identified with God's very presence. They turn up more persistently in the literature of the First Testament written after the exile of part of the Jewish people to Babylon, where they came into contact with the Iranian culture. The Iranian religion was a sister of the Vedic religion, and besides the Absolute God it believed in the minor gods and indeed also the devils, the asuras and devas of the Vedic world, although, strangely, with contrary characteristics: the asuras are the good gods and the devas the evil ones! The biblical world may have imported both of them as angels and demons, although some may have been picked up from primeval local cultures. The New Testament takes for granted the popular beliefs of the period and authors like Luke use angels freely to explain, for instance, the mystery and beauty of the birth of Jesus. Jesus is also presented in the Gospels as having contact with angels, and also as the great warrior fighting against evil spirits or evil forces that diminish human beings either by disease, injustice or temptation.

Are angels and demons just projections of the psyche? Are they literary creations representing aspects of the divine reality that is ever transcendent but about which we must somehow speak? Are demons mere personifications of evil, not 'real' beings? Popular religion and the official churches generally maintain the biblical realism and consider them as real beings, in some ways superior in power and intelligence to human beings, but created and limited. There was also a popular belief, generally sanctioned by the Church, that each human being (and at times also each town and country) has a 'guardian angel' as protector on God's behalf. Devils were not created evil, but were believed to be angels who had *decided* against God. Their influence in our lives is limited to 'instigation' to evil, subject to our willing assent.

The modern world view discarded angels and devils as popular imaginations, at times clinically helpful, more often harmful. Esoteric literature is filled with such beings under different names. The postmodern world is less dogmatic about the non-existence of intelligent non-human beings. Using the terminology of transactional analysis, Jesuit writer Carlos Valles (1997, 31–32) says that angels belong primarily, but not only, to the child in us, a very real dimension of our human existence. When we kill the child under the repression and stern control of the parent and the adult, as modern culture has done, angels disappear. 'The angels are real beings in God's creation,' he says, accepting the orthodox position, 'and their place in our lives is enhanced with the contribution of our own creativity. We all have our angels; then what each angel becomes for each person depends on what this person may want them to be in his or her life. The more space we give to them around us, always within the limits of common sense and orthodoxy, the better it will be for us and for them. They will fly more freely.' Today theologians speak much less about angels or devils, although both continue to live in popular imagination as friendly and unfriendly beings. The Christian groups in India emerging from the tribal world are comfortable with the belief in angels and devils as it conforms not only to the New Testament world but also to their original religion filled with bhoots, benevolent or contrary.

THE CHRISTIAN CALENDAR

The memory of angels and saints is spread throughout the year of the Christian calendar. Time is not uniform; every religious calendar introduces rhythm and variation to the flow of time. The variations depend first on natural rhythms: day and night, the agricultural seasons with the annual cycle of heat and cold. The civil calendar has its own high points like independence days, victory days, martyrs' days and significant heroes' days. The personal calendar is also marked by important days going from birthday to wedding and other anniversaries. Similarly the religious calendar is punctuated by the memory of the saints and other beings that surround us as reminders of their ongoing divine presence.

In the Christian calendar, apart from the celebration of saint days, there are three main cycles that cover the whole year. The first lasts about seven weeks and is built around the most popular of Christian feasts, Christmas or the celebration of the birth of Jesus (Khristjayanti) on 25 December. There is no historical record of the date of Jesus' birth. The choice of 25 December was probably a Christian adaptation of a Roman feast related to the celebration of the winter solstice, when the sun begins its return from its lowest position in the sky to the highest, and the days therefore become longer. The early Christians incorporated the symbolism of that feast into their celebration of the birth of Jesus, the 'Unconquered Sun'. Christmas Day itself is preceded by four weeks of preparation called 'Advent' (the 'Coming') and followed by about three weeks of celebration of the stories about the infancy of Jesus recorded in the

Gospels. During this period, Christians celebrate the New Year on 1 January.

The second cycle lasts nearly fourteen weeks and is built around the celebration of Easter, the day when Jesus, according to Christian faith, 'rose from the dead'. The feast occurs generally in April (rarely in the last week of March) and is calculated with the help of the lunar calendar. This feast corresponds to the chronology of the death of Jesus which fell around the feast of the Passover of the Jews on 14 Nissan, in springtime. The feast was celebrated in remembrance of the escape ('Exodus') of the Jewish slaves from Egypt, eventually to find a home in Israel. The Christian Easter is always on a Sunday, as this is the day when the Gospels tell us the disciples discovered the empty tomb of Jesus and saw him alive. Actually it is because of this event that Sunday became the most important day of the week: before that, in Jewish culture the feast day was the Sabbath, Saturday.

Just before Easter Sunday the whole community celebrates the Holy Week in which the last days of the life of Jesus are recalled, especially his death on the cross, seen by Christians not as a black tragedy but as the day of 'salvation' for humanity. This is why it is appropriately called 'Good Friday'. Holy Week is the last of a period of forty days of preparation leading to Easter, during which Christians are encouraged to intensify almsgiving, prayer and fasting or other forms of spiritual activity. In olden times (and in some conservative communities even today), the fasting was strict and socially controlled. Today it is left in great part to the freedom and imagination of the faithful, who may choose other forms of austerity, not just in food and drink, but also entertainment, or by doing additional works of charity or compassion, over and above the usual ones. These forty days of preparation for Easter are called Lent, deriving from the old English for 'lengthening', a word applied to springtime when days 'lengthen'.

Easter is followed by fifty days of celebration of the significance of the resurrection of Jesus, and the Easter cycle ends therefore on Pentecost Sunday, in memory of the beginning of the Church's preaching when, according to the Bible, the Spirit of God filled the hearts and minds of the disciples of Jesus and gave them the courage to be as witness to the risen life of Jesus and to preach his message to the whole world and 3000 people were converted to the way of Jesus. A week before Pentecost Christians celebrate 'Ascension' day, when according to St Luke the risen Jesus departed from the disciples in his visible form, although he remained invisibly with them.

The third yearly cycle consists of the weeks called 'ordinary time'. More than a cycle it is really the background against which the two important cycles of Christmas and Easter are structured. It consists of two separate periods: the first runs from mid-January (at the end of the Christmas cycle) to mid-February or March (the beginning of Lent); the second from Pentecost (May or early June) till Advent (end of November). During this time many Christians traditionally celebrate two important feasts in honour of Mary: her birthday or Nativity (8 September), her Assumption into heaven (15 August, coinciding with India's Independence Day).

Akbar the Great actually celebrated 15 August with devotion. We have at least two reliable contemporary accounts, one from a Greek deacon, Father Leon Grimon, who was at Akbar's court in Lahore in 1580:

> On the day of the Assumption of Our Lady, the emperor held a festival setting forth in an elevated and public place a picture of Our Lady which the Fathers had given him when they went there the first time. He called everybody to touch the picture and kiss it as a sign of reverence. And he granted the privilege of being knights of the house to all those who would touch the picture. His relations asked that the Prince his son [Salim, the future Jahangir] should be the first to do so and so he was (see Maclagan 1896).

FOOD AND DRINK

We return to the day in the life of the Indian Christian. The morning prayer is normally short. Pious families might go to a daily Eucharist in a nearby church; other families, especially Protestant, might have a common or private Bible reading at the morning prayer or at other times. This reading might be part of a continuous reading, or chosen according to the need of the time. The reading may be explained by family members.

Like his or her neighbours, the Christian generally has a morning breakfast and, hopefully, a noon and an evening meal. The fare of these meals depends on the local culture and the economic level of the family or the individual. It is generally not different from those of the neighbours, although in certain localities the community might develop specific dishes, whether home-made sweets or cooked dishes. Life in cities tends to discard specific traditional dishes if they involve much labour. Christians have no food taboos imposed by religion; only local custom might dictate that some food be avoided. In his Gospel, St Mark said that by his words and practice Jesus 'declared all foods clean' (Mk 7:19), conspicuously departing, in this, from Jewish orthodoxy. In a vision related to his meeting non-Jews, the orthodox Peter was bidden by God to eat of various animals shown to him. At his refusal to eat anything 'unclean' he heard three times the declaration of freedom: 'What God has made clean, you must not call profane' (Acts 10:15). Christians claim this freedom: they are not obliged to eat any specific food, and they are not forbidden by religion to eat of any one. They may be vegetarians or non-vegetarians. They may eat vegetables, or grain, or eggs, fish, meat, pork or beef. They are asked to be guided only by two higher principles: freedom and love. The broadness of the first is restricted by the second: not to give offence to anyone by insisting on our freedom. If our choices hurt the feelings of others we should avoid them, even if we have a right to our freedom, says St Paul to his Christians.

The same principle applies to drink. Most Christians do not consider drinking sinful in itself. Sin is found only in drinking in excess so that we lose control of our human freedom and dignity. Actually a small quantity of wine is part of the most central form of Christian worship, the Eucharist. Moreover, according to St John's Gospel Jesus offered a generous contribution of wine to a family at whose wedding wine had run short (Jn 2). And in the Bible a letter attributed to St Paul recommends to Timothy, 'No longer drink only water, but take a little wine for the sake of your stomach and your frequent ailments' (1 Tim 5:23). As in matters of food, the traditions of the family or community are a better guide than any blanket prohibition or guideline.

Even with this freedom in food and drink, the churches may,

and some do, declare some days in the year as days of fast (no eating at all or moderate eating) and/or days of abstinence (traditionally no eating of meat). But this does not mean that particular foods are impure; it is simply a collective exercise of penance to counteract human excesses.

FRIENDS AND RELATIONS

The Indian Christian does not live in isolation. The communitarian sense is primary in his or her view of life. We were created for community and only in community can we find full salvation. They do not define the liberated state as *kaivalya*, although some of the mystic writers have spoken of being 'alone with the Alone'. The typical biblical word for salvation is rather *koinonia*, which in Greek literally means 'commonness' and involves community. This is the origin of the expression at the end of the traditional Christian creeds, 'I believe in the communion of saints,' 'saints' being the word with which St Paul often refers to the members of the community.

The koinonia of the Christians is not restricted to fellow believers. This is the temptation of communalism that threatens all religions in their self-perception. A mature Christian knows that the primary referent of community is the whole human family, the family of God. 'Adam', the first human according to the biblical myth, includes all human beings, just like Eve is 'the mother of all living' (Gen 3:20). The whole human family is the authentic community. But there is danger in universality as there is in particularity. As the joke goes, we may 'love humanity but hate humans'. Jesus called us to love the neighbour, the concrete reality.

And thus God has given most of us a family as the primary school of love. Like other Indians, Christians love their families intensely and maintain close contact with a broad range of relatives, especially on the occasion of major religious festivals and family celebrations. It is also normal and helpful that there is an extension of the blood relationship into the whole family of believers. We regularly meet each other in worship, we share the same belief and conscious relationship with Jesus Christ, our Lord, and with his mother and the saints. We share a common hope and a common love. We form one family. And so the Indian Christian will have his or her circle of fellow believers with whom he or she shares much of life. They are in a very true way his or her brothers and sisters.

There is also in the Church a common 'father'. Of course God is the Father of all; but sociologically the role of father of the concrete Christian community is filled by the priest in charge of the community, or parish, whom many Christians call 'father' (a title extended by courtesy to all ordained priests, and oddly used, as it is at variance with explicit prohibition of Jesus, reported in Mt 23:9). Other Christians address their leaders as reverend or pastor or minister. A close relation with the priest, especially the parish priest or pastor, is quite typical of Christians. They will visit him on occasions, either as a sign of support and gratitude, or to ask for specific help. The priests or pastors are important social personages in the Christian communities. They themselves are supported by the love and financial help of the community. In many traditional places they visit the homes of Christians and bless them at least once a year. They also organize the community for various activities, both in the line of internal well-being and in the area of outreach to others. Priests have the role of gurus or spiritual guides, the role of intermediaries of the divine, the role of social organizers of community relationships and the role of helpers in crisis situations. But their scope goes beyond their Christian community and extends to all people, especially the poor in their locality.

Priesthood is not hereditary, even where the law of celibacy does not apply. In the Catholic Church priests are usually recruited on the basis of voluntary offer normally by young people around twenty years of age. Their offer for Church service has to be approved by the community during a fairly long period of study and testing. If after this period the bishop thinks that the person is fit for the role of leadership of the community, he agrees to ordain him and the candidate becomes 'incardinated' into the diocese under the bishop, or works within an approved religious order.

Similar kinds of close bonding take place between rural communities and their 'catechists' or lay leaders, although the quality of the relationship of the Christian faithful to them may be different from the relation with the ordained priests. One may ask whether this strong bonding of families with the celibate priest (in the Catholic tradition) does not foster an excessive dependence, which in the case of poor families has at times been criticized in missionary literature as 'mabapism'.

RITES OF PASSAGE

Baptism

In every family the birth of a baby brings joy and responsibility. The sacrament to celebrate a new life in the Christian community is baptism, or the 'christening' of the candidate whom the family asks to be made a Christian. It is the most important ritual, administered a few days or weeks after the actual birth. By itself baptism is not really a sacrament of birth or infancy, although sociologically it works in this way. Biblically baptism is the sacrament of personal conversion, of acceptance of the way of life proposed by Jesus through incorporation into the community of his followers. At some periods baptism was exclusively administered in adulthood. But infant baptism had also been a practice in very ancient times and became generally accepted by most churches. However, Baptist churches consider child baptism illegitimate and accept only what they call believers' baptism, conferred at a mature age.

Interestingly, some ancient Christian communities in India have retained rituals of infancy and childhood inherited from the local tradition. Some observe the Hindu customs connected to naming the child, piercing the ear, giving the first solid food or cutting hair for the first time. In Kerala, traditional Christian families have also kept, at least till recently, the ancient practices related to the first learning of the child, and indeed the pandit in this ceremony was not seldom a Hindu Brahmin. Some Christian communities have also preserved their tradition of joyfully and publicly celebrating the menarche of their daughters.

Whether given in childhood or in mature age, the core baptismal rite consists of a ritual bath (which may consist of merely pouring water on the head) accompanied by the biblical formula '[Name], I baptize you in the name of the Father and of the Son and of the Holy Spirit. Amen.' Baptism is never self-administered. It is normally conferred by a priest; in cases of need a deacon, a catechist and even any layperson may confer it validly and licitly. The significance of the 'bath' (*baptô* in Greek really means 'to dip') is not primarily the washing idea, although this is also found in the ritual, which speaks of the washing of sins, particularly for the infant the 'original sin'. In its primary meaning, the 'dip', as St Paul explains in the letter to the Romans (6:3–11), is a symbolic enactment of the death–burial of Jesus and of his resurrection, for the candidate was dipped into the water and raised out of it. Therefore baptism is a ritual and mystical identification with the Lord Jesus in his death and resurrection. It marks the pattern of life for the new Christian: to live in the same way and by the same values as Jesus. At baptism there are, besides the parents, godparents, adult Christians who make a formal commitment to help the child or the new Christian to grow in Christian life.

There are many other rituals associated with the sacrament of baptism: making the sign of the cross, exorcisms, readings from the Bible, anointings, a new robe, new light, etc. It is not possible here to explain each ritual. All are meant to reinforce the central symbol of the 'dip' into water to rise again 'new'. Water is the central symbol signifying birth and death, womb and tomb, both pointing to a new life in Christ. Traditional Catholics used to have water blessed by a priest for use as exorcism in the many moments of danger in life.

Catholic children in India as elsewhere often treat with great solemnity the first reception of the Eucharist or 'the first Holy Communion'. They are prepared for it by an intense doctrinal formation adapted to their age and by spiritual instruction on the significance of the sacraments of Eucharist and Reconciliation. The occasion is generally a source of much festivity and joy in the family. In Catholic schools it is generally prepared in group and celebrated when the children are about eight years old.

There is another less important rite of passage in most churches called either chrismation or confirmation. It is related to baptism, but generally it is given when the young adolescent comes out of the 'womb' of the family and faces the world at large. It is the rite of passage into the adult world. Catholics tend to confer it earlier, even in childhood; other churches delay it to when the young person can personally accepts all the demands of Christian life. The ceremony is preceded by a course of instruction on the Christian faith. It is conferred through a laying on of hands by the bishop, an anointing with oil specially blessed during the Holy Week and the invocation of the Spirit or power of God. The idea is to empower the adult to be a witness of her or his faith in a world whose values are often at variance with those of Jesus.

Education in the Faith

It is the responsibility of parents and of the leaders of the community to see to it that children receive proper Christian education, not only with regard to values and an ethical life but also regarding religious themes and heritage. In both areas the role of the parents is primary. Every child learns not only the common prayers of the community together with the 'creed', a brief summary of the Christian beliefs, and the 'ten commandments' of God as recorded in the First Testament, but also some basic Scriptural texts and the outline of the life of Jesus Christ and of the Christian understanding of God. Children also learn stories of the lives of saints. This learning takes place first by participation in family worship, by the teaching of the parents (especially the mother) and grandparents, by the regular preaching in churches on Sundays and other occasions, and in Christian schools by the teaching of the Bible and of what Catholics call the 'catechism' or the explanation of the Christian faith, formerly printed in the form of questions and answers but nowadays made more pedagogical with participative learning.

When the children cannot go to Christian schools, and at times even if they go, the churches provide 'Sunday school' organized specially around the time of the reception of the sacraments of confirmation and Holy Communion. There are often also a pre-marital instruction course to prepare couples intending marriage for a full understanding of the religious significance of marriage.

It is worth noting here that in general the Christian community values the girl child highly. Christians were the first to open schools specially for girls. That the girl is loved intensely finds reflection in the Census of India where the Christian community is ahead of other communities in the sex ratio. In the 1991 Census, the sex ratio of Christians was 994 females per 1000 males. Another point this Census makes is that contrary to what happens in other communities the proportion of women is higher in the Christian urban population (1001) than in the rural population (991). This would seem to indicate a rather open attitude to female migration to cities. There are, for instance, a great number of Christian female nurses or domestic workers in the cities.

How do Christian boys and girls, and men and women, deal with each other in their daily lives? This too depends very much on the tradition of each community and the level of education. In general, gender relations are socially controlled. In modern times there is more free exchange between boys and girls where there is more education. Both the family and the Church structures try to inculcate a sense of respect for the other sex. Social communication between them generally remains open. Marriage is not allowed before the age of twenty-one and eighteen for boys and girls respectively as per common civil law. In many Christian communities, marriage is arranged or at least facilitated by parents, as in most other Indian communities. The educated layers of the population will more easily tolerate or encourage love marriage, though even here the parents have an advisory role.

Marriage

As in other communities, marriage is generally the most elaborate rite of passage. The marriage customs of each Christian community vary and are most often influenced by the traditions of the surrounding cultures and religions. As marriage is both a religious and a secular institution, the norms of the civil code must be taken into account. At the same time the Christian churches have a long tradition of internal legislation in the matter and the Indian law respects the personal laws of various religions.

There are differences among Christian churches on the meaning and religious status of marriage. All accept that marriage must be monogamous. Most Protestant churches accept the legitimacy of divorce for serious reasons, especially when both partners demand it, and of the marriage of divorcees. In this they more or less follow the common civil codes. The Oriental churches are more attentive to the apparently strict views of Jesus: 'What God has joined together let no man set asunder' (Mt 19:6). They tolerate divorce only in difficult circumstances, out of mercy, so to say. They agree to a religious marriage of a divorced person, but if the first partner is still alive the second marriage can only be a simple ceremony without church solemnity.

The Catholic Church is known to be very strict regarding marriage. It takes the words of Jesus literally. It says that they imply what most religions seem to assume, that there is a divine sanction in the institution of marriage, that marriage is not just a casual contract between two persons in which they may introduce whatever clauses they wish. Human nature reveals the divine design, and inscribed in nature there is a script of what marriage must be: when man and woman seek each other to be united in marriage, their search must be first of all an offer of *love*, by which they give themselves totally to one another, so as to find the complement in their lives which both their bodies and their psychology have demanded for years.

Such love is life-giving. There is an intrinsic societal aspect to marriage. Marriage is not just a private adventure of two human beings; the whole species has a legitimate stake in it. For the sexual union sanctioned by marriage clearly leads also at the perpetuation of the species, and if this aim is consciously excluded, then, whatever rituals may accompany a wedding, there is no marriage. The Bible presents the story of the creation of man and woman in such a way that God is seen to be the source and ultimate authority in marriage:

> God blessed them, and God said to them: 'Be fruitful and multiply, and fill the earth and subdue it; and have dominion over the fish of the sea and over the birds of the air and over every living thing that moves upon the earth' (Gen 1:28-29).

On the basis of this text and because of the life-giving meaning of marriage, openness to nature's ways of providing new human beings through the marital act is implicit in marriage. Going further, the official Catholic doctrine declares the use of artificial means of preventing conception of a human being unethical, in spite of the popular culture of birth control. In practice, many couples ignore this teaching of the Church; others try to obey by following, when necessary, natural methods of spacing births.

The love promised in marriage must be unconditional. Only total love can form the basis of the most stable and satisfying relationship a human being can have. Hence marriage involves a mature promise of fidelity unto death that goes well beyond an agreement based on the infatuation of an instinctual attraction. Underlying the obvious emotional load that marriage has, there is a mature and free decision. 'Love is a decision' is one of the slogans used and meditated upon by the marriage encounter groups that have recently sprung up among Christians and others as well.

It is often asked whether human beings, especially those at the stage of civilization and of individualism in which we presently find ourselves, can ever make lifelong commitments. The constant fluctuations of our emotional life as well as of the external conditions of our existence, which always open possibilities of new relationships, suggest, it is said, that human decisions may be realistically made only for a time span within our immediate control. We can never promise anything for a remote future. Lifelong commitments are not possible.

Inspired by the teaching of Jesus, the Catholic doctrine rejects this limiting view of the human person. It teaches that the authentic spiritual nature of the human being implies the capacity to take the whole of one's existence and life into one's hands and to offer it in freedom and love. We can assume responsibility for our doings and for our future. We are not playthings of fate or of social determinism. Of course ultimate commitments require courage, a leap into the unknown, yet such commitments can be made and are being made. And this is the kind of commitment which the heart of a lover dreams of having and is not satisfied if it does not have. 'I love you as long as it lasts' is not a very complimentary proposition! We want to find in the other person not only a temporary friend but truly the complement of our existence, the 'other half' that brings us the assurance of a new wholeness.

Catholics are of course aware of the fragility of even the most serious and mature commitments. They would not dare to make any except at the foot of the altar, that is, counting on the power and grace of the divine reality to guide our steps and strengthen our decisions. This trust in the divine presence within us is an expression of the belief of the Holy Spirit, that is, of God as antaryamin, the Inner Guide. Catholics therefore consider marriage a sacrament, a sacred commitment entered into under the inspiration of God.

The churches try always to make sure that marriage is a free decision, not one forced on either partner by parents or society in general. It must also be an enlightened decision in which no fraud has entered. In the West the choice of partners is done by the partners themselves; the greater socialization between men and women and fewer barriers of caste or class make this possible. In India many Christian marriages, like other marriages, are at least partly arranged and inspired by the parents through the normal channels of inter-family relationships. However in most cases the negotiations include the participation of the prospective partners. There are on the part of the official churches no caste barriers for an acceptable marriage, but many Christian communities do observe ancient taboos in this area. Similarly, demands of dowry are made in some communities, though frowned upon by the Church authorities.

One of the hardest decisions of the Catholic Church is not to recognize divorce. The hope is that the love promised in marriage is of such quality that even if the couple breaks up and separates it remains as a bond. The vow given at marriage remains irrevocable. (Many plots and subplots in the Indian epics are based on the power of a vow.) A partner may be innocent and not responsible for the break-up, but even then, especially then, the decision of love remains as a longing and a commitment to overcome the crisis. No remarriage is recognized as long as the legitimately married partner is alive, even if she or he has remarried. The love given to a partner remains faithful to the end!

In spite of this highly idealistic doctrinal position, the practice of indissolubility of marriage as taught by the Catholic Church is not as absolute as it looks. There are in practice break-ups of marriages. When the cohabitation of husband and wife becomes impossible because of a deep incompatibility or because of the violence and injustice of one or both parties, the Church allows and even advises a courageous separation of the partners. Battered wives have a right to get out of the house, if they can! In most such cases a supportive group is necessary, and in some places the community provides it. The marriage bond is not thereby dissolved, but both the partners may live with a great sense of security and peace of mind. Meanwhile they may seek ways to restore human and mature relationships through counselling or other means.

There are occasionally cases when the marriage that has broken down is studied by experts in law and psychology. If they find that either partner did not enter into marriage with sufficient freedom, or that one of them or both did not have the psychological maturity to make a lifelong commitment and assume family responsibilities, the Church through its own tribunals and at the advice of experts can declare such marriages null and void from the beginning, after which the partners are free to marry another partner. Other grounds for annulment include impotency or the physical incapacity of the man to perform the sexual act, a serious deception about the identity of a partner, very close blood relationship between partners and insufficient age at the time of marriage.

The principle of an absolute indissolubility of marriage applies strictly only to marriages of baptized Christians that have been ratified and consummated. For here a specific Christian value is at stake. The Christian marriage is seen in a mystical dimension: husband and wife symbolize the mutual love of Jesus Christ and the Church. This is a sacrificial love unto death. The Christian marriage is a witness of such love in a world where self-sacrifice is discounted. No authority can dissolve such 'quality marriage'. Other marriages may be dissolved in exceptional cases. For example, when one of the partners converts to the faith and the other refuses to live with him or her in peace and mutual acceptance, the marriage can be dissolved so that both the persons are free to remarry.

'Until death do us part': marriage is obviously an institution of the world and it lasts as long as both partners are in this world. If one dies the marriage ceases to exist. All Christian churches permit the remarriage of widows or widowers, even in old age. Love can always be given. They also respect a decision of the widow or widower not to remarry and remain faithful to the memory of the partner, provided she or he can live in peace in the new situation.

Like most religious communities, the Church prefers that its members marry members of the community. This need not be seen as a case of communalism. It is rather a realistic preference. Religion enters deeply into the psychological and sociological make-up of many Indians, and a common faith lived within the same church ensures a greater likelihood of achieving the union of hearts and minds which makes marriage a joyful experience. But life is unpredictable, and human beings have a God-given freedom that no human institution can thwart. Hence men and women of different churches and different religions fall in love and want to marry, and are often ready to marry according to the Church's laws and views on marriage. In some cases even an atheist and a Christian may fall in love. Church authorities and relatives often try to dissuade the partners from such a union, but if the partners profess a serious commitment to love and lifelong fidelity and promise to respect each other's religious positions and grant the freedom to practise them accordingly, the Church authorities may grant dispensation for such a marriage.

'Mixed marriages' as they are called, or interfaith marriages, are becoming more common in cities today. Although there are possible pitfalls in such marriages, a number of them are successful. They require a very clear understanding of the position of each regarding their respective faiths, the freedom to profess it, relationships with the extended family, income, and children and their future education. The Christian partner assumes the responsibility of respecting the faith of the other partner and of sharing his or her faith with the children. Education in the Christian faith means sharing one's understanding of the message of Jesus and his values and of the person of Jesus himself. Such education and its expression must be done in such a way that the non-Christian partner's faith is not thereby belittled and that no threat is posed to the unity of the family. Family prayers may also be so structured that they reflect the faith of both partners.

Celibacy as a Value

Like other ancient religions, Christianity or at least some of its branches value celibacy as a special divine call given to some of its members. Not everyone is meant to be a celibate. But the presence of celibate people in the community has a message for all. In most of the Catholic tradition, celibacy is a condition for being made a priest or bishop. Moreover, the religious take a vow of perpetual celibacy, among others. The value given to celibacy is in no way a condemnation or devaluation of sexual life within marriage. It rather suggests that marriage itself is a special divine vocation to be freely accepted, not a 'necessary' stage in life one has to pass through. Celibacy if properly lived is also a witness to the fact that human beings are free even in the most radical of their drives. It offers them scope for styles of life that demand a universal openness to all others, without bias. In Christianity the option for celibacy is generally in view of a wider service.

However, recent public revelations of cases when celibacy has not been lived properly and is a cloak for secret sexual activity have brought out the enormous dangers of the celibate life. Although these revelations do not refer by any means to the majority of priests and religious, the numbers who have abused their status as celibate are significant enough to suggest the need for great caution in undertaking the life of celibacy and, for the Church, in approving it. The modern culture of individualism makes social controls less effective and the authentic life of celibacy more difficult. Celibacy has meaning if it is governed by a spirit of generous dedication to a worthy cause and a great love for the Lord of all beings.

CHRISTIANS AND OTHER RELIGIONS

How do Christians relate to people of other religious communities in India? Much depends on the history and character of each community. Generally speaking, relations are peaceful, though not always warm. Traditional Christian communities that are well established may tend to live in isolation from other communities. They respect the ways of living and religious practices of other communities and few criticize other religions. There is also nowadays a tendency to take part in some of the festivals of other religions, like Diwali, Holi, Id and the festivities of Durga Puja. There are often mutual visits among friends and/or exchange of gifts. There are also invitations to celebrate Christmas and other festivals. Family festivals like birthdays and weddings offer many opportunities for mutual celebration and help. Newer Christian communities may find it difficult to relate with neighbouring communities, if they formerly belonged to them. There may be tensions due to their conversion not being accepted by others, or other sources of conflict.

We may ask also what are the *views* of Christians regarding other religious communities. This is a difficult question because this is one of the areas where most churches have changed their popular and even their official views in the last fifty years—but one finds Christians holding views that have been discarded by their own churches.

There is no doubt about biblical and medieval Christianity's views regarding other religions. They were partly inherited from the Jewish background. Although there are universalist trends in the First Testament (for instance, in the Book of Genesis there is God's covenant with the whole of humanity), as a whole Judaism took a very dialectic position regarding other religions. Yahweh was the God of Israel, and the gods of other nations were his rivals. Yahweh would defeat them and emerge victorious in the perennial struggle between Israel and the powerful nations around it. The gods of the others were also ridiculed. As the psalmist sang, 'The idols of the nations are silver and gold, the work of human hands. They have mouths, but they do not speak; they have eyes, but they do not see; they have ears, but they do not hear, and there is no breath in their mouths. Those who make them and all who trust them shall become like them' (Ps 134:15–18).

Christians inherited these attitudes, which became closely linked to their basic creed. Yet Jesus was remarkably sensitive to the non-Jews he met, and although he did not speak of their worship he admired the spirit of faith found in some of them, 'such as I have not found in Israel'. The Catholic tradition of the Middle Ages had solved the problem of images that had bothered the Semitic world and had accepted that images were not 'idols' in the sense of being themselves 'gods', but symbols that help us to be in contact not only with Jesus Christ and the saints, but also with the divine reality itself. The contempt expressed by the psalm cited above had no place in the medieval understanding of images.

And yet the negative attitude towards other religions remained till the nineteenth and twentieth centuries even in the mainstream churches. 'Idolatry' was still criticized and condemned in biblical tradition. Idolatrous nations were seen to be in the wrong. But not only they. Non-idolatrous Islam was also wrong because it rejected that Jesus was the Son of God. There was little effort to understand the vocabulary of each theological tradition. The other religion was condemned wholesale. There was certainly a political dimension in this rejection. Christendom had been at war with Islam from the time when the Arab armies invaded West Asia and north Africa and even penetrated deep into continental Europe, first through Spain and later through Turkey and south-east Europe. At sea, too, the Islamic power confronted the emerging maritime skills of Portugal and other European nations in the Mediterranean Sea and later in the Indian Ocean. The fifteenth-century victory of the Christian kings in Spain on land and the 1571 battle of Lepanto at sea weakened and finally broke the stronghold of Islam on Europe.

The influence of this history was felt in India: the early missionaries and many later Christians found themselves closer to Hindus than to Muslims, although Muslims did not have 'other gods', 'the work of human hands'. However, the negative attitude to all religions remained and was part of the motivation for the missionary enterprise: the worship of false gods was seen as evil for the nations themselves, and a road to final condemnation, or a block to the only chance of salvation.

With the rise of the Enlightenment on the one hand, and of more objective studies on Orientalism on the other, the attitude of scholars to other religions started to change. They began saying that they could be tolerated, and that their people would change when they knew better. They also discovered not only authentic ethical values but also theological insights that were either parallel to those of the Christian tradition or could even complement them. The study of other religions became not merely cultural and historical but also theological. By the end of the nineteenth century and during the twentieth these attitudes slowly seeped into the communities of the faithful and finally into the official teaching of the churches.

Most Indian Christians had different lived perceptions of other religions from those that the missionaries tended to import and at times impose. As a whole Indian Christians had lived in peace with neighbours of other religions and were accustomed to respect their religious practices. They had seen outstanding examples of ethical goodness and spiritual refinement around them in members of different religions and could not therefore have the totally negative attitude to the religions and their gods they found in the Bible and the Western Christian tradition. They did not believe less in the Bible, but they were instinctively aware that the writings were culturally conditioned and had to be read differently in a different culture.

The new attitude of the Church to other religions was expressed almost dramatically by the official teaching of the Catholic Church during the Second Vatican Council (1962–65). We will quote two significant texts. The first comes in the Degree on Religious Freedom, no. 2, and affirms it as a human right:

> This Vatican Council declares that the human person has a right to religious freedom. Such freedom consists in this, that all should have such immunity from coercion by individuals, or by groups, or by any human power, that no one should be forced to act against his or her conscience in religious matters, nor prevented from acting according to one's conscience, whether in private or in public, whether alone or in association with others, within due limits. The Council further declares that the right of religious freedom is firmly based on the dignity of the human person as this is known from the revealed word of God and from reason itself. This right of the human person to religious freedom should have such recognition in the constitutional order of society by law as to make it a civil right (Flannery 1996, 552–53).

Those who know something of the history of Christianity will realize what a revolutionary statement this was for the community, although its content was already at least implied in the UN Declaration of Human Rights of 1948 and other secular statements. The new attitude is now mandatory in the Catholic Church. It is complemented by the Declaration on the Church's Relation to Non-Christian Religions. This document affirms that 'in its task of promoting unity and love among people, indeed also among nations, it (the Church) now turns its attention chiefly to what things human beings have in common and what things tend to bring them together' and that all human beings have similar basic questions which religions strive to answer. The document goes on to recall that all humanity has one origin and one goal, which it calls God. It then describes in a few selected words primal religions, Hinduism and Buddhism, and adds that '[I]n like manner, too, other religions which are to be found throughout the entire world strive in various ways to relieve the anxiety of the human heart by suggesting "ways", that is, teachings and rules of life as well as sacred rites'. Islam and Judaism are treated later on. Then the Council affirms the following:

> The Catholic Church rejects nothing of those things which are true and holy in these religions. It regards with respect those ways of acting and living and those precepts and teachings which, though often at variance with what it holds and expounds, frequently reflect a ray of that truth which enlightens everyone. Yet, without ceasing it preaches, and is bound to preach, Christ who is 'the way, the truth and the life' (Jn 14:6), in whom people find the fullness of religious life and in whom God has reconciled all things to himself (ibid., 569–74).

One could quote several similar positive allusions to other religions found in the Vatican II texts, and indeed in the statements of other churches and the World Council of Churches.

Four years after the conclusion of the Vatican Council in Rome there was a significant meeting in Bangalore called the All India Seminar: The Church in India Today, 1969. It was significant because bishops, priests, religious and laity, men and women from all over India participated. It produced a good number of guidelines and resolutions. Among others we quote the following from the Declaration of the Seminar, read on 25 May 1969:

> WE BELONG TOGETHER: Our commitment to Jesus far from separating us from our brothers and sisters puts us at their service after the example of the Master. The Christian fellowship is an open fellowship, open to all men and open to every human value. With the Second Vatican Council we recognize the wealth of truth, goodness and beauty in India's

religious traditions; it is all God's gift to our nation from ancient times. Moreover, we believe not only that God is the source of the inspirations of the past, enshrined in sacred writings and alive today in manifold spiritual traditions, but that his saving love is manifest in the great movement of renewal, of solidarity, of special responsibility and self-sacrifice for the underprivileged, which cut across all barriers of caste and creed and make us feel one in selfless dedication (All India Seminar 1969, 240).

Other Christian churches especially those of Asia have in recent years taken similar positions regarding religions. A theological consultation organized by the World Council of Churches in Chiang Mai, Thailand, April 1977, recommends that:

Approaching the theological questions (of the significance of peoples of other faiths and ideologies) we felt strongly the need to proceed . . .

With repentance, because we know how easily we misconstrue God's revelation in Jesus Christ, betraying it in our actions and posturing as the owners of God's truth rather than, as in fact we are, the undeserving recipients of grace;

With humility, because we so often perceive in people of other faiths and ideologies a spirituality, dedication, compassion and a wisdom that forbid us making judgments about them as though from a position of superiority . . .

With joy, because it is not ourselves we preach; it is Jesus Christ, perceived by many peoples of living faiths and ideologies as prophet, holy one, teacher, example; but confessed by us as Lord and Saviour, Himself the faithful witness of the coming one (Rev 1:5–7) (*Dialogue in Community* 1977).

These texts articulate what seems today the outlook on other religions of most Christians in mainstream churches. It is true that there are still some Christians, especially in fundamentalist sects, who keep the ancient and medieval misperceptions and seem to see them as the work of the devil. By far the majority of Indian Christians in the mainstream churches have at least a respectful attitude towards other religions as they have known them from their childhood. Many go further, an attitude summed up in the remark of a young Jesuit to a friend, 'Now I do not go to temples and mosques and gurdwaras as a tourist, to see the building or to see the people. I go there to find God.' Sacred places of all religions are vibrant with the faith of millions and that faith makes them sacred. What the *Narada Bhakti Sutra* says about the great bhaktas can be said of any group of authentic believers: *tirthikurvanti tirthani*, they make sacred places sacred. In the vicinity of other believers Christians experience the presence of the divine.

This does not mean, however, that Christians easily accept the slogan that all religions are the same because all rivers lead to the same sea. There are surely Indian Christians who are comfortable with such a pluralism. The majority may not formulate their faith quite in this manner and would be more attuned to the way Vatican II expressed the relation in the texts quoted above. In other words, they certainly accept that religions in many ways complement one another and that all can learn from all. But they see Jesus Christ in a special light. For them Jesus Christ is not just a manifestation of the divine reality in our world, nor merely a teacher of the path to salvation that helps all human beings. Jesus is this and more than this. He is the one in whom the whole human race reaches the innermost depths of God, because he is the human manifestation of what it means to be Son of God eternally. It is in union with the risen Jesus that humanity becomes one and shares in the privilege of the divine life.

Of course Indian Christians know that other believers perceive themselves and others differently, and would by all means defend their right to do so, and want also to learn from their perceptions. But at the same time they do claim the right to give witness to what is most precious in their life and explain why they are in the Christian fold and how that does not make them lesser but rather better Indians. They approve of the option of conversion and do not object to anybody endeavouring to give witness to his or her faith and attract others to it, if done with respect and humility.

With the change of attitudes to other religions the meaning of mission has also undergone a deep change in the last century. On the one hand it is seen as dialogue, as sharing of the insight about the ultimate concerns. Second, it is service: it is not directed to take people to heaven—this is the work of God and the responsibility of each individual—but to bring about a better earth, a place where justice, equality, fraternity and freedom are experienced and offered to all human beings. Mission is about building a true human community among us, a reflection on earth, as perfect as possible, of the kingdom of God. A true human community is one that lives the values of faith, hope and love. Christians just say that faith in Jesus Christ is a powerful help to reach this goal.

THE LAST RITE OF PASSAGE: DEATH

The last Christian rite of passage is common to all human beings. Death is the fundamental human destiny that colours the whole life. Every religion offers its own interpretation of death. Christians draw their interpretation primarily from the death and resurrection of Jesus. In its light, they first affirm that death is not the absolute end. Death is the entry into the new stage of existence that is no longer subject to change or decay. There is something in the human being that endures, is not subject to death and will be recreated. There are two ways of reflecting on the next life: one insists on the immortal nature of the spirit or the soul in terms similar to those found in the Gita. The other focuses on divine action and stresses the resurrection as a kind of new creation, although in continuity with the old existence. Immortality and resurrection are not necessarily incompatible, but they do qualify each other.

The Christian believes that not only our 'soul' or the spiritual component of our existence but our whole personality as we experience ourselves, with our spiritual–material polarity, will live eternally. It will be a transformed personality, as was that of Jesus seen by his disciples after his resurrection, but it will be the same personality. Christians generally do not believe in reincarnation or the transmigration of souls. They think that this belief diminishes the importance of the body in the human constitution (bodies cannot be changed as if they were shirts). They hold that all individual human beings are called to resurrection. All must rise: every man and woman that has lived on this earth from the beginning of human history. This rising is beyond time, and therefore the question of 'When?' has no meaning. This rising is simultaneously a seal on the choices we have made during our life on earth and a judgement on what we have made of ourselves after we received the gift of life.

Great care is taken in Christian communities that as far as possible the dying are accompanied till the last moment by those who love them, and that they also have the assistance of religion. For the majority who die of sickness either at home or in a hospital, when the time of death appears near the relatives call a priest to assist the sick person through the appropriate sacraments in his or her passage to eternal life. Priests consider it one of their primary duties to respond to this request, whatever the cost. At a convenient time he comes and speaks words of hope and acceptance to the sick person. He offers her or him a last chance to make a private confession of sins and express regret for them, asking God's forgiveness. The sick person receives from the priest a sacramental absolution, which is normally a source of great peace to him or her. The priest also sees to it that he brings to the sick person as soon as possible a share of the sacramental bread, 'the body of Christ', that has been shared in the Eucharist, which the dying person must have celebrated so often in his or her Christian life. The Eucharist given under these conditions is called the *viaticum*, literally 'the supply of food for the way (*via*)', death being mythically conceived as a long and arduous journey, as it is described in many literatures, for instance in the *Kausitaki Upanishad*.

Besides the two sacraments of Reconciliation and Eucharist, there is in the older Christian churches another sacrament formerly called 'Extreme Unction or Anointing', now more properly the 'Sacrament of the Sick'. It consists of applying a special oil blessed by the bishop to the various parts of the body of the sick person and praying for her or his recovery (oil as medicine) and for strength (oil as massage) for the journey of death. The sacrament therefore faces two directions: physical recovery, in response to the prayer for the health of the sick person, and death as a passage to another and definitive form of life. Both directions include a prayer for forgiveness of sins.

The priest concludes his services to the sick person with a blessing imparted in the name of God and of the Christian community. If the agony is already taking place the priest may continue reciting prayers by the side of the sick person until she or he expires. If death is not imminent these last prayers are normally recited by the relatives and friends who accompany the sick till the last moment.

After death there are special prayers for the departed person and normally some form of Eucharist will be celebrated in the church. The disposal of the body in the Christian tradition is by burial, not cremation. Cremation however is also allowed in most churches and in some cases recommended for reasons of ecology and economy. The sick person may have expressed her or his wish about that, in which case it would be respected. If not, it is for the immediate relatives to decide on the matter. The prayers designed to be said in the cemetery can also be said in the cremation place when cremation is chosen. In some communities special prayers or the Eucharist will also be offered a few days after the death and at the end of the month or at other times according to the local culture. These customs remind us of the tarpana of the Hindu tradition.

This is how a social anthropologist describes the death ceremonies of the Catholic Mukkuvar community of South India:

> Death . . . is ritualised by the officiating of the priest, and congregational singing. The body itself is cleaned, dusted with white powder and sprinkled with rose water, to be then dressed in new clothes. This is as far as purificatory ceremonies go. The family does not observe 'death pollution' after the funeral. The death is commemorated with special prayers after intervals of eight and thirty days, but there is no evidence that mourners keep to a special regime during this thirty-day period. Subsequently, death anniversaries are marked only by prayer (Ram 1992, 80).

There is another aspect of death that in the Middle Ages found vivid mythological expressions. It was then that the celebration of All Souls' Day on 2 November, immediately after All Saints' Day, was started. All Souls' Day remembers all the dead of the community. On that day even today many Christian families in India visit the cemeteries where their dear ones are buried and adorn their tombs with flowers and candles and ask from the priest a special blessing of the tombs, while they remain united to them in remembrance and prayer. At home they may also put garlands around the photographs of the departed, besides those placed on holy pictures. There is a real sense of communion with all the departed. This is in tune with the tribal sense of unity of the tribe with the ancestors.

In many Christian families the dead are not only fondly remembered but their blessings are sought. Before important occasions, for example the marriage of a daughter or a son, there is a tradition of celebrating special masses recalling the dead members of the family and asking their blessings for the young people to be wed. There is also a custom in some Indian communities on the anniversaries of the death of the parents to invite poor people, who in a sense represent the departed, and offer them a meal at home, and at times also new clothes. Only after these poor have eaten and given their blessings to the family will the family members have their meal.

The prayers offered on behalf of the dead and theological reflection led to the idea of what is called Purgatory. In so far as death is a passage to life in God, it presupposes a high degree of purity of heart. Our experience, on the other hand, is that even in old age we are not spiritually pure, and therefore we need purification to enter into communion with God. This purification is an aspect of the mystery of death. In the past it was pictured as a place where the souls of the dead persons were purified 'through fire' or suffering. It was called Purgatory. It was taken for granted that there is a great bonding between the living and the dead, and that the prayers of the living could hasten the purifying process of the dead and enable them to reach heaven 'sooner'. An enormous amount of popular and fictional literature developed on this theme. In the Middle Ages it made the 'masses for the dead' immensely popular, a practice against which Martin Luther protested vigorously. On the other hand in the nineteenth century Cardinal Henry Newman in his *The Dream of Gerontius* gave a new poetic expression to the purifying process that happens at death. In this little drama we may hear echoes of the epic journey of the soul to the seat of Brahman described in the early chapters of the *Kausitaki Upanishad*. The process of death itself is a purification.

The entry into new life is understood by Christians to be

determined not by fate but by God's gracious will, which is accepted by the individual concerned. St Augustine has a powerful saying about this: 'He who created you without you, will not save you without you.' Creation is a gift to be received; salvation is the completion of that gift through our personal freedom. If a person refuses the love of God to the last moment of his earthly existence, his or her refusal determines the status in the final form of existence. There is a great hope rooted in the picture of God given us in the New Testament that the mercy of God will overcome human resistance to his grace and that the immense majority of mortals, perhaps all, are saved. But speculations about the next life remain speculations: the next life is really a mystery hidden in God. Hell in the Christian tradition is the status of those who would permanently reject the love of God in their lives and whose free choice God respects. We do not know if anyone is really in such a hell.

Heaven on the other hand is the destiny marked for all humanity: to be with God. The ancient Indian descriptions of the stages of salvation could be applied in some way to the Christian interpretation of it. There is a salokya or being in the same world as God, there is the samipya or the nearness to the divine, there is the sarupya of receiving the same form as the divine, and there is the sayujya or perfect union with the divine, without loss of one's individual personality. We need a quasi divine form to be united to God, but it is that union that produces in us the 'divine form'. A characteristic of the Christian language about heaven is that it is *koinonia*, a community: indeed a community built around Jesus, the Son of God, in whom we participate in the divine Sonship. What this means in concrete remains shrouded behind the veil of faith.

GOOD NIGHT!

The day of an Indian Christian will often conclude with night prayers—if television allows for them! They may be very short, a prayer before going to bed. They may contain a short 'examination of conscience', highly recommended by spiritual writers like Ignatius Loyola and many others. It consists in thanking God for the graces received during the day and of reflecting on what the person has done that day, right or wrong, and what the peak experiences have been. This may be followed by an 'act of contrition' or a prayer asking for pardon, either memorized from the catechism book or spontaneously articulated. Such daily examination of conscience if taken seriously is a great help for personal spiritual growth.

Night prayers may also include a request for the blessings of God on the family and friends. Children may go to the parents for their blessings before going to bed. In more traditional families this may be the time for longer prayers like the rosary offered to Mary or a Bible reading period. There is no uniformity in these practices; they depend on traditions within each community and, of course, on personal preference.

12

The Christian Mind and Soul

The Christians as bearers of the memory of Jesus ~ The resurrection of Jesus and his presence ~ The Christian understanding of history ~ Christian materialism ~ The presence of God in history ~ The goal of history ~ Obsessed by sin? ~ Confession ~ Easter and victory over sin ~ The mystery of the Trinity ~ Root intuition: God is Love ~ Saccidananda ~ Approaches to contemplation ~ Christian ashrams ~ Faith as commitment and as belief ~ Excesses of orthodoxy ~ Hope as eschatological and as historical ~ Love of God and love of neighbour ~ Hymn to love

As we come to the last chapter of this survey of Indian Christianity, we hope we have conveyed that this religious tradition has shown a remarkable dynamism throughout its long history in India, developed a great variety of forms and made a rich contribution to the life of the nation. Recent studies in popular Christianity in India have stressed both its distinctiveness in various parts of the country and the many forms of religiosity that Christians share with their neighbours. The representations of divinity may be different, but the chariots of the gods are often quite similar.

Just as Christmas and Good Friday are today part of the national calendar, the memory of Jesus and his message are also intimately interlocked with the Indian understanding of life, of history and of God, in many subtle and fruitful ways. Christian communities in all corners of the country understand themselves as the official carriers of that memory and that message. The memory of Jesus is pregnant with a special insight into the divine mystery. The message spells out the memory particularly as it relates to human beings and their history and offers to them gifts of faith, hope and love. Many Christians wish to share this memory and message with others, regardless of whether they would join the community or not. For neither is essentially communal.

THE RESURRECTION OF JESUS

If we ask a Christian what is the core of the Christian belief system, few will hesitate to say that it all starts with the Christian affirmation that Jesus has risen from the dead. To the outsider this may look strange: they would consider this belief a quite derivative and secondary explanation of the experience of Jesus. Indeed critics often think that this affirmation obscures the high ethical content of the life of Jesus and lowers the message to the level of mythology rather than history. To the Christian the resurrection of Jesus is central to the understanding of history itself.

The event is of course closely related to the death of Jesus on the cross on Good Friday. On the third day, says the New Testament, the disciples, women and men, found his tomb empty and sighted him in various ways. It is all very confusing, and the accounts cannot be easily put together. But the details matter little. The basic fact attested to in multiple independent sources is that many early disciples testify to seeing him alive and communicating with them. What can the meaning of this be? According to an account in the Book of Acts, the significance became clear to the disciples fifty days later, on Pentecost Sunday, the 'Feast of the Weeks'. A nucleus of friends and disciples of Jesus were gathered around Mary, his mother, and some relatives in the upper room of a house in a corner of old Jerusalem. Luke writes that a great sound like the rush of a mighty 'wind' exploded upon them and that 'tongues as of fire' appeared on each one of them. The symbolism suggests an enormously transforming experience in which they were 'all filled with a Holy Spirit' and began to speak in various tongues as the Spirit enabled them (Acts 2:1–5).

The outcome of this experience was a strange message that the Greeks would later scoff at. The gist of Peter's discourse that followed the experience is that the crucifixion of Jesus, a man attested to by God, was 'according to a definite plan and foreknowledge of God'. Further Peter affirms that 'God raised him up, having freed him from death, because it was impossible for him to be held in its power . . . and of this we are all witnesses.' Finally 'exalted at the right hand of God', he first received himself from the Father the great promise of the Holy Spirit and then poured it on the disciples, as his listeners could see. This means that Jesus, the crucified one, is Lord and Christ. 'Lord' was a Hebrew and Greek title often applied to kings, but also to God himself, or to the husband or any person of superior rank. 'Christ' was a Greek translation of the Hebrew word messiah (hence the Hindi word *masih*), meaning 'anointed', and was also applied to kings and priests. The message may not seem very clear to us, but it was to the listeners then. It said that Jesus had a role in the divine order of history as the fountainhead of the Divine Spirit, which is the power able to transform the world. This basic insight would develop in the Christian community which constantly refers to Jesus as the source of blessing for the human family. In one form or another this message pervades the whole Scripture of the New Testament and is also supported, in the ancient Christian interpretation, by the First Testament.

To understand what makes a Christian tick one needs to unravel what is implied in this affirmation about Jesus at the core of the Christian creed. It is first of all an affirmation of the reality of an Absolute Sovereign Being, whom we call 'God'. Second, it is an affirmation that, in some way or other, God is not merely the Creator of the universe but is also related directly to the history of Jesus, and by extension to the history of the religion which Jesus followed, Judaism; and because Jesus has a universal significance, God is related to the history of the whole world. Third, this 'Absolute' Being is personally involved in history. Jesus always referred himself to 'It' and called upon 'It' as 'Abba', Father. In his view the world is not a puzzling enigma. It is not 'a tale told by an idiot, full of sound and fury signifying nothing'. It is embraced, one would say, by a mystery of love, a personal reality that reaches out to the whole existing reality and is the source of its meaning. Relating to that Divine Presence was for Jesus, as it is for all believers, the core of their religious experience. Fourth, Jesus is alive: the disciples saw him and experienced his presence and power in their lives. As an ancient text says, 'And they went out and proclaimed the good news everywhere, while the Lord worked with them and confirmed the message by the signs that accompanied it' (Mk 16:2). That he is alive the disciples had no doubt: they experienced his power among them, they had sighted him on various occasions, individually and collectively, and his body was not in the tomb where they had laid him. The conviction informs the whole of the Second Testament.

There is a divine purpose running through the events of history. The human search for God had found a new meaning when it discovered a God who is Love. This God, the Christian faith says, is not only guiding human history as reported in the story of the First Testament but is present within history in the person of Jesus of Nazareth. The history of Jesus now revealed a transcendent and absolute meaning for the human race. The divine reality flashes in the history of Jesus most evidently at the very moment when his life ended in the apparent tragedy of the cross. The resurrection of Jesus is the divine intervention that affirms the eternal value of Jesus' history and, by association with it, of all human history. God has made that wandering preacher of Galilee, that compassionate guru who 'went about doing good and healing all who were oppressed by the devil, for God was with him' (Acts 10:38), the symbol of God's acceptance of history even when history fails: when it ends in the murder of the weak and the persecuted One. God made him the universal sign of God's forgiving love.

Read within the philosophical world view of the Indian tradition, both Hindu and Buddhist, Peter's speech affirming that Jesus is 'at the right hand of God' can be seen as equivalent to saying that the man Jesus, our brother in the flesh and part and parcel of our history, shares in the Absolute Truth of God, or that he belongs to the paramarthika world. His existence was not an evanescent phenomenon limited to the vyavaharika history, destined to be lost when the final vision of the divine reality dawns on us. Rather, human though he is, Jesus 'is exalted at the right hand' of the Father, at a level sharing the divine glory, now and forever.

What is of absolute importance in the Christian faith is that this position of Jesus is not a private privilege granted to Jesus only because of his faithful obedience or because of his love: his place belongs by right to all humanity, to all with whom he is in solidarity, to all who are his brothers and sisters and accept making their lives meaningful. If he is raised 'at the right hand of the Father', he is there as representative of the whole human family. In other words, the belief in the resurrection of Jesus so central to the Christian experience involves also an affirmation of the 'resurrection of the flesh' or 'of the dead', that is, of all human beings, as affirmed at the end of the Creed. It is a belief in the value of all history, including all personal histories. All the good that human beings do to themselves and others and to the world that surrounds them is preserved in the divine *now* of eternity; all the evil they do is redeemed by love. Human history and, by association, nature and its evolution are not passing gifts that time will erase forever, but symbols and manifestations eternally accepted and loved.

A distinctive characteristic of the Christian belief is the way each individual is viewed. An individual is not valued merely for the impact he or she has had on history, but first and foremost because she or he is a unique image of God, irreplaceable. The faith understanding of most Christians is that there is no rebirth after this life, and no repetition of an individual's history. Every person born in this world is a new reality whose personal existence is to endure forever. We know of course that many of them do not come to fullness of humanity in this world because of various circumstances: infant mortality, crippling disease or abject poverty. Many have not been able to make free personal decisions and their passing through history seems incomplete and even irrelevant. This is true, and the mystery of such persons remains for us unexplained. But it would not be an explanation in the right direction to think of them as 'coming back', as if their bodies were merely the external package of their persons. Each individual is defined by his or her place in history. He or she is what nobody else can be. Each is also destined to flower beyond history as a beautiful reflection of God. If they could not bloom in this imperfect world, they are still part of the human history and when that history is made complete they remain personally 'at the right hand of the Father'.

The understanding of each life as unique, unrepeatable and a gift for eternity creates a great sense of responsibility for the world in which God has placed us. Although it is God's gift, eternal life will be the fruit and the transformation of our history. We are responsible for this world and for the world beyond. The unique nature of each human existence adds a tragic edge to human life. This life is the only one in which our own eternity and our contribution to human history has to be played out. We cannot delay. There is urgency in our historical existence.

At the same time, the Christian tradition puts a distance between the human and the animal world. This distance is found in the Creation accounts of the Book of Genesis and in the Bible more generally. The distance is not merely because of the obvious greater intelligence of the human, but because only the human has the obvious responsibility of freedom. While animals and other living creatures have an instinct that makes them struggle to survive, the human also has the ability to take decisions that are ethically good or evil. The ecological movement has certainly helped Christians to soften the harsh expressions of this distance between the human and the non-human world, but it does not do away with the Christian perception of the central responsibility of the human for nature and for history.

The Christian faith is not primarily a doctrine about the nature of God, but about the value of the human reality that is related to God. It is a revelation about humanity and its world. It is less about who God is and more about who we are because of God. The resurrection of Jesus tells us about the hope of our own resurrection, the intrinsic value of our lives, the meaning of history, the importance of matter and the meaning of suffering. For the resurrection is of a piece with the cross: it reveals the ultimate significance and power of human suffering. It reveals hope in the midst of apparent hopelessness.

The resurrection of Jesus also points to a certain 'materialism' in the Christian tradition. Christianity has never been comfortable with gnostic doctrines that exalt the spirit and despise matter. Matter is sacred, and in a sense it is the 'mother' of us all, as the French Jesuit P. Teilhard de Chardin insisted: Does not the Genesis story say that God made Adam out of the clay of the earth? The importance given to the material pole of the universe does not mean that Christianity denies the need for asceticism and detachment; it only means that such need is not linked to a pessimistic view of the material world or of its pleasures, but rather to a need to protect the freedom of the individual, who must remain master of her or his actions and not a slave of drives one cannot or does not want to control.

This importance given to matter in the Christian perception finds expression in several Christian beliefs. There is first the affirmation that God is the Creator of the whole world, material and immaterial. This is the first affirmation of the traditional Christian 'creeds'. Matter is neither evil nor a source of evil, nor an eternal entity parallel to the divine reality. It comes as a gift from God. God created it. Creation means that God, eternally free and pure, *nitya suddha, buddha, mukta swarupa*, as Sankara would say, wills the universe into existence and wants it associated with God's own being. This will of God has no explanation, except divine love itself. Love needs no reason to justify itself. Love is the outpouring of goodness and goodness is the essential characteristic of a pure existence.

We believe also that God guides human history. God is not an absentee Lord. He is antaryamin to creation, the inner controller. The faith in the presence of God in the human being Jesus Christ, who like us was tempted and suffers in his humanity, who lived a life of responsibility like our own in all things (but sin), is also an affirmation of the central place of matter in the Christian configuration. Even more, the experience of the resurrection of Jesus underlines the sacredness of the bodily dimension of human existence, for it shows us that in some way the body remains in the liberated existence. In the Eucharist, Christians come into spiritual contact with 'the body and blood' of Jesus Christ, present in the symbol of a meal. In all other sacraments too the material world reflects and radiates the light of the spiritual realities. Marriage itself, with its sexual element, is a sacrament. And the last theme of the Christian creed affirms the belief in the resurrection of the body unto life everlasting. This whole and holistic vision of the world and its history draws from the root experience of the resurrection of Jesus.

There is more to it. The faith in the resurrection is not only the lens through which Christians view and understand themselves and the world. Properly understood, it also provides a programme of action. On the basis of Scripture and their experience Christians believe that the risen Lord is the source of a new divine power, a spiritual shakti that is released into those who are willing to act according to the divine demands. Christians call this power the Holy Spirit, the energy of God diffused to all men and women in the universe. Implicit in this energy is a divine programme of action calling for human acceptance. St Paul speaks of a 'plan of God', a plan that covers all human history and has been 'published' in the resurrection of Christ. In one place he puts it like this: 'For God has allowed us to know the secret of his plan, and it is this: he purposed long ago in his sovereign will that all human history should be consummated in Christ, that everything that exists in heaven or earth should find its perfection and fulfilment in him. In Christ we have been given an inheritance, since we are destined for this, by the One who works out all his purposes according to the design of his own will' (Eph 1:9–11, translated by J.B. Phillips).

The Christian perception of history is that it leads to its being 'consummated in Christ': other translations explain the implications of the word: it will be 'recapitulated' or 'united' in Christ, or he 'will gather up all things'. The verb used in the Greek text involves both completion and convergence, or unification. This text is the root of de Chardin's metaphor of the Omega Point (named for the last letter in the Greek alphabet) as the goal of all evolution and history, coinciding with the historical and transhistorical person of Jesus Christ. Sri Aurobindo has a similar vision, but he could not give a name or a historical shape to the 'Overmind' or the centre of human oneness.

But we must not overlook the significance of the crucifixion: the one who is declared to be the pivot of history is a man defeated, a man crushed, a victim of history. He is not only the embodiment of the divine meaning for humanity but also represents all those who, like him, are victims of history. Here is where present-day theology understands the special role of the poor in the mystery of history. God's plan is certainly for all human beings, but it is a plan that affirms the dignity and value of those most rejected in our history and restores to them their place in history: and all those who want to be part of God's victorious outcome for history must align themselves to God's preferential choice and side with the victims of history.

The 'divine plan' for history does not involve the destruction of human cultures, religions or civilizations, but is rather a divine acceptance for them, signified in the very resurrection of Jesus. They all bring their unique contribution to the wholeness of human growth. They are an indispensable part of the process. This is the vision that commands the Christian understanding of our world and its direction. This does not, of course, deny the right of other people to propose different visions and to live according to them. Even if we do not understand how, we think that the various visions will be somehow integrated into the divine purpose. This plan is a call to action which extends to all human beings: a call to work for reconciliation of all polarities, for the overcoming of all enmities, for equality and freedom for all, a call to bring together, to make peace, to preach forgiveness of sins for people who are alienated from one another or from God. This is what makes the Christian tick.

OBSESSED WITH SIN?

Christians have at times been accused of being obsessed with sin. The myth of the 'Fall' of the original human couple of Adam and Eve presented at the beginning of the Bible and so magnificently portrayed in later art and literature, especially in Milton's *Paradise Lost*, seems to paint a gloomy picture of the Christian world view. Swami Vivekananda, with others, protested, 'It is a sin to call a man so [a sinner].' If our picture appears gloomy it is because we, Christians, have not been able to reproduce the thrill experienced by the first community, as reported in the New Testament. The good news they proclaimed was not that we were slaves of sin but the opposite: we have been liberated from sin! They said that God has taken the initiative to do away with evil in the world, that the love generated on the cross could overcome all sin, and that we could experience this divine activity in the measure in which we agreed to fall in with God's plan.

The experience of being liberated from sin is common among Christians even today. Among Catholics and some Oriental churches it is embodied in a beautiful ritual called the sacrament of reconciliation, or penance, popularly known as 'confession'. This characteristic Christian practice can be observed in churches all over India, especially on the eve of or during the great festivals. Many believers come to church to pray and ask forgiveness from God for the evil they have allowed in their lives. We all recognize the presence of sin among and around us. Christians penitently pray, reflect on their lives and then approach a chair in the church where a priest is sitting clad in his vestments. A metal or a wooden grille separates the priest from the kneeling believer. After some greetings and blessings, the penitent mentions what in his or her perception has been sinful in the recent or not-so-recent past and, through the service of the ordained priest, asks pardon and absolution from God. A short dialogue of spiritual advice may follow, and some symbolic act of charity or self-deprivation to be done or special prayer to be said is suggested to and accepted by the penitent. The priest then pronounces God's forgiveness. The sacrament ends with a blessing by the priest and a word of thanks from the penitent. In recent times this traditional practice has become less frequent, but it is also found in less ritual format, in ways that may look similar to counselling sessions but which are not devoid of the 'sacramental' or religious element.

This ancient practice may look frightening to an outside observer and can indeed give rise to abuse. One may think of the danger of creating a sense of dependence on the other. One may perhaps find the revealing of one's innermost conscience to another person something demeaning. One may even see it as an instance of the Church's control of its members. We do not think that this is the general experience of the vast majority of Christians. The experience is rather one of inner joy, of a deep peace at the assurance that the forgiveness from God which we all long for is real and has been pronounced in a human way. One feels inwardly a new person. One starts life anew, so to speak. Not that the evil done is forgotten: it remains a regretted and acknowledged part of our personal history. But it is no longer a cause for negative feelings about oneself. God has somehow intervened in our personal lives by enabling us to start again. Unlike human forgiveness, which reaches only the level of ignoring evil done, God's forgiveness reaches the depth of our personalities and renews them from within. It also creates or strengthens the desire to grow in human and spiritual maturity.

One must add that the practice is as far as possible protected against abuse. The most elementary but the strongest protection is that the priest is not allowed under any circumstances whatsoever to reveal anything he has heard in confession to anybody, directly or indirectly. He cannot even act differently because of what he has heard in confession. Any possible infringement of the 'sacramental seal' would be punishable by the most serious excommunication which among Catholics only the Pope can absolve. Most judicial systems even of secular governments respect the absolute confidentiality of sacramental confession, as they normally do for other professional secrets of the service professions (doctors, counsellors, psychiatrists, etc.).

The role of forgiving sins had a primary place in the understanding of the early Christian community. When St Luke's Gospel reports the conversation of the risen Jesus with the group of the earliest disciples, he explains the meaning of his death in terms of what the Scriptures had foreseen about the role of the Messiah: 'that the Messiah is to suffer and to rise from the dead on the third day, and that repentance and forgiveness of sins is to be proclaimed in his name to all nations, beginning from Jerusalem. You are witnesses of these things' (Lk 24:46–48). Repentance and forgiveness are linked up in this text. Repentance is the human side, forgiveness the divine. Repentance is actually our acceptance of the divine forgiveness that renews us.

It must also be recorded that from the earliest times of Jesus' preaching God's forgiveness of our sins was linked to the forgiveness we are ready to give to one another. This is very clear in many passages, for example, in the way in which St Matthew records the teachings of Jesus in the Sermon on the Mount, especially when the evangelist records the early Christian prayer, the second part of which is mostly on forgiveness. Addressing 'Our Father in heaven' the Christian is taught to pray, 'Forgive us our debts as we also have forgiven our debtors. And do not bring us into temptation but rescue us from the evil one!' After this Jesus is said to have commented, 'For if you forgive others their trespasses, your heavenly Father will also forgive you; but if you do not forgive others, neither will your Father forgive your trespasses' (Mt 6:11–15).

This should not be construed as if the forgiveness of God was reluctantly offered or conditional. The God of compassion wants to forgive, whenever the sinner wants to be forgiven. Forgiveness is a serious affair. The sacrament is not an easy way out of evil. It requires commitment to change. Forgiveness of sins does not make evil banal or cheap. It is not an easy grace that requires a few words and involves no further responsibilities. We are forgiven if we want to fight against evil and the evil consequences of our actions, individual or communitarian. We need to repair a broken world. Commitment to justice is integral to the process of forgiveness. It is symbolized in the 'penance' which the priest imposes on the penitent: that is only a symbol of a major obligation whose responsibility falls on the reconciled penitent.

The practice of confession and all prayers for forgiveness express an attitude of personal responsibility for spiritual growth. Confession is the starting point for what is called 'spiritual direction', a practice Christians have in common with other religions. With them too the role of the guru or the master for spiritual guidance and growth is recommended. Perhaps, however, the traditions of the Hindu guru, the Buddhist bhikku or the Muslim Sufi are more charismatic in character: they depend more directly on the spiritual quality of the person who is able to awaken others to truth and guide their spiritual growth. In the Catholic Church this role has perhaps been over-institutionalized and fused with the role of the ordained priest, to the loss of some of its power. A deeper dialogue with other religious traditions would surely benefit the Christian community in this area. Outstanding charismatic gurus like Father Tony de Melo (1931–87) are too rare, though not absent, in the Indian Christian community. Tony had a great gift for tapping the spiritual resources of the people he met, and even of many who merely read his books, whether Christians, followers of other religions or agnostics.

Does not the practice of confession, together with other traditional prayers and the teachings of the Bible, prove that the Christian faith is obsessed with sin? The answer is that 'obsession' is not the right word in this context. There is among spiritually mature people a regret that in modern culture we suffer a certain loss of the sense of sin. Anything seems to be permissible provided we are not caught. Yet paradoxically much of what is reported in the news media and in literature has to do with various forms of sin: war, corruption, terrorism, murder, infidelity, cheating, lying. The Christian tradition takes this world seriously, and at the same time affirms our responsibility to change what is evil in our midst, and offers the possibility to do so. Even the classical formulation of 'original sin' as the tragic evil of the first parents (the first human generation) which somehow affected the whole human race and its history cannot be used as an alibi for our failure to change the world. If the Indian tradition saw the world pervaded by avidya, an all-embracing ignorance blocking the path to liberation, the biblical tradition has rather spoken of *sin* as evidence that not all is well with the world. But, like ignorance, sin does not have the last word. Redemption is at hand; repentance is possible. With God's grace we can change the world.

THE MYSTERY OF THE TRINITY

One of the most puzzling things about the Christian doctrine for those who look at it from the outside is the famous formulation of God as 'Trinity'. Believers who make monotheism the basic tenet of their faith cannot understand how Christians could apparently have receded from the ancient Jewish belief in one God to the complex Trinitarian dogma. Muslims and Sikhs, especially, find this Christian belief highly objectionable. For many Hindus the belief in a divine Trinity can only make sense in relation to the popular myths of the Trimurti, three personifications of the creative, conserving, and destroying or consummating aspects of the divine. But they see the Trimurti as a human projection of multiplicity into a divine mystery that ('who') is beyond all mental categories and 'who' must always be meditated upon as 'one only without a second'—*ekam eva advitiyam*, a fortiori without a third.

Many Indian Christians do vibrate with these objections and are aware of how inadequate all language about God is, including their traditional Trinitarian language. In fact, in the Bible God is never 'counted', never described by the number three or any other expression of plurality. Christians consider themselves monotheists, indeed strict monotheists! Jesus was a Jew, and because his religion was monotheist to the core, so must the Christian's be. Towards the end of Jesus' life a scribe came up to him and put him a blunt question: 'Which commandment is the first of all?' Jesus does not hesitate one moment to repeat the basic Jewish prayer, the 'Shema Israel' from the ancient text in Deut 6:4–5: 'Hear, O Israel: the Lord our God, *the Lord is one*; and you shall love the Lord your God with all your heart, and with all your soul, and with all your mind, and with all your strength' (Mk 12:29–30 and parallel passages). Such was the faith of Jesus, a faith no Christian wants ever to change, but rather to share. This one God is nearer to us than the jugular vein, in the classical expression of the Muslim tradition.

Jesus experienced the nearness of this one God not simply as a spatial nearness, but as an affective nearness. God is a God not merely to be thought about or contemplated or affirmed philosophically, but to be loved. God is to be loved precisely because God is, as Jesus says, not merely a Creator but a loving Father— Abba, in Jesus' Aramaic language. This perception of God as loving need not pull us down to the level of mythology. God's love means that God relates to us as we are involved in our history. He is a source of strength and protection for the weak, the poor, especially those who have no other support. All of us experience at times the need for such support. At the end of the New Testament a letter attributed to St John puts it clearly: 'God is love, and those who abide in love abide in God, and God abides in them' (1 Jn 4:16).

In a very special way Jesus experienced himself as the beloved; the early tradition calls him the 'beloved Son'. After the horror of his death on the cross the disciples saw him alive as truly the beloved son. They understood that in his life and his presence in the world God himself had become infinitely close to the human family. In Jesus Christ humanity was the family of God in a new way.

In a letter to the Christians in the Greek city of Corinth, written in the year 57 CE, St Paul alludes beautifully to the Creation account of Genesis and reflects on Jesus: 'It is the God who said, "Let light shine out of darkness", who has shone in our hearts to give the light of the knowledge of the glory of God in the face of Jesus Christ' (2 Cor 4:6). The 'glory of God' is reflected on the face of Jesus. There is a bimba–pratibimba relation, to use the old Indian way of speaking, between God the Father and Jesus: the divine reality is 'reflected' in Jesus. Jesus makes God's love and therefore God himself present within history, and indeed present in the form of suffering. In Jesus, the beloved Son, God himself became in a sense even closer because now we can see him suffering with us. 'Whoever has seen me has seen the Father,' Jesus is reported to have told Philip (Jn 14:9).

We are here at the heart of the Christian faith. We believe we have a glimpse of the mystery of God because we see God through the prism of the life of Jesus. For us God is not just the 'unmoved first Mover' as Aristotle thought. Nor is he just the mysterious 'I-am-who-I-am', as Moses heard it in his vision of the burning bush on Mount Sinai. Nor is God just the 'One-alone-without-a-second' of the *Chandogya Upanishad* or the 'ever-pure-conscious-free' described by Sankaracharya. For us God is best known as Love. As St John wrote, 'God is love, and those who abide in love abide in God' (1 Jn 4).

Love means life in its deepest sense. Against the background of the life of Jesus, Christians see that *God is alive with love*. It is only in this context that the so-called Trinity can be meaningful, for it offers a certain insight into the ineffable mystery of God's own life. The Trinity means that God, infinite Love, gives himself or projects himself as an eternal Word. The substance of this Word is nothing different from God. It is rather the eternal expression of God's self. God and God's Word are one Being internally related—as knower–knowledge, also called Father–Son, linked by a shared love called the Spirit.

It took the Christian church and its theologians several centuries before they could reach a certain agreed understanding of the mystery of God revealed in Jesus. They articulated it in a language derived from Greek philosophy. The formulation was monotheist: there is only One God and God's pure substance is internally related as Father–Son–Spirit, meaning that there is life in the divine reality which is both Knower and Word, and Bond of union. They chose also a misleading term by calling these internal relationships 'persons'. Whatever its value, Christians are convinced that this formulation sums up what God revealed in Jesus Christ means.

In this context Indian theologians have spoken of the a-dvaita of God, 'not-two'. The Spirit, bond of love in Western theology, the divine advaita, is the one substance of God, not different from God, the union of Father and Son, Knower and Knowledge. The language of Father–Son must be taken as symbolic and must be stripped of any sexual connotation ('who is the mother?' The Father is also 'Mother' because God is beyond sexual dualities!).

The misunderstandings that flow from the classical biblical

language of Father, Son, Holy Spirit make a number of Indian theologians prefer a language derived from our tradition but adapted to the Christian faith: the God of the Bible is *Saccidananda*. In the medieval and late Vedanta and bhakti traditions Brahman is referred to and invoked as Saccidananda, that is Being, Consciousness and Bliss. Here, too, the tradition denies that these three realities are either qualities in Brahman or different components of the Absolute Being. The Christian follows this lead but is convinced by the experience of Jesus that these three ways of speaking of the divine mystery are founded in the very self-disclosure of the Supreme Being, and that the mystery of love involves a divine life in God, whom, for want of more adequate terms, we call Father, Son and Spirit.

Although unavoidably mysterious, this language suggests for Christians and, we believe, for humanity at large a powerful insight. Created in the image and likeness of God, we too are essentially related beings. Relation to the other is not an additional trait of our being. It is central, essential to our personality. We are not, and cannot be, monads floating in the sea of existence; nor can we really be just one, without relation to one another. Essentially we are interconnected. This has been the Christian teaching regarding human beings as persons. Persons are not merely subsisting individual substances, as the old philosophers defined them, but *relations*. We are all related, and in being related we are. We exist *because* we are related. And so the Trinity becomes in the Christian understanding the basis of a new anthropology, a new vision of human beings.

If our relations to others are part of ourselves, essential to our very personal existence, the question of reincarnation does not arise. Every point in history is the interlocking of many relationships, and the point I occupy is unique and cannot be repeated. I am unique. Elsewhere in history there can only be somebody else, not I. Each one occupies one place in history. We cannot be another person. José Ortega y Gasset (1887–1955), the Spanish philosopher, put it this way: 'I am I, and my circumstance.' This gives a unique character to the body–soul polarity as understood within the Christian world view (although we must be rather hesitant here, as there is not just one possible Christian world view: the Christian faith does not impose a philosophy on anyone, and Christians have developed many ways of looking at reality). In general Christians will understand the body–soul polarity not in terms of two substances coming together to constitute a human being but as one bipolar reality created by God where the soul seals the reality of the body, and the body gives concreteness to the soul.

I must therefore assume responsibility for my life. I cannot blame somebody else in the past, or even myself in past lives. I am unique and responsible for my present. Of course we know that our freedom is limited and that our body is subject to the laws of physical nature. There are inherited physical and psychic traits that specify and limit our area of freedom. But, within limits, free we are and free we must remain, using our freedom for responsible love.

CHRISTIAN ASHRAMS

As we have seen, there is in the Christian tradition a long history of spiritual search of inner purification and of a striving after a deeper consciousness of the presence of the divine within the human heart. The search for God reflected in the Jewish prophetic tradition continued in Christianity and the other great Semitic religion, Islam. This search has many parallel movements in the Oriental traditions, including the practices of inner purification, yoga, meditation and contemplation.

In Christian history we had movements of renunciation and flights to the desert in the third and fourth centuries, the appearance of monastic institutions both in the eastern and western parts of the Roman Empire, the discovery of the divine 'energies' by the Oriental tradition, its sadhana of icon painting to come to a mystical union with God, the *Hesychasm* or the way of silence and concentration with the help of breathing exercises, close to the Indian yoga. Later came the Benedictine way to God through liturgical prayer, reading of the Scripture and work, and later still the mendicant orders in many ways so similar to the Indian sanghas, the 'advaita' mystics like Eckhart and others in the Germanic world. In the Middle Ages there was a movement of the Beguines and the Beghards, followed by the orders oriented to service and the preaching of the Gospel, all trying to recover the 'purity' of the Gospel. The 'Reformation' was also an expression of this spiritual and mystical search.

There is indeed much lofty teaching on the spiritual paths marked by the masters of the spirit in the Christian world. In India these contemplative traditions have been present in various forms from the earliest times, and there are contemplative houses devoted exclusively to inner growth. What Indian Christianity has contributed of its own to the Christian contemplative tradition is the institution of Christian ashrams, patterned after models found in Indian culture, both in ancient times and during the renaissance of Hinduism (Keshub Chander Sen, Tagore in Santiniketan and Mahatma Gandhi). Ideally, in these institutions the search for the divine and inner purification go together with a simple style of life, the presence of a guru who can guide the seekers, silence and an open way of living freer than the rigid style of life of Western monasteries or convents.

The Christian ashram movement emerged from Indian Christians as new ways of living the Christian mission and offered models where Jesus' ideas of 'the kingdom of God' could become a reality. The movement started possibly at the end of the nineteenth century with the attempt of Brahmabandhab Upadhyay to establish in Jabalpur what he called a Hindu-Catholic monastery. Ecclesiastical interference blocked this first attempt, but in the early part of the twentieth century ashrams began to flourish in all the main branches of the Church in India. The idea was already raised in a meeting in Delhi 1912 of the National Missionary Society (founded in 1905). N.V. Tilak started an ashram in Satara in 1917; Christukula in Tirupattur was started in 1921; in the 1940s Animananda Brahmacari started one in Ranchi and in 1950 the Saccidananda Ashram in Kulittalai. About the same time Kurusimala was started in the hills of Kerala, and there was a Bethany movement in the Syro-Malankara Church. Many others followed and the movement flourished. Generally accepted by Hindus, the movement has, however, been virulently criticized by Sita Ram Goel (1994).

It is worth noting that a good number of Christian ashrams have been founded and are run by women, like Vandana Mataji, with a call to contemplative life. Not every institution labelled 'ashram' has the basic characteristics of an ashram, but many do and most consider Jesus Christ as their real guru. There is also at least one Zen centre run by Father A.M.A. Samy, S.J., a qualified

Indian Zen master, situated in Perumalai near Kodaikanal.

Sociologists have studied the Christian ashram movement and found two patterns which they have called kavi-ashram and khadi-ashram. In the first the inspiration is rather scriptural and the stress is on contemplation and withdrawal from the world. The classical Hindu ashrams is the ideal striven for. The khadi-ashrams fall under the inspiration of the ashrams of Gandhiji and Vinoba Bhave, and in them the leading inspiration is social concern and involvement with the poor. Both types are still functioning in the churches, the former more prominently in the Catholic Church where the contemplative tradition is strong, the latter more prominently in the Protestant churches.

FAITH, HOPE AND LOVE

Perhaps the main focus of the spiritual path of Christians has not been so much on meditation—although this has been a permanent feature of the tradition—but on the attainment of those basic attitudes summarized in the New Testament as the triad of *faith, hope* and *love*. It is precisely towards the growth in these attitudes, as they are seen in the life of Jesus, that the Christian spiritual growth is measured. In the classical tradition these are called 'theological virtues', that is, God-given powers that develop the divine life within us, attitudes that, so to speak, put us in direct contact with God.

Faith does not mean primarily the belief system that one must hold to be a Christian. This meaning is there, but is only derivative. Faith means primarily a commitment to God and a total trust in the love that God has for us. Faith is commitment and trust, and all forms of meditation and contemplation should enable us to grow in faith. Without faith there is not salvation, say Christian theologians inspired by Paul and following the teachings of Martin Luther. The human being is not fully human unless she or he is committed. Commitment to the higher values of life is faith. This commitment supposes of course a trust in reality, which a theist translates as trust in God. We cannot commit ourselves without that trust. But the act of trust involves always a leap in the dark. It relies on the other, not on oneself. This is faith: reliance on and commitment to God.

The Christian commitment is to God as revealed in Jesus Christ. Because of this historical angle, the acceptance of the history of Jesus is essential to the Christian faith. The commitment therefore articulates itself into a creed about Jesus Christ, his life, his role, his relation to God and his relation to the whole of humanity. It is therefore not too surprising that a right perception of historical truths is intrinsic to the Christian faith. Orthodoxy has always meant this, that in our commitment to God, done within the community of faith, the Christian accepts a correct understanding of who Jesus was. Without this acceptance of the historical truth of and about Jesus, faith would lose its anchoring and would cease to be Christian.

It is acknowledged that this stress on 'correct' faith ('orthodoxy') has been exaggerated in Christian history so that correct doctrine seemed more important than sincere commitment. This has led Church authorities and governments guided by the Church to such abuses as the burning of heretics, inquisitions and excessive excommunications. Today, the community regrets these historical mistakes and confesses its sinfulness in this area. This regret found official expression during the Jubilee Year when the Catholic Church officially asked pardon for wrongs committed in heresy-hunting. This theme was introduced by a cardinal in a service of repentance for the sins of the Church, on 12 March 2000. Cardinal Joseph Ratzinger, the head of the Congregation for the Doctrine of the Faith (formerly known and much feared as the Holy Office) said:

> Let us pray that each one of us, looking to the Lord Jesus, meek and humble of heart, will recognize that even men of the Church, in the name of faith and morals, have sometimes used methods not in keeping with the Gospel, in the solemn duty of defending the truth.

Then the Holy Father prayed:

> Lord, God of all men and women, in certain periods of history Christians have at times given in to intolerance and have not been faithful to the great commandment of love, sullying in this way the face of the Church, your Spouse. Have mercy on your sinful children and accept our resolve

to seek and promote truth in the gentleness of charity, in the firm knowledge that truth can prevail only in virtue of truth itself. We ask this through Christ our Lord, Amen. Lord, have mercy; Lord, have mercy; Lord, have mercy.

Indians may hear echoes of *satyam eva jayate* in this prayer!

Hope is not really so different from faith, but hope looks at the future. Hope means never to be broken down by disappointments or by doubts. Hope includes that strength involved in the Indian virtue of abhaya, fearlessness. Hope means continuing our journey even when we do not see the end. Abraham 'hoped against hope': this means that he never gave up his trust in God in the difficult moments of his life. Hope has two dimensions that are interconnected, one historical, the other eschatological. The latter is the assurance that life has an ultimate meaning, that death does not have the last word, neither the death of the individual nor the death of culture and civilizations, nor even the end of the world. There is an assurance of victory over death. The basis for that certainty for the Christians is the collective and individual experience of the resurrection of Jesus. Because Jesus has risen from the dead, we also, the whole of humanity, have risen with him, in hope.

But hope does not offer 'a pie in the sky when we die'. Hope is also historical, this-worldly. It consists in the confidence with which we struggle against evil in ourselves and our society. Hope calls on us to build both collective and individual programmes of reform, plans for action so that justice and love may prevail in the world. Hope is also rooted in the experience of the risen Lord, but does not take us out of the struggle for life, rather it calls us to life precisely because the risen Lord accompanies us in these struggles. This is clearly indicated in a beautiful old text quoted earlier which summarizes the experience of the early community. After recording the command of the risen Lord, similar to the one found in Matthew, Mark says:

So then the Lord Jesus, after he had spoken to them, was taken up into heaven and sat down at the right hand of God. And they went out and proclaimed the good news everywhere, while the Lord worked with them and

confirmed the message by the signs that accompanied it
(Mk 16:19–20)

'The Lord worked with them': this is the basis and the meaning of
the Christian hope. It is a hope that refuses to get discouraged by
any opposition or failure, because 'the Lord works with them and
strengthens the message'. Such hope is available to all who honestly
work for the improvement of the world.

Finally, if faith is rooted in the experience of the love of God
offered to us in the past especially in the history of Jesus, and hope
looks forward to the future we do not yet grasp, *love* means a
constant self-giving in the present so that we reflect divine love in
this world of ours. Love is the supreme Christian norm. St Augustine
expressed it boldly when he said, 'Love and do what you want!'
This in a sense is similar to what St Paul meant when he said that
the Gospel has replaced the law. Love means that we grow in such
a way that we do the right thing not because it is commanded but
because we want everybody to share in the blessings of salvation
we have received. Love does not mean attachment but self-gift. It is
a real overturning of our normal patterns of behaviour. Love means
ceasing to put ourselves at the centre of our concerns and striving to
make the other the centre—for the other is always the stepping
stone and the symbol of the presence of God. This must not be
misunderstood. It is not that we make the other a means whereby
we get united to the divine love, a means to our perfection. Rather,
we love the other absolutely because every human being shares in
the divine reality. Jesus made it clear that we cannot love God
without loving all our brothers and sisters. The conscious exclusion
of anyone from our loving concern is automatically the exclusion
of God. As St John says, 'If we do not love the brother or sister that
we see, how can we say that we love God whom we do not see?'
(1 Jn 4: 20). When Jesus answered the scribe's question about the
first commandment by recalling the need to love God with all one's
heart, he significantly added, 'And the second is this, "You shall
love your neighbour as yourself". There is no other commandment
greater than these' (Mk 12:31). Many of the parables and other
teachings of Jesus remind us of this goal of all spiritual growth: to
grow in love.

Love is easy in a restricted circle. Loving *all* is an almost impossible task. Only God's power can enable us to do this. It does not mean going out to do good to everybody in the world: we know we cannot do this. Jesus made it more concrete: love your neighbour. And who is my neighbour? asked the scribe. And Jesus replied with the well-known parable of the good Samaritan. The neighbour is the one in need who crosses your path. The Samaritan, a kind of Dalit in the Jewish culture, was the only one who stopped on the road to attend to the man wounded by the robbers: neither priest nor Levite had done that.

Jesus went even further: 'Love your enemies,' he commanded, and showed the way by asking God's forgiveness for those who crucified him.

At times love is seen in opposition to justice. Love seems to bypass justice and imply an attitude of tolerance of injustice and oppression. This would not be a Christian understanding of love. Love must include justice as a minimum and vital requirement. The search for justice, including social justice, has been a theme of the biblical teaching and has also been a dominant theme of Indian Christians, especially in their defence of the poor and the Dalits, in their protection of the tribals and their fight for the rights of women in society, in their political involvement. Love includes these concerns, even if at times it goes beyond them and reaches to the levels of forgiveness, total generosity and self-gift.

In modern theological language this teaching has been articulated among Christians as the need to have a 'preferential option for the poor'. The expression has its roots in the context of a society in which a powerful minority is seen as oppressing the powerless majority. In a dialectic of this kind it is necessary to opt for the oppressed, not in order to exclude the oppressor but to call him or her to change sides and live with compassion and a sense of fellowship. In India, many Christian groups have spelt out this option for the poor by making the Dalits, the tribals, women and unorganized labour the primary concern in social and political activism.

We can do no better than conclude this exposition of the spiritual ideals of Christianity by quoting the celebrated poem on love in St Paul's first Letter to the Corinthians, chapter 13. It is just as fresh and beautiful today as it was in 55 CE.

If I speak in the tongues of mortals and of angels,
But do not have love,
I am a noisy gong or a clanging cymbal.
And if I have prophetic powers,
And understand all mysteries and all knowledge,
And if I have all faith so as to remove mountains,
But do not have love,
I am nothing.
If I give away all my possessions,
And if I hand over my body to be burned,
But do not have love,
I gain nothing.

Love is patient, love is kind;
Love is not envious or boastful or arrogant or rude.
It does not rejoice in wrongdoing,
But rejoices in the truth.
It bears all things, believes all things,
Hopes all things, endures all things.

Love never ends.
But as for prophecies, they will come to an end;
As for tongues, they will cease;
As for knowledge, it will come to an end.
For we know only in part,
And we prophesy only in part;
But when the complete comes, the partial will come
to an end.
When I was a child,
I spoke like a child, I thought like a child, I reasoned
like a child.
When I became an adult,
I put an end to the childish ways.
For now we see in a mirror, dimly,
But then we will see face to face.

Now I know only in part;
Then I will know fully, even as I have been fully known.
And now faith, hope and love abide,
These three;
And the greatest of these is love.

References

Agur, C.M. 1990. *Church History of Travancore.* 1903. Reprint, New Delhi/Madras: Asian Educational Services.

Aiya, V. Nigam. 1906. *The Travancore State Manual.* Trivandrum: Government Press.

All India Seminar. 1969. *The Church in India Today.* New Delhi: CBCI Centre.

Amaladass, Anand, and Richard Fox Young, eds and trans. 1995. *The Indian Christiad: A Concise Anthology of Didactic and Devotional Literature in Early Church Sanskrit.* Anand: Gujarat Sahitya Prakash.

Anderson, Gerald H., ed. 1998. *Biographical Dictionary of Christian Missions.* Grand Rapids, USA, and Cambridge, UK: W.B. Eedermans Publishing Co.

Badrinath, Chaturvedi. 2000. *Finding Jesus in Dharma: Christianity in India.* Delhi: ISPCK.

Bailey, G.A. 1999. *Art and Jesuit Missions in Asia and Latin America.* Toronto: University of Toronto Press.

Benjamin, Joshua M. 2001. *The Mystery of Israel's Lost Tribes and the Legend of Jesus in India.* New Delhi: Mosaic Books.

Bernier, François. 1972. *Travels in the Mogul Empire A.D. 1656–1688.* Revised ed. Archibald Constable: New Delhi.

Boxer, C.R. 1969. *The Portuguese Seaborne Empire 1415–1825.* London: Hutchinson & Co.

Boyd, R.H.S. 1989. *An Introduction to Indian Christian Theology.* 1965. Revised 2nd ed. Delhi: ISPCK.

Buckland, C.E. 1906. *Dictionary of Indian Biography.* London: Swan Sonnerschein & Co.

Clarke, Sathianathan. 1998. *Dalits and Christianity: Subaltern Religion and Liberation Theology in India.* Delhi: Oxford University Press.

Cross, L.F., and E.A. Livingstone. 1977. *The Oxford Dictionary of the Christian Church.* 3rd ed. Oxford: Oxford University Press.

D'Costa, Anthony. 1962. The demolition of temples in the islands of Goa in 1540 and the disposal of temple lands. *Neue Zeitschrift fur Missionswissenschaft* 18: 161–72.

da Silva Rêgo, Antonio, ed. 1947–57. *Documentacio para a historia dos missoes do Padroado Portugues do Oriente, India, 1499–1542.* 12 vols. Lisboa: Divisao des Publicacoes e Biblioteca, Agencia Geral das Colonias. (Index volume. 2000. Lisboa: Fundacao Oriente.)

———. 1961. *The Christianization of the Goa Islands.* Translated from the Portuguese by Anthony D'Costa. Bombay: St Xavier's College.

de Melo, Carlos Merces. 1955. *The Recruitment and Formation of the Native Clergy in India (16th–19th Century).* Lisboa: Agencia Geral de Ultramar.

de Nobili, Roberto. 1971. *Adaptation.* Translated by S. Rajamanickam, S.J. Palayamkotti: St Xavier's College.

———. 1972. *On Indian Customs.* Translated by S. Rajamanickam, S.J. Palayamkotti: St Xavier's College.

Devi, Filomena Saraswati. 1939. *Vidyajyoti Journal of Theological Reflection* 53: 343.

Dhagamwar, Vasudha. 2003. Freedom of religion. *Economic and Political Weekly* (17 May): 1996.

Dialogue in Community. 1977. Geneva: World Council of Churches.

Diwakar, R.R. 1956. *Paramahamsa Sri Ramakrishna.* Bombay: Bharatiya Vidya Bhavan.

Downs, Frederick S. 1992. *North East India in the Nineteenth and Twentieth Century.* Vol. 5, Part 5 of *History of Christianity in India.* Bangalore: Church History Association.

Ekka, Alexius. 1999. Hundred years of Christian missions in Chotanagpur. *Indian Church History Review* 33: 79–117.

Fernando, Leonard. 2001. Christian response to the situation of poverty in India. In *Profiles of Poverty and Networks of Power*, edited by Anand Amaladass. Madurai: DACA Publications.

Flannery, Austin, ed. and trans. 1996. *Vatican Council II: Constitutions, Decrees, Declarations.* Northport, NY: Costello Publishing Company, and Dublin: Dominican Publications.

Gandhi, M.K. 1941. *Christian Missions: Their Place in India.* Ahmedabad: Navajivan Press.

———. 1958–94. *The Collected Works of Mahatma Gandhi.* 100 volumes. New Delhi: The Publications Division, Ministry of Information and Broadcasting, Government of India.

Goel, Sita Ram. 1994. *Catholic Ashrams: Sannyasis or Swindlers?* New Delhi: Voice of India.

Gonzalez Faus, Jose I. 2001. *Subversive Memory: Subjugating Presence.* Barcelona.

Hambye, E.R. 1997. *History of Christianity in India: Eighteenth Century.* Vol. 3 of *History of Christianity in India.* Bangalore: Indian Church History Association.

Hardgrave, Robert L.J. 1979. *Essays in the Political Sociology of South India*. Delhi: Usha Publications.

Hartmann, Anastasius. 1939–48. *Monumenta Anastasiana*. 5 vols. Luzern: Kapuziner Kloster Wesemlin.

Hosten, H. 1917–18. Glimpses into the conversion of the first Dacca Christians (1663–1750). *The Catholic Herald of India*, New Series 15(35–52) and 16(1–4).

Hunter, W.W. 1886. *The Indian Empire*. 2nd ed. London: Trubner & Co.

Indian Christians. 1928. Madras: G.A. Natesan & Co.

Jayakumar, J. 1999. Protestant Christians in Tamilnadu and the question of the communal electorate, 1917–1935. *Indian Church History Review* 33(2): 78–117.

Kanakaraj, K.A. 2000. *The Lighthouses of Rural Reconstruction*. Delhi: ISPCK.

Kersten, Holger. 2001. *Jesus Lived in India*. New Delhi: Penguin Books India.

Lalsawma, Reverend. 1994. *Revivals: The Mizo Way*. Aizwal: Lalsawma.

Leonard, G. 1985. Psycho-cultural dynamics of pilgrimage. *Ignis Studies* 3(3): 40–42.

Lloyd, J. Mairion. 1991. *History of the Church in Mizoram*. Aizwal: Synod Publications Board.

Lossky, Nicholas, et al., eds. 1991. *Dictionary of the Ecumenical Movement*. Geneva: WCC Publications, and Grand Rapids: W.B. Eedermans Publishing Co.

Maclagan, E.D. 1896. The Jesuit Missions and the Emperor Akbar. *Journal of the Asiatic Society of Bengal* 1: 38–113.

———. 1932. *The Jesuits and the Great Mogul*. London: Burns Oates and Washbourne Ltd.

Majumdar, R.C. 1962–63. *History of the Freedom Movement in India*. 3 vols. Calcutta: Firma K.C. Mukhopadhyay.

Nair, Patrick. 1963. *Sardhana: Its Begum, Its Shrine, Its Basilica*. Meerut: Prabhat Press.

Nehru, Jawaharlal. 1949. *Glimpses of World History*. 4th ed. London: Drumond.

Neill, S. 1984. *History of Christianity in India*. Vol. 1. Cambridge: Cambridge University Press.

New Catholic Encyclopedia. 2003. 2nd ed. 15 vols. Detroit: Gale.

Notovitch, Nicolas. 1895. *The Unknown Life of Christ*. Translated from the French. London: Hutchinson & Co.

O'Connor, Daniel. 1990. *Gospel, Raj and Swaraj*. Frankfurt im Main: Peter Lang.

Pachuau, L. 2002. *Ethnic Identity and Christianity: A Socio-Historical and Missiological Study of Christianity in North East India with Special Reference to Mizoram*. Frankfurt im Main: Peter Lang.

Panikkar, K.M. 1963. *The Foundations of New India*. London: Allied & Unwin.

Paradkar, Balwant A.M. 1969. *The Theology of Nehemiah Goreh*. Bangalore: CISRS, and Madras: CLS.

Philip, T.V. 1982. *Krishna Mohan Banerjea: Christian Apologist*. Bangalore: CISRS.

Phillips, J.B. 1972. *The New Testament in Modern English*. Revised ed. London: Collins.

Pickett, J. Waskom. 1933. *Christian Mass Movements in India*. 2nd ed. Lucknow: Lucknow Publishing House.

Ponnumuthan, S. 2003. Impact of Christianity as a liberative force in the social milieu of Kerala. *Vidyajyoti Journal of Theological Reflection* 67: 599–608.

Prakash, Louis. 2000. Bettiah mission, tribal mission and Dalit mission in Bihar: Three streams but one socio-religious movement. *Indian Church History Review* 34(2): 117–52.

Priolkar, A.K. 1958. *The Printing Press in India*. Bombay: Marathi Sanshodhana Mandala.

Rajamanickam, S. 1972. *The First Oriental Scholar*. Tirunelveli: de Nobili Research Institute.

Ram, Kalpana. 1992. *Mukkuvar Women*. New Delhi: Kali for Women.

Rao, B. Shiva. 1968. *The Framing of India's Constitution*. Select documents. 5 vols. New Delhi: The Indian Institute of Public Administration.

Sauliere, A. 1995. *His Star in the East*. Anand: Gujarat Sahitya Prakash.

Schurhammer, Georg. 1977. *Francis Xavier: His Life, His Times*. 2nd vol. Translated from the German by Joseph Costello, S.J. Rome: The Jesuit Historical Institute.

Scott, David C., ed. 1979. *Keshab Chunder Sen: A Selection*. Madras: The Christian Literature Society.

Sebastian, Joe. 2004. *The Jesuit Carnatic Mission*. Secunderabad: Jesuit Province Society.

Sen, S.P., ed. 1972–74. *Dictionary of National Biography*. 4 vols. Calcutta: Institute of Historical Studies.

Sharma, V.N. 1995. *Sawai Jai Singh and His Astronomy*. Delhi: Motilala Banarasidass.

Singh, K.S. 1998. *India's Communities*. 3 vols. Vols. 4–6 of *People of India National Series*. Delhi: Anthropological Survey of India/Oxford University Press.

Sitaramayya, K.B. 2001. *The Marvel and the Mystery of Pain: A New Interpretation of the Book of Job*. Bangalore: MCC Publications.

Smith, W.C. 1981. *Towards a World Theology*. Maryknoll, NY: Orbis.

Soares, A., ed. 1957. *Truth Shall Prevail: Reply to the Niyogi Committee*. Bombay: Catholic Association of Bombay.

Studdert-Kennedy, Gerald. 1998. *Providence and the Raj: Imperial Mission and Missionary Imperialism*. New Delhi: Sage.

Subramanyam, Ka Naa. 1970. *The Catholic Community in India*. Madras: Macmillan & Co.

Sundaram, V. Lawrence. 1986. *A Great Indian Jesuit: Fr Jerome D'Souza: Priest, Educationist and Statesman (1897–1977)*. Anand: Gujarat Sahitya Prakash.

Taylor, Richard W. 1975. *Jesus in Indian Painting*. Madras: The Christian Literature Society.

Tete, Peter. 1990. *The Kharias and the History of the Church in Biru*. Ranchi: St Albert's College.

Thakur, Rabindranath. 1934. *Car Adhyay*. Santiniketan: Bisvabharati Granthalay.

Thekkedath, Joseph. 1982. *History of Christianity in India: From the Middle of the Sixteenth to the End of the Seventeenth Century (1542–1700)*. Calcutta: Church History Association of India, and Bangalore: TPI.

Thomas, George. 1979. *Christian Indians and Indian Nationalism 1885–1950: An Interpretation in Historical and Theological Perspectives*. Frankfurt im Main: Peter D. Lang.

Toscano, Giuseppe. 1984. *Il 'Byun K'uns'*. Opere Tibetane di Ippolito Desideri, S.J., Roma: Istituto Italiano per il Medio ed Estremo Oriente.

Valles, Carlos. 1997. *Angels in My Life*. Anand: Gujarat Sahitya Prakash.

Vargas-Machuca, S.J., A. 2002. La investigacion actual sobre el Jesus historico. *Estudios Eclesiasticos* 77: 3–71.

Webster, John C.B. 1992. *The Dalit Christians: A History*. Delhi: ISPCK.

Wicki, J., ed. 1948. *Documenata Indica I (1540–1549)*. Monumenta Historica Societatis Iesu Series. Rome: Monumenta Historica Societatis Iesu.

———. 1950. *Documenata Indica II (1550–1553)*. Monumenta Historica Societatis Iesu Series. Rome: Monumenta Historica Societatis Iesu.

Winternitz, M. 1927. *History of Indian Literature*. Vol. 1. Calcutta: Calcutta University Press.

Young, Richard Fox. 1981. *Resistant Hinduism*. Vienna. De Nobili Research Library.

Zaidi, A. Moin and Shaheeda Zaidi. 1976. *The Encyclopaedia of Indian National Congress: 1885–1890*. Vol. 1. New Delhi: S.Chand & Co.

Select Bibliography

Aerthayil, James. *The Spiritual Heritage of the St Thomas Christians.* Bangalore: Dharmaram Publications, 1982.

Bayly, Susan. *Saints, Goddesses and Kings: Muslims and Christians in South Indian Society 1700–1900.* Cambridge: Cambridge University Press, 1989.

Chakravarti, Uma. *Rewriting History: The Life and Times of Pandita Ramabai.* Delhi: Kali for Women, 1998.

Clark, S.J., Francis X. *Asian Saints.* Quezon City, Philippines: Claretian Publications.

Correia-Afonso, S.J., John. *The Jesuits in India 1542–1773.* Anand: Gujarat Sahitya Prakash, 1997.

Farias, Kranti K. *The Christian Impact in South Kanara.* Mumbai: Church History Association of India, West India Branch, 1999.

Firth, C.B. *An Introduction to Indian Church History.* Revised ed., Delhi: ISPCK, 1976.

Harper, Susan Billinton. *In the Shadow of the Mahatma: Bishop V.S. Azariah and the Travails of Christianity in British India.* Grand Rapids: W.B. Eedermans Publishing Co., 2000.

Hedlund, Roger E., ed. *Christianity Is Indian: The Emergence of an Indigenous Community.* Delhi: ISPCK, 2000.

How They Found Christ. Series of Biographical Pamphets by ISPCK, Delhi.

Hudson, D. Dennis. *Protestant Origins in India.* Grand Rapids: W.B. Eedermans Publishing Co., 2000.

Lipner, Julius J. *Brahmabandhab Upadhyay: The Life and Thought of a Revolutionary.* Delhi: Oxford University Press, 1999.

Paul, Rajaiah D. *Triumphs of His Grace: Lives of Eight Indian Christian Laymen of the Early Days of Protestant Christianity in India.* Madras: CLS, 1967.

Raj, S.J., and G.C. Dempsey. *Popular Christianity in India.* New York: SUNY, 2002.

Robinson, R. *Christians of India.* New Delhi: Sage Publications, 2003.

Soares, Aloysius. *Catholic Church in India: A Historical Sketch.* Bombay, 1964.

Teilhard de Chardin, Pierre. *Hymn to the Universe*. London: Collins, 1965.
———. *Le Milieu divin*. London: Collins, 1960.
———. *The Heart of Matter*. London: Collins, 1978.
Tete, Peter. *A Short History of the Expansion of Catholic Missions in North India*. Ranchi: St Albert's College, 1997.
Thazhat, Andrews. *The Juridical Sources of the Syro-Malabar Church*. Kottayam: Paurastya Vidyapeetham, 1987.
Thomas, Abraham Vazhayil. *Christians in Secular India*. Rutherford: Fairleigh Dickinson University Press, 1974.
Thomas, George. *Christian Indians and Indian Nationalism 1885–1950*. Frankfurt im Main: Peter Lang, 1979.
Thomas, P.J. *100 Indian Witnesses to Jesus Christ*. Bombay: The Bombay Tract and Book Society, 1974.
Tisserant, Eugene. *Eastern Christianity in India*. Calcutta: Orient Longmans, 1957.
Velinkar, Joseph. *India and the West: The First Encounters*. Bombay: Heras Institute, St Xavier's College, 1998.
Vivekananda, Swami. *The Complete Works of Swami Vivekananda*. 8 vols. Almora: Advaita Ashram, 1931–51.
Webster, John C.B. *The Dalit Christians: A History*. Delhi: ISPCK, 1992.
Zachariah, Mathai. *Inside the Indian Church*. Delhi: ISPCK, 1994

Index